*Public Relations
and Presidential Campaigns*

# Public Relations and Presidential Campaigns:

## A CRISIS IN DEMOCRACY

## Melvyn H. Bloom

*Thomas Y. Crowell Company*
*Established 1834*
*New York*

See Copyright Acknowledgments on page 351.

Copyright © 1973 by Melvyn H. Bloom

*Designed by Ingrid Beckman*

Manufactured in the United States of America

ISBN 0-690-00090-1
1   2   3   4   5   6   7   8   9   10

Library of Congress Cataloging in Publication Data

Bloom, Melvyn H.
    Public relations and presidential campaigns.

    Bibliography: p.
    1. Presidents—United States—Election.   2. Public relations
    and politics.   I. Title.
    JK524.B57   1973        659.2′9′32901        73-10057
    ISBN   0-690-00090-1

*For Priscilla and Our Sons*

# Acknowledgments

The gestation period of this book has been a long one, and so is the list of those who helped, in one way or another, to make it a reality.

My work on this topic began as a paper for a seminar on the American presidency under the guidance of a great and sensitive scholar, Professor Saul K. Padover of the Graduate Faculty of The New School for Social Research. And if this book is to make any contribution to the study of American politics, then it is to Dr. Padover that the credit must go for recognizing that there was a contribution to be made, and for encouraging me to pursue it with vigor and develop it into a book worthy of publication.

Other sources of inspiration were the extraordinary observations, wisdom, and scholarly indignation of Professor Howard White and the incisive comments of Professor Hans Morgenthau, with both of whom it has been my privilege to study the crisis of democracy and the politics of America at the Graduate Faculty.

Education is a long process. I was trained as a newsman before I was trained as a political scientist. And it is my early instincts and concerns as a reporter which probably led me to view the process of choosing a President through the spyglass of a communicator. For this, I thank mainly the faculty of that unique institution, the Medill School of Journalism of Northwestern University. A most special note of gratitude must be reserved for a most outstanding and innovative advocate of professional, socially conscious journalism, Professor Emeritus Curtis MacDougall. For it is that distinguished teacher who taught me what to look for and how to find it, and to care about what I discovered.

The preparation of this book, as the notes and bibliography will indicate, relied heavily on the firsthand observations and thoughtful insights of a wide cross-section of scholars, journalists, and public relations and communications professionals. I am especially indebted to the pioneering works of Professor Stanley Kelley, Jr., and James Perry, and the unparalleled campaign reporting of Theodore White. Particularly helpful also have been the campaign accounts of Lewis Chester, Godfrey Hodgson and Bruce Page; Joe McGinniss; Karl A. Lamb and Paul A. Smith; and Daniel M. Ogden, Jr., and Arthur L. Peterson.

The final stages of a book like this one are perhaps more difficult than the writing and research itself—the inquiries and placement, the shifting and honing, the editing and rewriting, the mechanics and legalities. For their invaluable help in those labors, I am grateful to Mira Berman, President of Allerton, Berman and Dean, and her colleague Karl Engel; Sanford Schlesinger of Rose and Schlesinger; and my agent, Arthur Pine. A long procession of interested and capable secretaries, too numerous to mention individually, had a hand in typing and retyping and correcting the manuscript, aiding with the intricacies of its preparation. Special thanks must be reserved for Felicia Morales, through whose typewriter passed nearly every page of this manuscript in its earliest stages.

My wife, Priscilla, carried a lion's share of the retyping duties. But I am grateful to her for much more than that, for without her patience and encouragement while I was at work on this book—and her impatience with my procrastination when I was not—I never would have reached this stage. I thank her for her understanding and insight —and, with our sons, Jeffrey, Alan, Steven and Bradley—for the sacrifices in our family life over a long period which gave me the time I needed for my own fulfillment.

New York
June 1973                                        MELVYN H. BLOOM

# Contents

"Whenever the people are well-informed, they can be trusted with their own government; whenever things get so far wrong as to attract their notice, they may be relied on to set them to rights."

—Thomas Jefferson
1789

". . . We pledge ourselves . . . to be guided in all our activities by the generally accepted standards of truth, accuracy, fair dealing and good taste."

—Declaration of Principles
Public Relations Society of America

# *Public Relations and Presidential Campaigns*

# Introduction

Public sentiment is everything. With public sentiment nothing can fail; without it, nothing can succeed. He who molds public sentiment goes deeper than he who enacts statutes or pronounces decisions. He makes statutes or decisions possible or impossible to execute.

—Abraham Lincoln
Ottawa, Illinois
August 24, 1858

If I am ever profoundly thankful for any instrumentalities, it is for the editor and his paper. They furnish the winds for my sails.

—P. T. Barnum
*The Life of P. T. Barnum*
Written by Himself, 1855

One hundred years ago it would have seemed ludicrous to attempt to divine any relationship between the views of Abraham Lincoln and those of P. T. Barnum with regard to the significance of public opinion. But within fourscore and seven years of Mr. Lincoln's death, those who succeeded him and those who attempted to do so were looking increasingly to the latter-day heirs of Mr. Barnum to help put the wind in *their* sails, too.

Lincoln's classic quotation on public sentiment can be traced to Rousseau, who developed the term *public opinion* as we use it today. In his discussion of the general will, *volonté générale*, Rousseau said that "whosoever makes it his business to give laws must know how to sway opinions and through them govern the passions of man."[1] The

*1*

technique, the know-how to which Rousseau alludes, is the core of what we now know as the practice of public relations. Public relations is a process in which contemporary Presidents have placed a good deal of faith.

Lincoln and Rousseau were speaking of the importance of effective public relations techniques as a tool in the effective conduct of high office. It is the purpose of this book to illustrate and assess the significance of those techniques, as they have now evolved, in the *attainment* of office, specifically, the presidency of the United States.

"Public relations" has become a rather commonly used term in America, but it cannot always be understood, since, as a concept and practice, it is still in the state of defining itself. As public relations professionals know, the literature and shoptalk of the craft are filled with an overabundance of definitions and redefinitions.

Public relations does not mean the same thing to everyone. Some see it as a form of black magic, others as a cure-all for the difficulties that are faced by all sorts of institutions and individuals. Then there are those who scorn public relations with sweeping denunciations, condemning it as prostituted journalism, organized misinformation, or worse.

As Scott M. Cutlip and Allen H. Center point out, "The calling, like most professions, suffers from the fact that its misdeeds are more widely heralded than are its accomplishments. The specialized knowledge and skills of the calling are available to fools, knaves, and saints alike."[2]

These authors, whose book *Effective Public Relations* is professionally regarded as the "bible of public relations," point out that "Public relations thinking has served to deepen the sense of social responsibility in our public enterprises. It has contributed to public welfare. It has improved the communications required in our society."[3]

Robert Heilbroner had difficulty defining public relations in 1957 when he said, "In a word, public relations covers a lot of acreage— blurring out into advertising, slopping over into selling, dipping down into publicity, and touching—or at least aspiring to—the 'making' of public opinion itself."[4]

Public relations is often confused with some of its functional parts —and is often used as an equivalent term for those parts: propaganda, publicity, institutional advertising, press-agentry, speechwriting, the organization of special events, opinion sampling, community relations, and many other tools. All are parts of the whole, but none are its equivalent. For the sake of clarity, the term *public relations* might best be restricted to Cutlip and Center's professionally accepted definition, *"The planned effort to influence opinion through acceptable performance and two-way communication."* Thus, the term encompasses "the performance and communications used to build profitable relationships with the public," and does not confuse the means with the ends, which relate to the quality or status of public *relationships.*[5]

This book will try to illuminate a widening view on the part of both practitioner and client of the aims and methods of public relations in presidential campaigns. It will further demonstrate that while public relations is increasingly considered a technical, specialized activity, public relations men tend to be broad-gauged, flexible counselors who have assumed a variety of roles in campaigns not necessarily confined to their traditional function as specialists in communications.

The significance of public relations in presidential campaigns has not received much attention from political scientists. This lack of scholarly attention to the problem will not be unraveled here. But it is offered as an explanation of the fact that the principal sources for this study have been books written by journalists, news accounts, articles in professional public relations and advertising journals, and personal interviews.

Professor Stanley Kelley's book *Professional Public Relations and Political Power*[6] appears to be the most recent volume exclusively devoted to this field by a political scientist, and his original work is now seventeen years old. As we shall see, political public relations has come a long way in the last seventeen years.

When Kelley wrote his book in 1956, he pointed out that the political activities of public relations men had attracted little attention, and that introducing these activities into consideration invites a rethinking of a number of our conceptions of American politics. "Historically, political techniques have modified profoundly the practical effect of our institutions of government. There is every reason to believe that those techniques involved in political public relations will be no exception to this rule."[7]

Public relations professionals themselves have pointed to the importance of what they are doing to the study of American political campaigns and elections. One of them has put it this way:

Political scientists a few years hence may well view the introduction of "professional public relations" into U.S. politics as the most significant development in government since the late nineteenth century. In fact, not since the emergence of machine politics in the 1870's and the rise of the so-called "ward boss" has there been a transition more noteworthy in the political mores of America.[8]

American democracy goes as far as any system in attempting to accommodate itself to public opinion. It provides, through the campaign and election system, devices through which citizens can control the personnel and policies of their government. "It is into this fundamental relationship between politician and electorate, between those who seek power and those who bestow authority, that the public relations man inserts himself, seeking to guide the action of the politician toward the people and the people toward the politician."[9]

And, as we shall later see, the public relations man has been followed into the political battlefield by a veritable army of technicians —campaign consultants, pollsters, advertising men, market analysts, data processors, simulators, and others—under the banner of what James Perry—a masterful journalist in the forefront of the chroniclers of this phenomenon—has called "The New Politics."

The public relations man is not involved in presidential campaigns for what might be considered traditional political reasons. He is involved because he belongs to a group with unique skills. So when we study the public relations man and his colleagues, we assume, with Harold Lasswell and Abraham Kaplan, that "skill, like wealth or prestige or position, is a basis of power in society and changes in the skills used in political action will have discoverable consequences for the distribution of power and influence."[10]

Many of these new professional managers and organizers call themselves "campaign consultants" or "political consultants" rather than "public relations consultants." As we have pointed out, public relations as a field and public relations men as individuals are increasingly characterized by considerable flexibility. The public relations field includes such functions as the development and structuring of new organizations and the creation and implementation of programs of public affairs in a number of areas, backstopped by skills in research, administration, management of personnel, budgeting, and so on. Although many specialists in these individual areas would never dream of calling themselves public relations men, many public relations men, on the other hand, can see themselves—or a team of their fellow professionals—doing virtually everything that needs to be done as a function of a campaign organization. Often, they take on these near-total organizational responsibilities—indeed, they often have a role in the design of the organizations themselves.

For example, in Senator Barry Goldwater's 1964 presidential campaign, there were five principal subdivisions under the direction of Dean Burch: finance, public information, research, administration, and field operations. Public relations professionals could feel at home in any of these areas.

In a conversation with the writer, Nick Kostopulos, then special assistant to the chairman of the Democratic National Committee, agreed that there is no longer any question about the trend toward the development of such political technicians at all levels of the electoral system:

> Sometimes they are public relations men, sometimes they are professional campaign consultants—often they play both roles. They are thought of as the men most able to deal efficiently with the media, and in such a way as to use the limited number of available dollars to the greatest effect. . . . They have added new layers to political organization. They are part of the effort of political organizations to move away from the "political hack syndrome." Bossism is a thing of the past. Party leadership is being constantly upgraded. . . . The emphasis is on professionalism, and the p.r. man is a professional.[11]

There is a certain mystique about the political public relations man —perhaps public relations men in general. It may not always be clear to the nonprofessional just what it is they do, how they do it, and just how the effectiveness of all of this can be measured in terms of victory or defeat. But, as Professor Howard White has put it so well, "Whether or not these people brought their candidates a single vote, they have become some of the professionals of politics. They are not only respectable; they are believed to be indispensable. . . ."[12]

Linked closely to our hypothesis of the increasingly significant role of the public relations professional in presidential campaigns are two other factors that should be mentioned briefly before we proceed to trace the historical development of that role: the constantly increasing significance of the mass media, particularly television, in presidential campaigns and the ever-growing importance of personality and "image" in American politics.

The mass media, as they have grown, changed, and multiplied, have called for new methods and new skills. As for the importance of television in a presidential campaign, Theodore White has said that of all those matters in which organization is important, "the direction of television in a political campaign is comparably the most important. Here is where the audience is; here is where the greatest part of all money is spent; here is where creative artistry and practical commercialism must join to support the candidate's thrust."[13]

White might have added: here is where the public relations man is. For a large part of his career is spent in calculating just how to obtain the maximum impact for a particular story in an age in which technological advance has made the conveying of information a highly technical field.

Closely related is the question of personality and image. In the American two-party system, political parties are no longer supported by the electorate primarily because of ideological loyalties. And, when political parties cease to be ideologically distinctive, the personalities of their candidates assume much greater—in fact, overriding—significance.

Scholars such as Daniel Boorstin and Marshall McLuhan have engaged in some pioneering attempts to deal with this question of personal charisma, particularly as it is reflected in the visual images that have become so important in political campaigning. Boorstin contends that national politics has actually adopted the Hollywood "star system" and is dominated further by that system with every election. Some of the evidence presented in this book, particularly with regard to the rise to the presidential arena of such individuals as Ronald Reagan, would seem to bear this out.

The importance of personality in politics, it might be noted, has produced some curious anomalies. Kostopulos told the writer that he has been particularly struck by the way in which certain constituencies, in complete disregard for neat ideological stereotypes, elect both liberal and conservative representatives with equal aplomb: "[Estes] Kefauver was elected in Tennessee and [Ralph] Yarborough in Texas by large margins after each of them had refused to sign the 'Southern Manifesto.' Illinois had [Everett] Dirksen and [Paul] Douglas; Wisconsin had [Alexander] Wiley and [William] Proxmire. Senator Fred Harris is a liberal from a conservative state, and so is [Representative] Carl Albert . . . and all of them are popular with their constituencies. It's all a question of imagery."

Imagery, personality, the star system, and the mass media are among those major issues with which this book will deal in tracing the role of the men and the techniques of public relations and related specialties in the process of choosing the President of the United States. Our method will be to:

> 1. Trace the history of some earlier applications of public relations to politics, particularly the presidency, through about 1940.
> 2. Survey the emergence of modern public relations in presidential campaigns since the 1952 election (a milestone in this field, particularly because of the advent of television), analyzing some of the professional practices and principles followed, largely as public relations men themselves explain them.
> 3. Discuss the role of public relations in presidential campaigns from 1952 to 1968.
> 4. Attempt to evaluate just what all of this means to the process of choosing the President of the United States and, therefore, to American democracy.

The accounts of specific presidential campaigns in this book are by no means intended to be complete either as to historical records or to political analyses. Rather, they consist only of highlights, sometimes scattered, which, in sum, serve to illustrate the role of public relations professionals, techniques, and considerations. In beginning this effort, we might bear in mind Theodore White's observation:

> The transaction in power by which a President is chosen is so vastly complicated that even those most intimately involved in it, even those who seek the office, can never know more than a fragment of it. For it is the nature of politics that men must always act on the basis of uncertain fact, must make their judgments in haste on the basis of today's report by instinct and experience shaped years before in other circumstances. Were it otherwise, then politics would not be what they are now—the art of government and leadership; politics would be an exact science in which our purpose and destiny could be left to great impersonal computers.[14]

# One:

# The Early History of Political Public Relations

The idea of "public relations" had its origin in American business. As Stanley Kelley and others have pointed out, the businessman's dominant attitude toward the press was long one of indifference. Public reaction to what he and his corporation did generally played little part in his decision-making process.

Eventually, concentration of economic power in a few enormous corporate empires brought about sharp reaction from government, labor, and eventually, sharply persistent attacks in the daily press, the muckraking magazines, and books such as Upton Sinclair's famous work *The Jungle*. Articles by well-known journalists appeared with titles such as "Making Steel and Killing Men," "Railroads on Trial," "De Kid Wot Works at Night," "Frenzied Finance," and "Can This Be Whitewashed Also?"[1]

In his *McClure's* article of 1906, "Railroads on Trial," Ray Stannard Baker quoted James Russell Lowell:

> "All free governments . . . are in reality governments by public opinion and it is on the quality of this public opinion that their prosperity depends. . . . With the growth of democracy grows also the fear, if not the danger, that this atmosphere may be corrupted . . . Democracy in its best sense is merely the letting in of light and air."[2]

As the attacks persisted, attitudes began to change. Businessmen sensed a need and recruited those who could help them fill it. Public relations pioneers such as Ivy Lee, Edward Bernays, and Pendleton Dudley went to work for major corporations and individuals in the business world.

In time, the emphasis moved from defensive reactions to continuing campaigns. By 1924, Ivy Lee, whose most famous client was John D. Rockefeller, Sr., was able to say: "I do not view publicity as 'press-agentry.' . . . Publicity comprises . . . *everything involved in the expression of an idea or an institution including the policy or idea expressed.*" And, at another point: "The great publicity man is the man who advises his client what policy to pursue, which, if pursued, would create favorable publicity."[3]

Lee thus stated forty-nine years ago essentially that view expressed earlier in this book—that public relations involves "acceptable performance," and that this implies counseling on policy, at the management level, with publicity itself serving as an operational tool of the counselor.

Early works on American politics and political campaigns, as Kelley has pointed out, give minimal attention to the role of political publicity. But the situation apparently changed in politics, as it did in business, around the turn of the century, when commentaries on political campaigns began to note that newspapermen were serving as press agents to candidates.

Cutlip and Center demonstrate how what we now label political "public relations" had its origins in the work of Samuel Adams, Franklin, Hamilton, Jefferson, and Paine, who organized and promoted the American Revolution. They were men whose knowledge of the importance of public opinion and the techniques for molding it was intuitive. One historian has said: "Samuel Adams owned no superior as a propagandist. No one in the colonies realized more fully than he the primary necessity of arousing public opinion, no one set about it more assiduously."[4]

Adams and his colleagues used in their campaigns techniques still in use today by public relations men: mass-circulation pamphlets, the creation of action-oriented organizations, oratory, staged events. Newspapers were fed articles by these men—who, as public relations men do today, remained in the background and left their material unsigned. One of the earliest of many "created events" in American history was the Boston Tea Party.

> Samuel Adams and his associates between 1748 and the Revolution centered a propaganda exchange about Roberts and Fowle's *The Independent Advertiser* (Boston) until 1750 and Edes and Gill's *The Boston Gazette* from 1775; . . . Adams supplemented

his work by building up committees of correspondence in more than 80 towns; . . . The manner in which Adams, the press agent, publicized the Boston Massacre of March 5, 1775, and the Boston Tea Party of December 16, 1773, characterizes this potent work. In both cases Adams hustled his eye-witness account—carefully biased—throughout the colonies.[5]

Cutlip and Center contend that America's most important contribution to political thought, *The Federalist Papers,* can, "without stretching the point . . . be called public relations documents." Indeed, they quote David Truman's statement that "The entire effort of which *The Federalist* was a part was one of the most skillful and important examples of pressure group activity in American history," and Morrison's and Commager's contention that "unless the Federalists had been shrewd in manipulation as they were sound in theory, their arguments could not have prevailed."[6] This is an interesting view of the history of American political thought. Although the ideas of *The Federalist* are what we properly study today, it gives one pause to speculate on what might have happened had its authors been less concerned with assuring that their arguments reached the proper public or less skilled in seeing that they did so.

The turbulence of the era of Andrew Jackson produced Amos Kendall, another early political public relations man. As a member of Jackson's Kitchen Cabinet, Kendall, former newspaper editor, served as the President's informal ghost-writer, press agent, poll-taker, and advisor. In fact, several members of the Kitchen Cabinet were editors who aided Jackson, not the most articulate and educated of men, in communicating his ideas.

Kendall played a role in Jackson's administration not unlike that of Pierre Salinger under John F. Kennedy and Bill Moyers under Lyndon Johnson. He worked at the highest levels of government shaping strategy and writing presidential speeches and other documents. The official news organ of the administration, *The Globe,* was organized by Kendall and set a new pattern for the partisan press of the era.

Kendall wrote and widely distributed numerous press releases to a national press which, by the time of Jackson's election, had more readership than that of any other nation. Kendall was able to sense the growing impact of the press on public opinion. In his own way, he polled that opinion and made careful analyses for the President of the way in which newspaper comment and content reflected the disposition of the people.

Kendall influenced policy by determining, as best he could, the desires of the people, and by helping Jackson offer the citizens ideas they found congenial. He was one of the first to sense the shift in the balance of power from the traditional political aristocracy of the East to the growing frontier population and the urban working classes. In true p.r. style, Kendall operated anonymously, serving in the obscure post of fourth auditor of the Treasury, and using political organization, rallies, and staged events, as well as the press, on behalf of Jackson. All of this caused John Quincy Adams to observe of Jackson and Martin Van Buren that "Both . . . have been for 12 years the tool of Amos Kendall, the ruling mind of their dominion."[7]

The campaign techniques instituted by Kendall and the Kitchen Cabinet changed little for more than half a century. Following the acrimony and dissension of the Tilden-Hayes campaign, political leaders looked for new ways to win voters in a rapidly growing population, substantially changed in its composition by mass immigration. By the time of the presidential campaign of 1880, improved printing machinery, an increasingly abundant supply of cheap paper, and the desire to "enlighten" new immigrants had brought about the introduction of mass-produced campaign literature.

In 1900 *Munsey's Magazine* said that campaign literature was carefully prepared and read:

> Expert and experienced managers. . . . Men who are learned as regard to the issues at stake, and who have that requisite of the successful politician which might be termed a knowledge of applied psychology, hold the blue pencil. Paragraphs, sentences, and words are weighed with reference to their effect on the mind of their reader.[8]

The Bryan-McKinley campaign of 1896 set a pattern that remained more or less unchanged until the first use of radio as a campaign device in the 1920's. During the '96 campaign, both Republican and Democratic headquarters gave forth a torrent of pamphlets, news releases, posters, and other materials now thought of as routine in political campaigns. Obviously, the population had grown, and campaigning had become less direct as voters moved out of the hearing range of conventional campaign oratory. "By 1900, the managers of the political press bureaus, both national and state, had assumed most of the functions which characterize today's practitioner." The first emergence on the national scene of pioneer public relations man Ivy Lee was as publicity man for Judge Alton B. Parker in the presidential campaign of 1904.[9]

Lee had worked for *The New York Times* and the New York *Evening Journal* as a reporter. He then left newspapering and served as publicity man in the New York mayoralty campaign of Seth Low and in the press bureau of the Democratic National Committee (an affiliation that is particularly interesting in view of his later association with John D. Rockefeller). After the 1904 election, which his client lost to Theodore Roosevelt, Lee joined with George F. Parker, a Buffalo, New York, newsman who had worked as Grover Cleveland's press agent. Lee and Parker created what they called at first a "press bureau," dedicated to the purpose of fighting the negative publicity that business was receiving with positive publicity, and of explaining and defending business to the public.[10]

The winning candidate, Theodore Roosevelt, was frequently accused by his opponents of attempting to rule the country from the front pages. His first act upon returning from William McKinley's funeral was to summon the Washington chiefs of the three news associations to work out a new pattern for White House press relations. A *Harper's Weekly* article during Roosevelt's first term carried the title "Theodore Roosevelt: Press Agent." Teddy Roosevelt was eminently accessible, and this endeared him to the press. He tried to determine popular opinion on important issues, or, as he once put it, he "collected and reflected doctrines of the day." He is also credited with perfecting the "trial balloon" technique, which has since become a standard device of Presidents and lesser politicians as well. Cutlip and Center have said, "with the growth of mass-circulation newspapers, Roosevelt's canny ability to dominate the front pages was a newfound power for those with causes to promote. He had a keen sense of news and knew how to stage a story so that it would get maximum attention."[11]

This latter sentence is one which, to this day, might be used to describe a number of Presidents who followed Theodore Roosevelt to the White House. Lyndon Johnson, as we shall see later, particularly relished this kind of staging of news.

In 1911 Frank Parker Stockbridge was hired as a press aide to

Woodrow Wilson and had an important role in Wilson's pre-convention campaign for the Democratic presidential nomination. Stockbridge arranged Wilson's tour of the West; distributed speeches, photographs, and other information to a large mailing list; got out advance copy on Wilson's speeches, and organized press conferences for his candidate, who was far from thoroughly convinced of their value.[12]

George Creel, a newspaperman with muckraking credentials, worked as a public relations man for the Democrats in the 1916 presidential campaign and was appointed by President Wilson in 1917 to head a federal Committee on Public Information. Creel and his committee argued that the World War did not necessitate enforced censorship, and that *"expression, not suppression,* was the real need. The printed word, the spoken word, motion pictures, the telegraph, the wireless, cables, posters, signboards, and every possible media should be used to drive home the justice of America's cause."[13] Two other leading public relations pioneers, Edward L. Bernays and Carl Byoir, received some of their early experience with Creel's organization.

The Democratic Party, according to Stanley Kelley, organized what was apparently the first full-time, permanent political party publicity bureau after Alfred E. Smith's defeat in the 1928 elections. Charles Michelson was hired to head the bureau, and his appointment was announced in June, 1929. The Democrats, out of power since Wilson's administration, apparently feared that the publicity resources available to government could well lead to a permanent disequilibrium between the party in power and its opposition. Indeed, the Republicans seemed to adopt the same point of view in following and elaborating upon Michelson's example in the period from 1932 to the election of Dwight Eisenhower twenty years later.

Michelson's training grounds for political public relations were the Hearst newspapers in San Francisco and New York. He wrote in his autobiography that he considered his job with the Democratic Party one of making news that might prove damaging to the Hoover Administration. He said that the import tariff issue was one of those he selected for such a negative campaign because "It was easy to get before the country a picture of slavish legislators closeted with the representatives of those industries whose owners had contributed most largely to the Hoover campaign fund and fixing rates as they were told to do by Big Business."[14]

With the beginnings of the Depression, Michelson's task became one of making political capital out of social unrest. His material referred to the early days of the Depression as the "Hoover Panic" and to the tar-paper shacks of the unemployed as "Hoovervilles." His techniques included feeding material to Democratic senators and congressmen whose names helped assure it a place on the front page; sending to newspapers clippings of news items and editorial ideas, and circulating published cartoons lampooning Republicans.

Kelley indicates that by the time Michelson's publicity bureau operations had reached this stage, the Republicans perceived a need for a similar organization and proceeded to establish their own bureau, headed by another former newspaperman, James L. West.

At the time of the 1932 presidential campaign, Michelson became part of the campaign strategy board that also included Franklin Delano Roosevelt. This pattern continued in the succeeding campaigns of 1936 and 1940, and, as we shall see later, public relations men have continued to hold one or more seats on the central strategy board of virtually every presidential candidate since that time. As Kelley points out, "Just as in an earlier period the career of Ivy Lee had dramatized the usefulness of the public relations counsel's talents to captains of industry, so now did Charles Michelson's to the world of politics."[15]

The title of "public relations director" made its formal debut in presidential politics during the 1936 campaign, when that appellation was given to Hill Blackett, a Chicago advertising man hired to work on the campaign of Republican candidate Alf M. Landon. There were some of the first glimmers in this campaign of the application of the merchandising and commercial advertising experience of business. For example, Blackett mounted a radio spot announcement campaign and distributed campaign movies, along with large quantities of printed material.[16]

Meanwhile, the "ins" were stimulating rapid growth of government public relations, for as the Depression increased the interest of private business in public relations activities, the New Deal did the same for government. In 1935 Elisha Hanson observed that the F.D.R. Administration had "set up new publicity divisions and expanded old ones, hired more newspapermen than were working for the newspapers, retained commercial advertising agencies to promote its programs, and created and enforced procedures for the dissemination of official news." What was true in general was especially true of the National Recovery Act. "With the NRA, propaganda became not only a tool for promotion, but a way of governing."[17]

Despite these developments, Pendleton Herring was able to observe accurately in 1940 that "In comparison with commercial advertising, political propaganda is still crude. The politician in this country has not taken advantage of . . . [the] more subtle ways of manipulating public opinion."[18]

That year, 1940, witnessed an overwhelming demonstration of the impact of political public relations on the heart of the Democratic process when Wendell Willkie, the Indiana farm lad whom Harold Ickes once called "the barefoot boy from Wall Street," won the Republican presidential nomination on the sixth ballot. Thomas E. Dewey, Robert A. Taft, and possibly Arthur Vandenberg were the leading contenders for the Republican nod. With an apparently hopeless deadlock between Taft and Dewey on the fourth ballot, a claque in the spectators' gallery at the Philadelphia convention took up an incessant "We want Willkie" chant. Two ballots later, the convention stampeded to Willkie.

Curtis MacDougall has assessed the pre-nomination campaign this way:

> Wendell Willkie did not become the Republican party nominee in 1940 because the galleries screamed his name. . . . His campaign was long and skillfully planned and brillantly executed. It *was* precedent-breaking, but not for the reasons fed to the gullible public. . . . The business and industrial leaders who decided upon Willkie sometime between six months and a year in advance of the convention skillfully divided the nation and induced their local equivalents in all of the states to unloose the deluge at the proper moment.[19]

Just where and when the Willkie for President idea emerged is unclear. It has variously been attributed to "Old Iron Pants," General Hugh S. Johnson; Thomas W. Lamont, then chairman of J. P. Morgan and Company, and columnists Arthur Krock and David Lawrence. In any case, the Willkie idea snowballed after November 20, 1939, when General Johnson made the first serious public mention of it at the New York Bond Club. When reporters sought out Willkie for comment, he said, "In view of the speed with which the federal government is taking over my business, I'll probably have to be looking for a new job shortly. General Johnson's is the best offer I've had thus far."[20] (Willkie, who was president of Commonwealth and Southern, had managed to sell a subsidiary, the Tennessee Electric Company, to the Tennessee Valley Authority for $78,600,000 —$23,000,000 more than the government's original offer.)

The following February, Oren Root, Jr., gave up his law practice to organize Associated Willkie Clubs all over the country, and a Willkie Mailing Committee was established. Russell Davenport, managing editor of *Fortune* magazine, resigned on May 2 to manage the Willkie pre-convention campaign and brought along a large group of professional public relations and advertising men. The publicity buildup was well-timed, and feature articles on Willkie began to appear in mass media reaching a variety of audiences.

In the *New Republic* an article defending civil liberties appeared with Willkie's by-line. *Look* and *Life*, which both ran series on potential candidates, included Willkie. He was endorsed by the Scripps-Howard newspaper chain and by such syndicated columnists as General Johnson, Westbrook Pegler, and Raymond Clapper. Endorsing him also were the Des Moines *Register* and *Tribune*, owned by Gardner and John Cowles, who also counted *Look* magazine among their properties. The papers were full of news of Willkie's "underdog" campaign and the activities of his followers as the convention grew near. The week before it opened, the *Saturday Evening Post* contained an article by Willkie, "Five Minutes to Midnight," and another by General Johnson, "I Am Not Nominating Him."

As the delegates assembled, Governor Harold Stassen of Minnesota, the "boy wonder" of the Republican Party since his victory the previous year over the Farmer-Labor organization in his state, emerged as Willkie's floor manager. Then, from all over the country, delegates began receiving thousands of wires, letters, and telephone calls. The communications came from bankers to whom many of them were obligated. They came from a variety of prominent industrial and financial figures, stockbrokers, railroad officers, manufacturers, publishers, society leaders, and so on.

As Curtis MacDougall put it: "The pressure came from exactly the right sources and there was enough of it to impress the professional politicians that not to respond to it would be equivalent to spitting in the eye of the golden goose."[21]

It was not long before this episode that Judge Learned Hand had observed:

"The day has clearly gone forever of a society small enough for its members to have a personal acquaintance with one another. . . . Publicity is an evil substitute and the art of publicity a black art. But it has come to stay. Every year adds to the potency, to the finality of its judgments."[22]

The Willkie campaign, while making considerable use of the "black art" of publicity, relied rather heavily on professional techniques that related hardly at all to "public opinion"—*to volonté générale*, the "general will" of Rousseau. That it is still possible to "seize" a presidential nomination was demonstrated by the Goldwater forces in 1964, as we shall discuss in a later chapter.

After the 1966 Congressional elections, Arthur Schlesinger, Jr., taking a cue from Learned Hand, is reported to have called Senator Charles Percy a product of "the black art of public relations." What are some of the techniques of this "black art," and how are they applied in presidential campaigning?

# Two:
# The Emergence of Modern Public Relations in Presidential Campaigns

Successive presidential campaigns have shown increasingly elaborate concern with the attitudes of the electorate and with the means for influencing those attitudes. Before examining contemporary public relations at work in several recent campaigns, it will be helpful to discuss some of the strategies, methods, techniques, and philosophy that are being put to work on behalf of those who would be President and to cite some examples of the new professionals who are doing the job. For, as Kelley has said, "With the techniques have come technicians: the propaganda function in politics has more and more moved out of the hands of the lay politicians into those of the propaganda specialist."[1]

Kelley points also to an interesting paradox: that early public relations programs of business were, to a certain extent, a borrowing by the private sector of the political techniques used by its partisan opponents. As business programs matured, they were, in turn, reflected by party politics. This development came full circle, as commercial advertising and corporate public relations eventually began to furnish the standards by which the efficiency of political public relations efforts were judged.

In 1922 Robert C. Brooks was able to say:

> Considering the large sums constantly spent for political propaganda, it is rather remarkable that we have no better guides in this field than certain traditional rules of thumb and the idiosyncracies of the campaign manager in temporary command. By the employment of research methods similar to those applied in analyzing business concerns, efficiency experts should be able to throw light on the relative value of . . . the principal methods of campaigning.[2]

In both politics and business, the evolution has been from press-agentry to professional public relations in the sense we have defined it. As Edward L. Bernays put it forty-six years ago, "This profession has developed from the status of circus stunts to what is obviously an important position in the conduct of the world's affairs." And the contemporary public relations man is constantly at work to determine the ways in which the resources of increasingly complex modern systems of communications can be used to organize and direct public opinion.

In Bernays' words:

> The public relations counsel is first of all a student. His field of study is the public mind. His textbooks for this study are the articles printed in newspapers and magazines, the advertisements that are inserted in publications, the billboards that line the streets, the railroads and the highways, the speeches that are delivered in legislative chambers, the sermons issuing from pulpits, anecdotes related in smoking rooms, the gossip of Wall Street, the patter of the theater and the conversation of other men who, like him, are interpreters and must listen for the clear or obscure enunciations of the public. . . . But he is not only a student. He is a practitioner with a wide range of instruments and a definite technique for their use.[3]

There are, as we have seen, a number of factors that have helped to make public relations experts a commonplace feature of political life. The media—and their degree of sophistication—are expanding steadily; the costs of campaigning are growing constantly, so as to make efficient use of available funds a critical factor in campaign organization; it is an increasing strain upon the skills and resources of the campaign organization to establish national identification of candidate "image" because of the expansion and mobility of the population and the consequent difficulty of conducting traditional whistle-stopping, baby-kissing, hand-shaking campaigns for high office. In view of these and other factors, the need for professional coordination of all phases of a major campaign becomes increasingly evident.

By 1956 *Business Week* was able to report:

> The Democratic National Committee is advising party candidates . . .: "If you can afford it, you should have professional advertising and publicity experts to assist you," because "the assistance is well

worth the cost." . . . Indeed, it's a brave candidate for any office nowadays who can afford not to have such counsel.[4]

In the same year Robert Humphreys, the campaign director of the Republican National Committee, was quoted as saying:

> "I used to say a campaign was 10 percent public relations, 60 percent candidate, and 30 percent organization. Now it's hard to measure. . . . Good p.r. is the difference between good sparkplugs and bad ones in an auto."[5]

Both major parties have had national public relations directors and staffs of p.r. specialists in a direct line of succession from Michelson and West. Kelley feels that the public relations departments of the Republican National Committee and the Republican Congressional Campaign Committee "are, in effect, commercial public relations agencies performing political functions."[6] It should also be pointed out that many of the administrative and legislative assistants to potential presidential candidates, such as governors and senators, are, by experience and training, public relations men.

Despite the weight of such evidence, the meaning for the American democratic system of having political discussion increasingly given over to the members of a restricted skill group has not come in for very much serious analysis by political scientists. As the 1956 *Business Week* article, stimulated at least in part by the publication of Professor Kelley's book, stated: "Whatever you call the art, it is firmly entrenched in American political life—though it has so far received skimpy attention."[7]

To the extent that such analysis has appeared, it has aroused, as might be expected, a good deal of defensiveness on the part of practitioners. Writing in *Public Relations Quarterly*, Morton B. Lawrence said of the critics:

> These very dedicated political scientists . . . seem to feel that a political television program or a brochure in which complex issues are presented in an interesting or "easy-to-take" manner constitutes a fraud upon the voter . . . [but] the choice is between popularized versions and no voter interest at all.[8]

Another practitioner, Paul A. Theis, public relations director of the Republican Congressional Campaign Committee in the 60's, rested his case upon the impression that a candidate seeks to make on editors and broadcasters. In the quest for limited newspaper space and air time, the candidate may find himself ignored if his releases are "sloppily written or phrased like legal briefs." On the other hand, "if . . . the approach is professional, then the editor or broadcaster is impressed that the campaign should be taken seriously."[9]

Ray W. Fenton says that the costs of campaigning are the principal justification for professional public relations guidance. He contends: "The good public relations man is expected to save money by suggesting spending funds where each dollar will do the maximum good, preventing the waste of money on ineffective things." Rising costs, says Fenton, help impress candidates that they need sound advice and a firm hand in the expenditure of their campaign war chests.[10]

Indeed, costs of presidential campaigns are becoming astronomical. The Chase Manhattan Bank, seeking to inform more people of this problem, produced a film demonstrating that Abraham Lincoln's presidential campaign cost less than $100,000, less than today's price for thirty minutes of prime network television time. In the 1960 election, the film pointed out, the major parties each spent nearly $200,-000,000 on campaign costs. (The Chase film, by the way, was no "cheapie" itself. The thirteen-minute production by Film Counselors, Inc., of New York, was narrated by former National Broadcasting Company commentator Chet Huntley and cost an estimated $45,-000.)[11] Figures for 1968 indicate total expenditures in excess of $250,000,000.

Concern with the rising costs of presidential campaign expenditures—when television first became a major factor, as early as 1952—was sufficiently great to prompt an investigation by a special committee of Congress. In December 1952 Representative Clarence J. Brown of Ohio told the committee that the total expenditures by both major parties in that year had risen to more than $80,-000,000.[12]

A veteran campaigner, Michigan Democratic Chairman Neil Staebler, explained the growing costs and their likely consequences as follows:

> ". . . Our main problem comes from the modern development of the mass media of communication. These media are expensive and grow more so all the time. . . . [They] are not merely expensive, but for them have been developed new advertising techniques,

requiring professional skills that are also expensive. . . . If present tendencies continue, our Federal elections will increasingly become contests not between candidates but between great advertising firms."[13]

Indeed, the Federal Communications Commission estimates that outlays for political radio and television broadcasting rose from $20,000,000 in 1962 to $32,000,000 in 1966, or 60 percent in four years. Expenditures for political advertising in magazines and newspapers have been only about 10 percent of those for radio and television in national campaigns. Television costs have increased because of a much higher volume of units purchased, as well as increasing prices for such units.[14]

So, as campaign costs and the complexity of the mass media escalate, it follows that candidates for the presidency will no longer rely upon amateurs. The circumstances of the times, in fact, reduce some of the traditional political leaders to the category of amateur campaigners. The same holds true for many of the dearest friends of the candidates and some of the most devoted party workers. Television, with its special requirements, expense, and limitations of time, calls for the services of experts. To a degree, therefore, the public relations man in political campaigning is "a product of the electronic age."[15]

With regard to this matter of television, at least two other points —one operational, the other theoretical—deserve mention.

First, although vast amounts of money are the primary requirement for maximum television exposure of a candidate, the simple availability of cash does not in itself assure that candidate the use of the airwaves during prime time. Radio and television stations have no obligation to sell time for political broadcasts. The candidate for President must wait his turn for time availabilities, and he may find himself lined up behind the weight-reducing salon, the brewery, the hemorrhoid remedy.

Federal law does require that stations make available "equal time" to all contenders for a given office. This means that each radio or television station that grants free time, newscasts and news interviews excepted, to one candidate must provide equal time to each opposing candidate. But the fact that one candidate may be in a financial position to purchase available time does not mean that the same will be true of his opponent.

A notable exception to this whole procedure took place during the

1960 campaign when Congress temporarily suspended the "equal time" requirements (Section 315 of the Communications Act) for the "Great Debates" between Richard M. Nixon and John F. Kennedy. The major networks made available four hours of prime time for the two candidates at no cost. We shall examine those debates in more detail during our discussion of the 1960 campaign, but suffice it to say here that former presidential press secretary Pierre Salinger, in his book *With Kennedy*, states flatly that television enabled John F. Kennedy to defeat Richard Nixon in 1960.

In subsequent presidential campaigns, Section 315 was in force, and radio-TV coverage, outside of newscasts, was confined largely to paid broadcasts. Some observers have suggested that one reason why Section 315 remains in operation is that it gives an advantage to incumbents. Their activities are more likely to be covered "for free" on regular news broadcasts, while challengers tend to attract somewhat less attention.

Secondly, along with radio, television has been a catalyst in bringing about a new era of more intensive public participation in presidential politics. But it has also, in the words of Samuel Archibald of the Fair Campaign Practices Committee:

> ... [made] possible the instantaneous spread of lies and distortions to the furthest reaches of the country, with little chance of the truth catching up to the falsehood—at least not in time to counteract the damage to a politician's reputation and prospects for election.[16]

Let us next look at the nature and extent of some of the commercial organizations—the public relations firms—as well as some of the individual consultants who operate on behalf of the candidates for public office.

Paul Cain, the head of one such organization in Dallas, Texas, pointed out that there are a number of "fringe operators," generally headquartered in state capitals, who call themselves public relations men, but who are in reality professional campaign managers or lobbyists. Cain estimated that some 10 percent of the counseling firms with membership in the Public Relations Society of America, the national accrediting organization, have political clients. These, he said, generally fall into three categories:

(a) The larger firms, such as my own, who give complete campaign management to state office races, but who stay out of district or local races (for example, in the last two years, we have handled two gubernatorial races, one senatorial race, and one Presidential campaign)....

(b) Each large community usually has one particular public relations firm which handles the local city administration's politics, bond issues, school board elections, and that sort of thing. These firms usually also will handle candidates in the primary elections for the legislature and occasionally for Congress.

(c) There are also in large communities three or four one-man shops, usually calling themselves John Doe & Associates, who will take on campaigns for the state legislature, local judgeships and that sort of thing.

... It would be my guess that there are one or two politically competent PR firms in most major cities and states. Texas and California are a little more conspicuous than the others, perhaps, because they are so large and their politics so heterogeneous that it is really like running six or seven different campaigns at once and requires professional planning and a large staff.[17]

Despite what might appear to the layman and student of politics alike to be an underground surfeit of political public relations specialists, Paul A. Theis complained during 1968 in *Public Relations Journal* that there is "a crying need for competent, experienced professionals to handle public relations in political campaigns."[18]

Theis said that the campaign committees of the two major parties receive "uncounted requests" from candidates for public offices at all levels to help find them public relations assistance for their campaigns, and that each year most such requests go unfilled.

A "lucky candidate," according to Theis, might persuade a local newsman to gamble on quitting his job and joining a campaign as public relations director. Or, he may be able to convince a friendly corporation president to give a member of his public relations staff a leave of absence to handle the campaign; or he may be able to afford a campaign management firm. For every "lucky" candidate, however, there are dozens who are not.

Nevertheless, Theis points out, *presidential candidates can usually afford the best men available.*

Theis's rundown of the ideal qualifications for political public relations seems somewhat obvious: News reporting or writing experience, an ability to prepare press releases in the proper style, and insight into the problems of the media, including television stations and their handling of news. In addition, he should know the news outlets and their deadlines and be on good terms with the media people—especially the political writers, reporters, and commentators—and familiar with their problems and needs.

The motives of public relations firms in taking on political candidates vary considerably. Paul Cain, in the letter quoted previously, said that "very few successful public relations firms regard political campaigns as preferred business." He indicated that his own firm, which has been "moderately successful" in political campaigns, takes them on for two reasons. First, because he sometimes feels he cannot keep out of the race if he believes that the election of a particular candidate is extremely important. Secondly,

> I am willing to get into races at the level of governor or United States senator or attorney general, simply *for the friendships I will make that will be useful to me in my business.* I don't mean influence peddling; I simply mean that *it is frequently useful and convenient to be on a first-name basis with public officials* [italics mine].

As for the fees involved, Cain said, "the financial side of political campaigns is not at all attractive to a firm like ours." He complained that campaigns "clog up" his entire shop, take too much staff time, often require that temporary staff be hired, induce a flood of "time-wasting" telephone calls, and cause the firm to neglect some of its regular clients. He observed that two Texas firms specializing in this kind of work were nearly out of business, partly because, in his opinion, they depended upon the seasonal and temporary activity of political campaigns.

Perhaps the first of the modern professional consulting firms devoting itself exclusively to political public relations was Whitaker and Baxter of Los Angeles. James M. Perry, of the *National Observer*, in his book *The New Politics,* points out that the two essential ingredients of the "new politics" were actually born more than thirty years ago when the late Clem Whitaker and his wife, Leone Baxter, organized their firm. And, says Perry, "some of the work they did many years ago is, in some ways, superior to anything being done today."[19]

Perry's two "essential ingredients" are:

> 1. Appeals should be made directly to the voters through the mass media.
> 2. The techniques used to make these appeals—polling,

computers, television, direct mail—should be sophisticated and scientific.

Whitaker and Baxter was new in its time because it was a *professional firm* of political managers. Campaigns, of course, have always been run by *someone*—often a friend or associate of a candidate, such as Mark Hanna. Later on, Perry points out, some of these men, such as James Farley, who worked for Franklin Delano Roosevelt, and Murray Chotiner, who worked for Richard M. Nixon, became more professional in their activities. "But Whitaker and Baxter was a company, and its business was managing political campaigns for corporate profit. That was a new kind of politics." The firm appealed directly to the voters through the mass media, although the many "scientific" campaign techniques treated at length by Perry had not yet been refined.

Whitaker and Baxter, whose operations are also treated at some length by Stanley Kelley, managed seventy-five political campaigns between 1933 and 1955. They won seventy of them.[20]

Perry quotes Clem Whitaker:

> "It was Patrick Henry who said, 'Give me liberty or give me death.' That's what we call laying it on with a ladle. . . . Even in these modern times, that is the kind of dynamic sloganeering that molds public opinion and wins campaigns."[21]

He also quotes a critic of the Whitaker and Baxter methods:

> "The sad fact is that their manufacture of slogans and wielding of ladles has led to a grievous debasement of political debate. . . . Whitaker and Baxter's peculiar contribution, however, has been to make a precise art of oversimplification, to systematize emotional appeals, to merchandise the images they create through a relentless exploitation of every means of mass communication. Compared to these virtuosos, the old-time politician seems like an amateur."[22]

Of course, there were no "old-time politicians" in California in the sense in which that term would be generally recognized in the East, and Whitaker and Baxter "moved in to fill *all* the vacuums."

> Using mass media in a highly sophisticated way, they took their clients' messages directly to the voters. . . . They were the first to find the way to the voter in the absence of the party machine.[23]

As both Perry and Kelley point out, Whitaker and Baxter, once retained by a candidate, gave all the orders. They were in charge, and the campaign was to be conducted as they saw fit. No one else ran the show, and the man who was to hold office, if elected, was not the one whose judgments dictated the course of the campaign.

> [Whitaker and Baxter] developed the issues; they created and placed the advertising; they wrote the scripts. It was the candidate's responsibility to pay for what Whitaker and Baxter decided was best. They made their point with clarity. . . . There was a certain inherent arrogance, which the two partners tried not at all to cover over.[24]

One of the growing number of current operators in this field at the presidential campaign level is Joseph Napolitan. We shall later touch upon his role in Hubert H. Humphrey's 1968 presidential campaign. Napolitan came to national attention in 1966 when he managed the campaign of Milton Shapp, who defeated Robert P. Casey, the state senator for Pennsylvania's Lackawanna County and the official organization candidate for governor, in Pennsylvania's spring Democratic primary.

The Shapp campaign was, according to an official of the Democratic National Committee with whom we talked, a national political classic. It demonstrated how the right mixture of financial backing, media exposure, and technical skill can combine to bring victory to an individual virtually unknown to a large electorate before his entry into a campaign.

"There are some cases where money, exposure, and the ability of technicians can make the difference between winning and losing," the official told us. "I know Milt Shapp, and I respect him, but I think it's safe to say that without Joe Napolitan and his techniques, Shapp wouldn't have had a chance for the Democratic nomination."[25]

Casey, the first official Democratic candidate for governor of Pennsylvania to have been beaten in a primary, apparently agreed. He assessed the campaign this way:

> "You have to do what he [Shapp] did. You have to use the new sophisticated techniques, the polling, the television, the heavy staffing, and the direct mail. You can't rely any more on political organizations. . . . We're at the tag end of an era."[26]

Napolitan sees today's political campaigns as big business:

> "Each year, they're more expensive. I figure that campaigns for the

U.S. Senate and governor in each of the ten biggest states now cost at least one million dollars apiece. If you were to invest that much in business, you'd want a consultant. If you were going to spend that much for a building, you'd want an architect. It's the same thing with campaigns. I think every campaign that costs $1,000,000 will be professionally managed within the next ten years. It's just bound to happen."[27]

Another of the new consulting firms, Campaign Consultants, Inc. (CCI), is headed by David Goldberg, who served as national director of the Draft (Henry Cabot) Lodge Committee in 1964. We will have occasion to examine that committee's activities later on, but Perry indicates—accurately—that Goldberg was probably chiefly responsible for Lodge's upset victory in the 1964 New Hampshire presidential primary. Another principal in CCI is John Deardourff, a former director of research for the New York Republican State Committee, who also worked for Nelson Rockefeller and John Lindsay. CCI, with offices in Boston and Washington, D.C., advised Edward M. Brooke during his successful campaign to become a Republican senator from Massachusetts and Vice President Spiro T. Agnew in his race against George Mahoney to become governor of Maryland. The firm also counseled Governor George Romney of Michigan in connection with his 1968 Republican presidential primary campaign in New Hampshire until Romney decided to withdraw. One of CCI's techniques in the Romney campaign was to punch IBM cards for all of New Hampshire's 148,000 registered Republican voters for use in direct-mail activities.[28]

Another new firm, U.S. R & D, was, along with Joseph Napolitan, one of the few professional campaign consulting firms working nationally for Democratic candidates exclusively. The firm was notably unsuccessful, and it has already gone out of business.

This firm was headed by two one-time Kennedy associates, William Haddad and Robert Clampitt, and was headquartered in New York City. Their loss record included the campaigns of the late Robert King High, who was defeated in the 1966 Florida gubernatorial election by Claude Kirk; Detroit Mayor Jerome P. Cavanaugh, who lost the Democratic senatorial primary in Michigan to G. Mennen Williams, and New York City Council President Frank O'Connor, soundly defeated by Nelson Rockefeller in his attempt to become governor of New York in 1966.[29]

Another new firm, which has carried the political applications of the Hollywood star system to its logical conclusion of insanity, is headed by Hal Every and appropriately domiciled in Los Angeles. Every calls his firm the Public Relations Center. He has an interesting approach, which sounds like a W. C. Fields aphorism: candidates, says Every, should never be seen or heard. "Unless the guy is an experienced speaker," Every told the *Wall Street Journal*, "he's going to do himself far more harm than good getting out there where people can ask him questions."[30]

Every, perhaps to the good of the democratic system, has yet to manage a presidential campaign. Under his strategy, as Perry points out, voters would make their decision on a candidate based on a slogan such as "Three Cheers for Pat Milligan." Every dreams up such a slogan, mails it to people, puts it on bill-boards, runs it in the newspapers, and then asks people to elect his client for no reason which bears any relation to the candidate's capacity to do the job.

Despite the mixed record of some of these firms, it should be borne in mind that the political public relations man is like a football coach: he operates under a tremendous compulsion to win for his clients. The old master, Clem Whitaker, who, by the way, worked only for Republican candidates, once told a professional gathering:

> If you launch a campaign for a new car, your client doesn't expect to lead the field necessarily in the first year, or even the tenth year. If you're in third, fourth or fifth place, that's good enough; you're still *one of the big five!* But in politics they don't pay off for PLACE OR SHOW! You have to win, if you want to stay in business.[31]

So while there are great similarities between the public relations techniques used politically and those used commercially, there is often a wide gulf in the quantitative goals. A commercial program can be a great success if it "sells" 5 percent of the market. A political program will probably fail if it does not "sell" more than 50 percent of the electoral market.

This compulsion to win is perhaps one reason why political public relations men see themselves as coordinators of ideas and not simply as the promoters of political commodities which, from their professional point of view, may not be salable. As the coordinator of ideas, one practitioner has pointed out, the public relations man is often the one who develops the central theme of a campaign. In such a role, he determines which issues will take precedence, and which will be subordinate, and he molds them into the candidate's basic approach to the voter. Whenever possible, he develops a slogan which "in a few words brings the central theme home to the voter."[32]

In many ways, this is a logical development in the role of the public relations man. If men seeking public office regard mass persuasion as the road to success, then the specialist in that technique obviously is going to be very influential in political campaigns. As the public relations man goes farther into the heart of the electoral process, he is not likely to stop short of crucial political policy formation.

As Robert P. Casey pointed out after his defeat by Milton Shapp, the old-fashioned political leader aimed at control through patronage rather than policy. But the professionals of public relations affect the candidate in areas much more central than his eventual selection of personnel.

Paul Theis, for example, says that as one of a candidate's key people, the public relations director must sit in on daily strategy sessions, assessing the effect of every campaign decision from a media point of view. From his news experience, he determines, for example, whether statements which his client or employer plans to issue "will make the candidate look good or bad." Thus, it is imperative that he have access to the candidate at all times.[33]

Given this responsibility for at least that part of the campaign which appears above the surface—the candidate's statements, speeches, and news releases; his radio and television exposure; his public appearances; his advertising activities—with concomitant authority for the expenditure of campaign funds, the public relations man emerges as perhaps the leading influence in the shaping of the candidate's public image and often that of his party as well.

This means that the practitioners have a great responsibility indeed. In the words of one professional: "No longer are they dealing with competitive soap flakes, but with programs and personalities that may have a profound and lasting effect upon the well-being of the nation."[34]

This question of the increasingly profound responsibility borne by the political public relations man has disturbed some practitioners and scholars alike. Martin Hauan, who served as public relations director of the Democratic National Committee in 1968, has said that it is dangerous for candidates to rely too heavily on their public relations advisers, and that the candidates should always make the basic decisions, because "they're more qualified to do so."[35]

Howard White has written that the public relations men:

> . . . do not run for office. They are not officers, they are not neces-
> sarily members of the parties they are aiding. Yet they are at least
> trying to play a dominant role in determining the issues. If they
> succeed, and there is some reason to believe that their star is
> rising, they can be a far more dangerous force than the old-style
> political boss was. The Theodore Roosevelts and the Clevelands
> scorned the old professionals. In the new-style campaign the par-
> ties seem eager to compete for the new professionals.[36]

Morton Lawrence has warned his fellow professionals that it is not their job to reshape policy so that it conforms with the position having the greatest appeal to voters. Lawrence is clear in his conviction that the public relations man serves the candidate best by confining his function to presenting the honest opinion of the man who is seeking office "in the most cogent manner and favorable light."[37]

By definition, however, one of the public relations man's jobs, Lawrence agrees, is to gauge the likely public reaction to anything a candidate plans to say publicly, to any position he plans to take on any issue. However, presenting a candidate's views, in light of the adviser's findings, so that they will gain the greatest possible public acceptance can lead to a kind of sterilization of a campaign. The easiest way not to offend anyone is to say very little that is forthright, to avoid controversial issues, and to modify one's position subtly to suit what the statistical analysts tell the candidate is the primary audience of the moment. Numerous political writers feel that this is precisely the course chosen by the "new" Richard M. Nixon, both before and after his ascendancy to the White House.

This is not to say that the public relations man is reluctant to interject issues into a political campaign. Issues are one of the tools of his trade. It is a measure of his skill to express his client's position on issues so as to influence the greatest possible number of people to see things the way his candidate sees them. The crucial question for American democracy, however, is whether the public relations man's product is a legitimate contribution to the deliberative process or just so much slick talk.

Kelley feels strongly that the place given to issues in a campaign by the public relations man is a prominent one, but he does not raise a warning flag against the possibility of "political sterilization" mentioned above:

> Public relations politics is issue politics: parking tickets cannot be fixed by newspaper, radio or television. Issues are weapons and must be managed as such. Though this does not mean that the public relations man is free to choose only those issues that suit his purposes, it does mean that he has certain criteria which guide him in their selection, delineation, and the stress he gives them.

Kelley contends that the public relations man is always on the attack when dealing with campaign issues:

> To attack is to press on the public the issues that are to one's own advantage. To attack is not just to give one's own side of the question, but to *define* the political situation.[38]

Issues are often, for the practitioner, an approach to a theme—a unifying thread which runs through the campaign. A review of presidential campaigns since 1952 indicates a consistent tendency to choose three or four issues and pound away at them for the duration. The issues may relate to a theme such as "The Mess in Washington," a phrase which is sufficiently vague to cover a multitude of alleged sins, or "The Great Society," which is meant to cover a multitude of alleged virtues.

Issues, once selected, tend to be put in rather simple terms and are repeated as frequently as possible in precisely the same terms, much as an advertising slogan for a commercial product. The contribution of this standard approach to rational political deliberation, let alone the virtue of eloquence, would appear, to say the least, highly suspect.

One prominent practitioner repeats for his colleagues the advice of an unidentified "famous psychologist" that a sure way of putting an idea into people's heads is "through affirmation, pure and simple, kept free of all reasoning and proof. The conciser the affirmation and the more destitute of every appearance of proof, the more weight it carries."[39]

Another professional says that the effectiveness of political sloganizing "has been demonstrated by its becoming a major target of . . . critics, who seem to forget that slogans have played a major part in the development of world history and have spurred men on to great achievements."[40]

This kind of thinking is a clear reflection of the influence of commercial public relations in the realm of politics. It is, in fact, a technique more of advertising, packaging, marketing, and hard-sell sales promotion than of public relations. *Business Week* once quoted an anonymous politician as saying that "politicians have finally realized [that] the skill, training and experience which daily move millions of dollars in merchandise must have something to do with helping people make up their minds."[41]

In the words of another practitioner: "Reduced to the basics, the problem of promoting a candidate for any office is really one of packaging and marketing. There is a distinct difference between selling a candidate and marketing him, just as in the case with a commercial product. Selling is much more direct. It is an effort to convince people to buy whatever you have to offer them. Marketing, on the other hand, involves finding out just what it is the public most wants to buy and then making it available to them."[42]

One of the key differences, on an operational level, between a political campaign and a commercial marketing and packaging campaign is time. Product promotion usually involves a long-range, thoroughly laid-out campaign, preceded by a period of trial-and-error test-marketing. Political campaigns are of necessity much more compact and tense. But, from a professional point of view, some of the packaging techniques are similar. Both involve an effort to gain public acceptance and approval. Furthermore, if the analogy is complete, both involve finding out what people are buying this season and then altering the product to suit their taste.

Paul Theis divides the process into three parts:

> 1. *The label.* In politics, this involves the party and what it is thought to stand for. This presumably includes the party platform. It also includes labels which cross party boundaries, such as "liberal," "moderate," "law and order candidate," etc.
>
> 2. *Past performance.* Like a General Motors car or Heinz ketchup, the party and candidate must be generally well thought of.
>
> 3. *The package itself.* The product is the candidate—the potential President. Of course, as Theis recognizes, to the degree that the package is human, it is something of an unpredictable quantity.[43]

Theodore White has also recognized the analogy. The process of becoming known, of becoming identifiable to voters, he points out:

> is perhaps the most expensive and necessary condition of American Presidential politics. People cannot vote for a candidate unless they recognize him; this problem of POLITICAL marketing dwarfs any comparable problem of mercantile marketing.[44]

There are, White confirms, several ways to market a potential President through the political process. The simplest way, if one is wealthy, is to purchase renown. Another route is through the endorsement of an incumbent administration, which puts a man on national display, perhaps through a Cabinet position, diplomatic assignments, or various special projects. Obviously, if you control the White House, you have the power to give any individual an opportunity to become a national star. Roosevelt did this for Truman, Harriman, and several others. Eisenhower did it for Nixon. Nixon did it for Agnew and Kissinger.

White also points to a possible third course. If your political fame is primarily regional, and you are unable to win national stature in either of these first two ways—because you are not wealthy, and/or because the opposition is in power—then you must show some muscle at the polls. This is the difficult route of the primary elections, which was chosen by such individuals as Estes Kefauver in 1952 and 1956, John F. Kennedy in 1960, Barry Goldwater in 1964, Eugene McCarthy in 1968, and George McGovern in 1972.

Paid advertising is an important part of a coordinated public relations marketing campaign. News coverage, which cannot be purchased directly, is more believable, and many presidential candidates have displayed considerable ingenuity at garnering editorial space and broadcast time. Advertising may be less believable, but if it is copious and consistent, it influences people.

Furthermore, as Fenton observes, political public relations men know that buying time and space is the only way to be positive that their message will reach the voters in precisely the same form it left their office. Although most public relations firms and individual consultants do not themselves handle the production and placement of advertising, many of them will not accept a political candidate as a client unless they control the advertising copy and scheduling. Since the responsibility for maintaining consistency rests with the public relations adviser, it is usually accepted practice that those who write for candidates and advise them on their relationships with the media should also retain supervisory responsibility for their advertising.

Lewis Chester, Godfrey Hodgson, and Bruce Page, three British correspondents who produced a large volume on the 1968 presidential campaign, came away convinced that American admen have "pushed the technique and ambitions of their craft further than anywhere else in the world."

> . . . The great Bullshine Machine rolls forward, extending the field of fire for its shiny product from the advertising pages to the news columns, from skinless sausages . . . and mass-produced cakes . . . to the personality of candidates and the great issues that divide society. The constant exposure to this shower of matter—half-true, or even true, but always simplified, always loud, always self-serving—induces a peculiar mixture of gullibility and cynicism that is close to neurosis. It is not an attitude that is well adapted for distinguishing between bullshine and brass tacks, rhetoric and reality.[45]

The three English observers raise a nice issue: the way in which the commercial approach to presidential politics—the hard sell—may eventually affect the attitudes of voters toward the electoral process itself. When presidential candidates are sold like soap flakes, the effects upon the heart of the democratic process—the judgment and deliberative abilities of the electorate—may be profound indeed. When voters are sold candidates via the "Bullshine Machine," are they likely to take would-be Presidents and their claims with a great deal more seriousness than they would a new brand of toothpaste and *its* self-proclaimed assets?

We have made frequent reference to the process of finding out what the voter wants in order to mount a campaign that responds to his needs and desires. This means that the public relations practitioner generally turns to opinion sampling as a first step in the campaign process, and one which is repeated as the campaign moves along.

To p.r. executive H. Zane Robbins, the difference between telling the voters what they want to know, once you have learned this from the polls, and telling them what you want them to hear is "the difference between communicating and just making noise." He quotes columnist Marquis Childs as observing that a politician is "a man who identifies the sound of his own voice with the infallible voice of the people." Says Robbins: "Good research prevents a candidate from making this fatal error."[46]

Campaign opinion sampling, however, does not concentrate on issues alone. It attempts also to discover what the voters think of the candidate and his opponent. This kind of information, according to Robbins,

> ... can often be a valuable guide in helping the candidate present himself in a more favorable light. It can also reveal weak points in the makeup of his opponent. Dealing in personalities, of course, is out. It isn't ethical in the first place, and it will cost you votes in the second place.

On the other hand, if your opponent is "too young," it is permissible to "hammer away at youth and inexperience." If he is too far left or right, it is proper, Robbins says, to underscore his associations.[47]

Howard White was concerned about the implications of this point of view, several years before Robbins wrote the words above, when he said:

> By studying the weaknesses, the prejudices, in a public, you may convince the public that it is getting just what it wants. This is precisely what the "new" men, managerial men, must do, and they must do it with the help of political scientists and other scholars.[48]

Playing upon the emotions of the electorate in this fashion is a technique primarily directed at the nonvoter and the politically inactive voter in an effort to involve them in the campaign. As is the case with the public relations man's involvement in issues, his involvement with emotions also works against disciplined, machine-oriented votes in determining an election. If disinterest is the ally of the political boss and his machine, then emotional involvement is the ally of the "new" manager. Thus, he strives to inspire love, hate, fear, respect, anger, admiration, and—when he is fighting off a challenger—one of the most politically effective emotions of all: doubt.

Doubtful images of mysterious origin sometimes grow up around men at the presidential level. Once a presidential candidate is so cast in a public role, it is a formidable job for him to attempt to change the characterization. It is, according to Theodore White, "as if once someone has assembled personality traits into a convenient pattern, no writer ever re-examines it; it is easier to use the accepted pattern." Sometimes the author is traceable: for example, Westbrook Pegler's creation of "Bubblehead" Wallace. But more commonly, White points out, the pattern will grow by itself and is then even more difficult to break: "Adlai Stevenson as the Egghead Hamlet of politics and Dwight D. Eisenhower as the Patriot Above Politics were roles so quickly and completely cartooned and accepted that no one could trace their origin."[49]

Theodore White has also made some helpful distinctions between the various audiences the presidential candidate and his advisers attempt to reach during the course of a campaign (and we are indebted to him for much of the following analysis).[50] Each of these audiences requires distinct skills in public relations, organization, and management.

The largest, most obvious audience is the national one—the general public. A presidential candidate is routinely linked to this public through the dozens of reporters and correspondents who follow his every movement during the course of the campaign. The candidate's public relations staff are the shepherds to this flock. Twice a day they supply the waiting newsmen with speech texts or press releases. Thus, both the morning and the afternoon newspapers are assured that they are getting fresh material.

The public relations men who travel with the candidate must also tend to the sea of microphones and television and film cameras that bob before the candidate each time he speaks, in search of brief audio-tape excerpts for the evening news. Through all of these media, the candidate reaches his national audience—the casual watchers, the preoccupied listeners, the hasty readers.

The candidate and his managers and advisers also pursue what Theodore White calls the "strategically calculated audience," known in public relations textbooks as "special publics." Every presidential campaign has, for example, selected certain states, strategic because of their electoral votes, to be worked intensively and repeatedly.

In every one of these states, the public relations staff of the candidate must service and cultivate the local media, seeing to it that they treat the arrival of the candidate as a truly major news event. Citizens are aware of his visit throughout the urban and rural circulation area of the state's larger newspapers and the coverage areas of the major radio and television stations. If the candidate speaks in Milwaukee, the speech may rate only the briefest treatment in New York media, but in Wisconsin it's front-page material. Thus, a direct impact is made on an important state, and local dignitaries and volunteers have had their enthusiasm aroused so that they might light fires under other potential supporters once the candidate has moved on.

The third audience, which White calls the "personal audience," is dwarfed in size by the other two. The membership of this group consists of those lucky enough to set eyes on the candidate—at airports, at crossroads, lining curbs, waiting at whistle stops. The candidate's public relations staff includes people who help turn these crowds out.

White feels that this smallest audience, in a special way, is the most important of all for the candidate:

> . . . These are the people who count most. . . . only the personal audience . . . can give the candidate the one thing he needs most; response of warmth or frost, of applause or indifference. Its laughter, its scowl, its silence, its cheers, its yearning, its measuring eyes, are the only clues in the mystic communication between the leader and the led, to tell truly whether he has reached those he seeks to lead. . . . The candidate must feel the beat of the people he hopes to lead; their heart is his target. And no public-opinion poll or analysis can tell him half so well whether he has reached that target as can the people themselves, giving him the beat of their response.[51]

But the fact of the matter is that in the age of mass communications, every audience for a Presidential candidate is a national audience. If any candidate and any audience think otherwise, they need only turn to the press corps, the cameras, and the microphones for a reminder of who is out there.

Obviously, the art of scheduling a campaign so as to reach all of these publics at the most propitious time is an intricate one. The public relations operatives have an important role to play in the effective allocation of the candidate's time, virtually every minute of which is accounted for from the time of the convention to his victory or concession statement on election night. Schedules have to be integrated and geared to political need and news requirements, as well as to the demands of transportation and time and the diverse problems of the pack of newsmen who dog the heels of major candidates and often require a good deal of care, feeding, and mothering while on the road. Groundwork is laid ahead of the traveling entourage by a team of unique public relations specialists, the advance men. They arrange the tours of presidential candidates down to the last detail; indeed, whether they remember that last detail and get it right is often the measure of their effectiveness. As Theodore White says: "A good advance man must combine in himself the qualities of a circus tout, a carnival organizer, an accomplished diplomat and a quarter-master general."[52]

A major candidate's public relations staff is also involved in the creation of events that help assure the candidate maximum favorable news coverage. Even regularly scheduled events are "staged," or managed, in such a way as to keep the name and picture of the candidate up in front of the electorate. Practitioners are fond of using the Boston Tea Party as their historical prototype of the staged political event. But often the events they plan are slightly less momentous. For example, Paul Theis advises:

> Don't wait for events to just happen. Stage activities for news and photo coverage during the "dog days" to keep the candidate's name and picture before the voters. . . . Photos of the candidate helping volunteer workers stuff envelopes, inspecting a new bus planned to carry his campaign to the people, or a picture of a carpenter removing the door of the candidate's private office, with a caption stating that he pledges "an open door policy" . . . if elected.[53]

The introduction of electronic technology into most aspects of American society has not left political campaigns untouched either. A number of devices in data processing, telecommunications, and computer gaming long ago made their debut in the field.

One such device is the recorded telephone call. Voters in selected crucial areas receive letters over the candidate's signature saying that he will be calling them. Meanwhile, back at headquarters, the operator dials the number, waits until a light goes on to signal that the phone has been answered, then switches on the recorded message. While it is running, the operator dials another number. One machine can make twenty-five hundred calls a day. This gimmick was used by the Romney organization in Michigan on behalf of five Republican candidates for Congress. In one district, two machines completed 52,213 calls. When the polls showed the technique was having some impact, a third machine was rushed in and completed 9,308 calls in eight days. Under a contract with the Telectraphonics Corporation, which owns the gear, the calls cost four cents each.[54]

Computers are also kept busy by political public relations men. One of the outstanding users over the years was Governor Winthrop Rockefeller of Arkansas, who, according to Perry, was "the only politician in America who maintains his own private computer expressly for political work and who pays, out of his own pocket, a stable of experts to run it. . . . Mr. Rockefeller's aides freely admit that without the computer (and all those exotic spare parts), he would never have been elected governor in 1966. And, it was partly because of the computer that he was heavily favored to win re-election in 1968" (which he did). A tremendous amount of money is involved in such efforts. Perry reported that another computer, which Winthrop Rockefeller began using in 1967, leased for $10,000 a month.[55]

The Democratic National Committee began using data processing experimentally in 1960. By 1967 it had graduated to an IBM 1401 and, like Winthrop Rockefeller, was planning to switch to the larger, faster Model 360. "By 1967 . . . the pace was suddenly accelerating. New firms were being created to specialize in political data processing. And new ways were being found to use computers in politics."[56]

One such firm is Datamatics, Inc., of Los Angeles, partly owned by and located down the hall from Spencer-Roberts & Associates, a campaign consulting firm which has worked for presidential candidates Nelson Rockefeller and Ronald Reagan, among other Republicans. Perry quotes the head of Datamatics, Vincent P. Barabba, as saying:

> "The candidate who does not avail himself of modern campaign techniques may be as unfortunate as the physician who shuns the latest diagnostic instruments or the businessman who disregards new methods of merchandising. It is a truism that in an era of innovation he who does not move forward is left behind."[57]

Barabba's firm goes beyond the Winthrop Rockefeller-type applications of electronic data processing to direct mail, list keeping, registration, and fund-raising. Datamatics also provides detailed demographic and political analysis. According to Perry, "The Republicans are leaders in both areas."[58]

Perry also points to other possible uses of the computer in political campaigns. It can place advertising, presumably making "scientific" decisions about the impact of the various media and the types and locations of advertising to be placed. A computer can be programmed to prepare an entire advertising budget, schedule the advertising program, and even send out the mail. A computer can also schedule all of the events of a political campaign, a process known as the "critical-path method."[59] Computers were so employed in scheduling Richard Nixon's "surrogates" in the 1972 campaign.

Another political use of electronic data processing is simulation, first used in a presidential campaign by John F. Kennedy's organization in 1960. Simulation is an imitation of reality. The computer records millions of bits of data, and then estimates what actually will happen if a number of different courses of action are followed. Perry points out that while an opinion poll indicates a perception at a given moment in time, and is therefore static, a simulation estimates mathematically the entire range of human behavior hypothetically possible in a make-believe situation and is therefore dynamic. He feels that simulation "may turn out to be the computer's most important contribution to American politics," and quotes Harold Lasswell, who wrote. "This [simulation] is the A-bomb of the social sciences. The breakthrough here is comparable to what happened at Stagg Field."[60]

Perry's explorations of the technological frontiers of political campaigning may seem esoteric to the public relations man, the student of politics, and the lay voter who finds himself on the other end of the process. He drew this composite picture of a presidential campaign under the new political technology:

> The candidate's travels . . . will be scheduled by a computer. The campaign will be laid out by the critical-path method. Polls will be taken over and over and analyzed and cross-analyzed. Spot commercials will be prepared weeks in advance of the election, and their impact will be almost subliminal. Researchers will read the polls and study the data from a "simulator"; the issues they develop will . . . be aimed like rifle shots at the most receptive audiences. Researchers will systematically investigate the opposing candidate, and the new techniques will be used to destroy his credibility. . . . And the candidate? He will be out front, moving from state to state with robot-like precision, being fed the data from the polls and the simulator. He will no doubt be articulate and probably he will be handsome and vigorous. And he may or may not be qualified to be President of the United States.[61]

When Perry made these predictions, sounding like the Jules Verne or H. G. Wells of presidential campaigning, he said that no one had yet put together a political campaign successfully employing *all* the new techniques. But he predicted that *someday* a presidential campaign would be organized this way, bringing all of these technological tools into play. He wrote the words quoted above in 1967, and the events of the following year proved him perhaps a better prophet than he would have dared to expect. For—except for the simulator (which had, indeed, been used eight years before)—all of the techniques Perry listed were, evidence indicates, employed by the major presidential candidates in 1968.

We turn now to some highlights of the presidential campaigns of 1952–1968, in an attempt to further illustrate the influence and significance of public relations practitioners and the techniques of their craft upon the process of choosing a President.

# Three:
# The Eisenhower Campaigns:
# 1952 and 1956

## The 1952 Campaign

### The Republicans

A few days before the inauguration of Dwight D. Eisenhower as President of the United States, Wayne J. Hood, executive director of the Republican National Committee, showed committee members a book marked simply "Campaign Plan." He told the National Committee that the book was ". . . the most complete blueprint ever drawn up in advance of a presidential campaign."[1]

The plan, prepared in format typical of advertising and public relations agency presentations, outlined the basic organization and strategy of the 1952 Republican presidential campaign. It dealt with campaign appeals, speeches, literature, advertising, radio and television broadcasting, the relative emphasis to be given to various communications media, the types, places, and times of public events and campaign trips, and the regions of the country upon which campaign efforts would be focused. The plan had been drafted by Robert Humphreys, public relations director of the campaign, who had previously served the Republican Congressional Campaign Committee in the same capacity. A draft of the plan had been considered by the Republican Strategy Committee in Washington shortly after the 1952 convention, and then flown to Denver, where a final version was worked out in consultation with General Eisenhower and his staff.[2]

The "Campaign Plan" focused first on mending the rifts within the Republican Party. There was a danger of a political sitdown by the embittered supporters of Senator Robert A. Taft, "Mr. Republican," and the reintegration of this largely midwestern contingent was the first goal of the campaign. Humphreys' plan said, "We must start with people who are now Republicans—the 20 million voters who have stuck with the Republican Party through thick and thin. *They must not be alienated.*"[3]

Eisenhower and his running mate, Richard M. Nixon, took various measures to allay such alienation, including early campaign trips through the Midwest. But the most important single step was a rapprochement breakfast meeting of Taft and Eisenhower, held at Morningside Heights on September 12, 1952. Following breakfast, Senator Taft issued a statement saying that the two men agreed on most issues; that any differences were differences of degree, and that in the naming of appointments after January 20, no one would be discriminated against for having supported Taft. There would be no purge of Taftites.[4]

Democratic candidate Adlai E. Stevenson, in one of the few formal press conferences of his campaign, reacted immediately: "Now we have the spectacle of the candidate who won the nomination seeking out his defeated rival and begging for a kind word. It looks as if Taft lost the nomination but won the nominee."[5]

Professor Stanley Kelley, to whom we are indebted for much of this account of the 1952 campaign, says that for Democrats, the Taft-Eisenhower meeting was one of the single most important developments of the entire campaign. For thereafter, Ike's "capture" by his party's conservative wing became a principal public relations theme of the Stevenson campaign.

The "Campaign Plan" identified four potential sources of votes: Republicans, Independents, Democrats, and Stay-at-Homes—

> *"those who vote only when discontent stirs them to vote against current conditions.* . . . It is not assumed that either the Independent or Stay-at-Home vote is necessarily a 'liberal' vote. A safer assumption is that both, like all other voters, are a cross-section of various political philosophies. . . . The pertinent fact is that Stay-at-Homes outnumber the Independents by approximately forty-five million to an estimated three or four million. . . . The recommended strategy is: *Attack! Attack!* and *Attack!*"[6]

Kelley identifies four noteworthy pieces of strategy inherent in this statement:

1. The common assumption that a big vote is a Democratic vote was rejected outright.

2. To go after the Stay-at-Home vote meant targeting citizens who had probably been uninvolved previously with political organizations. Further, and most importantly for our interest, it was assumed that the Stay-at-Home voter could be reached through the mass media, even if he hadn't been approached by precinct workers or reacted to such approaches in the past. Therefore, public relations was posited as a major weapon.

3. It was assumed that the Stay-at-Home vote was primarily a negative vote, which could be moved to the polls on Election Day by a campaign designed to stir and crystallize discontent.

4. The *attack* strategy is important in that it is through attack that one takes the initiative in establishing the issues. Attack gives one the edge in choosing the battleground and the weapons.[7]

The plan went on to stress personalities, emphasizing the "friendliness" and "human" qualities of the Republican candidates. Said the plan:

> "Both Republican candidates have warm and winning personalities. Both have a high degree of salesmanship in their manner. They are individuals who would normally be welcomed visitors in almost 100 percent of the living rooms of America. . . . Obviously the thing to do is gain entrance for them into the homes of America by every means possible so that the warmth of their personalities can be felt."[8]

Data on whether the Stay-at-Home vote actually contributed a disproportionate number of votes to Eisenhower's ultimate victory is unclear. The University of Michigan Survey Research Center found another recruiting ground that contributed a significantly large number of votes to Eisenhower: those who had supported Democratic candidate Harry S. Truman in 1948. Twenty-four percent of those interviewed who said they voted for Eisenhower, said they had voted for Truman in the last election.[9]

Pollster Louis Harris' study of the Roper polls for 1952 concludes that there were sizable defections of Democrats in 1952. It also calls attention to the rapid growth in the population of suburban areas in the 1948–1952 period, with the overwhelming proportion of the votes in those areas going to the Republicans.[10]

In retrospect, it appears that Kelley was correct in his assessment of Republican strategy as indeed well calculated to win support among marginal Democratic voters. As he pointed out, the Republican public relations men concentrated their campaign efforts on marketing the personalities of their candidates and attempting by persistent attack to set the issues. One of the reasons why the 1952 campaign is a classic among presidential contests is that the importance of Eisenhower's personality as a determinant of the election was an obvious lesson for future nominations of candidates.

Kelley points to the emphasis that this places on the political advantages accruing to someone in the spotlight, a point also stressed by Theodore White, and underscored by common sense. Such glamour almost inevitably attaches to an incumbent; however, it also accompanies a man such as General Eisenhower, a national hero. Wendell Willkie's candidacy may have demonstrated that it is possible for a man outside the spotlight to attract a good deal of attention, but not without the benefit of a tremendously elaborate and expensive public relations program.

According to a Roper poll of March 1952, Dwight D. Eisenhower was the most admired living American. It was probably inevitable that politicians would be tempted by the political capital to be made from this goodwill. During the pre-convention campaign, a Citizens for Eisenhower leaflet stated the case bluntly:

> "The Republican Party must not take a chance! *With* Eisenhower, the victory will be sweeping. *Without* Eisenhower, the outcome is doubtful. . . . If you *are seeking Republican office*, would you

> rather add to your strength the surging wave of Ike Eisenhower, or have a doubtful candidate in on your coattail. . . . The odds against a Republican victory are *huge*."[11]

Thus, as Kelley points out, given the popularity of Senator Taft's opposition, the senator's methodical delegate recruiting drive was made by Eisenhower's publicists to seem almost anti-democratic.

The issues selected for the principal Republican attack were the Korean war, subversion in government, and corruption.

In his speech at Chicago accepting his party's nomination, General Eisenhower told the country that:

"Our aims—the aims of this Republican crusade—are clear: to sweep from office an administration which has fastened on every one of us the wastefulness, the arrogance and corruption in high places, the heavy burdens and anxieties which are the bitter fruit of a party too long in power."[12]

In January 1952, the Roper polls showed that one-fourth of the respondents named the Korean war as a major national problem. One-third of those interviewed selected this issue voluntarily in September and one-half by late October.[13]

The Korean situation had not changed, but the public's perception of it apparently had. Peace negotiations were at a standstill throughout the 1952 campaign. Kelley suggests that the voters were by this time "reacting to their verbal environment, which [the professional public relations men working for the Republicans] had done much to shape."[14]

By the end of the campaign, polls indicated that a majority of the people believed Communist infiltration in the federal government was one of the country's most serious problems. Those interviewed also believed, four to one, that only the Republicans could effectively stem the red onslaught on Washington.[15] Here, the public was responding to no objective situation at all, but simply to an issue that had been created professionally for political purposes—including those of the Republican presidential campaign.

As for the corruption issue, in early September, one-third of Roper's respondents were concerned with dishonesty in high places; nearly 50 percent of those who were thought Adlai Stevenson could handle the problem. But by the close of the campaign, a majority of those who considered corruption a leading issue also felt that it would continue in a Stevenson administration.[16]

On October 24, General Eisenhower brought the war issue to a head when he pledged to "bring the Korean war to an early and honorable end. . . . That job requires a personal trip to Korea."[17] Kelley states that the idea for the "I shall go to Korea" pledge was born in the mind of Emmet J. Hughes, a senior editor of *Life*, who was working as a speech writer for Eisenhower.[18] (Hughes was later to perform similar duties for Governor Nelson Rockefeller of New York in his campaigns for the Republican presidential nomination.) Adlai Stevenson later commented on the pledge: "The ghost-writer who provided the proposal failed to give it content. The general was to go to Korea, but nobody indicated what he should do when he got there."[19]

Organizationally, the Republican campaign had several divisions[20] in 1952:

> 1. The Republican National Committee and the Senatorial and Congressional Campaign committees, coordinated through a strategy board, which included Robert Humphreys, public relations director of the Republican National Committee.
> 2. Citizens for Eisenhower, the pre-convention Eisenhower organization, became Citizens for Eisenhower-Nixon.
> 3. The personal staffs of Eisenhower and Nixon, of which Sherman Adams was the informal leader.

Kelley demonstrates that public relations men could be found throughout all the divisions in a variety of capacities. Murray Chotiner, who had previously handled Richard Nixon's campaigns for Congress and the Senate, and had served as campaign manager for California governor Earl Warren and Senator William Knowland, worked with the vice presidential campaign. (Chotiner, who stayed in the background throughout the 1968 campaign, was later appointed counsel to the President's Special Representative for Trade Negotiations.) General Eisenhower's headquarters staff included Abbott Washburn, former public relations director of General Mills and director of organization for the pre-convention Citizens for Eisenhower. (Washburn became director of the United States Information Agency during the Eisenhower Administration and later a partner in a public relations consulting firm.)

Robert R. Mullen, former p.r. man for the Economic Cooperation Administration, became public relations director of Citizens for Eisenhower-Nixon. James C. Hagerty became Eisenhower's personal press secretary. Harold E. Rainville, a Chicago public relations man, was designated executive director of the Senatorial Campaign Committee, and another public relations man, Harold Slater, became public relations director of the Congressional Campaign Committee. Finally, Whitaker and Baxter of Los Angeles moved from the American Medical Association's National Education Campaign, which a short time before had coordinated a successful effort to defeat President Truman's health proposals, to direct the National Professional Committee for Eisenhower-Nixon.[21]

Robert Humphreys' public relations division of the Republican National Committee was the largest single public relations organization of the campaign. Humphreys had been publicity director of the Indiana State Republican Central Committee, a radio sports commentator, publicity man for sporting events, an International News Service correspondent, national affairs editor of *Newsweek*, and public relations director of the Republican Congressional Campaign Committee. Drawing a monthly salary of $2,044 in 1952, he was the highest paid member of the National Committee staff.[22]

The division that Humphreys headed in 1952 had general responsibility for radio and television programs; visual aids; motion pictures; newspaper, billboard, and other print advertising; buttons and banners; and other variegated campaign devices. His department worked with two advertising agencies: the Kudner agency and Batten, Barton, Durstine and Osborne (BBD&O). Kudner's responsibility was for the print media, with both agencies handling radio and television. BBD&O also worked with the Citizens group, an account which also commanded the services of another advertising agency, Ted Bates and Company. Kudner and BBD&O came to the campaign with political experience as well as technical expertise. Kudner had worked with Robert A. Taft in his 1950 senatorial campaign. BBD&O had helped Dewey in his 1948 presidential campaign and his 1950 gubernatorial campaign, and John Foster Dulles in his 1949 senatorial race.[23] According to Kelley,

> Only a few of the professional propagandists working for Eisenhower in 1952 were hired specifically and only for the occasion. The others came into the campaign as more or less permanent members of already existing political teams. In this latter category one would certainly put Murray Chotiner, James C. Hagerty, and the men of BBD&O.[24]

Members of the Republican public relations and strategy teams were agreed that General Eisenhower lacked the polished speaking ability of Governor Stevenson. His speeches were hardly classics of dynamism. As the campaign progressed, his advisers emphasized radio and television programs presented as discussions or informal reports. All along, he stressed that he was not a "me-too" candidate. On the other hand, he assured the electorate that a vote for him would not be a vote to repeal recent history.[25] The general called for a "middle way," assuming "that all Americans of all parties have now accepted and will forever support what we call social gains."[26]

Louis Harris may, therefore, have caught the spirit of the image for which the Republican public relations men were striving when he described Eisenhower as "the white-collar man's Roosevelt."[27] Bernard C. Duffy, the president of BBD&O, referred to the approach as one of "merchandising Eisenhower's frankness, honesty and integrity, his sincere and wholesome approach."[28]

With the theme selected, the public relations men went to work on sloganeering. A favorite Republican campaign slogan became "The Mess in Washington." This was a kind of code for the three key Republican charges against the incumbents:[29]

> 1. That they had been responsible for widespread corruption;
> 2. That they had been "soft on Communism," allowing "reds" to infiltrate the government;
> 3. That they had "bungled" the country into the Korean war and could not get it back out.

Other slogans became "the scandal-a-day administration," the "top-to-bottom mess," and the need for a "new broom." Doubt was frequently engendered by referring not only to known malfeasance, but also to what "none of us will ever hear about." Confidence in the Democrats was also undermined with innuendo about a lack of concern with the dangers of internal Communism.[30]

Above all else, it was television which made the 1952 campaign in so many respects unlike those which had gone before. The political use of television in 1952 began a revolution in presidential campaigning that has only intensified in the years since. And a most significant effect of that revolution was the new political strength with which the public relations and advertising professions emerged from the 1952 campaign. They might have been consulted in previous years, but there was now a totally new element in campaigning. The traditional politician, at best, was vaguely uncomfortable about television—only the specialists understood it and what to do with it. Of course, in 1952 even the specialists had a lot to learn. But it was they alone who possessed that esoteric skill which was, in and of itself, a sufficient basis for the creation of a new brand of political elite. The television audience had grown significantly large between 1948 and 1952, and those who made the decisions were convinced that the audience was now sufficiently large to warrant giving it a place in the Republican presidential campaign plans.

Kelley points out that advertising men had calculated that by mid-October of that year, television stations would cover almost all of the populous areas of some of those states most critical politically. Nineteen million television receivers were in use, with some fifty-eight million people watching them. *The New York Times* reported on August 28, 1952, that the Eisenhower campaign organization had budgeted about $2,000,000 for television and radio.

Those who wrote the Republican "Campaign Plan" felt that television was the best way to bring Eisenhower and Nixon before the public. The plan recommended televising speeches on public policy, but also went on to say, "Informal, intimate TV productions addressed to the individual American and his family, their problems and their hopes, are necessary to make the most of the ticket's human assets."[31]

The Republicans, it was apparent, were searching for a form of political expression that would make fuller use of television's potential than the conventional political speech. The Republican Congressional Campaign Committee had televised a program entitled "The Case for a Republican Congress" in May 1952. In this production, the Democratic Party was put on "trial" by a combination of Republican Congressional leaders and professional actors. Later in the campaign, a Republican governors program and the election eve "Report to Ike" were also inspired by this same motivation to produce a "show."[32]

The Democrats were less innovative in their approach to television in 1952. On June 2 *The Democrat* promised in an editorial that the party was going to use television and radio "in a more exciting, more dramatic way than any political party ever dreamed of. . . ." But, according to one study, the Democrats devoted some 96 percent of their television time to paid coverage of traditional political speeches.[33]

Part of the reason for such widely varying results, given the fact that both parties had turned to professionals for help with television, may have been the different ways in which the two parties approached the buying of network time.

Time-buying for the Republicans was in the hands of BBD&O executive Carroll Newton. He concentrated on simulcasts (simultaneous radio and television broadcasts, then in fairly wide use because of the number of radio owners without television sets) during the closing weeks of the campaign. Newton bought time mainly during those periods that already had the largest established audience (such as those of Arthur Godfrey and the Saturday night Sid Caesar-Imogene Coca "Your Show of Shows") on the theory that political telecasts could not successfully compete for a large audience with well-liked entertainment features. The BBD&O theory was that it was necessary to reduce competition to a minimum by preempting the most popular shows and at the same time attempt to capture at least part of their audience.[34]

This approach is still a subject for lively debate in professional circles, for there are also those who contend that a viewer is antagonized by a candidate or a cause—or, for that matter, anything from a football team to a President-in-power—which forces his favorite program off the air.

BBD&O executive Jock Elliott told his agency's annual meeting on February 27, 1953, that many political broadcasts were tuned in accidentally. "We knew that people were more interested in Godfrey, for instance, than a political speech," he said. Elliott said that "Lesson Number One" was to "buy the best time periods you can get, even if it means paying through the nose to preempt a high cost show."[35]

According to *The New York Times* of September 15, 1955, Vice President Nixon preached the same theme to an audience of radio and television executives: "Sell [the candidate] the best time for drawing an audience, even if it costs twice as much."

The Republicans also put a good deal of stress on radio and television spot announcements. These were concentrated in the closing days of the campaign, beginning in the last week of October.

Rosser Reeves, a partner in Ted Bates and Company, was an early enthusiast of the spot announcement project, something of an innovation in presidential campaigning, and was closely involved with its execution. Reeves' premise was that the presidential race might be close, and that spot announcements in key areas might prove a decisive factor in its outcome. A former Ted Bates associate, Michael

Levin, was asked by Reeves to draw up a plan to be sold to Republican leaders. The Levin plan, according to Kelley, was largely a digest of Samuel Lubell's *The Future of American Politics*. It called for a special effort to switch forty-nine counties in twelve states from Democratic to Republican majorities, and thus give General Eisenhower the election. It called for a saturation spot campaign costing $2,000,-000 over a period of three weeks. The recommended format was one of citizens asking the general questions, to which his answers would display "complete comprehension of the problem and his determination to do something about it when elected. Thus, he inspires loyalty without prematurely committing himself to any strait-jacketing answer."[36]

The plan was accepted by General Eisenhower and Walter Williams, and the Citizens organization retained Ted Bates and Company to produce the spots, with BBD&O purchasing time for them. A group including publisher John Hay Whitney and Fred Rudge, a public relations man, worked to raise the additional funds for the spot campaign.[37]

The results demonstrated further the reliance by the Republicans on the experience of professional advertising and public relations consultants and technicians. It also demonstrated the sterilization of a presidential campaign that such total reliance often tends to produce.

Levin's plan pointed out that the spots would be broadcast too late for any effective rebuttal by the opposition. After further consultation with pollster George Gallup concerning the themes on which the Democrats were most vulnerable at this stage of the campaign, it was decided to concentrate the spots on corruption, high prices and high taxes, and the Korean war. Listeners, for example, would hear the announcer say, "Eisenhower Answers the Nation!" and then:

> VOICE: Mr. Eisenhower, can you bring taxes down?
> EISENHOWER: Yes. We will work to cut billions in Washington spending and bring your taxes down.
> or
> VOICE: Mr. Eisenhower, what about the high cost of living?
> EISENHOWER: My wife, Mamie, worries about the same thing. I tell her it's our job to change that on November 4.[38]

*Business Week* reported on June 30, 1956, that the 1952 Republican "blitz" of last-minute thirty-second radio-television spots cost the Citizens for Eisenhower-Nixon organization about $1,500,000 over a three-week period. The magazine referred to the campaign as "the height of simplicity in execution," and (in consonance with our thesis), a demonstration of the "political strength" of the "adman-publicist."

The Republicans also followed a unique approach to radio and television in the party's final one-hour election eve simulcast. A progress report on the program, circulated at BBD&O, outlined it as follows:

> "Theme—A report to the General on the work of the Citizens for Eisenhower Committee.
> Concept—A people dedicated to a cause.
> Production—A minimum of professional actors, high echelon people in political or private life, and staged acts."

The program was produced by Arthur Pryor of BBD&O at a cost of about $267,000.[39]

Quoting the BBD&O script, Kelley reports the show opening with the announcer saying:

> "During the next hour, we will take you to San Francisco, Los Angeles, Seattle . . . to Cleveland and to Philadelphia and to New York City. We will bring you the people who have devoted months of time and labor to a Crusade led by a man with humbleness of spirit. . . . What inspired this spontaneous demonstration of sincere devotion? An old American habit! A matter of principle, a matter of issues!"

The program followed with fast-paced film sequences: cash registers ringing up increased costs; Alger Hiss; the Rosenbergs; the Korean war; Eisenhower's home in Abilene; the general with Winston Churchill, with GI's, with his family at the birth of his grandchild. In all, there were eighty-one switches from live telecast to film, from city to city. One saw a remarkable variety of symbols: an attractive secretary in San Francisco's Chinatown; Korean veterans; John Roosevelt; a ballet dancer; Dr. Kelly Yamada of Seattle talking about "Nisei for Eisenhower-Nixon"; a prayer at a Los Angeles "Coffee for Eisenhower"; a Negro; aircraft workers; a foreign-born laborer; a ten-year-old who had organized "Tykes for Ike." The program closed with the Eisenhowers cutting a victory cake. The A. C. Nielsen Company's tabulations showed the Republican broadcasts outdrawing those of the Democrats.[40]

Measuring the effectiveness of such political promotion is, of course, an approximate science, at best. Before the first public relations and advertising men went to work on the 1952 campaign, Eisenhower's unusual personal popularity was already at work for him, as was a general restlessness with twenty years of Democratic control of the federal government, and a search for quieter times following a Great Depression and Great War.

Although it is difficult to determine just how much the efforts of BBD&O, Kudner, and Ted Bates contributed to the Republican victory, it is important to recognize the strength of the conviction of political leaders that it *would* contribute and *did* contribute. Likewise, no one can really tell whether the Democratic defeat would have been greater—or, for that matter, less—had it not retained its own agency, The Joseph Katz Company.

It is also important, in examining the differences in the ratings obtained by Eisenhower and Stevenson, to recognize that the parties followed different guidelines in placing candidates' speeches on the air. The Republicans used periods normally held by the most successful commercial entertainment shows. Kelley points out that on the two occasions when the Democrats followed this practice—once for Stevenson and once for President Truman—ratings showed that the audience surpassed Eisenhower's average.[41]

Republican public relations man Robert Humphreys has described the introduction of new techniques into politics as a contribution of public relations professionals to campaigning. One such technique—used exclusively by the Republicans in 1952—was that of the visual aid. Humphreys' devices were like those used by advertising and sales agencies: cartoon film strips projected on portable screens and synchronized with tape-recorded narration. The Republicans had six such films: *Korea—The Price of Appeasement, America's Creeping Socialism, Inflation, or Our Fifty Cent Dollar, Taxes, Scandals,* and *Ticket to Freedom.*[42]

The cartoons were executed by professional artists, and the narration was performed by professional announcers. Party workers were charged with encouraging the use of the material by local organizations and volunteers, as well as by churches, service clubs, and other nonpartisan groups. It was a medium that could be used efficiently by volunteers who were untrained as speakers or public relations experts. It also provided a means by which industry could make a contribution to the Republican cause through the loan of audio-visual equipment. The John Deere Company, for example, kept its state representatives busy showing one of the films during the final two weeks of the campaign. According to a report to the Republican National Committee, the films reached an audience of some three million people.[43]

The new emphasis on television did not put a stop to Republican political rallies in 1952, although it certainly can be said to have added another dimension to such events. Considerable efforts were made to assure visual appeal. "The Advance Man" by Richard L. Williams in *Life* magazine reported on October 6, 1952, that a blueprint for the occasion of the formal opening of the Eisenhower campaign before eighteen thousand persons in Philadelphia filled thirty-nine pages. It advised that as the "throng enters Convention Hall" on September 4, "the following will be provided for them: fresh-cut red roses (25,000) . . . noisemakers (3,000) . . . flags (5,000) . . . programs (25,000)." The blueprint also advised the candidate to place himself with his right hand on the Liberty Bell in Independence Hall for photographic purposes.

BBD&O issued instructions to radio and television advance men for the Eisenhower and Nixon road tours, spelling out personal contacts to be made, the kinds of facilities to be used, arrangements for introducing candidates, and so on. Murray Chotiner's set of instructions for Nixon's advance men contained 125 separate points, "ranging from types of hotel accommodations desired to procuring a Korean war veteran to lead the pledge of allegiance."[44]

Much of Eisenhower's preliminary scouting was performed by John B. Quinn, a Nebraska public relations man. He was followed by a task force called Young Industry for Eisenhower. This group was charged with insuring crowds for the candidate. Women were signed up to invite local residents by telephone to each event. The general traveled more than forty thousand miles, making more than three hundred speeches. And each of his stops was accompanied with what Kelley has called "probably the most meticulously planned and sustained ballyhoo yet shown in a presidential campaign tour."[45]

As the candidates traveled, the press coverage they received was monitored by nine BBD&O staff members, charged with analyzing the reporting of the campaign and suggesting ways to keep the Republican message on the front page. This group reported daily to Hagerty and Chotiner on the previous day's publicity, including Democratic utterances and editorial comments. The group also drafted running comments and strategy suggestions for the campaign.[46]

Campaign literature was by no means eliminated because of the new emphasis on television in the 1952 campaign. It was a task carried out by the publicity division of the national committees of both parties, and included the expected speech kits, background material and manuals for party regulars; special-appeal materials for Blacks, veterans, farmers, and other interest groups, and leaflets, posters, streamers, and so on for the public in general. The Republican "Campaign Plan" advised against long, slick leaflets, suggesting instead greater use of pictures. One Republican pamphlet, imaginatively titled "Ike and Dick, They're for You," showed the candidates in a variety of poses by themselves and with their families, captioned with phrases assuring voters who might have wondered that they were "God-fearing men" and "regular guys," even though they were "scrappers." The Republicans also put out a comic book, "From Yalta to Korea," "explaining" the "tragedy that has cost over 100,000 American casualties and countless billions of dollars." The cast of characters included Dean Acheson, Owen Lattimore, and Alger Hiss.[47]

The use of professional public relations and the new campaign medium of television received a severe test when an unexpected and potentially severe crisis arose just two weeks after the formal opening of the Republican campaign. On September 18, the New York *Post* reported on an $18,000 "secret" fund established for Senator Nixon by a group of well-to-do California constituents, to be used for expenses incurred while holding senatorial office.

Almost immediately, Democratic National Committee Chairman Stephen Mitchell demanded Nixon's resignation as the Republican vice presidential candidate.

On September 20, Nixon went on with a planned western tour after he had explained that the fund was used for mailing and political expenses that he felt should not be incurred by the taxpayers. In the midst of a campaign speech, he was interrupted by a heckler who asked about the fund. The senator (according to *The New York Times* of that day) told the audience he had been warned at the convention in Chicago "that if I continue to attack the Communists and the crooks in this government they would continue to smear me. . . . They started it yesterday."

General Eisenhower reportedly spent most of that day in meetings on the new crisis. The Washington *Post*, a supporter of the Republican ticket, demanded that Nixon withdraw, and the demand was picked up by such other giants of journalism as *The New York Times* and the New York *Herald Tribune*. Kelley reports that the nation's papers disapproved of the Nixon fund by a 2-to-1 ratio, and that the general was receiving telegrams expressing disapproval in about the same proportion. On the afternoon of September 20 (according to the *Times* of the next morning), Eisenhower announced that his running mate's report would need to be "clean as a hound's tooth—or else."

Nixon's staff, meanwhile, decided that there was only one way for the senator to effectively make his case: a television "report to the nation." BBD&O bought half an hour of time for the program, to be telecast on September 23, at a cost of $75,000. Nixon has since said that one consideration in selecting the date was to allow sufficient time for a full buildup of the story.[48]

Then, on September 22, the sharpness of the Nixon story began to diminish as reports from Chicago appeared in the press disclosing a fund used by Governor Stevenson to supplement the salaries of some Illinois state government officials. Stevenson explained that the fund consisted mainly of leftover money from his gubernatorial campaign, and that it was being used to attract more able men into the service of the state. On September 23, Postmaster General-to-be Arthur Summerfield echoed Nixon's "smear" charge of three days earlier by claiming, according to *The New York Times*, that the candidate was being attacked by "men who have promoted Communism, supported traitors, and never fought so much as one day for their country." He called upon the nation to tune in the senator that night.[49]

Perhaps the most important figure at this point in Richard Nixon's fight for his political life was Edward A. "Ted" Rogers. Rogers was serving as Nixon's television adviser. He was on leave as manager of the Hollywood office of the advertising agency of Dancer, Fitzgerald and Sample, and a seasoned television producer, with commercial credits that included "The Lone Ranger," "Beulah," and "Double or Nothing." Murray Chotiner had asked Rogers to serve as Nixon's television consultant in the 1950 Senatorial campaign. The producer traveled with the candidate, analyzing his potential and his mistakes with the new medium, working out signals and advising him on facial expressions, lighting, and so on. Rogers, in Nixon's Portland hotel room, carefully went over the speech for that evening with the candidate. Meanwhile, a Los Angeles law firm was asked to report on the legal status of the senator's fund, and Price Waterhouse and Company was given the task of auditing its expenditures.[50]

Nixon went on the air at 6:30 Pacific Standard Time. Twenty-five seconds later, Nixon began to answer the question "What about the $18,000?" He said there was no secret about it. "Not one cent of the [money] or any other money of that type ever went to my personal use." He said he had used it to pay the ". . . political expenses of getting my message to the American people and the speeches I made—the speeches I had printed for the most part—concerned this one message of exposing this administration, the Communism in it, the corruption in it. . . ."[51]

Talking more about himself than the fund, the senator explained that he had no personal wealth, and had started working as a boy in his parents' grocery store, working his way right through college. Then, in 1940, "probably the best thing that ever happened to me happened. I married Pat. . . ." He practiced law while she taught school. Then the war came: ". . . My service record was not a particularly unusual one. . . . I guess I'm entitled to a couple of battle stars. . . ."

After the war, Nixon said, he had gone into politics. His homes in Washington, D.C., and California weren't paid for. He couldn't afford a mink coat for Pat, but "I always tell her that she would look good in anything." Nixon had accepted another gift that he hoped politicians wouldn't start talking about—his dog, Checkers. "The kids, like all kids, loved the dog . . . and regardless of what they say about it, we are going to keep it."

The senator returned to his earlier theme that there was more to the attacks than the fund issue.

"The purpose of the smear, I know, is this, to silence me, to make me let up." He would continue to fight the smears, "Because, you see, I love my country. And I think my country is in danger. . . ."

The broadcast was a professional job. And it got a professional rating—Nielsen indicated that Nixon had been seen on nine million television sets. The Republican National Committee, by the afternoon of September 25, said it had received nearly a quarter of a million letters and telegrams, overwhelmingly supporting Nixon's retention on the ticket. A great many newspapers, including some that had favored the senator's withdrawal, indicated that they had been satisfied by his explanation. And the day after the television program the BBD&O Eisenhower-Nixon Research Service reported that in the five days since the story had broken Nixon had pushed Stevenson from the front pages. From West Virginia, General Eisenhower announced that Nixon had been fully vindicated. The vice presidential candidate immediately took the offensive, challenging Stevenson to make a public accounting of his own fund. If he did not, said Nixon, this would be "admission that he has got something to hide."[52]

Not only did Nixon grab the headlines and establish a new platform from which to attack the opposition, but the whole operation, from a public relations point of view, was even more effective, in that he had now established himself firmly as a television drawing card. Nixon's first television broadcast of the campaign had reached "only" 968,000 television sets. But his "Checkers" speech enlarged that audience by ten times. The Hollywood star system had operated to Nixon's benefit and to the benefit of the Republican Party's chances in the November election. From an advertising man's point of view, it was all quite tidy and economical. Television had enabled the candidate to defend himself before an estimated eighteen million persons at a cost of $75,000. Apparently no one pointed out publicly at the time that, although television had made it technically possible for Nixon to explain himself, it had cost $75,000 to defend a fund of $18,000, which had been collected to cover expenses that the senator had been unable to handle in any other way. Furthermore, the $75,000 price tag (which would be considerably higher today) would have effectively denied a similar opportunity for coast-to-coast self-defense to anyone not supported by a treasury whose administrators were willing and able to spend that amount of money—not to mention the cost of the professional consulting services that went into the project.[53]

Senator Joseph McCarthy also did his share on television on behalf of the Republican ticket. It was possible for McCarthy, given his bent, to say things about the opposition during the course of the campaign that might have been inappropriate coming from one of the candidates.

The senator spoke in Chicago on October 27, and, according to *The New York Times* of October 28, told a national radio and television audience about Adlai Stevenson's "aid to the Communist cause." The Wisconsinite singled out members of Stevenson's staff as having alleged subversive connections. He "mistakenly" referred to Stevenson as "Alger" twice during his speech. Then he went on to say Stevenson feared a Republican victory because:

> "He and his whole camp, as well as every crook and Communist in Washington, knows that if I am chairman of that Committee [the Permanent Investigating Subcommittee of the Senate] and Republicans control the other committees, then we will have the power to help Dwight Eisenhower scrub and flush and wash clean the foul mess of corruption and Communism in Washington."

Reaction among the Republican leadership was mixed. On election eve, the Democratic publicity division released an analysis of the speech, detailing some eighteen errors of fact.[54] But the harm had been done, and it is unlikely that the belated Democratic rebuttal had much effect on voters who had been influenced by McCarthy's contribution to the campaign. There appears to be no record, by the way, of General Eisenhower or Senator Nixon formally dissociating themselves from the McCarthy address during the course of the campaign.

On Election Day, Dwight D. Eisenhower received more votes than had ever been obtained by a presidential candidate up to that time. With about 70 percent of registered voters at the polls, he received a popular vote of 33,936,252, as compared to 27,314,992 for Adlai Stevenson. The electoral vote was 442 to 89.[55]

As we have seen, the Republicans had applied, in 1952, the techniques of professional public relations, marketing, and advertising on a scale hitherto unprecedented in American politics. And, as the new administration settled down in Washington, it apparently did not forget the value of those techniques and the professionals who use them. For on August 19, 1953, the *Wall Street Journal* reported that Walter Williams was being given an office in the White House. His duty: to "sell" the President's policies to the public. An unnamed "high official" was quoted as saying: "We all suddenly realized we were busy manufacturing a product down here, but nobody was selling it."

## The Democrats

When the Democratic party chose Adlai E. Stevenson of Illinois as its presidential nominee on July 26, 1952, it nominated a man who had taken pains to indicate that he was not a candidate. Although he had not halted the pre-convention activity of his supporters, he had isolated himself from it.

From the perspective of public relations, the differences between Governor Stevenson and General Eisenhower were enormous. The general was a public relations man's dream, the governor what public relations men call euphemistically, "a creative challenge." Eisenhower's name had already entered the folklore of America; Stevenson, according to a spring 1952 Gallup poll, was known to only 33 percent of the electorate and 28 percent of the Democratic voters. President Truman, using a technique mentioned earlier, attempted to focus greater national attention on Stevenson in January 1952 by inviting him to a meeting at the White House, and again the next month, by mentioning him favorably during a press conference. At this point, however, the emphasis upon a public relations buildup for Stevenson was not as great as the emphasis upon his buildup among leaders of his own party.[56]

Stevenson's method of selecting campaign issues and the audiences before which he would deal with them contrasts sharply with that of his Republican opponents. In the introduction to his book *Major Campaign Speeches, 1952*, Stevenson said he decided what he would say, but left to others the decision on when and where he would say it.

Working with his Springfield staff, it was decided that each major issue would be treated separately in a series of speeches to be made in September. The Democratic strategy, while thus made on a generally informal and piecemeal basis, was pervaded by a general theme of defensiveness. Stevenson felt the "time for change" sentiment was the most serious of the hurdles he would have to overcome. Furthermore, the Democrats felt themselves wedded to the twenty-year record of their party and not as flexible as the Republicans in maneuvering in the selection of issues.[57]

The Stevenson campaign also contrasted with that of Eisenhower in the area of organization. The governor simply lacked the personal organization that had long since developed around his opponent. A number of groups were, however, set up to promote the Stevenson-Sparkman ticket, and operated more or less independently. Campaign headquarters in Springfield, Illinois, was headed by Wilson Wyatt, the campaign director. Stephen Mitchell, chosen by the candidate to chair the Democratic National Committee, ran that operation from Washington. Another group, Volunteers for Stevenson—the Democratic counterpart of the Citizens for Eisenhower-Nixon—established its main office in Chicago. Completing the organizational picture were the less formal personal groups that traveled with Stevenson, Sparkman, and President Truman.[58]

Public relations professionals were in leadership roles in each of the component groups in the Democratic Party's campaign structure. They were, however, with one exception, men who came directly from either the news media or government information posts and were less disposed than their Republican opposite numbers to draw upon the experience of commercial public relations.

In Springfield, Clayton Fritchey, assisting Wilson Wyatt, had responsibility for coordinating publicity. Samuel Brightman ran the publicity bureau of the Democratic National Committee and was responsible for most of the literature and film production and the committee's media relations. Stevenson's press secretary was William I. Flanagan, and Roger Tubby performed the same function for Harry S. Truman as the President campaigned. Porter McKeever served as publicity man for "Volunteers for Stevenson," aided and advised by Manly Mumford, the public relations director of the Borden Company, and thus the one member of the group with long experience in public relations. Finally, two advertising agencies were retained. The principal firm was The Joseph Katz Company, which handled space advertising, radio and television time-buying and production, and literature design and production. Katz worked for both the National Committee and the "Volunteers." The "Volunteers" also placed some advertising through the Erwin Wasey agency's Chicago office.[59]

And when it came to television, the Democrats, like the Republicans, turned to the professionals of the commercial advertising agencies for assistance, and were, in fact, dependent upon them. The Democrats, however, approached the buying of television and radio network time in a much different fashion than did the Republicans.

*The Democrat* reported on June 16, 1952, that during the previous month the Katz agency, which already had been retained by the Democratic National Committee, had purchased time for eighteen radio-television simulcasts from 10:30 to 11:00 P.M. on Tuesdays and Thursdays. Party Chairman Frank E. McKinney explained that this would allow for substantial savings from other campaigns, in which "we have had to pay to remove regularly scheduled sponsored shows to make way for political broadcasts. . . . This year, however, we have secured choice time periods on television and radio BEFORE commercial sponsors have signed their fall contracts."

As we have seen earlier, the Republicans were attempting instead to preempt the most popular shows with the largest audiences for their broadcasts on the theory that the large "accidental" audience would be well worth the additional cost. The theory paid off handsomely.

The Democrats, on the other hand, seemed convinced that the regularity of their proposed programming would build a habit in their audience. Thus, Joseph Katz of the Katz agency proudly reported an estimated savings of some $300,000 in preemption costs.[60]

In retrospect, the Democrats' approach to television seems to have had little to recommend it, save its economy. The Republican strategy was considerably more skillful and sophisticated in terms of professional communications. For the Democrats, with their plan for eighteen regularly scheduled half-hours of presentations by their candidates, could not realistically expect to reach far beyond those who were already committed to the party's cause.

The Republicans had also set the pace in their last-minute spot announcement campaign, and the Democrats were simply unprepared to deal with it. Instead of replying in kind, they made an issue of the technique itself, characterizing it as a "huckster's blitz." Volunteers for Stevenson had picked up news of the spot campaign, and had gotten a copy of the Levin blueprint. George Ball reacted on behalf of the Volunteers by saying the Republicans had:

> "conceived not an election campaign in the usual sense, but a super-colossal, multimillion dollar production designed to sell an inadequate ticket to the American people in precisely the way they sell soap, ammoniated toothpaste, hair tonic, or bubble gum. They guarantee their candidates to be 99.44/100 percent pure; whether or not they will float remains to be seen."[61]

The Democrats' next move was to file a complaint with the Federal Communications Commission, charging that commercial advertisers had unfairly made paid-up time available to the Republicans. Then the Democrats also put on some spots of their own. But the contrast was dismal. It was neither "huckstering" nor a "blitz." Time and funds were in short supply; while the Republicans spent as much as $1,500,000 on their spot campaign, the Democrats used only about

$77,000 of their radio and television budget for this purpose. Fur-thermore, while the Republican spots were capitalizing on doubt and discontent, the Democratic spots were confined to playing on the old Charles Michelson pre-1933 theme of the "Republican Depression."[62]

Once Richard Nixon made his "Checkers" speech and had emerged "clean as a hound's tooth" from the fund "scandal" of late September, he turned on Adlai Stevenson with renewed vigor. Steven-son had given a deposition in the perjury trial of Alger Hiss, testify-ing to the good character of the defendant. The matter of the deposi-tion was brought into the campaign by Nixon in a television speech on October 13. He said he was questioning Stevenson's judgment, not his loyalty. Stevenson, said Nixon, had acted voluntarily. There fol-lowed several other speeches in which Nixon branded Stevenson with such labels as "appeaser" and "dupe of Hiss." As in the case of the McCarthy attack, General Eisenhower was silent, but a group of twenty-two prominent lawyers, including supporters of both presiden-tial candidates, said that Stevenson should not be criticized for doing "what any good citizen should have done."[63]

Stevenson was visibly upset by this series of attacks, which fit right into the offensive strategy of Robert Humphreys' "Campaign Plan." In a speech at Cleveland, he said that he had been asked to testify as to the reputation of Alger Hiss and had done so: "I testified only as to his reputation at the time I knew him. His reputation was good. If I had said it was bad, I would have been a liar. If I had refused to tes-tify at all, I would have been a coward."[64] The governor said that he was somewhat incredulous that such an explanation of his "role" in the Hiss case would be required of him in a contest for the presidency with Dwight D. Eisenhower. He charged that the Republican crusade had now become "a systematic program of innuendo and accusa-tion."[65]

The final Democratic television program of the 1952 campaign was presented, like that of the Republicans, as an election eve simul-cast. It was a far cry, however, from the fast-paced documentary-style closing broadcast worked out for the opposition by their public rela-tions advisers, advertising consultants, and television experts. The Democrats' program included speeches by President Truman, Vice President Alben Barkley, Governor Stevenson, and Senator Spark-man.

Stevenson reviewed the campaign and reaffirmed his faith in the Democrats as the "people's party." He said he had tried "diligently, day and night, to talk sensibly, honestly, and candidly" about the nation's problems. He promised to be a good sport if he lost the election. And if he were to win, he said, ". . . I shall ask Our Lord to make me as an instrument of His peace."[66]

Many of Stevenson's radio and television appearances demonstrated not only the absence of public relations advice, but an apparent absence of any technical assistance at all. They were simply sloppy productions. For example, the bad timing of his presentations at times led to the Democratic candidate suddenly finding himself being awkwardly cut off the air.

> . . . Some critics have felt that his typical forms of expression were more literary than forceful and that his use of humor was as much a hindrance as a help. . . . For good or ill, it appears that the Democratic candidate's speeches owed little to the advice of public relations men.[67]

Some welcomed Stevenson's apparent disdain for public relations and professional broadcasting advice and even lauded it as courageous. But from a pragmatic point of view, it seems not to have served him very well on the air.

During the course of the campaign, Stevenson traveled somewhat less than his opponent, and his public appearances showed less evidence of the vastly detailed public relations planning described earlier in connection with Eisenhower's road tours. Secretary of the Interior Oscar Chapman and others served as advance men and helped to smooth relations with the news media and between Democratic factions.[68]

In many of his speeches, Stevenson used what public relations adviser Manly Mumford was later to call the "Blunt Truth Technique." The governor told a convention of the American Legion, that if elected he would "resist pressures from veterans, too . . ." if he deemed their demands to be excessive. He told a southern audience that he was committed to the civil rights plank of the Democratic platform. He told an AFL convention that political parties must maintain independence from the labor unions. The use of this technique by a presidential candidate would seem to illustrate the fact that, in the age of mass media, the candidate's audience is almost inevitably national.[69]

President Truman made up for some of Stevenson's apparent lack of enthusiasm for the campaign trail when he left for a nationwide whistle-stop tour on September 27. He operated in the "give 'em hell" tradition of 1948. The President's dynamic style, the contrast of his folksiness with Stevenson's more erudite approach, and the prestige of his office combined to give the Democrats a publicity advantage, putting Mr. Truman on the front page regularly, sometimes along with his two potential successors, sometimes without their companionship.

The President's campaigning was more akin to the partisan strategy of the Republicans than the more defensive tone that generally characterized the 1952 Democratic campaign. For example, *The New York Times* reported on October 5 that the President had called Republican criticism of his foreign policy a "wave of filth," and on October 7 that Mr. Truman had said that Eisenhower was a great general but that "he cannot be depended on to master the great political issues with which we are faced."

The Republican strategists' answer to President Truman was the organization of a "truth squad," which traveled in the wake of the chief executive. Its members included Senators Homer Ferguson, Bourke Hickenlooper, Francis Case, and Eugene Millikin. A series of press releases was issued in the names of these Republican leaders, charging the President with lowering the dignity of the campaign. Arthur Summerfield, the *Times* reported on October 1, charged that Mr. Truman had "lowered the great office of the President to the level of the cheapest politics." Senator Robert Taft spoke of the Chief Executive's "wild talk." Governor John Lodge of Connecticut called the President's speeches "gutter politics."[70]

All of this contributed further, in terms of sheer quantity, to the Democrats' publicity advantage. But after twenty years, unhappiness with the Democrats was apparently widespread and, simultaneously, the Republican Party had again made itself respectable to a large majority of the American voters. It had selected a national military hero as its candidate and successfully marketed him as the next President of the United States.

The findings of V. O. Key, Jr., confirm this observation that even when the dissatisfaction with the current trend of political events is marked, the opposition party must be perceived as an acceptable alternative; "the minority must not clearly threaten basic policies that have won majority acceptance." After examining the evidence of opinion surveys in elections from 1936 to 1960, Key depicted General Eisenhower's 1952 victory as a classic instance of the voters perceiving the party out of power as a "usable minority." The Republican campaign very carefully avoided doing anything to renew the old Depression-era image of a party opposed to social reform. Rather, the Eisenhower campaign was successfully designed to allow voters to act upon their displeasure with the Democrats' handling of the Korean war, and perhaps upon their doubts about honesty, and even patriotism, in Washington.[71] As Key put it:

> The entire episode throws light on the qualities that minority must possess if it is to serve its purpose. A minority led by radical conservatives probably would have had great difficulty in winning in 1952. This is not to say that a serviceable minority must be identical with the majority; it must be different. It must be different enough in the appropriate respect to arouse hope that it can cope satisfactorily with those problems on which the majority has flunked. It must not, though, so threaten accepted policies and practices that it arouses widespread anxieties. The circumstances of 1952 made the Republican party for the nonce a usable minority—in a country normally Democratic.[72]

Under the circumstances, then, the axiom that a big vote is automatically Democratic ceased to be an axiom. Kelley points out that those subscribing to that line of thinking hold that Republican-oriented groups, such as professional and upper-income individuals, have traditionally shown the highest degree of political participation. Non-voting is generally highest, proportionally, among low-income groups. Thus, if these non-voters can be guided to the polls, they would cast their votes along the same lines as other low-income group members, insuring a Democratic triumph. This theory, however, does not put great stock in the extent to which voting behavior can be influenced and issues shaped by a carefully planned public relations and propaganda program. As we have seen, the Republican strategists turned from this traditional reasoning, emphasized instead communications techniques aimed at the stay-at-home voters, and were proved correct.[73]

The positions held by professional public relations men in the strategy councils of the two parties show some interesting differences. The entire sweep of the strategy of the Eisenhower campaign demonstrated pervasive influence of public relations counsel. The Democrats, as we have seen, used fewer professional p.r. men, drew much less upon commercial public relations experience and techniques, and involved their public relations men much less in policy decisions during the course of the campaign. Not only did no one in 1952 play any role for the Democrats comparable to that of Robert Humphreys' for the Republicans, but no one was assigned a role comparable to that which the Democrats themselves had earlier given to Charles Michelson.[74]

Accounts of subsequent campaigns reveal some evidence that this contrast persisted, although neither consistently nor to the same degree as obtained in 1952. Increasingly, professionally experienced public relations men can be found well integrated in most Democratic campaign organizations. The Democratic National Committee uses such people on its own staff and advises candidates through the country to retain public relations and advertising experts of their own.

But one important difference remains. When one examines the background of such public relations people as have been used by Democratic presidential candidates, it would appear that their backgrounds tend to emphasize experience with nonprofit organizations, government, and the news media, rather than business and industrial corporations and commercal agencies. The Republican Party, given the strength of its traditional alliances with the business and industrial community, may naturally tend to turn more often in that direction, find more sympathetic counselors in those positions, and have an easier time recruiting men with commercial backgrounds. It may also be the case, however, that working for the Republicans is more lucrative—or potentially so—since fund-raising is traditionally less of a problem for the Grand Old Party.

## The 1956 Campaign

We shall not review the 1956 campaign in detail. Eisenhower and Stevenson were again the candidates, and the incumbent prevailed. It is, however, interesting to look just briefly at the attitudes of the two parties toward public relations techniques and their use in 1956, given the background of the classic campaign of four years earlier.

The incumbent has a virtually unbeatable advantage when he

decides to seek another term. Historically, he almost never loses, except under the most unusual of circumstances. In the twentieth century, President Taft failed in his bid for reelection because of a deep split in his party, which brought about the election of a minority President, and Herbert Hoover lost an election that took place in the midst of the most serious economic depression in the history of the United States.

As one public relations professional has pointed out, the incumbent has the advantages of a built-in campaign staff, instant recognition by the voters, relatively easy access to campaign funds, and the ready-made prestige, status, and political trump cards necessary to build effectively active volunteer groups. It would appear logical, therefore, that professional public relations would be called upon most vigorously and often on behalf of the challenger.[75]

As in 1952, Robert Humphreys and his staff were given the responsibility for blueprinting the Republican campaign strategy. Once again also, the advertising firm of BBD&O was retained to work with the National Committee. Carroll Newton was again responsible for buying radio and television time for the candidates' presentations.

BBD&O told *Business Week* before the 1956 convention that it would not put any staff members who were Democrats to work on the Republican account. The agency was reported "mum" on the amount of cash involved in its end of the campaign and would not reveal whether it intended to emerge from the effort with any financial profit. By June 30, Newton had already booked some $2,000,000 worth of television time, and at least three other advertising agencies had been signed up to help the Republicans at various levels.[76]

The success of television for the Republicans in the 1952 campaign so influenced the action in 1956 as to establish firmly a new pattern in presidential politics. As Cutlip and Center put it, "Full-scale use of television in 1952 and 1956 marked the beginning of the end of [the] historic pattern" of campaigning. President Eisenhower's intention to lean heavily—perhaps almost exclusively—on television for his campaign activities in 1956 was expressed in his significant statement that he would "wage no political campaign in the customary sense" but would "inform the American people accurately through means of mass communication."[77] Interestingly, statements made by the incumbent Lyndon Johnson in 1968, and Richard Nixon in 1972, were almost identical.

The Democrats, in January 1956, had engaged one of the smaller advertising agencies, Norman, Craig and Kummel. The firm's executive vice president, Norman Norman, told *Business Week* that his agency "went after" the Democratic account. Its motives in doing so were interesting. Norman said the agency saw it as a "profitable" and "prestige" account. Its contract with the Democratic National Committee was "ironclad," regardless of whom the party nominated. Norman indicated that fifty people would be assigned to the campaign on a full-time basis, but made it clear that their policy role would be limited. He said his men were "technicians," hired to work out the best techniques for implementing the policy and strategy decided by the party itself.[78]

Nevertheless, the public relations trade press felt able to report in the summer of 1956 that:

> Public relations has assumed new dimensions in the [Democratic] party's planning. In no previous Presidential campaign has it made such intensive application of the techniques of industrial PR. Never before has PR had so important a voice in the policy making of the political organization.[79]

Samuel S. Brightman, again serving as director of publicity for the Democratic National Committee, coordinated public relations for the 1956 Democratic campaign. Brightman, who was described by *Public Relations News* as a disciple of Charles Michelson, was formerly a newspaperman. He had been Washington correspondent for the Louisville *Courier-Journal* and a member of the staff of the St. Louis *Star-Times*, the Cincinnati *Post*, and radio station KSD in St. Louis. He had served as an Army public information officer and joined the Democratic National Committee's publicity staff in 1947, succeeding Charles W. VanDevander as its director in 1952.[80] Brightman described his function this way:

> Our whole operation is an exercise in PR. We're now more aware of PR and the potentialities of new techniques and channels of communication. We have a sophisticated electorate today. They want to know—and we're trying to provide a good information service.[81]

Brightman worked closely in 1956 with Clayton Fritchey, who had been made deputy chairman of the National Committee, and with the committee's director of research, Philip M. Stern. The Brightman staff numbered fifteen persons, and although he reported that a number of public relations professionals were cooperating with him during the campaign, apparently no outside public relations counsel was retained.[82]

Brightman concentrated heavily on intra-party training in the use of political public relations, in addition to his work on the public side of the campaign. One major communications tool was the party's official organ, *Democratic Digest*, of which Fritchey was editor and Brightman managing editor. During the campaign, the press run each month was 180,000 copies. Party workers were also given a ninety-six-page handbook on political publicity, which advised Democratic aspirants throughout the country to seek the services of public relations firms and advertising agencies. It said the fees would be well worth the cost, because "it is an investment which helps assure the most efficient use of each advertising and publicity medium."[83]

The handbook included chapters on the use of television, radio, newspapers, direct mail, leaflets, comic books, handbills, posters, and display material. It called "good publicity" the "cheapest weapon in the campaign arsenal." The publication listed the types of mass media; urged personal meetings with editors and reporters; set forth some rules for good press relations; told how to prepare a press release, hold a press conference, and stimulate feature stories; discussed the staging of events and warned that "bad stunts can be poison"; stressed the need to adapt to television's highly pictorial requirements; and even provided tabulations of the average costs for producing releases, photographs, and other materials.[84]

Public relations devices were also used internally to stimulate party morale. Each month party workers received a bulletin signed by Chairman Paul Butler containing such "inspirational" messages as "Victory is in the air. Hard work, cooperation, unselfish effort will accomplish this." Also included were reports on the speeches of the party leaders, women's activities, campaign preparations, staff changes, and so on. Each month Brightman supervised the mailing of 250,000 pieces of literature to the party's leadership list. In addition, his staff produced and distributed the usual speeches, policy statements, press conference reports, and so on.[85]

It seemed evident that if the Democrats had lagged behind in public relations activities in 1952, they had now been converted by a baptism of fire. The Democrats lacked, however, much of the experience, polish, and ready cash that was available to the opposition—along with the advantages inherent in the incumbency.

# Four:
# The 1960 Campaign

## The Pre-Nomination Campaigns

By 1960 professional public relations, advertising, marketing, and media technology had become well established aspects of presidential campaigning. The concern with "image" was paramount. The use of television was crucial. In fact, many observers feel that Richard M. Nixon lost his lead in the campaign, and quite likely the election, because of a single television appearance.

The 1960 campaign process began well in advance of the nominating conventions. The pre-nomination campaigns were active and bitterly fought. And in a sense never before known to the process of presidential selection, public relations played a most significant role in these campaigns. This comes through rather clearly in any review of the events of the 1960 campaign. Here, we have relied heavily on Theodore H. White's uniquely comprehensive work *The Making of the President 1960* as the principal source of information, and are deeply indebted to Mr. White for his monumental contributions to the study of American politics.

### The Democrats

Most prominent among the several candidates for the Democratic presidential nomination in 1960 were Senators Hubert H. Humphrey, Lyndon B. Johnson, John F. Kennedy, and Stuart Symington and the Democratic candidate of 1952 and 1956, former Governor Adlai E. Stevenson. It would appear that public relations considerations and techniques played a significant role in the pre-nomination campaigns of all of these men with the possible exception, interestingly enough, of Lyndon Johnson.

Senator Johnson's efforts at the nomination, spearheaded by Speaker of the House Sam Rayburn, were much more characteristic of the "old" politics than of the "new." It was an effort that took place within the leadership circles of the Democratic Party—an attempt by one group of political leaders, largely from the Southwest, to win over other political leaders, and, with them, the delegates they controlled and influenced.

Stuart Symington of Missouri had decided rather early in the game that virtually his only chance for the nomination lay in the possibility that he would emerge from a convention deadlock as a compromise candidate, a "dark horse" acceptable to conflicting factions. This was a conclusion apparently reached by the senator on the basis of his honest assessment, and that of his close friends and advisers, of his own image problem. The difficulty was threefold.

First of all, Symington was not at all well known outside of his home state. Secondly, many who did recognize his name did so because they thought of him as a one-issue senator, a specialist who had served as Secretary of the Air Force, and who knew and cared a great deal about defense but not much else. Thirdly, Symington's press contacts, unlike those of the men who were his rivals for the convention's plum, were weak, for the national press saw the senator as a kind of monomaniac on defense matters and something of a lightweight in other fields.[1]

Adlai Stevenson had made it clear to his supporters that although he would not turn the nomination down if it was offered to him, he would not make any active attempt to obtain it. Nevertheless, a campaign was under way, without his active involvement, beginning in early 1960. By April the various arms of Stevenson's campaign had combined forces and set up a Washington office. To many Stevenson supporters, the collapse of the Summit Conference in Vienna seemed to make the governor's nomination more urgent than ever.[2]

James Doyle of Madison, Wisconsin, who had "shepherded and restrained the volunteers," came to Washington, where he officially announced the launching of a Draft Stevenson movement. Draft Stevenson clubs were operating in forty-two states. The New York newspapers carried full-page appeals for funds. The first brought in $40,-000, more than the response to any single such ad in either 1952 or

1956. The Stevenson organization also launched a direct mail campaign, sending every delegate and politician who would be at the convention broadsides containing poll results, analyses, and pleas. The predominant theme was that only Stevenson could rescue the Republic from Khrushchev—and Nixon. In Los Angeles, Stevenson leaders leased a building across the street from the convention's headquarters hotel and put up a banner one hundred feet long and nine feet high imploring "Draft Stevenson." Planes were hired to tow banners bearing the same message over New York on Independence Day weekend. Then, volunteers from all forty-two clubs received their order to march on Los Angeles:

> This was the carnival coating of the movement, the necessary noise to pressure the politicians, the delegates, the press.[3]

White points out that although this frenzy of the volunteers and the hoopla and press-agentry was deemed necessary to stampede the delegates, more quiet efforts were also under way in an attempt to structure the convention so as to give in under the stampede. Those efforts were under the direction of Senator Mike Monroney of Oklahoma and John Sharon, a junior partner of the Washington law firm of Cleary, Gottlieb, Steen and Ball (who in 1956 had proposed the "open convention" approach to the vice presidential nomination). These efforts, however, simply were not enough to halt the more considerable offensive of John F. Kennedy, nor even to top that of Hubert H. Humphrey.

Public relations considerations had been part of Humphrey's early determination to pursue the nomination. He said later of his decision to make the try, reached at an afternoon conference in Duluth, Minnesota, on July 11, 1959:

> ". . . even then I was being compared to Kennedy instantly, and his publicity was incredible it was so good. It was in the right place, in the family magazines, in the good journals, in the quality spots. And I knew how I looked. I was always being talked of as being pro-labor, argumentative, testy, competitive, a far-out liberal. The only organization I had was in Minnesota, I had no money, no big press on my side, no public relations. *My Minnesota crowd doesn't know how to use public relations.* We had a certain pattern that worked in Minnesota, but they didn't know how the national press works . . ."[4]

The organization and talent assembled by John F. Kennedy in his quest for the Democratic nomation were quite different. Since 1952 he had been furnished ideas, information, and analysis by Harvard professors "to shape his national thinking." After his 1958 reelection to the Senate, a more formal group of a dozen or so scholars had been formed under the leadership of political scientist Earl Latham of Amherst. Kennedy assembled his "brain trust" at the Harvard Club in Boston for dinner in January 1960 and told them they were mobilized. During the summer, Professor Archibald Cox of the Harvard Law School established himself in Washington with a seven-man speech-writing force. They got ideas primarily from the pool of professors, who thought, analyzed, and prepared data on national policy, which was channeled from the universities to Cox to Kennedy's aide Theodore Sorensen, and thence to the senator.[5]

The Kennedy campaign had its equivalent of the Robert Humphreys "Campaign Plan" of 1952. It was the "O'Brien Manual," a 64-page book prepared by Kennedy adviser Lawrence O'Brien (later to become postmaster-general and eventually Democratic national chairman and the manager of George McGovern's 1972 campaign). The thrust of the manual was that every vote counts; every citizen likes to feel that somehow he relates to the power structure; making an individual seem useful and important to himself in the power system of American politics is a way to take advantage, as White had put it, of "one of the simplest and noblest urges of politics in the most effective way."[6]

This strategy grew out of the knowledge, based on experience, that Kennedy was, in fact, a glamorous candidate. It is not difficult for a glamorous candidate to arouse people, but quite another matter to convince those people that they are useful participants in the political process. Yet, it is sound public relations practice to give one's supporters that feeling of utility. In 1958 Kennedy's Senatorial campaign headquarters had been swamped by some eighteen hundred volunteers. O'Brien solved the organizational problem—and received a public relations plum—by employing the volunteers at sending thank-you letters to 256,000 signers of nomination petitions. This eminently good political solution made those who received the letters happy, and at the same time gave every volunteer the "illusion of service."[7] Of course, the whole process was illusory; no really meaningful political act was really taking place.

Public opinion polling was so important to the Kennedy operation as to be an indivisible part of the central campaign organization, with pollster Louis Harris serving as one of the candidate's key advisers. Harris, who had been running a successful market research firm, was first employed by the Kennedys prior to the 1958 Senatorial campaign in Massachusetts. Although that was a routine professional contract, Harris had been attracted by the Kennedy personality, and when the pre-nomination campaign was organized in earnest in 1959, Harris was not only a Kennedy zealot but also a member of the inner circle. In 1960 he polled more people around the country than had ever been surveyed by any political analyst in American history: ". . . upon his reports, upon his description of the profile of the country's thinking and prejudices as he found them, were to turn many of John F. Kennedy's major decisions."[8]

Harris's findings and his resulting recommendations for modifications in the Kennedy image to suit the burden of public opinion were apparently taken with the greatest seriousness. For example, Stephen Shadegg in his book *How to Win an Election* reported that in 1960 Kennedy's pollsters brought in the information that the senator's youthful appearance was a liability. Kennedy, according to Shadegg, then proceeded to change the style of his haircut, adopted more conservative clothing, "and deliberately attempted to appear older and more mature."[9]

It might be added here that this emphasis on appearance not only illustrates the kind of polling data that may influence a candidate, but also the importance of visual images, and the new demand that television imposes upon a candidate—and upon a political party in choosing its man.

Daniel Ogden and Arthur Peterson have pointed out that, traditionally, efforts have been made to secure a presidential candidate who would be at ease in small groups of powerful political leaders and at the same time eloquent and persuasive when facing large crowds. A candidate might frequently find himself facing fifteen thousand persons for a long oration in the days before the invention of microphones and loudspeakers. And many of those fifteen thousand may have been prepared to commit themselves to a course of political action following the speech or debate. In the 1960's, however, ". . . a party looks for a man who is at ease, articulate, and attractive when facing the television cameras and who likewise can spark the massive gatherings of a purely partisan nature. He must be an expositor as well as an orator."[10]

Kennedy and Humphrey had both chosen the primary elections as their route to the nomination. Indeed, with neither of them a national figure, and the opposition in control of the White House, other options were closed to them. The crucial battleground between the senators from Massachusetts and Minnesota became the West Virginia and Wisconsin primaries.

Wisconsin came first, and both candidates approached it energetically. Their liberal programs matched closely. With little political differentiation, image and personality and technique were likely to make the difference.

Although each of them spent about $150,000, Hubert Humphrey said he was like a "corner grocer running against a chain store." Humphrey had billboards, advertisements, radio and television time, literature, a campaign bus—all his technical needs were satisfied. But his campaign team consisted of Minnesota men who had busy full-time jobs outside of Wisconsin and couldn't give their candidate more than weekend help. At the national level, Humphrey headquarters consisted of six men in four Washington hotel rooms. Kennedy, on the other hand, had prepared for months. He got around on his own plane. And he had Louis Harris, whose polling of 23,000 Wisconsinites was the largest ever done in a single state. "Above all, Kennedy had organization and the beginning of a national press cult."[11]

Humphrey had two staffed offices in Wisconsin, Kennedy had eight. Humphrey leaned on labor support and help from the regular Democratic organization when he could get it. The Kennedys relied on themselves for funds and manpower, which included the candidate's sisters, brothers, classmates, Senate staff, and friends. They had a freewheeling organization with independent techniques—a staff free to set its own targets and decide on how to reach them.[12]

Theodore White has summed up the public relations impact of this kind of operation:

> It is activity that creates news, and activity in Wisconsin lay chiefly with Kennedy—in the flight of his personal plane . . . ; with the candidate's glamorous family, with his revolving circus of Ivy League performers and organizers. The press, charmed by Kennedy, entranced by the purr of his political machinery, slowly fastened on the candidate from Massachusetts as the winner.[13]

In West Virginia, the Kennedy organization itself made news. It was handed some very valuable services free of charge. Eight head-quarters and eight sub-headquarters offices were staffed by talented men of independent wealth: advertising men, attorneys, and artists, among others. And while the one Kennedy team was being deployed in West Virginia, the second squad was simultaneously fielded in Maryland, a third in Oregon, and a fourth team was warming up in Indiana.[14]

O'Brien built an organization of some nine thousand volunteers in West Virginia. Meanwhile, the public relations buildup was in full swing. In the newspapers, Kennedy advertisements were devoted to the senator's heroic war record or to attacking Hubert Humphrey as the "puppet of faceless men" afraid to show any courage of their own in the contest. The Kennedy family traversed the state, making news as they went. Kennedy appeared frequently on the television screen. A major Kennedy television biography opened with a picture of a PT boat, switched to the senator holding a book in his large library and receiving a Pulitzer Prize, then went to a shot of him reading to his daughter on his lap. In seconds, images skillfully portrayed the candidate as war hero, eminent scholar and author, and devoted father.[15]

Kennedy's staff had been divided on how to handle the religious issue, and the candidate took the advice of his West Virginia consultants and Louis Harris, attacking the issue via television. The strategy was to make the religious question a morality play. It was to be tolerance versus intolerance. Thus, no voter could easily satisfy his own conscience that he was displaying tolerance by voting for Humphrey. Sorensen spent a sleepless weekend in Nebraska answering Kennedy's request for the four or five questions about Catholics that most bothered Protestants. Armed with this information, FDR junior, who had been touring the state with the "clan," went on the air with Kennedy in West Virginia, playing the interlocutor and asking the candidate about his religion.[16]

Humphrey, feeling overwhelmed by the Kennedy campaign budget, attacked the "politics of big money" in West Virginia. This seemed reasonable, in view of the fact that Humphrey had to spend about half of his own time raising funds for his campaign. He barnstormed in a bus, carried his own bags. The Wisconsin primary had run him into heavy debt, and his labor support seemed to have evaporated. There was something depressing about the whole operation. White reports that Humphrey "exhausted every resource of friendship" to raise money. His total expense in West Virginia, peanuts in presidential politics, was $25,000. By the final Saturday morning of the primary campaign, Kennedy had spent $34,000 on television alone. When the time arrived for Humphrey's final Sunday night half-hour program, the television stations threatened to cancel him out if he did not pay for his time a day in advance. Humphrey responded with a personal check for $750, under circumstances which Theodore White describes with great poignancy. And, somehow, Humphrey came up with another $750 to toss into thirty last minutes of television time for a telethon the day before election.[17]

A telethon is a televised public relations device in which a candidate, in theory, opens himself to any question from any voter who can get a call through to the station. A well-produced telethon requires a large and competent staff to screen incoming questions and put them in sequence, so as to convey the feeling of spontaneity while at the same time giving the candidate an opportunity to develop his central themes. White has said the telethon "is commonly one of the most spurious and obnoxious devices of modern political gimmickry." When a telethon is conducted with real authenticity, and the candidate is fed unscreened questions, "the effect is comic."[18]

On election eve, Humphrey sat before a manual telephone in a television studio, and the viewing audience heard the unfiltered questions and the senator's answers. None of the questions hit anywhere near the central areas of his campaign issues, and some came from far-out crackpots. Some callers rambled on without asking questions. A party line operator got on the phone and demanded the lines be cleared for an emergency. "The telethon lost all cohesion—proving nothing except that TV is no medium for a poor man."[19]

If television contributed to Humphrey's downfall in the primaries, it was later to help Kennedy, as his party's nominee, capture the presidency. But as Kennedy accepted the nomination, his rival for the White House, Vice President Richard M. Nixon, by now an old TV hand, saw nothing to fear in the senator's electronic image. He watched from Washington, with two advisers, as John F. Kennedy delivered his acceptance speech at the Los Angeles convention. The three Republican viewers were pleased:

> The Vice-President offered the observation that he thought it a poor performance, way over people's heads, too fast. He could take this man on TV—so he felt. Already the Republican and

Democratic parties had been exchanging an interfire of telegrams over a proposal for a series of national TV debates between the candidates. The Vice-President, according to those who discussed it with him, was not worried by the tired image on the screen before him that night; he could not foresee what time, illness and strain would do to his own image on such a screen in the fall; he looked forward to the meeting.[20]

## The Republicans

The most spectacular pre-nomination campaign on the Republican side was, from a public relations point of view, not that of the eventual nominee, Richard M. Nixon, but rather the elaborate effort of Governor Nelson Rockefeller of New York. As Theodore White has described it:

> By mid-December [1958], when the private staff of the Rockefeller family had been combined with the political resources of the New York Governor, the Rockefeller Presidential exploration was a thing of political wonder, large enough to make even the Kennedy operation seem like a Montana roadshow.[21]

Specifically, White indicates that the organization included:

> —a *political* division, in charge of relationships with state Republican leaders around the country;
> —a *speech-writing* division, which researched and drafted statements on world and national affairs;
> —an *"image"* division of high-level public relations talent, which dealt with problems of personal public relations [a leading figure in the "in-group" was the late Frank Jameson, whom White characterizes as "a genius at public relations"];
> —a *logistics* division, which scheduled and arranged the governor's trips almost like the advance men of a full-scale presidential campaign.

Routine press relations were handled by Rockefeller's press secretary in Albany. There was also a citizens' division in touch with grass-roots Citizens for Rockefeller Clubs, which were ready to sprout around the country. A campaign biography was in preparation, as was a history of the governor's long career in public affairs and philanthropy.[22]

The first official pre-nomination Rockefeller campaign, from a public relations point of view, lasted about eight weeks, from early October to early December 1959. As the governor went around the country, making news with his speeches, Leonard Hall, operating on Richard Nixon's behalf out of the Sheraton-Park Hotel in Washington, was doing an astute job of counter-newsmaking. If Rockefeller discovered a pocket of support, Hall, an astute and tireless defender of Nixon, would quickly spring an announcement from a Republican leader or group of them, displaying equal or greater enthusiasm for the governor's rival.[23]

Somewhat discouraged by this scouting trip, Rockefeller retreated from the race in December. But by May 1960, with the disarmament conferences with Russia breaking down in Geneva, and with America's position in foreign affairs looking increasingly worse in much of the world, the governor apparently became increasingly obsessed with the feeling that the presidential term of office beginning in 1960 would be one of constant crisis. Rockefeller presumably discussed these matters, as well as the ability of Vice President Nixon to cope with them, at a long conference with his "chief thinker," Emmet Hughes, on May 30, 1960, at the immense Rockefeller estate in Pocantico Hills. The meeting resulted in a Rockefeller decision to attack what he considered American complacency.[24]

This second pre-nomination effort, then, ran from about June 1 to July 19, 1960. It included a number of public appearances and radio and television efforts, as well as the issuance of nine major papers, which White has called "one of the most remarkable collections of political documents in American campaign history." The study papers covered American economic growth, civil rights, foreign affairs, national defense, government reorganization, health care for the aged, disarmament and arms control, education, Latin American unity, and a general summation prepared for the Republican Party platform. They carried implicit across-the-board criticism of the Republican Party's conduct of the affairs of state during the eight previous years of G.O.P. hegemony and could thus not be expected to make many friends among party leaders.[25]

William M. Brinton of San Francisco, who had been laying the groundwork for the organization of a national network of Citizens for Rockefeller organizations when the governor withdrew late the previous year, flew to New York on June 27 to ask the Rockefeller staff to allow him to go ahead and set up a national Draft Rockefeller movement. He was allowed to proceed, but without formal authority. By July 8, Brinton had run a newspaper ad seeking support in twenty-nine papers in the twenty-one states where Citizens for Rockefeller groups had been reorganized. He received forty thousand replies by July 11. Although solvent and operational, it was too late to organize pressures similar to those of the Stevenson movement. But Brinton did run another round of national newspaper ads, urging Republicans around the country to write, wire, and phone state delegations in Chicago to demand the nomination of Rockefeller. There were additional appeals on television. The use of the media in this case brought on a display of the politics of participation, during which, within fifty-six hours after the first television spots appeared, more than a million pieces of mail and telegrams poured into the hotels, special post offices, and convention facilities, swamping mail delivery and slowing down mail sorting in some of the hotels by forty-eight hours. But without regular organizational efforts behind the scenes, activity like this really does not have much hope of gaining a presidential nomination.[26]

Personal image was a matter of major concern to Richard M. Nixon and his advisers as the Vice President contemplated his forthcoming nomination. From a public relations point of view, Nixon's staff saw as assets his famous "kitchen debate" with Nikita Khrushchev; his courage in the face of a barrage of rocks and saliva during his tour of Latin America; and his apparent role in handling the affairs of state during President Eisenhower's illnesses. On the other hand, there were strong negatives, such as the reaction to tactics employed by Nixon during his early campaigns for the House and Senate—the old charge that he used unfair accusations against his opponents in both campaigns. Some had come to refer to Nixon as the "parlor McCarthy."[27]

Nixon's public image had been a concern long before the campaign formally began. In 1958 public relations man Herbert Klein, a former southern California newspaperman (who would become, in 1968, the American government's first "communications director") was recruited, following a December strategy meeting at the Key Biscayne home of Florida realtor C. B. "Bebe" Rebozo. Klein came to Washington the following June.[28]

The Volunteers for Nixon offices began to issue Question and Answer Sheets dealing with a variety of topics—civil rights, economic policy and philosophy, Africa, social welfare, labor, education, Latin America, and so on. Each document was five to twelve pages long, and they were issued in a packet entitled "Become Better Acquainted with Richard Nixon." In the view of one author who was closely connected with the Nixon campaign, these documents, issued long before the convention, were part of an effort to "impress thought leaders in particular with the Vice-President's breadth and depth of vision and to reveal his concern over major issues of the day and his reasonable position on them. Their political position was variously described as "moderate liberal" or "liberal conservative"[29] (adjectives used in 1968 to describe the "New Nixon").

The policy pronouncements of both Nixon and Rockefeller were to have more significance at the Chicago convention than one might have expected. For the principal dramatic clash at Chicago was not one of men so much as of ideas—of the Republican Party's approach to the issues.

The clash was resolved in the famous Nixon-Rockefeller "Pact of Fifth Avenue." The "Pact" was an agreement reached after Nixon, on the Friday before the Republican convention, flew to New York for a meeting with Rockefeller. The governor was raising the possibility of an open fight on the convention floor, charging that the draft of the party platform was not strong or specific enough to satisfy him.

Nixon's tactics in negotiating this accommodation with Rockefeller served, very early in the game, to undermine his relations with the press. For the Vice President had left his entire personal staff, as well as the press, ignorant of what was going on. And when the first rumor of the New York meeting began to circulate in Chicago on Saturday, July 23, Herbert Klein, now officially Nixon's chief press aide, was denying that any such meeting had taken place. Klein sincerely believed this to be true, but found himself being denounced as a liar by newsmen, who had previously trusted him as a colleague.[30]

The Nixon-Rockefeller agreement became final during a three-hour telephone conversation between the two men in New York and Charles Percy, Melvin Laird, and other platform committee officials in Chicago. The language already prepared for consideration by the committee was, it should be pointed out, endorsed by Rockefeller in a number of cases. But, according to Karl Lamb and Paul Smith, "Manipulation by Governor Rockefeller's public relations staff gave the impression that the agreement represented a capitulation by

Nixon. [Senator] Barry Goldwater labeled the outcome a 'Republican Munich,' and the resulting feud in the Platform Committee required all Nixon's skills to resolve."[31]

Nixon's independent action was a foretaste of a method of operation that was to plague his public relations staff throughout the campaign. It illustrates the dangers that can occur when a candidate, who previously had worked through a staff of public relations men, suddenly moves on his own, without either consulting or informing the experts. This sudden inclination to bypass the public relations professionals can, as it did in this case, seriously disrupt the orderly process of public communication.


## After the Nomination: the Presidential Campaign

### John F. Kennedy

The campaign of John F. Kennedy for the presidency of the United States was characterized by a style that had become rare in American politics. When Abraham Lincoln eulogized Henry Clay, he spoke of the eloquence of the man as one of his great virtues. This quality of eloquence is one not often found in contemporary American politics. The demands of a modern campaign, coupled with the new methods of packaging, marketing, and promoting presidential candidates, have made eloquence, to a large degree, an anachronism. Clay, like Lincoln himself, wrote his own material, and through the speeches of both men ran philosophical threads that indicated a commitment to an ideology that went far beyond the immediate objective of office-seeking.

The style of John F. Kennedy was of another sort. As Theodore White has pointed out, there is considerable doubt as to whether any historian will one day find it a truly worthwhile pursuit to reproduce the speeches over which the senator from Massachusetts labored with assistants such as Theodore Sorensen and Richard Goodwin. For speeches such as that on government ethics at Wittenberg University, on national defense at Miami, on Latin American affairs at Tampa

> passed through the dutiful typewriters of the press corps who followed the campaign; all were dutifully reproduced in the press

across the nation; yet by that time specifics and issues had all but ceased to matter; only "style" was important. [But the Kennedy style], for those who have an affection for American political performance . . . was a thing of beauty.[32]

Now, with the nomination in hand, the Kennedy campaign was unified to a degree under the Democratic National Committee. The committee included the Kennedy Research Team, directed by Myer Feldman; the Kennedy Speech Writers' Division, under Archibald Cox; the National Committee's Research Division (which served mainly Congressional, state, and local candidates), directed by Robert Oshins; and the Publicity Division, handled by Roger Tubby and Samuel Brightman. The entire operation was managed by Sorensen, Kennedy's principal policy adviser, who went with the campaign party on the plane, and Feldman, who stayed in Washington to supervise the four divisions and personally approve every National Committee statement which carried the candidate's signature.[33]

Feldman recruited for his Research Team five full-time specialists in various substantive fields. These men explored key issues, selected by the candidate. They developed briefing memoranda for speeches and, eventually, the television debates with Richard Nixon. The team also worked on brochures, statements, and other special materials for various branches of the National Committee. Roger Tubby, in his slot as campaign coordinator for publicity, divided his assignments with Brightman, the committee's pre-Kennedy public affairs director. Both men, as we have seen, were Stevenson-Eisenhower campaign veterans. Brightman ran regular National Committee publicity, while Tubby handled releases on the Kennedy speeches, telephone requests, news conferences, and a series of rebuttal pamphlets entitled "Correction Please." He also prepared many by-lined articles for the senator for publication in national magazines and newspapers.[34] Meanwhile, Pierre Salinger, traveling with the campaign plane, handled the candidate's on-the-spot relations with the traveling press party.

An effort was made to involve professional writers, rather than public relations technicians exclusively, as a supplement to Archibald Cox's speech-writing staff. A Writers' Bureau was established in New York to draw upon a number of distinguished authors and writers. But apparently neither of these Cox efforts proved very useful during the heat of the campaign. Kennedy did not speak to the specialized audiences that would have appreciated the addresses-in-depth on public policy questions that the speech writers were preparing under Cox. These formal addresses were severely edited, rewritten, or discarded. By mid-October, the Writers' Bureau had been abandoned and the Washington speech-writing staff greatly reduced. Some of its members went to work for Adlai Stevenson, who was at that point campaigning for the senator, and others went on the road as advance speech writers for Kennedy. Members of this latter group would visit a city before the candidate's scheduled speech and work with the campaign advance man and local Democrats to pick up some local color and issues for the senator to work into his remarks.[35] Among the distinguished journalists in this group were John Bartlow Martin of the *Saturday Evening Post* and Joseph Kraft, author of *The Struggle for Algeria.*

White saw Kennedy's campaign staff as divided, *informally,* into three parts:[36]

> 1. The *"Personal Brain Trust"* of Sorensen, Goodwin, and Feldman ("Although somewhat aloof with outsiders," White wrote, "this trio has a fey, intellectual quality that is quite captivating").
> 2. The *"Academic Brain Trust"* of Arthur Schlesinger, John Kenneth Galbraith, McGeorge Bundy, and Walt W. Rostow.
> 3. The *"Political Brain Trust"* of Kenneth P. O'Donnell, Lawrence O'Brien, Richard F. Donahue, and Ralph Dungan (otherwise known as the "Irish Mafia").

In addition, the Democratic National Committee retained the advertising agency of Guild, Bascom and Bonfigli to handle national advertising for the presidential campaign. The agency's role in content was apparently not major, and its task was mainly one of time- and space-buying. The Democratic Party paid nearly a quarter of all its campaign expenditures to its advertising agency—an official total of $2,413,227.[37]

Kennedy's youth, per se, was not his principal image problem as the campaign got under way. His name needed to become better known, but there was confidence that this name familiarity could be gained with advertising, barnstorming, and, hopefully, by debating Vice President Nixon. "His real needs were to establish that he was mature and experienced and that he was a moderate liberal who wanted action."[38]

From a technical point of view, the first ten days or so of the Kennedy campaign proved discouraging and rather dull. The senator's speeches were not especially well delivered and attracted little press attention. According to White, the advance work in such states as Washington and Oregon "was atrocious and resulted in humiliation for the candidate." In California, Kennedy was badly scheduled and underexposed. He was booked for a Los Angeles speech in the Shrine Auditorium, one of the smaller of the halls available in that enormous city. But the Kennedy style and theme were developing. The reporters heard the five-minute "all-purpose" speech repeated several times each day, but heard it change from city to city and grow easier. For example, the candidate began to make oblique reference to his wife's pregnancy—and, in the course of a day, his wife's condition ended up as a press-conference question to which the senator replied with great confidence that the baby was to be a boy (which it was).[39]

It was during this period that Kennedy developed what White calls the "grand theme" that permeated his campaign: "America cannot stand still; her prestige fails in the world; this is a time of burdens and sacrifice; we must move." His standard phrases included: "The importance of the presidency"; "the world can not exist half slave and half free"; "only the President can lead"; "we must move"; and "I ask your help." The pattern shaped itself into a theme as the candidate and his advisers observed where applause indicated the senator had hit a vital target, and indifference that he had spoken over the heads of his audience.[40]

The evolution in the uses of television in the 1960 campaign, given the background of the revolutionary changes begun in 1952, was most interesting. The lessons of repetitive brand-name advertising had taken root firmly in presidential politics. Spot announcements were the rule of the day. The advertising logic was simple. For the price of one thirty-minute telecast, which might have attracted only a limited, and perhaps already convinced, viewing audience, a candidate in 1960 was able to flash his face and his name on the screen many times over many days in ten-, twenty-, and thirty-second spots, which members of the viewing audience would be far more likely to see, sandwiched as they were in between their more usual fare. Kennedy and Nixon both used numerous spots and avoided using any formal thirty-minute studio programs to present themselves and their views.[41] As we shall see in our discussion of the "Great Debates," later developments in the campaign dealt a firm and nearly final blow to the thirty-minute campaign program.

Kennedy's relations with the press were characterized by an unusual intimacy—and one that could not have been promoted by the finest of public relations men acting on their own. As a Pulitzer Prize-winning author and former reporter, the senator was known to have enormous respect for the press and to seek the company of newsmen on a personal level.

The candidate would read news stories and tell reporters if he particularly liked a passage of theirs, as he proceeded to quote it from memory. Although he seldom took the advice of newsmen, he flattered them by asking for it. He made a point of being available for quick conversational exchanges, as he stopped for a cold drink or got on or off a plane. White tells of JFK borrowing reporters' combs and pencils and filching their candy bars. Furthermore, Senator Kennedy's p.r. staff replicated this approach. Pierre Salinger, Don Wilson, and Andrew Hatcher would ride the press buses and serve as constant sources of information, passing on little exclusive background items to new correspondents. It all paid off handsomely. In White's words:

> There is no doubt that this kindliness, respect and cultivation of the press colored all the reporting that came from the Kennedy campaign . . . [The press] felt that they, too, were marching like soldiers of the Lord to the New Frontier.[42]

As the election approached, the candidates and their public relations staffs felt great pressure to provide more and more newsworthy copy each day. But there remained less and less to say, "and as the news demands grew and the content dropped, the efforts to keep up the appearance of novelty were prodigious." The normal news file from correspondents with the Kennedy camp grew from an average of sixty thousand words a day to an average of ninety thousand words a day in the final week.[43] The phrases were the same, the theme had not changed, but the press, serving their readers and listeners and viewers, and the public relations staff, serving the candidate, worked together to find more and more to say.

One of the public relations innovations in the Kennedy campaign, which simplified the work of the press, was the nearly immediate availability of a stenotype transcript of what the candidate had to say each time he spoke. Stenotypist "Chick" Reynolds, who had the added asset of being "a good companion of the road" for the press corps, traveled with the campaign party and ground out the transcripts. This device allowed reporters to relax during the course of the Kennedy oratory, knowing that they would have an accurate transcript at their fingertips within an hour. No equivalent service was provided by the Nixon public relations staff, by the way, until much later in the campaign.[44]

Another campaign innovation by the Kennedy organization was the building of the first political simulator to be used in presidential campaigning. The project was an innovation of three professors—William McPhee of Columbia University, Ithiel de Sola Pool of MIT, and Robert P. Abelson of Yale. These men had presented their idea to Edward L. Greenfield, a New York businessman and sometime adviser to liberal Democratic politicians. Greenfield discussed the possibilities of simulation with the Democratic Advisory Council, and the working politicians, including Democratic Chairman Paul Butler, agreed to proceed with the project. James M. Perry gives an interesting account of the simulator's application to the campaign.[45]

The data fed to the simulator came from the Elmo Roper Public Opinion Research Center at Williams College, where there resides a collection of all the old IBM cards used by Roper and other pollsters. The Roper center agreed to the use of its archives on the condition that all basic data tabulated would be available to the center, where the Republicans would have a similar opportunity to use it, and, secondly, the center and the social scientists involved in the project requested that all its results be available for scholarly publication following the election.

These social scientists, along with Greenfield, organized themselves as the Simulmatics Corporation. Data came from sixty-six surveys, representing more than one-hundred thousand interviews. Respondents were classified into 480 types; for each type, information was recorded dealing with voting behavior, election turnout, and attitudes on some fifty different issues. Altogether, the simulator was fed about one million individual pieces of information.

Once the simulator was geared up, it was asked a practical question: What would happen on Election Day if the anti-Catholic criticism of Senator Kennedy were to grow significantly? The Simulmatics report was delivered to Robert F. Kennedy on August 25, 1960, and said, in its key section, as quoted by Perry:

If the campaign becomes embittered [Senator Kennedy] will lose a few more reluctant Protestant votes to Nixon, but will gain Catholic and minority group votes. Bitter anti-Catholicism in the campaign would bring about a reaction against prejudice and for Kennedy from Catholics and others who would resent overt prejudice. . . . On balance, he would not lose further from forthright and persistent attention to the religious issue, and could gain.

When this did, indeed, become a real situation, Senator Kennedy did, indeed, choose to meet the religious issues head-on, and most post-election analyses seem to indicate he made the right choice. As for how much weight the candidate gave to the simulator report, Perry quotes Abelson and Pool: "Neither we, nor the users, nor even John F. Kennedy if he were alive, could give a certain answer. . . . [But] our own contribution, if any, was to bolster by evidence one set of alternatives."

Kennedy aide Theodore Sorensen later wrote of the simulator:

Neither speeches nor debate preparations were based on any "people machine." Considerable self-advertising by a group called the Simulmatics Corporation has given the impression that their computer analyses of public opinion research were read and adapted by Kennedy and all his top advisers. In truth, their reports, when read at all, were no more valuable than the issues polls that were fed into their computers. They contained all the same faults: they restated the obvious, reflected the bias of the original pollsters and were incapable of precise application.[46]

Nevertheless, as Perry points out, "A simulator was built and it did supply information that was read by the 10 or 15 men who actually ran a Presidential campaign. More importantly, the simulator seemed to be at least partly effective."

In any case, the "scholarly" efforts of the professors gave birth to the Simulmatics Corporation. Perry describes it as an operating commercial firm with a healthy list of clients, including some federal government agencies. Although the corporation was quite willing to build a simulator for the 1968 presidential campaigns, nobody asked for one. But Perry feels it is just a matter of time: "Most politicians are still skeptical about using computers to handle payrolls, much less to construct models to imitate hypothetical, make-believe situations."

Simulators aside, it seems apparent that Kennedy and his advisers were much influenced by the results of public opinion polls—particularly those conducted by the house pollster, Louis Harris—in choosing issues to be attacked during the campaign and in determining the strategy for the attacks.

In October, for example, Kennedy decided to hit hard at the traditionally Republican suburbs around the major cities. He pursued suburban votes around Chicago, Philadelphia, New York, and Baltimore, appealing to younger voters in these outlying areas. The central issue for this phase of the campaign was determined after a Harris survey indicated that while less than 30 percent of American families were then sending their children to college, at least 80 percent hoped to see their children so educated in the future. So in the suburbs, the Democratic candidate went after educational issues, and the young couples, struggling with too many bills and simultaneously concerned for the future of their children, apparently listened. In the suburbs of the fourteen largest northeastern metropolitan areas, Kennedy was able to increase the Democratic vote percentage from the 38 percent polled by Stevenson in 1959 to 49 percent in 1960.[47] Harris, playing the p.r. man as well as pollster, also warned his candidate to prepare for a last-minute Republican television blitz, the campaign debut of President Eisenhower—and a recurrence of religious sentiment. Like the simulator, Harris urged Kennedy to face the religious issue head-on. And, according to White, he suggested that a nationwide television show be devoted to that purpose.[48]

The nature and timing of the religious issue was taken out of Kennedy's hands by the Reverend Norman Vincent Peale, when the New York clergyman, author of *The Power of Positive Thinking*, issued a statement questioning the ultimate loyalty of any Catholic aspiring to the presidency and the wisdom of putting an adherent of that faith in the White House.

Kennedy dealt with the issue by accepting an invitation from the Greater Houston Ministerial Association to discuss his religion. He told the Texas group that if he found any conflict between his conscience and the responsibilities of the presidency, he would resign his office. White feels that in this statement Kennedy went far toward a philosophical definition of "the personal doctrine of a modern Catholic in a democratic society." But the philosophizing done with, public relations took over its exploitation. The television networks broadcast portions of the Kennedy performance nationally the next day. Kennedy volunteers used the filmed record of the statement over and over again during the next seven weeks. "It was to be their basic document; no measure is available of how many millions saw the film played and replayed, still less is there a measure available of its effect.[49]

There was at least one other instance in which the candidate's involvement in a passionate social issue was turned to his considerable public relations advantage. This involved Senator Kennedy's intervention in the case of the Rev. Martin Luther King. Dr. King had been sentenced, on a technicality, to four months of hard labor in the Georgia State Penitentiary at Reidsville, an institution in which Mrs. King and others felt the prospects of a lynching were not unlikely. At the suggestion of Harris Wofford, a member of the campaign's civil rights staff, Kennedy called Mrs. King from Chicago's O'Hare Inn. He expressed his interest and concern and assured her he would try to do whatever he could for her husband. Word reached the media that the candidate had intervened to protect the Reverend King. The senator's campaign manager–brother, Robert, on the following morning telephoned a plea for the civil rights leader's release to the Georgia judge who had sentenced him. Dr. King was released from jail the next day, and "in the Negro community the Kennedy intervention rang like a carillon." Scores of black Protestant leaders, beginning with Dr. King's father (until then, a Nixon supporter), began to endorse the Democratic candidate. The candidate's staff made further public relations capital of the incident when, under Wofford's direction, a million pamphlets describing these events were printed and, on the Sunday before election, distributed outside black churches all over the United States.[50]

This favored public relations technique of creating news—or of riding piggyback on "natural" news stories—continued in expert fashion right down to the wire. Even the small touches were not forgotten. For example, twelve registered voters of Hart's Location, New Hampshire, who always vote at midnight, only minutes into Election Day, were each the owner of an autographed picture of John F. Kennedy. The candidate's men had canvassed the village several days earlier and made the presentation. "It was worth the effort, for Hart's Location's results would be the first flash of news on the wires to greet millions of voters as they opened their morning papers over coffee."[51]

John F. Kennedy's campaign in 1960 is a difficult one to categorize in terms of its use of professional public relations. The techniques were certainly all there. Television and polling, for example, were in many ways the keys to the campaign. On the other hand, there were few, if any, professional public relations men—in the sense of men experienced in commercial techniques—who were thoroughly involved in prominent policy positions (Louis Harris was one notable exception). Rather, the central Kennedy staff, composed of generalists rather than technicians, included men with a keen sense of public relations methods.

There is evidence that the candidate himself was keenly aware of the importance of his own image and heeded the advice of those who spoke with authority on this subject. But the Kennedy campaign—indeed, the Kennedy presidency—was characterized by a unique sort of "in-groupism," which looked to the outside not so much for guidance as for very specific technical assistance to fulfill needs that those close to J.F.K. could not themselves satisfy. Even then, they may not have been convinced that they *could not* satisfy every need if they *had* to—only that even such exceptional human beings had to admit that they had just so much time to do what had to be done.

## Richard M. Nixon

Richard Nixon's pre-nomination concern with his rather pugnacious image continued to be translated into concrete political and public relations measures once the nomination was in hand. Nixon's campaign was paced differently than that of Kennedy. If hard punching was to be necessary, the Republicans would save it for the last weeks of the campaign, where, combined with a media barrage, it could overtake the more evenly paced Kennedy campaign.

But, ultimately, such decisions were those of the candidate himself. Unlike Senator Kennedy, Nixon was a solitary operator. He had nothing like the Kennedy "brain trust" at work for him. Not only was there no "Nixon Mafia," but many experts were ignored or their advice disregarded.

Nixon's choice of a running mate seems to have been part of his concern with promoting a "positive image." Henry Cabot Lodge did considerably more than "balance the ticket." Lodge was chosen as a respectable internationalist. He had been the Republican member of the 1950 Tydings Senate Subcommittee investigating Joseph McCarthy's charges of Communists in government. Lodge had been critical of both Democratic laxity and McCarthy's irresponsible accusations.[52]

Lodge was to have a specific supplementary function in the building of the Nixon "national image." Nixon felt that his only sound strategy was to run as an across-the-board, fifty-state "national" candidate, appealing to the voters on the issues of "experience in government" and the Eisenhower record of "peace and prosperity." Therefore, the Vice President did not want to speak to groups of Negroes, Jews, Puerto Ricans, or other minority groups; this job was left to Lodge.[53]

In the first weeks, Lodge did well from the point of view of the Nixon advisers. Then, in mid-October, the ambassador provoked the outrage of his running mate's staff by pledging to a Harlem audience that if Nixon were elected he would name the first Negro Cabinet member in history. The campaign advisers felt that if the pledge were allowed to stand, Nixon would be committed to a course of action that would gain him few additional votes in the North and might lose him millions in the South. (White quotes one Virginia congressman as saying, "whoever recommended that Harlem speech should have been thrown out of an airplane at 25,000 feet.") Following this incident, Lodge's enthusiastic cultivation of minority groups was curtailed.[54]

Another tactical step in the promotion of a positive Nixon image was the establishment of a dual campaign organization. The labor pains of the nomination gave birth also to a massive, cross-country Citizens for Nixon-Lodge organization. Signals would be called from this headquarters, rather than those of the Republican National Committee. The public relations advantage of this maneuver, in the candidate's eyes, was that many independents and Democrats who might want to work for him (and he was convinced that many did) would feel more comfortable under the aegis of the Volunteers than that of a more strictly partisan organization.[55]

The Nixon organization went to work on a series of Position Papers. These somewhat pretentious pseudo-academic documents were issued from August 31 to mid-October in an effort to reach the nation's "thought leaders," as well as special interest groups. The statements were reviewed before release by a prestigious Policy Advisory Board, which included a number of academics in its membership. Position Paper subjects included national purpose, the meaning of Communism to Americans, education, the scientific revolution, housing, and medical research. They were "designed to convince recipients that the candidate was thoughtful and well-informed and as President would be advised by qualified leaders from the business and academic communities."[56]

Another of the advisory groups in the Nixon campaign was the Washington Plans Board. This board had nominal authority over campaign details and scheduling, once the candidate had determined policy and principles. The Vice President was to consult the group before making commitments, and to meet with it weekly. Board members included Campaign Chairman Leonard W. Hall; Campaign Director Robert Finch; Planning Director James Bassett; National Committee Chairman Thruston B. Morton; National Committee Public Relations Director L. Richard Guylay; Director of Television Operations Carroll Newton, and a liaison man from the Eisenhower staff, Robert Merriam (the political scientist son of political scientist Charles Merriam, and a veteran of an unsuccessful mayoral campaign against Richard J. Daley of Chicago). These men were to operate "the nationwide machinery of the Republican Party in support of the candidate and feed into the master plan of the campaign such personalities as Eisenhower, Rockefeller, Goldwater, Dewey, Percy, Lodge, Mitchell, and Judd wherever such names would do most good."[57]

The campaign plan had been blueprinted well in advance. After telling the Republican convention that his campaign would start immediately and go to every state, Nixon took off and covered Illinois, Rhode Island, Nevada, California, Hawaii, and Washington state in the first ten days. The candidate and his advisers felt they had scored a public relations coup as a jet stream of newspaper headlines shot news of the Vice President's vigorous activity before the public's attention. The Gallup poll reversed itself for the first time since January and showed Nixon with a 52 to 47 percent lead over Kennedy. The Vice President's advisers had planned an intensive nine-week campaign schedule starting September 12. All Republican state chairmen had been asked to fill out questionnaires on the key issues they wanted to stress in their states and to turn them in for screening at the convention. The public relations experts had meanwhile decided that regional, rather than national, television would be used extensively by the candidate. As in the case of Senator Kennedy's campaign, it was decided to go after the suburban areas in a big way. All travel and television scheduling was to be buttoned down efficiently before September 12, leaving only the last two weeks of the campaign uncommitted.[58]

But Nixon alone was running for President. And in his role of solitary leadership he sentenced the elaborate campaign plan to death by abortion. The Plans Board had just four sporadic meetings before being abandoned altogether by the candidate. As the campaign continued, this tendency of Nixon to make decisions personally, to abandon staff and advisers—or never to use them once recruited—became increasingly evident. "By the end of the campaign, disaffection from the candidate had become general," according to White. It was understandable. Nixon's high-level volunteers, planners, and advisers were talented men, and many had taken leave from ranking jobs in American commerce to help the candidate. But they often could receive no hearing from the Vice President, and efforts to contact him degenerated ". . . into both the bizarre and the humiliating as they tried to penetrate through his inner court to his attention. . . . One of the men of the command staff said, "he reduced us all to clerks."[59]

One cannot help but observe this early indication of an operational style of isolation which, during Mr. Nixon's eventual tenure in the White House, was to become something of a national issue.

Among the advisers who found themselves awaiting word of the candidate's judgment were two ever-popular Republican television experts, advertising man Carroll Newton and the man behind the "Checkers" show, Ted Rogers, Nixon's personal television consultant. Both men, according to White, wanted to see television used more creatively in 1960 than had been the case in the past. They recommended avoiding old-style programs in which the Vice President would face the camera and talk of hard political matters. They proposed instead five political spectaculars:

> 1. "Khrushchev as I Know Him," which would include film clips of Nixon abroad and in conflict with the Soviet Premier.
> 2. "You and Your Family in 1960," in which the Vice President would try to present himself as an ordinary family man with ordinary family problems.
> 3. A program devoted to Nixon's first week of cross-country campaigning.

    4. A closing show featuring film clips of campaign high-
lights.

    5. A well-planned telethon on election eve.

It would be interesting to speculate on just what such shows would add to the national dialogue. In any case, Newton and Rogers apparently waged their own intramural campaign for these and several other television ideas, including a pictorial analysis of the Democrats' lack of legislative success in Congress during 1960, and various regional television shows stressing the candidate's concern for local problems in important electoral areas. Here again, the Vice President "suspended judgment" and as his advisers waited for orders, it became increasingly apparent that the course of the campaign would be whatever Richard Nixon personally decided.[60]

White stresses throughout his account of the Nixon campaign that one of the candidate's driving personal goals was to be liked, and not thought of as the cruel, hard-nosed, vengeance-seeking man who had been portrayed rather widely in the media during the fifties. Nixon was seeking to identify with people, to communicate in such a way as to evoke human warmth and empathy. Although his press releases were standard political prose, Nixon's personal appearances showed his effort to communicate with the "regular guys": ". . . his style was homestyle. . . . He would point his finger at the audience, the way the man in a white smock selling an analgesic does on the television screens."[61]

There were echoes of the personal history that Nixon had first bared coast-to-coast in the 1952 "Checkers" speech in much of the Vice President's 1960 campaign oratory. He liked to evoke memories of his mother arising at five o'clock in the morning to bake pies for sale in the family grocery store, so that her five sons could have the education their father hadn't had. The man seeking the presidency of the United States confessed that he had wanted to be an engineer and piano player; he had also wanted a model train, but nothing worked out right. Once he told the story of how his older brother, who died when Richard was quite young, had wanted a pony so very badly. But it cost $75, and his parents had to decide that he couldn't have it, since they wouldn't have money left over for food and clothing for the other boys. The press corps, according to White, couldn't decide whether to call that day "Maudlin Friday" or "The Day the Pony Died." Yet, he adds, ". . . it must have been impossible, seeing him just once at a railway station, not to want to comfort or to help this man, who, like so many of his listeners, was one of life's losers."[62]

Nixon's humble, folksy approach and his lone-wolf strategy continued beyond the early stage of the campaign. Republican regulars began to attack him for his kid-glove campaign, and in early October, he seemed to confirm and explain his search for personal acceptance by the people when he reportedly replied to party leaders, "I have to erase the Herblock image first." Herbert Block (Herblock) is a nationally syndicated political cartoonist for the Washington *Post*. He was fond of cartoons showing Nixon with droopy jowls, dark eye circles, a heavy black beard, and banana nose. White contends that Nixon's sensitivity to such barbs is greater than anyone outside of his inner circle recognizes—that he wanted, above all, to be accepted by the eastern world, which had always seemed so strange to him, as it was also to seem strange to Lyndon Johnson, during his presidency. But this was to be the "New Nixon" (not to be confused with the later "New Nixon," c. 1968), and yet no speech, no behavior pattern of his had ever seemed acceptable to this group. White quotes one Nixon friend:

> "The trouble with Dick is that he's been brainwashed by the Eastern liberals. If he lives to be a hundred, he'll never forget that Herblock cartoon of the welcoming committee, and him climbing out of the sewer to greet it, all covered with that stubby beard of his."[63]

Nixon, to say the least, had a serious problem in his relations with the press during the 1960 campaign. The press, in order to act in its role as educator of the public, must first be well informed itself, and understand the matters about which it is obliged to write. If complex matters—say tax reform or farm subsidies—are to be touched upon by a presidential candidate in a speech or policy statement, then the press should be clear as to his meaning and purpose. Otherwise, save for one or two expert reporters, the harried campaign press corps can do little more than a mundane summary of what they are handed by the candidate and his staff. White cites the handling of Nixon's farm policy speech of September 16 as an example of lack of concern for what is perhaps the most basic area of public relations—the quality of one's relationships with key media representatives. Nixon and his advisers worked intensively on the farm speech for two days, but no one attempted to explain it in advance to correspondents. Reporters following the Nixon plane received a copy of the text after 10:30

P.M., somewhere between Virginia and Iowa, the night before it was to be delivered. White describes the feverish atmosphere as reporters went to work on the Vice President's complicated suggestion for disposing of farm surpluses, which he felt was the essence of the nation's agricultural problems. Their work completed to the best of their abilities, reporters amused themselves with imaginary leads such as:

> Vice President Nixon said today farmers should eat their way out of the surplus problem;
> Vice President Nixon said today that farmers are too blankety-blank greedy. He suggested they get what he called "honest jobs" in urban industries.[64]

These diversions were facetious, but the malice in them seems evident, and White agrees it may have been there. It was malice that could be traced to the candidate and his staff, who had decided early in the campaign that the press was fighting them and that the way to reach the emotions of the American people was through television—by paying for the time you need to say what you want to. Although White feels confident that the malice of the correspondents did not penetrate their press dispatches, it is a strong man, even though a thoroughly trained and experienced journalist, who does not in some way show his feelings in his copy—especially when they stem from persistently difficult working conditions.

Accessibility—then as now, for press as well as others, even close associates—was a continuing problem. Reporters' efforts to meet privately with the candidate were rebuffed. Even Theodore White admits to being denied personal contact and to having to distill his interpretations from personal observations of someone with whom he could not talk.[65]

Journalists are professional people, and in 1960 Richard Nixon and his staff abused their professional pride. This appears not to have been an accidental decision. Apparently, the Vice President's public relations advisers, rather than mounting a campaign to win the affection of the press, began with an assumption that the press was an anti-Nixon cabal—almost by definition—and that nothing could be done about it.

The result of this staff attitude was to make things as difficult as possible for reporters. Prepared speeches were not handed out, thus forcing correspondents to take extensive notes. Transcripts of the

Vice President's remarks were also withheld for most of the campaign, until Kennedy's instant transcript service finally was duplicated by the Nixon staff. It was as though the Nixon staff was punishing the press by making life difficult for men who had serious assignments to carry out. White says that although most of these reporters were probably inclined to vote Democratic, they were anxious—even for purely selfish reasons—to write vividly, substantially, and objectively about the Vice President. But he held himself apart; while Kennedy had a rotating pool of reporters in his personal plane at all times, Nixon would sometimes allow, and at other times forbid, any reporters aboard. He simply kept to himself. It was probably a serious error for him to attempt to reach the voters completely without the press, despite his extensive efforts via television. For even though Nixon won the editorial endorsement of 78 percent of all newspapers supporting a presidential candidate in 1960, he made no effort to tell the press what he really thought and felt.[66]

Nixon, of course, did have a press staff. But its members apparently were far from the traditional public relations mold that we have cast in this book. Rather than compensating for the candidate's reticence, press secretary Herbert Klein, according to White, was all the things a press secretary is not supposed to be: "elusive, uninformative, colorless and withdrawn." He viewed the press with suspicion, and

> . . . it was more difficult to elicit information from Klein than from John F. Kennedy himself. As much as any man, Klein was responsible for Nixon's bad press. Robert Finch . . . was the source of almost all warm and positive information about the Vice President, as was Nixon's planning director, James Bassett of the *Los Angeles Mirror*, who was left behind in Washington throughout the campaign.

So by the end of the campaign, the prevalent mood among the reporters assigned to the Nixon trail was the mood the Vice President had feared all along—hostility.[67]

Some of the problems may have come from the fact that Nixon himself felt some author's pride in his work. For although there were several speech-writing aides in and around the Nixon headquarters, "no complete speeches were ever written for the Vice President. He wrote his own." There were, of course, some people around who might do some research and even turn an occasional bit of word-smithing. They included Charles Lichtenstein, a University of Notre Dame political scientist; George Grassmuck, an international relations expert from the University of Michigan; James Shepley of *Time-Life*; newspaperman John Franklin Carter; New York political public relations man Charles Kline, and others.[68]

Meanwhile, the Republican National Committee was grinding out advertising. Time and space-buying was in the hands of Campaign Associates, which was paid an official total of $2,269,578 by the committee during the course of the campaign.[69]

Campaign literature also came rolling out. The most elaborate mailing piece on Nixon's behalf was a thirty-two–page newsprint pamphlet in *Life* magazine–type format. The cover featured a friendly Nixon and was followed by President Eisenhower's letter of endorsement and a picture of the two men in deep and thoughtful conversation. Most of the booklet was filled with a pictorial history of Nixon's family, boyhood, and service in the Navy, Congress, and as Vice President. Only three pages were devoted to the Nixon-Lodge team and the campaign itself.[70]

When Nixon met with his key advisers on October 16 to plan the final stage of his campaign, he found himself rejecting a good deal of the professional advice given him by his own strategists. They wanted him to abandon his pledge to campaign in all fifty states and felt he could do so honorably because of the two weeks he had been hospitalized during the course of the campaign. Despite the impact the Vice President might have made by concentrating only on certain crucial big states in the last twenty days of the campaign, he refused to do so. Many Republicans also believed that it was time for Nixon to address himself to the religious issues, which Kennedy had not raised personally after his Houston statement. Kennedy's associates had been discussing "tolerance," and some of Nixon's Protestant lay advisers, such as Arthur Flemming and Fred Seaton, were ready to stimulate a call by Protestants to Catholics for equal tolerance. Nixon did not want the issue raised in any fashion. The Vice President's advisers pressed for some of the stiff-punching tactics of the "old Nixon"—for example, attacks upon Kennedy's irregular attendance record on the floor of the Senate and in his committee sessions. But Nixon liked Kennedy (White says Kennedy exerted over Nixon "the same charm that a snake charmer exerts over a snake"), and even if that was not reciprocally true, the Vice President would not assault or dissect his opponent. Instead, as White sums it up, the principal thrusts of his counterattack became:

> 1. Kennedy was "running America down" by repeatedly asserting that the U.S. prestige around the world had reached a new low.
> 2. The Democratic platform (not so much Jack Kennedy personally, as the Nixon advisers suggested) would raise the price of everything the housewife buys by 25 percent.
> 3. In these grave times, America could not experiment with inexperienced leadership.[71]

Two other major factors need to be considered in focusing upon the public relations aspects of Nixon's 1960 campaign: the belated intervention of President Eisenhower and the last-minute, all-out television effort of the Republican Party.

President Eisenhower had left the Vice President to his own devices. He had felt that Nixon would have had a better base campaigning as secretary of defense or state, but Nixon had chosen in 1956 to retain the vice presidency rather than move to a cabinet post. The President had appeared at the 1960 Republican convention in Chicago, but did not remain long enough to see his associate nominated. When the nomination came, the President congratulated Nixon on being "at last free to speak freely and frankly in expressing your views." The two men met at Newport four days after the convention, and the nominee's advisers came away with the impression that Nixon would concentrate on the solid Republican vote during the course of the campaign, and the President on the independents and what he himself liked to call the "discerning Democrats." The President had agreed to make three national television appearances: a closed-circuit fund-raising effort in Chicago on September 29; an early November campaign program; and a closing show on election eve. He also made a general commitment to various "nonpolitical" appearances around the country in which he would stress the "national peace and prosperity" theme. Apparently, no more was asked of the President by Nixon's staff. White quotes one member of Mr. Eisenhower's staff as saying, "all of us expected the President would get into the campaign one hell of a lot more than he actually did."[72]

That no call to participate ever came would seem to indicate a rather major public relations blunder on the part of the Nixon organization. The President's tremendous popularity had grown and prospered during his eight years in office, and by 1960 his coattails might have been broad and powerful enough to carry a Republican successor into the White House. But the Nixon organization had chosen to go its own way.

And as it did, the President apparently found cause for irritation. The first television debate had been scheduled, with Nixon's consent, for an evening on which the President was to be on national television addressing the Catholic Charities banquet in New York, thus competing with the Chief Executive for public attention. Furthermore, Eisenhower grew increasingly disturbed by Senator Kennedy's attacks on his administration. He expected that Nixon would counter his opponent immediately, and if not, would invite the Chief Executive to pick up the cudgel. But it was not until October 31 that the President and Vice President got together once again—at a White House luncheon arranged on barely forty-eight hours' notice. This time, the President agreed to make personal appearances in Pittsburgh and Cleveland and to devote an entire day to barnstorming in New York City and its suburbs. White feels that the President's active force during the last ten days of the campaign contributed mightily to the last-minute surge for Nixon which brought the Vice President to within a whisper of victory.[73]

Another mighty contribution to the Nixon upswing was undoubtedly the final television burst of the Republican campaign. It began with a nationally televised Nixon rally in Cincinnati on October 25, continued with an Eisenhower telecast out of Pittsburgh on the 29th, and was followed by another national television rally featuring Nixon, Lodge, and the President in New York on November 2. This last-minute binge was followed each night by a live fifteen-minute Nixon television show. Then, on election eve—November 7—the Republicans, as White puts it so vividly, "let the purse strings pop in what was certainly the most expensive and probably the most effective burst of television electioneering since the medium invaded American culture." Costing an estimated $200,000 (the Democrats insisted it was $400,000), the finale gave Nixon a way to hold "national attention on the ABC network from Detroit in a four-hour telethon that mixed schmaltz and substance in equal proportions, showing the Republican candidate at his best (talking of peace) and at his worst (discussing the high cost of living with Ginger Rogers, who said she, too, had to live on a salary)." The telethon was followed by a fifteen-minute presentation by former New York Governor and presidential candidate Thomas E. Dewey, then a three-way, half-hour hookup between Nixon, Lodge, and the President. That day—November 7—cost the Republicans about $500,000 for television. The total cost to the Republicans for these last ten days was about $2,000,000—spent for what White felt was, at least up to that time, "the greatest electronic effort ever made to move men's minds."[74] Certainly there had been nothing like it before in the history of communications—let alone public relations.

This television blitz, however effective, did not turn out the way the public relations experts and television technicians had planned it. Experts who had expected to be taken quite seriously were barely, if ever, consulted in mounting the communications side of the campaign.

For when Nixon began his campaign, he had theorized, along with his enthusiastic communications specialists, that he could carry his message to the people of America by the most imaginative use of the video tube ever displayed in the history of American politics. Thus, the experts and technicians, assuming the freedom to experiment in this creative use of the medium, prepared "a basket of tricks and special shows designed to use the medium as it had never been used before." The candidate, however, as we have seen, was indecisive about those plans. He was sensitive about being labeled a "Madison Avenue" candidate. One result of this uneasiness was that some of the volunteers in the media field—first-rate personnel of a number of first-rate firms—had to install themselves in an unmarked office, which was located on Vanderbilt Avenue, a short block east of Madison Avenue, but far enough away from that notorious street to avoid the label.[75]

The Vanderbilt Avenue staff grew to realize they were not being consulted. Three months went by from the time of the July 25 acceptance speech during which Nixon had never once appeared on national television under circumstances which he controlled. When he did appear on television, the Vice President did so in the old-fashioned manner of a televised radio program, facing the camera, trying to squeeze the usual all-purpose speech into a little parlor talk. On the Saturday before Election Day, however, the television staff in New York was prodded out of its usual, relaxed status and given forty-nine weekend hours to get a complete telethon on the air. Apparently the Vice President, who had at the start of the campaign rejected his public relations advisers' suggestions for a well-planned telethon, had now reversed himself, convinced that urgent measures were at last necessary.[76]

But these late measures were not enough. Nixon had played the campaign close to his vest, operating as a lone-wolf candidate. He seldom consulted most of those who were qualified, willing and ready to advise him, and even when he did, he often chose to ignore what they had to say. Even those with continuing responsibility on the firing line had problems in communicating with the candidate, and this was reflected in their management of such vital areas as media relations. At the end of the campaign, Nixon had not really molded himself into any discernible "image." His campaign, in White's words, had "neither philosophy nor structure to it, no whole picture either of the man or of the future he offered. One could not perceive . . . any shape of history, any sense of the stream of time or flow of forces by which America had come to this point in history and might move on."[77]

Just how much Nixon's decisions, late in the campaign, to heed the advice of his counselors with regard to the President's participating in the campaign and the last-minute deluge of national television contributed to bringing him within a hairbreadth of the presidency is difficult to say. By the same token, one might argue that had the Republican candidate heeded the counsel of his professional public relations advisers, had he made use of the assembled television expertise, had he been more open and accessible in his relationships with the media, had his press staff serviced and related to newsmen as Kennedy's had, Nixon just might have picked up sufficient strength to go the rest of the distance to the White House.

## The Great Debates

The four televised debates between Vice President Nixon and Senator Kennedy during the 1960 campaign have been described by a wide variety of observers in what seems, in retrospect, rather grandiose terms—"An episode . . . entirely fresh in the sweep of American political history" is Theodore White's characterization. Ogden and Peterson go so far as to call the video encounters "a major landmark in world history."

It may be true that the candidates' discussion, such as it was, was witnessed by more people at one time than had ever before sat in on an encounter between two men striving for the world's most powerful office. But by the same token, the nature of that encounter and the quality of the exchange were determined not so much in the spirit of true deliberation as in that of image-making for the candidates and entertaining television for the broadcasters. The issues in the campaign were hardly more clear following the four encounters than they had been before.

Theodore White feels that when, on September 26, 1960, the mascara and cigarette commercials gave way to a voice regretting the cancellation of the Andy Griffith Show, the screen

> . . . dissolved to three men who were about to confirm a revolution in American Presidential politics. . . . This revolution had been made by no one of the three men on the screen—John F. Kennedy, Richard M. Nixon, or Howard K. Smith, the moderator. It was a revolution born of the ceaseless American genius in technology; its sole agent and organizer had been the common American TV set. Tonight it was to permit the simultaneous gathering of all the tribes of America to ponder their choice between two chieftains in the largest political convocation in the history of man.[78]

There may be some doubt about how history will view the greatness of the convocation, although it certainly was a large one. The "Great Debates" were a boon to John F. Kennedy, who needed—and gained—great name familiarity and an image of seasoned experience and maturity. The Nixon camp was divided, but the candidate finally sided with those of his advisers who felt that the debates might help dispel his "cold and calculating" image. In any case, anyone running for President in 1960 would have found themselves caught up in a long series of circumstances begun in 1956 when Adlai Stevenson first broached the concept of debates by issuing a challenge to President Eisenhower. The White House had rejected the idea on the grounds that it would detract from the dignity of the presidential office. But following the 1956 election, Democratic National Chairman Paul M. Butler had kept the idea from dying. Working with CBS President Frank Stanton, he helped persuade all three major networks to jointly advocate the repeal of the equal-time provisions of Section 315 of the Communications Act in the case of presidential campaigns. Congress agreed, and voted a suspension of the Section 315 provisions for the presidential campaign of 1960. So the challenge to Nixon came not only directly from Senator Kennedy, but indirectly in terms of great pressure from the television networks and the public to use this newfound special freedom. Any excuse that Nixon might have offered for refusing to debate would have been turned by Senator Kennedy to his own political advantage. So Nixon gave in to the pressures. And then both candidates gave in to a new set of pressures—pressures by commercial television operators for a "good show"—and accepted a format that caused the debates to be reduced to a series of hastily made "generalizations on a wide variety of topics."[79]

One interesting change that the debates provoked was television's conversion from a strictly partisan to a bipartisan instrument. When political parties pay for their own air time to display their own candidates, it is probably fair to assume that the great majority of the viewers are already convinced; for the most part, Republicans watch Republicans, and Democrats watch Democrats. This is one reason for the emphasis on spot commercials—partisan viewers are much less likely to get out of their chairs to turn off the opposition candidate if he is on for only thirty seconds or a minute, and not replacing an entire program.

The audience ratings for the debates seem to bear witness to the success of the planners' objective in attracting Democrats, Republicans, and uncommitted voters to the same political program. The viewing audience for each of the debates averaged between sixty-five and seventy million persons—more than the most fanciful predictions by the television networks, and more than at any other time in previous television history, save the climactic game of the 1959 World Series, when some ninety million Americans tuned in to watch the White Sox play the Dodgers.[80]

Nixon's television advisers wanted as few debates as possible. They felt their man was the "master of the form," and that a single debate could deal a deadly blow to Senator Kennedy's chances. They felt that the insistence of the senator's advisers on five debates showed that they were scared; if they weren't, they would have been willing to risk all on a single encounter. But Kennedy's television team, who eventually allowed themselves to be negotiated down to four debates, felt that their candidate could only gain from such encounters. White quotes Kennedy television consultant J. Leonard Reinsch as saying: "Everytime we get those two fellows on the screen side by side, we're going to gain and he's going to lose."[81]

Kennedy's preparation for the first debate was characterized by long and thorough research and briefings by Sorensen, Feldman, Goodwin, Harris, and brother Robert. Possible questions were formulated, and the candidate and his aides spent hours doing a "cram" job. Nixon, on the other hand, tired and not entirely recovered from a two-week hospital stay, was incommunicado to his television advisers, who could not even reach press secretary Herbert Klein. He spoke to a hostile labor audience on the morning of the first debate, and was alone in his hotel room—except for one phone call and one five-minute visit—until he left for the television studio. The frantic Republican television experts had tried to get through to him all day, and one of them was finally allowed to brief the Vice President during the ten-minute ride to the CBS studio in Chicago. When the adviser suggested the candidate come out fighting, Nixon, according to White, rejected the idea with the implication that it had come from the network executives, whose primary interest was in a good show.[82]

We shall not attempt to relate here the nature and content of the debates, as White and others have done so well. Suffice it to say that they were debates in name only. They were planned by commercial television technicians, in consultation with political public relations technicians, and there seems little doubt that the format and production techniques were designed primarily for a program that would be judged effective by standards having more to do with show business than with political deliberation.

The debates did, however, demonstrate the enormous ability of television as an instrument in realizing the political public relations goal of bringing about broadened political participation by the electorate. They also demonstrated the stunning impact of electronic, visual images upon the minds of the voters.

Nixon had been viewed as the front-runner when the debates began; Kennedy had been a struggling underdog. When the debates ended, the positions had been reversed. There is no general agreement, however, as to just what, if anything, the debates really achieved in shaping public opinion. It was evident that the crowds greeting the senator literally grew overnight after the first debate. Nixon's "me-too" style in that encounter did not seem to leave many Republican leaders very enthusiastic, and telephones rang at Republican headquarters in Washington suggesting that someone tell the candidate that the "old Nixon" was the one who could win the election.

A case can be made that the debates stimulated a greater sense of personal participation on the part of the voters. This broadened participation is, in fact, a point at which the objectives of public relations and the American democratic system merge. Where they may part is to the extent that such voter choices are made on the basis of visual images, as opposed to political judgments based on reality. As White points out, the fact that 85 million or more Americans would give up their evening hours over the course of the four programs to watch Nixon and Kennedy give their glib one-minute answers to the pear-shaped questions of a trio of newscasters was more salient than anything the candidates actually said. "There certainly were real differences of philosophy between John F. Kennedy and Richard M. Nixon—yet rarely in American history has there been a political campaign that discussed issues less or clarified them less."[83]

Elmo Roper's extensive polling, based on a national sample, nevertheless estimated for CBS that 57 percent of those who voted in 1960 felt that the debates had influenced their decisions; 6 percent—more than four million Americans according to this sample—ascribed their final decision to the debates alone. Of this group, 26 percent voted for Nixon and 72 percent for Kennedy. Insofar as this data is even roughly accurate, then it can be calculated that two million votes for Kennedy were stimulated by the debates alone. The senator's popular vote margin was just 112,000. So perhaps it is all the more understandable why Kennedy stated on November 12 that "It was TV more than anything else that turned the tide."[84]

The debates, in addition to their impact on the voters, also brought about a major change in the Democrats' public relations strategy for the use of television in 1960. Originally, the Democratic National Committee had booked eight half-hour periods for major nationwide telecasts. It was felt, apparently, that Senator Kennedy needed this exposure, so that he might speak to national audiences on major issues of the day and at the same time familiarize more and more people with his name and visual image—as Stevenson had done in 1952 and 1956. But when the "Great Debates" were scheduled, most of that television time was canceled, with the exception of the election eve broadcast. Instead, certain Kennedy appearances in major cities around the country were telecast over regional networks, with the hookups paid for by participating state party organizations. It is interesting to recall that never during the 1960 campaign did Senator

Kennedy deliver a single nationwide televised address on a major policy issue.[85]

Such paid partisan political broadcasts have since been re-instituted in presidential campaigns, and at considerable expense to the candidates. Section 315 has not again been suspended. And, as one might expect, commercial broadcasters, many of whom charge premium rates for such broadcasts, have resisted—at least until a new proposal made in 1973—suggestions that they be required to donate time to candidates so that the size of the campaign budget does not become the sole determinant of how often the voters see a candidate on television. Generally speaking, broadcasters—who run their stations on federal licenses to use channels which are in the public domain—have retreated rather sanctimoniously from the notion that they be required to allot specified amounts of free time to candidates. For example, C. Wrede Petersmeyer, president of Corinthian Broadcasting Company, has said:

> "Television, radio and the print media already provide without charge substantial exposure for candidates and issues through various informational techniques. To require media to go beyond this by donating time or space to candidates to use as they please . . . would amount to a private subsidy for a public purpose. Such a requirement would be unsound as a matter of public policy and probably illegal."[86]

The future of televised debates in presidential campaigns is difficult to predict on any generalized basis. Whether or not such encounters take place, in some form, in future campaigns will really depend on the circumstances of each particular campaign. They have not recurred in twelve years; 1976 is sixteen years and five elections later, and it is probably safe to assume that things will not be the same as they were in 1960. It can be assumed also that any occupant of the White House will be unlikely to engage in such exchanges, and that therefore debates will probably not take place in those years in which an incumbent President is running for reelection. At other times, one or both candidates, as in 1960, may feel that for one reason or another, televised debates would be to their advantage.

Congressional leaders are likely to follow the lines of the candidates of their respective parties, and if both men want the debates, Congress will suspend the Section 315 provisions on a temporary basis. Permanent repeal of Section 315 is not likely, in that its very existence has its utility as a control and face-saving device in situations where only one candidate is enthusiastic about debating. Congress's refusal to grant a suspension can shift the blame from a candidate who does not want to publicly refuse to debate. By the same token, positive Congressional action can have the effect of embarrassing an otherwise reluctant candidate and perhaps forcing his hand by removing the only legal barrier to two-way debates.

# Five:
# The 1964 Campaign

## The Pre-Nomination Campaigns

### The Republicans

In early 1964, with Lyndon Baines Johnson settling in as President of the United States as the nation shook itself, breathed deeply, and took up its uncertain course again after the disaster and insanity of the assassination of its duly elected President, the Republican party began officially to turn its Grand Old Eye on the White House.

Two months to the day after the murder of John F. Kennedy—on January 22, 1964—the better-heeled Republicans of the nation donned their dinner clothes and went off to finance dinners in a number of key cities, where they were orated at by various prominent leaders of their party. It was clear from the divergent tones of those addresses that these Republican leaders had not huddled in advance to agree on the signals for the evening's cross-country play.

In New York City, prominent Wall Street attorney Richard M. Nixon was the featured speaker. It was not clear whether he was the Old New Nixon or the New Old Nixon, as he told his colleagues: "We shall not win by resorting to image-making . . . We shall win and deserve to win by standing on principle on one great issue. That issue is the initiative against communism."[1]

The same evening, Governor William W. Scranton of Pennsylvania, who had crossed Ohio for a similar occasion in Indianapolis, told Hoosier Republicans that the greatest hour of the G.O.P. was when it presented the American people not with a negative image, but with a positive program. And Indiana's neighbor to the north, Governor George Romney of Michigan, spent the evening in the nation's capital. Preaching to a Washington, D.C., audience, he advocated that the party give the nation new leadership to restore personal responsibility, individual morality, family life, public integrity, and faith in American principles.[2]

The battle that was to come was to be fought on two fronts. One was in the presidential primaries. Often, these internecine battles are unpleasant affairs. But in Theodore White's words, "The Presidential primaries of 1964 were to exceed in savagery and significance any others in modern politics." White put a good deal of faith in issues. These, rather than personalities, he averred, were to be the focus of the 1964 Republican primaries, where "For the first time, Americans were required, publicly, to decide their posture on war and peace in an age of nuclear war."[3]

The other battle—the covert battle for the votes of delegates to the 1964 Republican National Convention—had begun long before. It was a battle waged by the new professionals in politics—a battle of power brokers to seize the convention as it had not been seized since 1940. As Republicans in New Hampshire and Oregon and California were regaled at vast expense by the image-makers and their techniques, this more silent battle went on behind the scenes, as other professionals practiced their own peculiarly covert form of political black magic under the leadership of F. Clifton White, whose operations we shall examine shortly.

### HENRY CABOT LODGE

Henry Cabot Lodge, the proper Bostonian who had been turned out of the United States Senate in the fifties by the brash, young John F. Kennedy and was soon thereafter officially classified by *Who's Who* as a "statesman," was off in South Vietnam in 1964, serving as the ambassador of the Johnson Administration. But as the New Hampshire presidential primary approached, some of Lodge's fellow Republicans got to thinking that perhaps it was he who should be the next President of the United States. The campaign they proceeded to wage on his behalf has been described by the principal chronicler of the election year battle as "a madcap adventure, the gayest, the happiest, the most lighthearted enterprise of the entire year 1964."[4]

The proprietors of Operation Madcap were relative amateurs in politics, although at least one of them has since graduated to the status of a professional's professional. The group included David Goldberg, "who had grown bored with his law practice" (and now runs Campaign Consultants, Inc.), Paul Grindle, a former New York public relations man who had gone back to Boston to develop a successful scientific instrument firm, largely through the use of direct-mail techniques; and two pretty, young Boston ladies. Together, they had scraped up $300, which they used to open a Boston Lodge-for-President headquarters, which was promptly shut down under a Massachusetts law prohibiting such establishments without the approval of the candidate concerned. "They traveled as a do-it-yourself package . . . to compare them with the operations of genuine professionals like Lawrence O'Brien and Clif White is impossible."[5]

When the campaign was banned in Boston—an action that is supposed to help the national take for such items as books and movies —the Grindle-Goldberg operation dismantled the office, drove to Concord, New Hampshire, and set up a new Lodge headquarters across the street from the State Capitol. Using Grindle's direct-mail techniques, they obtained an old statewide list of registered Republicans and mailed out ninety-six thousand letters inviting recipients to write to Ambassador Lodge in Saigon—in care of the Concord office —and pledge their support of his candidacy. Theodore White has said that

> In politics, it is essential that a group give the impression of a force in being, for everywhere, in thousands of American homes, are individual citizens who believe themselves hopeless because they are alone. It is only when they find they aren't alone that they become a real political force.[6]

Operation Madcap apparently gave the right impression, because the response to its first direct-mail appeal brought back 8,900 pledges of support. The Lodge "organization" was encouraged and began in February to build its write-in campaign to a smashing climax. Their second mailing, asking each recipient to "pick up two more votes," brought an even more astounding response. For the original 9,000 responses multiplied by 3 figured out to 27,000 votes out of a total of 100,000—a hefty bloc, if it could be delivered. So a third mailing was dispatched, this one including a clear sample ballot that demonstrated to New Hampshire Republicans just how to write in the ambassador's name.[7]

Meanwhile, public relations man Grindle went back to New York to gather up some film clips showing Lodge with President Eisenhower during the 1960 campaign and produced a television show on a budget of $750. It reminded the viewer of some details about Lodge's career, his war record, his expertise at shouting down Russians in the United Nations, and so on. The campaign began to snowball. It received increasing considerable press attention. Correspondents who had said all they could about Goldwater and Rockefeller wrote about the sudden mobilization of Lodge volunteers. Public opinion analysts began to find a rising tide for Lodge throughout the month of February. And as this would succeed in making a new story,

> the four pranksters would whack the story up another degree with some new statement or device. And as the correspondents would come to visit them in Concord (as much to chat with their handsome young ladies as to escape the weight of Western civilization being debated by Goldwater and Rockefeller), new stories would appear.[8]

It worked. Republican voters in New Hampshire, apparently more responsive to the "pranksters" than to "the weight of Western civilization," gave 33,000 votes to their man, as opposed to just over 20,000 for Goldwater, just under that number for Rockefeller, and 15,600 for another write-in—Richard M. Nixon, who had forever retired from politics and getting "kicked around" by the press after his defeat by "Pat" Brown in the California gubernatorial election two years earlier.[9]

It was not only a political coup. It was a public relations coup. Lodge was now in charge of the headlines. He led the polls. His picture was on magazine covers (for New Hampshire, not Vietnam). According to the public opinion analysts, he was, by April, the apparent choice of the Republican rank and file. He had silenced Nixon altogether. He had caused Goldwater to abandon Oregon and concentrate his efforts on California. And for Governor Rockefeller,

> The name of the game was now Impact. From New Hampshire on, there was no longer any real chance of his becoming the Republican nominee. But to veto the choice of Goldwater, he must prove before the convention assembled that Republican voters would not have Goldwater on any terms.[10]

In view of Rockefeller's obvious desire to become President of the

United States, the resources that he continued to pour into the apparent effort to achieve that goal, and the techniques that were mustered on his behalf, White's analysis of his position after New Hampshire may seem a bit overdrawn.

But White is clear in his conclusion that if Lodge's name had not been entered in the New Hampshire primary, Rockefeller would have won by a flat majority, going on then to a larger win in Oregon, and probably carrying California, for a solid trouncing of Barry Goldwater.[11]

NELSON ROCKEFELLER

Nelson Rockefeller, still governor of New York as the maneuverings for the 1964 Republican presidential nomination got under way, had undergone a divorce and rapid remarriage since the 1960 election, and under circumstances that could hardly be counted upon to make his marital status a popular political asset. But the governor was still interested in becoming President of the United States.

With party leaders shifting their preferences to Senator Goldwater as early as the spring of 1963, Rockefeller decided to try the same route that had led John F. Kennedy to the White House in 1960—an appeal that went directly to the people through the primaries. On November 7, 1963—two weeks before the assassination of President Kennedy—Rockefeller announced from his Albany office that he was going to openly campaign for his party's presidential nomination. And then he went off to New Hampshire to begin his primary campaign. He was a man who knew what he wanted; he also knew that if he was to get it, he would have to demonstrate that his popularity with the voters was overwhelming. And he knew that the route to such popularity had a good deal to do with public relations and the staff and the money that all of this implied.

White has said of those recruited to aid the governor, "The crew that Nelson Rockefeller took into battle in New Hampshire was one of the most elaborate ever to enter political war in America in modern times . . . The Rockefeller staff in 1964 was a thing of splendor."[12] Among his key staff members, put together over some three years of effort, were the following:[13]

> —George Hinman, the trusted manager who had worked with him in 1960.
> —Dr. William Ronan, who "had found a way of combin-

ing his professor's knowledge of political theory with an administrator's knack for cutting to the heart of things." (While some politicians hire professors, Rockefeller, in Ronan, had gone one better and hired a dean.)

—Charles F. Moore, a former Ford Motor Company vice president, who "had volunteered as a strategist of public relations as much out of determination to stop Barry Goldwater as out of simple gaiety of spirit."

—Roswell Perkins, head of a new and very large research department.

—Robert McManus, who had been Rockefeller's press secretary in 1960, and "had by now acquired an almost encyclopedic knowledge of the important newsmen and news outlets across the continent."

—Henry Kissinger, another academic gone partisan who had replaced Emmet Hughes as "chief theoretician on foreign affairs."

—Hugh Morrow, who wrote speeches, and

—many, many others, including "second-string members . . . in such quality and such numbers as to staff several campaigns."

But something strange happened in New Hampshire. The behemoths were upset by an absentee, a write-in, a non-candidate—Henry Cabot Lodge. He had had no Kissingers, no Hinmans. But without the professors and the professional managers, a hotshot p.r.-man-turned-businessman and a hotshot attorney-turned-political-manager and a couple of pretty girls and some mailing lists and a lot of supporters in quest of something had divided the liberally inclined Republican vote of New Hampshire. It was a vote that might otherwise have given the governor and his campaign factory a 2-to-1 triumph over the Arizona senator, who had been getting standing ovations in medium-sized cities for preaching his conservative ideology, sewing up delegates, and, worse still, challenging the veracity of the Eastern Republican Establishment. Besides, Nelson Rockefeller, who had been used to getting his picture on the front pages in Chicago by eating bagels in New York, was being crowded from the attention of the national media.

When Rockefeller moved on to Oregon, his captain was a man

described by White as "one of New York's best political technicians" —Robert Price, campaign-manager-in-residence of the then Manhattan Congressman, John Lindsay. Price was released to Rockefeller for this one-time-only emergency and set up in Oregon a direct-mail campaign such as Lindsay had used within his New York constituency. Funds and personnel were virtually unlimited, and in three weeks Price was able to develop a statewide volunteer organization from his mailing lists. Price and the Rockefeller p.r. men then moved on to a carefully pinpointed newspaper advertising campaign and a blitz of television appearances, which reached its electronic orgasm in a series of paid and unpaid Rockefeller appearances that "totally dominated the Oregon home screen for the 48 hours before voting." The candidate sloganized about the "mainstream" and "responsibility," and appealed to Oregonian emotions with "He Cares Enough to Come." Goldwater, Nixon and Lodge were not there, but Rockefeller had come, and he won.[14]

California was next.

California is not known for stable politics. It is, to say the least, not politically homogeneous. Contemporary political mythology has it that California—southern California, at any rate—is populated by Birchers and socialists living next door to one another in $50,000 homes bought for $199 down. Whatever the sociology of the situation, political campaigns in California have traditionally been characteriezd more by Hollywood-type personality buildups, exciting public relations and publicity techniques, and one-time cause-oriented volunteer groups than by solid, permanent party organization with the ability to deliver votes.

Rockefeller found that in California he had the support of the moderate Republican leadership. But, as White quotes one California politician as saying, "moderates are the people who don't go to the polls on Election Day." It might be added that they also generally don't ring doorbells before Election Day. Goldwater, meanwhile, had the support of volunteers who worked California with the zeal of crusaders. And Rockefeller, throughout the midwinter and early spring, was on the bottom in the polls. His mammoth organization might have thought itself omniscient—almost. But its New York managers didn't know California. Campaign Manager Hinman needed some people who did, and he turned to a firm of the "new professionals": Spencer-Roberts & Associates of Los Angeles.

Spencer-Roberts, a firm which James Perry describes in some detail, is today perhaps the best known of the firms in the political management business. It emerged to fill an apparent void in the field about a year after the death in 1961 of Clem Whitaker of Whitaker and Baxter. Although that firm still operates actively, no competitors appeared in California while Whitaker and Baxter was at its height. Spencer-Roberts has had a variety of clients—more since it became better known through its association with Governor Rockefeller in 1964. The firm works only for Republicans—all kinds of Republicans. It helped John Rousselot get elected to Congress before he retired to go to work for the John Birch Society. It also worked for California's liberal Republican Senator Thomas Kuchel. In 1966 Spencer-Roberts, in their greatest achievement, managed the successful gubernatorial campaign of film star Ronald Reagan who said after his inauguration, "They supplied the know-how. I'd never run for office again without the help of professional managers like Spencer and Roberts."[15]

It is difficult to tell just what kind of Republicans William Roberts and Stuart Spencer are themselves. Roberts served as executive director of the Los Angeles Young Republican organization until its infiltration and then control by right-wingers. He then became executive director of the Los Angeles County Republican Central Committee. Spencer entered public life as director of recreation for the City of Alhambra, and then became a precinct director in Los Angeles with Roberts. Both men acknowledged to Perry that their overriding ambition is to someday manage a full-scale presidential campaign. "We are," Roberts says, "mercenaries."[16]

Spencer-Roberts works in a different relationship to the candidate than did Whitaker and Baxter. As we have seen, Whitaker and Baxter were the directors, the candidates their actors. They insisted on this inverted stance, and candidates who retained them signed away their rights—and, at least for the moment, their responsibilities. But Spencer-Roberts serves its clients as political technologists. It is a role that really goes farther than the traditional Whitaker and Baxter methods, which placed primary emphasis on hard-core propaganda. Says Perry:

> Political technocracy is sexless; it has no soul and a computer for a heart. The candidate, for whom the technocracy works, must supply the human elements. Sometimes he does, which is fine;

sometimes he does not, which is frightening. . . . The technocrats really don't care. Ideology, issues, human emotion—these are not their concern. Ray Bliss, [former] chairman of the Republican National Committee, is almost a caricature of today's technocrat. "Don't ask me about issues," he tells reporters, and then they all repeat together: "I'm just a nuts-and-bolts technician."[17]

Perry sees Spencer-Roberts' chief assets—which probably served to attract Rockefeller and Hinman—as:

1. Their political judgment, especially relevant in California, "is exceptionally sophisticated. . . . They support their own intuition with a careful appraisal of the polls."
2. Their ability to organize at the grass-roots level, which "continues to be without parallel. , , ."
3. "They keep their eyes and ears open; they keep learning." The firm, as we have seen, now owns a part of a political data-processing firm, Datamatics. It is also beginning to manage campaigns in other states.[18]

George Hinman had actually begun checking out Spencer-Roberts in California before President Kennedy's assassination, at a time when the polls showed Goldwater leading Rockefeller 63 to 28 percent. When Hinman hired the firm several months later, it quickly expanded its staff and even subcontracted to other, more specialized consultants. Gross, Roberts and Rockey, a San Francisco firm specializing in campaign finances, farm problems, and the black community was retained and coopted into the Spencer-Roberts organization. Ross Wurm and Associates of Modesto, a firm that concentrated on agriculture, was hired to set up a paid organization of field workers in California's rich and extensive farm country.[19]

Spencer-Roberts developed a full-fledged Rockefeller organization in California. Through their experience with right-wing Republicans such as Rousselot, members of the firm knew what the opposition could deliver. Some fifty Rockefeller headquarters were opened across the state. Money being no problem, the firm hired its own Rockefeller troops. Unfortunately for the governor, such helpers could not be paid enough to work up the same degree of frenzy as the Goldwater volunteers. The firm next developed an almost foolproof method for turning out crowds for Rockefeller's appearances. After selecting an area where they wanted to display their candidate, Spencer-Roberts would draw names from each neighborhood and send out thousands of formal invitations to a reception there, nominally hosted by some prominent local Republican who was to contribute only his name to the gala event. Rockefeller would then stand in a reception line for more than two hours running, shaking every hand thrust his way, answering the questions, signing the autograph books. "That Rockefeller was reduced almost to incoherent exhaustion was hardly noticed."[20]

The receptions were well attended and enthusiastic. The new media attention that the governor was receiving following his Oregon victory may have helped to boost the attendance, and Rockefeller began barnstorming the state, shaking hands at Spencer-Roberts' packaged receptions—sometimes as many as seven thousand or eight thousand hands a day—and speaking from early morning until late at night.[21]

Behind the scenes, Spencer-Roberts had managed to create an organization of some twelve thousand "volunteers." Each of them received a newsletter and, in turn, mailed out bales of Rockefeller literature, variously estimated at up to two million pieces in a single mailing. One mailing intended for all of the state's two million registered Republicans was entitled "Who Do You Want in the Room with the H Bomb?" It cost an estimated $120,000 to get out this piece, essentially a collection of authentic Goldwater quotes that, says Theodore White, were "savagely presented." Spencer-Roberts produced an expensive half-hour television program entitled "The Extremists," which told of the lot of some Californians who had been persecuted by witch-hunters from the southern part of their state. Rockefeller, calling it "McCarthyism-in-reverse," insisted on its cancellation.[22]

"Telephone mills" were another Spencer-Roberts device. These consisted of banks of operators who called large numbers of names on registration lists in an effort to locate and wrap up votes for Rockefeller. Some twelve hundred operators were at work in the state by the close of the campaign. Recruited on a commercial basis, operators were not volunteers either. Perry points to an interesting sidelight here. Rockefeller had insisted that the operators be hired on a completely non-discriminatory basis, and, as things worked out, black women were in the majority at the largest telephone "mill," Los Angeles, which was staffed by six hundred operators. So, for whatever the impact, many of the voices over the telephone were, therefore, identifiably Negro voices, talking to citizens in communities with records of considerable hostility to black people and civil rights efforts.[23]

There also seemed to be some confusion over money. In one sense, Spencer-Roberts was entrapped by the problem of spending money to good effect. Goldwater and his leaders were riding hard on the size of Rockefeller's fortune. And the governor's campaign manager grew shy of any last-minute drenching of the press, radio, and television with a planned, paid-up terminal barrage like the one which Price had brought off in Oregon. Says Perry: "The Rockefeller people didn't want to appear too loaded. Thus, in the last days of the campaign, they cut back on radio and television time. They also cut back on spending for high-visibility items like billboards. As things turned out, it was a mistake."[24]

Rockefeller, who seemed to be running ahead through late May, lost the California primary on June 7 to Barry Goldwater, who then went on to a first-ballot nomination at San Francisco's Cow Palace. Spencer-Roberts had completed its first big-time assignment—the closest the firm had come to a presidential campaign.

The Spencer-Roberts reception technique has since been widely used by imitators. Perry quotes one Rockefeller aide as saying, "They produced absolutely astounding results in turning out people for our receptions. . . . We couldn't believe it; we had never seen anything like it in the East." But the receptions had not been enough to reach the voters in a state where, of fifty-eight counties, one county alone is as big as Connecticut, Massachusetts, and New Jersey combined. There was apparently no real "master plan" for the campaign, and some normally standard public relations activities were simply overlooked by the professional managers. It was, for example, discovered eight weeks before Election Day that no one had remembered to design the highway billboards; and no radio scripts were written until the final days, when it was no longer clear just what the message should be.[25]

Apparently, Spencer-Roberts, with its emphasis on management and organization—the more strictly political aspects of the campaign —was weak in the area of professional public relations. They were more organizers than propagandists, image-makers, or salesmen. Said one Rockefeller staff member: "Spencer-Roberts' weakness is their inability to put together a total campaign and sell it to the voters. They don't understand the mass media. . . . They failed where Whitaker and Baxter always succeeded, in their ability to sell a candidate."[26]

Nevertheless, the Rockefeller organization paid for and got a professional job—probably more professional than anyone else could have delivered. And Spencer-Roberts learned some valuable lessons, which the firm was to apply two years later on behalf of Ronald Reagan in his bid to govern California, and again two years after that, when the matinee-idol-turned-governor sought the help of Spencer-Roberts in his covert efforts to wrest the Republican presidential nomination from the hands of ex-Californian Richard Nixon.

BARRY GOLDWATER

The march of Barry Goldwater to the Republican presidential nomination at the Cow Palace in 1964 was choreographed a long time before Rockefeller and his group or Grindle and Goldberg or even, in his heart of hearts, Richard Nixon began to tabulate their potential delegate counts. The score had been written by F. Clifton White. As far back as 1961, with John F. Kennedy newly installed in the White House, White and his volunteers laid their plans as carefully as any group of generals has ever mapped out a *coup d'état*. White and his colleagues marked out each state with its delegate count, dates, and procedures for choosing convention delegates. "Their planning," says Theodore White, "was more careful, more detailed, and earlier begun than that of any previous Presidential campaign; it was a masterpiece of politics."[27]

Clifton White is a political technician, one of the finest in America, in the estimation of Theodore White (who has aptly pointed out that ". . . some men become seized by the fascination of a specialty until they become technicians useful only to men of larger vision. . . ."). Clif White, an unsurpassed expert in such tactics as petitions, the organization of meetings, nominations, floor seating, and so on, had controlled the National Federation of Young Republicans and that group's conventions from 1950 to 1960. This he did as a hobby. As a professional, he found his services in demand by the Dewey organization in New York and then by industry. As a consultant to companies such as United States Steel, Standard Oil of

Indiana, and General Electric, White instructed aspiring executives—Republicans and Democrats alike—who had been dutifully assembled by their great corporations to learn how they might take part in public affairs.[28]

Clif White had done some technical work for the Nixon organization in 1960. He was unhappy with the way the campaign had gone, and began to think of what might come next. He was later to say: "I've probably elected more presidents of more organizations in back rooms than any other man in America. But after a while you get to think about the dimensions of the room. What's going on in the country?" And at a luncheon with some old Young Republican friends in the summer of 1961 White began to wonder out loud about his ability to use his fabled techniques at the presidential level—and whether he could seize the Republican Party much as he had seized and held for a decade the Young Republican organization.[29]

Were White's techniques similar to those of professional public relations? Clifton White, it should be emphasized, operated underground at first, but his initial objectives were the hearts and minds of the conservatives—a specialized, right-wing public, the "primitives," as some writers have called them. For he knew that, given the proper pressure points, the emotions of such people could be aroused to a state of political frenzy. White also knew that in his Young Republican organization he had a well-organized national net capable of moving into control once the rabble had stormed the party's gates. And this was, indeed, the group that eventually controlled the party, turned it over to Goldwater, and then lost its influence as the senator's inner circle took charge.

Clifton White began a series of secret meetings in Chicago on October 8, 1961, and he and his associates decided that they would form an *ad hoc* committee with the objective of grabbing the Republican Party for Goldwater and the cause of the conservatives. White obtained an appointment with Goldwater the following month. The senator was amused, but indifferent. In a posture remarkably similar to that of Adlai Stevenson in another day, he was unwilling to lend his name officially to the cause. But he also would not repudiate it. At a second meeting, then, the committee voted to divide the country into nine regions for the organization of conservatives, to establish an office to be run by White, and to raise $60,000. White had an office in New York by the spring of 1962 and travel funds to contact the nine regions in which volunteer directors were already at work preparing to garner Goldwater delegates for 1964. It was not until December 1962, however, that the press finally became aware of what was going on. The formation of a "cloak and dagger" Draft Goldwater movement was revealed just as the F. Clifton White coven of political wizards, now fifty-five strong, met again in Chicago. The next month, White saw Goldwater again. The senator, though now annoyed by the publicity, still refused to repudiate White and his new "movement."[30]

But the White group was pleased with the publicity and proceeded to take some overt public relations steps to keep the effort in the spotlight. They would now form the National Draft Goldwater Committee, to be chaired by Peter O'Connell of Texas. White would be the national director, and they would "draft the son of a bitch," regardless of whether he wanted to run. The committee called its first public event—a July Fourth rally in Washington, D.C.—two years after the organization's conception. Zealot-laden buses arrived, and the crowd of seven thousand that assembled at the Armory had been exceeded only by those attracted by the Eisenhower and Kennedy inaugurals and the preachings of Billy Graham.[31]

It all worked p.r. wonders. How could Goldwater remain publicly unmoved by all of this? Clifton White stirred up not just a covey of conservatives but a national mandate. Nelson Rockefeller had helped things along by his marriage to "Happy" and somehow, by the late summer of 1963, the senator from Arizona looked over his shoulder and saw TV cameras following him around. He saw himself on the cover of *Time, Life,* and *Newsweek.* And, come fall, the invitations to appear on the evening "talk" shows came with increasing frequency. The senator hadn't planned it this way. When asked if he was really running, he replied, "I'm doing all right just pooping around."[32]

But as Goldwater "pooped" in August, it was evident that he was giving the proposition some serious thought. The Draft Goldwater volunteers had now grown to a serious national movement, which White operated from his new headquarters in Washington, D.C. Goldwater, according to Theodore White, saw Clifton White accurately—as a technician, "loyal, but, in Goldwater's eyes, nonetheless limited. To take over the organization without offending White would be difficult. But the organization must be used." Goldwater moved to bring Denison Kitchel, a Phoenix lawyer and a close confidant, to Washington to coordinate with the volunteers. Kitchel was given the title of campaign manager, ostensibly for Goldwater's 1964 bid for reelection to the Senate, but his real mission was serious exploration of the possibilities of the presidential nomination.[33]

Goldwater's decision to run came sometime in December 1963. By Christmas, in Arizona, he was preparing to publicly announce his candidacy. The senator had made a serious attempt to secure the professional services of Leonard Hall to direct his campaign. But Hall, out of loyalty to Nixon, had turned him down, not wanting to make any commitments before it was clear the former Vice President was really out of it. On the evening of New Year's Day, Goldwater called another of his Arizona friends, Richard Kleindienst, and asked him to decide overnight whether he would come to Washington and manage the campaign which the senator would announce on January 3. Kleindienst was happy to be of service.[34]

Goldwater moved on toward the New Hampshire primary, where he was to be plagued by serious public relations problems. He and Nelson Rockefeller were the only two men on the Republican ballot. Their fellow party members in New Hampshire were going to have the opportunity, early in the 1964 presidential year, to witness a confrontation between representatives of distinctly different approaches to running the country—and to running a campaign. Nelson Rockefeller, with his enormous staff, gave complicated Emmet Hughes and Henry Kissinger–type responses to questions about the complex world in which we live; Goldwater had simple, direct answers for each highly complex question.

The senator's candor, as Theodore White puts it, is the completely "unrestrained candor of old men and little children." He had been used to speaking after dinner to audiences of devout conservatives. If remarks made to such groups appear on the public record, Goldwater considers this a breach of friendship and confidence. Goldwater, then, entered New Hampshire carrying the serious burden of such recent statements as his advocacy of the use of atomic weapons by NATO "area commanders"; a suggestion that the TVA be sold; a proposal to withdraw diplomatic recognition from the Soviet Union, and another to abolish the graduated income tax. Now a declared candidate, Goldwater was followed everywhere by reporters poised to write down, record, and film his candid remarks, which fell in rapid succession. For example, in his first week of campaigning in New Hampshire, Goldwater called United States missiles "undependable." Immediately, Robert McNamara's Pentagon public relations staff was after him.[35]

It should be pointed out that some of Goldwater's early phrase-making—calling the Eisenhower Administration a "dime-store New Deal" or suggesting we "lob one into the men's room of the Kremlin" —were, as Governor William Scranton observed, personal expressions of a private citizen, made before he had become a candidate. But Goldwater would say just what he had always thought. Reporters love a candidate like this, because he will give them some front-page copy almost any day of the week. Goldwater, however, would be furious when one of his frank thoughts was quoted in the newspapers, analyzed, and elaborated upon in the columns, commentaries, and editorials. He had expected a sympathetic hearing in New Hampshire, and yet, as he read of himself day by day, "it was another Goldwater he was reading about, a wild man seeking to abolish Social Security and go to war with Russia." Theodore White, who followed Goldwater around for a few days, says flatly that "it was quite clear he did not know what he was doing."[36]

Karl Lamb and Paul Smith, both of whom followed the 1964 campaign firsthand, sum it up this way:

> The New Hampshire primary was a searing experience for Goldwater and his associates. For the first time, the gay spontaneity of Goldwater's style, which had won such enthusiastic support on the Republican banquet circuit, was placed before the full view of small groups of a skeptical electorate and the hostile analysis of the national mass media. Goldwater placed himself almost completely in the hands of his New Hampshire manager. . . . The New Hampshire experience confirmed the decision to limit Senator Goldwater's informal visits with both voters and the press and to rely more completely on television and on formal campaign addresses.[37]

Goldwater, it appears, was sadly lacking in professional public relations counsel. There was a need here for such help, in its best sense. For the senator's conduct in the New Hampshire primary betrayed a kind of naïveté about the importance of the media—and the kind of national media attention generated by the first presidential primary of an election year.

Here, for example, is an excerpt from an interesting summary of Goldwater's first week of New Hampshire campaigning during January 1964 by Loye Miller of *Time* magazine:

> "He continues to roll out rather remarkable statements which sooner or later seem bound to get him into trouble. . . . Now that Barry Goldwater is a formally declared candidate for the Presidency, he can expect intensive scrutiny of every remark from the rest of the nation. And this week he got his facts so muddled on at least a couple of the leading issues of the day that it will be surprising if Nelson Rockefeller doesn't pick up the inaccuracies and imprecision and use it to portray Barry as an intellectual lightweight."[38]

By the time Goldwater began to concentrate his efforts on the California primary, his inner circle included Denison Kitchel as chief of staff, Karl Hess as an overworked speech writer, Clif White as head of a group of field operators, and Richard Kleindienst and Dean Burch of the Arizona group. "Here were plotted and prepared the tactics, the blows, the volley and counter-volley of public statements designed to answer Rockefeller in the headlines and on television." There was also, in California, a force dominated by Robert Gaston, the "undisputed and autocratic boss of the Young Republicans of California . . . the most engaging of the dedicated right-wingers in American politics. . . ."[39]

Goldwater did not correct his press problems in California so much as he avoided them. He simply stopped exposing himself to situations where dozens of reporters might follow him around waiting to seize upon one of his hyperbolic allusions. He appeared almost entirely at large gatherings, and these were held mostly in the southern part of California. He tended also to veer away from the kind of issues he had discussed in New Hampshire, speaking instead on what he called the "fundamentals"—"decency, patriotism, liberty, law and order." There was also an interesting turn toward a last-minute barrage of lavish campaign advertising. The Sunday before the primary election saw a virtual inundation of Goldwater advertising, particularly in southern California. In the Los Angeles *Times* alone, one of the most expensive of the nation's advertising outlets, the Goldwater organization bought four and one-half pages in the Sunday edition. Other papers also were flooded, and parallel efforts were carried out on radio and television. Rockefeller, meanwhile, was operating under the late-in-the-campaign restraint that caused some holding back in response to the "millionaire" campaign label.[40]

Throughout the pre-nomination campaign, and after the convention as well, Goldwater and certain of his lieutenants and supporters would blame the press for many of their difficulties and adopt a general attitude of hostility vis-à-vis the news media. The "Eastern Liberal Press" was to become synonymous with anti-Goldwaterism, anti-conservatism, and a vague sort of anti-Americanism in the Goldwater lexicon.

As the journalism student learns in his first reporting class, quoting a subject directly always comes within the boundaries of objective reporting; and yet there are times when it can be a surer way to condemn a man than the most malicious libel. Often quotes from public figures are so badly stated that they can seriously damage the speaker —and this is one of the reasons for the number of "off-the-record" and "background" meetings with the press held by many government officials, from the President on down.

In the case of Goldwater, who insisted on speaking political foolishness in public on frequent occasions, it was difficult for reporters to resist quoting him. But as the campaign wore on, Theodore White, himself a master journalist, reports:

> . . . When Goldwater would hang himself with some quick rejoinder, the reporters who had grown fond of him would laboriously quiz him again and again until they could find a few safe quotations that reflected what they thought he really thought. They were protective of Goldwater in a way that those zealots who denounced the Eastern press could never imagine.[41]

## The Democrats

There was, of course, never any doubt about Lyndon Johnson's claim to the Democratic presidential nomination in 1964. But the President sensed the need to steal at least part of the show from the Republicans, so as not to give the opposition the total benefit of the buildup in political interest on the part of the news media and public that takes place in an election year. And he knew just how much of an advantage the occupant of the White House has in putting on such a show for the voters. For Lyndon Johnson was rare, not only as a President but as a human being, in his uncanny, innate sense of public relations. Just as he developed a reputation for doing his own staff work and making his own decisions on many matters ordinarily handled by presidential staff, so too was he, in many ways, his own best (and worst) public relations man.

He had a keen interest in the press and a sensitivity to everything it said about him and his programs. It was a concern that was evident from his first hours in office when, in an action reminiscent of Theodore Roosevelt after McKinley's funeral, he called in editors and publishers, columnists and commentators after the Kennedy funeral. On the evening following the funeral, presidential assistant Walter Jenkins telephoned the State Department to say that the President wanted the international reception being held in the Benjamin Franklin Room to be televised live, and wanted to be sure that the camera took only his left profile.[42]

Johnson was somewhat irritated later in December as the country and the media became accustomed to the fact that he had, indeed, become President and his daily doings began to fade from the front pages. He called in the senior press officers of eight or nine government departments for a quick four-minute L.B.J.-style chewing out just before he went away for Christmas week. The White House, he said, had been on the front page with only one story all week—and that was the lighting of the Christmas tree. They had better get with it, and give press secretary Pierre Salinger as many stories as possible so that they could be released in Texas. The President told the government public relations people that he had been checking the federal budget, and that they had better start earning the billion dollars a year the government was spending on the members of their profession. Then, when Johnson got to Texas, he drove the sixty-five miles from the ranch to Austin to have some New Year's drinks with the press corps. And on the way back to the presidential plane upon departing for Washington, he told the correspondents he was going to make big men of all of them; they "were gonna get along fine together; if they played ball with him, he'd play ball with them—and he didn't expect to see it in the papers if they saw him with one drink too many under his belt."[43]

L.B.J. also moved quickly to prompt Congressional action on some fifty major pieces of Kennedy legislation still bottled up. One of the Kennedy people who remained for a while on his staff, said, according to White, "I don't think he's motivated by any greater desire than to please *The New York Times* and get a pat on the back from [Georgia Senator] Dick Russell—both at the same time." Others saw him as already looking toward the coming 1964 election and a desire to have his record written as quickly as possible.[44]

When Johnson's methods made no substantial difference in his press relations after the first few weeks in office, he moved into the alternating cycle of courting the press and being angry with it. This erratic public relations behavior, which would be anathema in the commercial world, characterized Johnson's behavior not only during the 1964 campaign, but throughout his next four years in office. Before long, L.B.J. had a new press secretary, as Pierre Salinger left for a brief sitting as senator from California. The President replaced him with a man with whom he felt considerably more at home, George Reedy:

> Reedy could not prevent Johnson from making mistakes, could not restrain him in dealing with the press. . . . But on those rare occasions when Reedy permitted himself to give a full-dress analysis of his master, he could explain the President better than anyone else, making him seem big and wise, cosmetizing away the warts on the giant he served.[45]

Even with his own man acting as a buffer between the White House and the press, the media occupied a major part of Johnson's time. James Reston summed up one such week in *The New York Times* in late April:

> In the last seven days, President Johnson has held two formal and two informal press conferences, made seven impromptu statements after White House meetings, delivered a major foreign policy address to the Associated Press, helped settle the national railroad dispute, opened the New York World's Fair and talked at a political rally in Chicago. . . .

Without having developed specific campaign tactics early in 1964, L.B.J.'s approach was simply to rack up his record of accomplishments as President. He also planned to make himself visible all over the nation, and traveled at an unprecedented rate. He left a long trail of speeches and front-page stories behind him as he moved around. He seemed to develop his themes not in mid-campaign, but on the road long before the convention. "There were two grand themes—

Prosperity and Harmony." After the Goldwater nomination, which the President and his advisers apparently had thought would not become a reality, the theme of peace replaced the other two.[46]

Thus, without the consultation of professional public relations men, the President succeeded in indoctrinating the country through the daily production of front-page stories and news film and tape "with such apparently artless simplicity that it was scarcely aware of the process." Union speeches would be balanced by appearances before business groups, a White House visit by labor leaders would be followed by one from a like number of industrialists, and so on. The speeches themselves took on a new polish as Kennedy speech writer Richard N. Goodwin joined the inner circle. L.B.J. also drafted Texas liberal Horace Busby and author Douglass Cater, who was assigned to prepare a book for the L.B.J. by-line.[47]

Then, on March 4, Goodwin wrote a speech—a draft which, though unused, contained a bit of sloganeering of which any member of the public relations or advertising fraternity would have been proud. It said something about a "great society." The President took to the phrase and used variations on the theme several times in March and April—sixteen times, according to one count—as he monitored feedback from the press and the reactions of his audiences. On May 22, 1964, at the University of Michigan, *the* "GREAT SOCIETY" (he had since elevated the phrase to all caps) speech was made. The President had found a distinctive political position which was his alone. He was no longer asking for sacrifice in the Kennedy spirit, but promising greatness. He had found, as Lamb and Smith have put it, "a phrase and set of ideas that would lend distinction and direction to his campaign and subsequent administration."[48]

The President was doing his best to take a "nonpolitical" or, more accurately, semi-nonpartisan approach to the coming campaign. For that fight for the presidency would, in effect, be the first truly partisan battle of Johnson's long political career. A Democrat in Texas who had risen to the high office of U.S. senator could run without significant opposition. And once in Washington, his politics were those of legislative manipulation and the battles of Capitol Hill. But in 1964 he finally would have to do battle with a genuine Republican. Months before that Republican was nominated, polls showed that Johnson's "nonpolitical" approach was having some impact. And in June the

Gallup poll showed L.B.J. would garner 81 percent of the vote against Goldwater if the election were held the next day; the Harris poll showed Johnson with 74 percent of the total vote.[49]

The black magic of polling, in fact, became a peculiar fascination of the President at about this time. And throughout the rest of his career in the White House, the pollsters would remain his court wizards, as he read their surveys as barometers of the American people's reaction to his personality. White House visitors would from time to time report on the President's tendency to whip polls out of his pockets and begin expounding on their meaning before captive audiences.

In the spring of 1964 Walter Jenkins commissioned a poll on the Maryland primary, from which George Wallace had emerged with 43 percent of the Democratic vote. Johnson read the fifty-five-page Quayle technical report overnight and called for more of the same. By June he had become an incurable poll addict. He learned all he could about the polls' public interpretations of attitudes. And he was especially interested to read results indicating that he could choose any running mate he pleased at the Democratic convention and not cut into his considerable projected margin of victory by more than 2 percent.[50]

By late March the President, a television station owner in his own right, began to turn his attention seriously toward the tube, with an obvious acceptance of the important role that television would play in his campaign. If the President was addicted to polls, he also suffered from an earlier and equally chronic addiction to television. It was well known that Johnson had a three-set bank of television sets installed in his bedroom—complete with remote controls—so that he could see all the major networks at one time, fading sound and pictures in and out at will from any point in the room.

John F. Kennedy had decided in 1963 to charge the huge New York advertising firm of Doyle Dane Bernbach with the direction of Democratic television activities during the campaign. L.B.J. put his imprimatur upon his predecessor's choice on March 19, 1964, directing the agency to plan and coordinate with him through Bill Moyers at the White House and Moyers' associate Lloyd Wright at the National Committee. Planning got under way quickly. The campaign had the advantage of a sure-thing candidate, plenty of lead time, and the guidance of one of the young men closest to the President and a man at the National Committee who had direct access to the White

House whenever necessary. Thus, "the New York specialists were able to begin on a political television campaign that fully warranted the hackneyed adjective 'creative.' "[51] We shall examine that campaign more fully below.

President Johnson's fondness for showmanship with the press reached what was probably its manic pinnacle on August 26, as the Democratic convention met in Atlantic City and prepared to nominate him as its presidential candidate—and whoever he might choose to serve with him as its vice presidential choice.

The Chief Executive discussed the campaign, the vice presidency, and the convention with reporters as he walked them through no less than fifteen brisk quarter-mile laps around the South Lawn of the White House in the oppressive 89-degree heat of a Washington summer. White has called the spectacle "a public circus that perhaps had never been equaled before anywhere." Asked about the campaign, the President said he was going to sit right there in that White House and do his job as he went along. He was worried about Goldwater though—the man was frightening people. By now an expert on opinion sampling, Mr. Johnson held forth on polls at some length—they were all overwhelmingly in his favor. He chided the press for talking so much of "backlash." And as for his health, the doctors had checked him over a little while before, and he was in good shape. In fact, he gave the press a copy of the medical report.[52]

The President also did an artful job of press-agentry in stage-managing the rather spectacular announcement of his choice of Hubert H. Humphrey to be vice presidential candidate. With consummate skill, the President ran the whole process associated with his announcement so as to be sure of achieving the maximum amount of media attention. Flights from Washington to Atlantic City were carefully scheduled according to the convention agenda. The planes would take off and arrive when it was not essential for television to be carrying the proceedings from the convention floor. Senators Humphrey and Dodd, along with presidential aide Jack Valenti, had to tour Washington for an hour so as to arrive at the White House at precisely the moment that would assure a live television pickup. The car was kept waiting another twenty minutes at the White House gate to assure that the President's acts of greeting them and taking them inside could be appropriately produced as a TV special event.[53]

This melodrama, which L.B.J. staged and produced on August 26, has been characterized this way by Theodore White:

> In its mixture of comedy, tension and teasing, it was a work of art; it was as if, said someone, Caligula were directing "I've Got a Secret." It is difficult to see it as any appropriate way for handling succession to the mightiest office on earth; but as excitement and a study of personality in power, it was unmatched. . . . There were perhaps 30,000 people assembled at Atlantic City, but all of them danced on the strings that ran from the White House. . . .[54]

# The Post-Convention Campaign

## Barry Goldwater

The 1964 presidential campaign of Barry Goldwater, like his campaign for the nomination of the Republican Party, fascinated the news media, but not in the way a professional public relations man would want to see them fascinated. For it was really the blunders of the campaign, rather than its proficiency, that intrigued the communicators. Democrats, of course, were pleased. Republicans—even many of those who loyally supported their candidate—were themselves not always sure about the campaign and often downright apprehensive.

Public signs of disunity had, of course, appeared at the convention itself. Any public relations man worth his salt would have told the candidate to heed them, but either no one around him did so advise, or the senator had chosen not to listen. Moderate forces led by Governors Nelson Rockefeller, George Romney and William Scranton (represented by his fellow Pennsylvanian Senator Hugh Scott) made public efforts to override the decisions of the Platform Committee, chaired by Wisconsin Congressman Melvin Laird, by a vote of the full convention. But any effort at compromise was summarily rejected. This worked to the political disadvantage of Goldwater during the course of the campaign, because it gave his Republican adversaries "public justification for abandoning the traditional practice of at least pretending to rally in support of the Party's nominee."[55]

For when Nelson Rockefeller took the rostrum in San Francisco to advocate the first of the three draft minority resolutions prepared by the moderate forces of the East, he was viewed by those in the galleries as the villain. Laird had delayed the debate until long past prime television time—at least in the East—by obtaining a ruling that the entire platform must be read into the microphones in order to place it officially before the convention. After the ninety-minute reading had ended, Rockefeller seemed almost to relish taunting the galleries, as they roared and raged, booing and screaming their hatred:

> They yelled back at him and strained in their seats as if trying to grab him and get him. . . . And as the TV cameras translated their wrath and fury to the national audience, they pressed on the viewers that indelible impression of savagery which no Goldwater leader or wordsmith could later erase.[56]

Suggestions have been made by members of the Goldwater forces that the gallery occupants who booed Rockefeller had actually been planted there by the Rockefeller-Scranton forces in an attempt to discredit the senator. Clifton White has made this charge, as has a conservative theoretician interviewed by Lamb and Smith. However, along with Theodore White, Lamb and Smith reject this contention on the basis of personal observations.[57]

It is true that when Scranton had decided, not long before the convention, to pursue his party's nomination—largely motivated by his personal convictions—he faced Clifton White's ironclad count of sewed-up Goldwater delegates. Making an impact on the convention would have required mobilizing every single uncommitted delegate and winning away about two hundred already pledged or leaning toward Goldwater. This would have called for a recapture of the party and convention in an effort akin to that of the Willkie team of 1940. But that 1940 team had had more time, and it had strong alliances, and it did not operate in an atmosphere of hostility as widespread and blatant as that of 1964. The Scranton operation, as Theodore White has observed, required both "a master plan and a master staff," and had neither.[58]

During the campaign, the Goldwater organization was to return to the convention's rejection of the moderate forces and the magnitude of Goldwater's first-ballot victory of more than eight hundred votes as validating his contention that he was indeed the candidate of the party rank-and-file. The charge that Goldwater was not really the choice of most of those in his own party seems, however, to have been confirmed by the polls. Philip Converse, for example, reports that public opinion data demonstrates that Goldwater was the choice of no more than 25 percent of registered Republicans. And of those interviewed after the election, "less than 20 percent of all Republicans recalled having preferred Goldwater at the time of the Convention."[59]

Such data was ignored by the Goldwater staff. Thus, opinion sampling, a central tool of political public relations—and one which was being amply employed by the opposition—was virtually disregarded. It can also be said that in the case of the opposition, the Democratic organization and the Johnson organization were coterminous. But this principle of unity simply did not apply to Goldwater and the Republicans.

Public opinion as a factor in shaping the senator's campaign, organization, and program was first put into rather unique Goldwaterite perspective by adviser Raymond Moley. Moley was a former economics professor and one-time speech writer for Franklin Delano Roosevelt. He had broken with the New Deal to become a conservative theoretician and consultant to Republican candidates. In a plan first given to Senator Goldwater on October 4, 1963 (the plan actually served as the basis for the organization of Goldwater's campaign), Moley said that earlier Republican candidates had gone astray by failing to present a consistently conservative philosophy.

> Each had been prey to the advice of minor politicians who were forever pressing him to take a stand on this or that issue in order to appease the demands of this or that interest group.

Moley gave the back of his hand to systematic public opinion studies as "a national obsession":

> In academic and business life this has assumed the fancy name of "opinion research." Those who pretend to leadership first determine what "the public" wants and then seek to give it, or at least, promise to give it . . . but the measurement of public opinion is still a cdude and fallible instrument. The perils such soundings face lie in sampling, in the large number of those interviewed who have no opinions at all . . . [in] the prevalence of prevarication, the changing of opinions from one day to another, and the shaping of questions which would induce predetermined answers.[60]

The Moley memorandum was notable for its failure to deal with the means through which the conservative philosophy of the Goldwater movement was to be communicated to the public. And evidence indicates that the campaign ended without the very practical questions of mass media ever having been settled.

However, as Lamb and Smith point out, the Goldwater campaign did include some professionally prepared political advertising. The Leo Burnett advertising agency of Chicago had been retained by the Republican National Committee, and this firm did have the opportunity to do some preliminary structuring of the Republican media campaign before the convention. It had, for example, scheduled a segment of Republican television time at the conclusion of the Democratic National Convention. Another advertising agency was retained by the Draft Goldwater Committee. "But the expertise of Madison Avenue was not represented on Goldwater's personal staff, and his organization functioned throughout the primary election period without a Director of Public Relations." Denison Kitchel had early been concerned with filling this position, but he was unable to find a well-qualified person to accept the job. Finally, after the convention, he obtained the services of L. Richard Guylay, a Republican National Committee veteran, who had worked in a similar capacity during the Eisenhower and Nixon campaigns. Guylay was already affiliated with a company in the communications field, and it now became the official advertising agency for the campaign. Thus, the "Goldwater account" passed into the hands of a third firm.[61]

This third agency was the Interpublic Group of New York, the world's largest group of marketing-communications companies. Guylay was later to become chief executive of Interpublic.

Apparently, Goldwater's staff eventually agreed to the need for coordinating the goal of articulating the conservative position with that of presenting that position through the mass media. Based on the experience of earlier campaigns, and the first principles of communications, such a need is incredibly commonplace, but for some reason it did not seem so to those initially charged with running the Goldwater campaign.

Charles Lichtenstein, deputy research director of the Republican National Committee, became liaison man between the campaign staff and the technical group charged with the preparation of Goldwater's television shows. Lichtenstein had a like assignment during the California primary campaign, and thus had some familiarity with the use of the mass media, but his assignment had been made on an emergency basis, and "After the election, several campaign organization members complained they got 'very little help from the experts of the advertising world.' "[62]

Had the standards proposed by Moley been followed, the tasks of the advertising agencies would have been thought of as strictly technical activities—without direct connection to the work of the principal "in-group," which was to be assigned to the articulation of conservative principles. But, as Lamb and Smith point out, it is difficult to separate the content of a campaign from its method of presentation. Although campaigning has, as we have seen, sometimes approached the unified marketing strategies developed for merchandising products such as toothpaste, the sound public relations coordination of a political campaign does not require that degree of manipulation. It does require, however, that the public relations professionals advise the candidate and those closest to him on the best means of capturing the attention, imagination, and loyalty of the voters. "At the very least, [they] will have knowledge of the expected attention span of the average voter and may suggest concentrating messages to fit within that span."[63]

Another unique aspect of the Goldwater organization with direct impact upon public relations and related activities was the existence of a powerful financial directorate (headed by former General Electric Board Chairman Ralph Cordiner) with strong veto power. Since campaign contributions flow in greatest volume toward the end of presidential campaigns, a finance chairman usually borrows against the credit of the party. This Cordiner refused to do. In the area of advertising, such power to refuse a request for funds on the basis of no ready cash in the treasury is especially significant, because the media do not work on the basis of credit, and all political advertising must be paid in advance. When payment was required for the time that the Leo Burnett agency had booked for the conclusion of the Democratic convention, the campaign treasury was empty, and Goldwater's financial advisers decreed that the time be canceled. This was only the first instance of an apparent tendency on the part of members of the financial directorate to fancy themselves as public relations and advertising experts. In any field of endeavor, such imposition of a need to pass muster by a group of non-professionals is the p.r. man's nightmare. The Goldwater finance group reportedly went so far as to propose which newspapers be used for certain ads and to suggest that the candidate take a stand on such matters as Proposition 14, the state constitutional amendment on the California ballot that repealed fair housing legislation. Cordiner also decreed the cancellation of precious network television time booked in advance for the last ten days of the campaign. Ironically, the Goldwater campaign finally finished in the black because of the large number of small contributions that came in at the last minute in response to national television appeals.[64] (This finance technique was aped in 1972 by the man in the U.S. Senate who, ironically, was about as sharply opposed to Goldwater as any member of the Upper Chamber —George McGovern.)

All of this helps explain Theodore White's characterization of the Goldwater campaign organization as absolutely first-class—in the sense of a sculptor's mock-up of a new model for Detroit's auto industry:

> It was meticulously designed, hand-sanded, striking in appearance —but it had no motor. It recalled the famous quatrain of the medieval poet Samuel Ha-Nagid about the crippled man who carved on a wall the engraving of a perfect leg and tried to stand on it, but fell.[65]

This striking difference between plan and reality is well illustrated by the existence of a strategy board which included p.r. director Guylay, Goldwater press secretary Tony Smith; speech writer Warren Nutter; Robert Smalley, William Miller's public relations man; and Clifton White, now director of the Citizens for Goldwater-Miller. The board was scheduled to meet each Sunday with the candidates to study the biweekly polls conducted by Opinion Research Corporation of Princeton and to review the general situation. The candidates never showed up at a single meeting.[66]

Super-organizer Clifton White's role had changed considerably once Goldwater decided to go seriously after the nomination and domination of his party. Before the convention, White served with Richard Kleindienst as co-chairman of field operations. He was later put in charge of those states where no primary campaigns would demand the unique educational advantage of exposure to Goldwater's political thought. The task of delegate-gathering in these states was seen as a job for a political technician, and White had earned his stripes on that field of combat.[67]

Following the convention, White's eye was on the chairmanship of the Republican National Committee, and he sought that post as a reward for his coup in seizing the nomination. But at the convention's close, White overheard a conversation, in a Mark Hopkins Hotel elevator, in which two men discussed the candidate's choice of Dean Burch as national chairman. White had received no notice, no peresonal message. But in August he was named national director of Citizens for Goldwater-Miller.[68]

The initial planning for Goldwater's use of television illustrated the exclusion of professional communicators from policy influence, the deep division in the campaign organization between the technicians and the theoreticans, and the notable lack of any channel for two-way communications essential to sound public relations programming. It was also an example of the "leg-on-the-wall" planning that Theodore White has described.

On paper, the television plans looked fine. When the task force finally got down to business on August 20, computers had completed their analyses of the three previous national campaigns by party, state, and ethnic group. Charts had been readied illustrating "swing states," and map overlays pointed up the two hundred major television markets, demonstrating how the largest audiences might be reached for the least amount of money. According to Theodore White, 1,700,000,000 bits of information had been fed through the Republican computers. None of the bits, however, included any information on the content of the candidate's forthcoming television appearances. Furthermore, the media specialists could not find out what the message was to be, because they could not reach their candidate, nor even Kitchel. Their contact was Guylay, whose every move was subject to a fiscal veto by Cordiner.[69]

As the initial planning meetings got under way, the advertising professionals favored the use of spot announcements. The more inveterate Goldwater types, however, felt that the senator's personality and ideas needed thirty minutes, not thirty or sixty seconds, to come through. This latter point of view prevailed. The decision was based upon a determination to expose voters to the conservative philosophy, as opposed to readiness to accept the advice of the media specialists on which techniques would draw the most votes. Predictably, the Goldwater programs—measured by the ratings they received— were sober discussions that attracted audiences that probably needed no convincing. The senator's major foreign policy program drew an audience of about seven million, while at the same time on another network twenty-eight million persons watched "Peyton Place." But the Goldwater audience was a devoted one. Trailers filmed by Hollywood actor Raymond Massey appealed for funds as each show concluded. The response constituted the largest number of small contributions ever received by a political campaign. It also bolstered the arguments of the staunch conservatives in the inner circle of advisers that the gloomy forecasts of the opinion surveys were hogwash, in that they did not reveal the "hidden conservative" voters who would emerge in November.[70]

The Republican leaders working with Goldwater had, in fact, decided at the start of the campaign that it would be what Theodore White has called "a majestic dialogue on the two American philosophies, the conservative and the liberal." Goldwater, as he traversed the Republic, would expose deep party differences on a wide variety of burning issues. But the Republicans were frustrated by the failure of the Democrats to join the game. Kitchel later spoke of this growing frustration: "Lyndon Johnson was so far away from it, we couldn't find an opponent. We were punching a pillow."[71]

Many students of American presidential campaigns, however, including professional public relations men, might have predicted that such an effort at pointing up genuine political differences was unlikely to succeed. The reason is simply that such sharp distinctions, generally, do not exist. The tendency of American voters is to side with moderate candidates, and their expectation is that most candidates will stay rather close to the center on most issues. In 1964 a candidate for the presidency was suddenly speaking to the issues from that the gloomy forecasts of the opinion surveys were hogwash, in a pronounced right-wing point of view, and it was evident that the voters did not react very positively to what he was saying. Thus, there was no political advantage to the party in power in being drawn into such a debate.

There is an irony here which depresses one with basic faith in American democracy. Theoretically, when one goes to the polls, he chooses between two men who represent two distinct approaches to the issues. To the extent that he has no real choice, the system is in a state of crisis. And yet, here was a candidate attempting to set forth such an approach, and finding himself foiled at every turn because of a refusal—a canny one, to be sure—of his opponent to supply the other side of the dialogue.

The men who would be writing Goldwater's speeches would

obviously be of immense importance in the kind of philosophical, substantive campaign that the Republicans had chosen to wage.

But as Theodore White has pointed out, ". . . no man, at this superior level of thought and direction, was more alone, more undermanned and understaffed, more deserted by friends, allies and associates, than Barry Goldwater." Professor Warren Nutter of the University of Virginia was perhaps the outstanding intellectual on the speech-writing staff. But Theodore White observed that Nutter was "haggard with exhaustion" by October. Tony Smith—in bad health but virtually the only experienced political public relations counsel with the Goldwater organization—bore the principal burden of the statements and reactions to which a candidate must give birth at least twice daily. Karl Hess was in a similar position as the only highly experienced writer accompanying Goldwater on the road, "editing and rewriting in weariness the erratic flow of research material that came to the campaign plane from Washington."[72]

The times and places chosen for Goldwater's speeches often seemed to bear no relationship to the issues on which he chose to focus. He spoke on crime to retired senior citizens in St. Petersburg, Florida, a quiet and peaceful city where it was no issue. The St. Petersburg *Times'* comment: "Right City, Wrong Speech." In West Virginia, one of the poorest, most depressed states of the nation, Goldwater chose to open fire on Johnson's anti-poverty program. In Atlanta, a city that was notoriously under-represented in the Congress and in the Georgia legislature, he made an anti-reapportionment speech. In Tennessee he referred hardly at all to the TVA, which residents remembered he had once offered to sell for a dollar.[73]

Furthermore, the senator's phraseology seemed to bear no evidence of any influence by those professional communicators who might understand the likely reaction of national audiences who would read of Goldwater's speeches around the country.

In Hammond, Indiana, for example, the candidate spoke to mill workers—largely of East European extraction—about "liberating Eastern Europe," "victory over Communism," maintaining a "superiority of strength" and a "devastating strike-back power," "suicide for the Communists if they should ever push the button," that the United States would "destroy them" if they ever did so, and so on. *New York Times* correspondent Charles Mohr stopped counting part way through the speech after ascertaining that Goldwater had used phrases such as "holocaust," "push the button," and "atomic weapons" thirty times. Even though Goldwater, in making such speeches, was trying to say that *he* would never push the button, it was impossible for the media to report his comments without some very warlike quotations. Thus, there seemed always to be a threat, a willingness to gamble with human lives, inherent in Goldwater's comments on national defense.[74]

As for the style of the speeches, Theodore White observes that Goldwater's best was characterized by a "yearning sincerity and indignation." He was convinced that government is the enemy of liberty. "One could not question the conscience of this conservative. Here was no ordinary politician pitching for votes; he was on a crusade to free America from enslavement." But, unfortunately, this kind of campaigning "could never make an audience chuckle."[75]

The Goldwater organization, which had failed at what professionals call "preventive public relations"—keeping your nose clean, seeing the crisis before it occurs and averting it, promoting your best image, and avoiding controversial situations—could not now solve its problem of "remedial public relations"—patching things up once the bricks come flying through the window.

Said Denison Kitchel:

> "My candidate had been branded a bomb-dropper—and I couldn't figure out how to lick it. And the advertising people, people who could sell anything, toothpaste or soap or automobiles—when it came to a political question like this, they couldn't offer anything either."[76]

It is one of Professor Stanley Kelley's principal contentions that public relations politics is issue politics. The Goldwater campaign was indeed built around issues, but, as we have seen, public relations considerations apparently played no part in the selection and presentation of those issues. The issues here were chosen and developed without public relations assistance. They were expressed in modes of which public relations men would not have approved. And when they got the candidate in trouble, there was no magic cure in the public relations men's bag. Furthermore, the issues were raised by one side, but not really dealt with by the other. There was no dialogue, but Goldwater persisted in his monologue anyhow. He did not try to tell the people what they wanted to hear, but he went on telling them what *he* wanted them to hear, anyhow.

Any hope the Republicans might have retained that the Democrats would join them in a "reasonable" dialogue on the issues had, in fact, vanished with the showing of the famous Democratic "Daisy Girl" television spot in early September. If the Republicans were disregarding their own Opinion Research Corporation data on the impact of the "nuclear issue" upon public thinking, the Democrats were very much aware of it. Many of the Goldwater statements that the Democratic advertising and public relations people exploited with such devastating effectiveness were actually made before the campaign. This included the candidate's pronouncements on Social Security, his suggestion that the eastern seaboard be "sawed off," and his proposals on defense, which sounded more like officers' club repartee than responsible campaigning. Lamb and Smith point out that Goldwater's advisers were aware of the existence of such statements through their information storage system. Yet they persisted in planning on a two-party dialogue based upon issues raised in Goldwater's formal addresses. This overlooked the attitudes toward the senator already held by the voters.

> They did not realize how easy it would be for the Democratic Party to campaign against the incautious Goldwater of the New Hampshire primaries, paying little heed to the Republican nominee. . . . He was placed in the curious position, for the candidate challenging the incumbent, of having to defend his record—not the record of what he had done, but the record of what he had said. This defensive posture kept the issues alive and reinforced the voting decisions of those who had selected President Johnson.[77]

As the campaign moved on, Goldwater had to sacrifice his attacks —the natural offensive posture of the challenger—in order to defend himself. In a sense, he was running two races. One was against the President, the other against the image of himself that he and the image-makers of the opposition, both Republican and Democratic, had created. Goldwater had thus to set about breaking the caricature which was drawn first by the men of his own party (with unwitting help from the candidate himself), then by Johnson and his helpers and Doyle Dane Bernbach. In Theodore White's words, "Rockefeller and Scranton had drawn up the indictment, Lyndon Johnson was the prosecutor. Goldwater was cast as defendant. He was like a dog with a can tied to his tail—the faster he ran, the more the can clattered."[78]

The Goldwater staff did their best to deal with the problem. They first used conventional techniques and turned out speeches and position papers. On September 22, they tried a televised Eisenhower-Goldwater conversation at Gettysburg, in which the general only reluctantly participated. The long conversation of the ex- and would-be Presidents was digested into half an hour, during which Ike blessed the senator's efforts, and called the talk of Goldwater's alleged desire to use the A-bomb, without much prompting, "tommyrot." But the program was an editorial more than an interpretation. And when the broadcast was over, the voters still didn't know just how the candidate felt about nuclear weapons—only that the last Republican to occupy the White House felt that whatever Goldwater thought, it was okay with him. Later, President Johnson proudly announced the Nielsen rating for Goldwater's half-hour. The senator and general had scored 8.6, against 27.4 for "Petticoat Junction," and 25.0 for "Peyton Place."[79]

As might be expected, the political professionals on the staff of the Citizens for Goldwater-Miller, under Clifton White, had grown restless over the campaign's failure to gain the offensive. They rejected the judgment of those on the Goldwater staff who were hoping for their "dialogue," and landed instead on their own issue—"Ethics." Its themes were "moral decay, bribery, violence in the streets, and the image of President Johnson as a political wheeler-dealer." In the tradition of political propaganda, Clif White and his people felt that since Goldwater was running against fear, he needed to stimulate counter-fear: the dread of domestic violence and a general decay in American morality.[80]

There emerged from the Clifton White analysis a filmed television documentary entitled "Choice," which was produced under the questionable imprimatur of "Mothers for a Moral America."

Clifton White said that Goldwater personally approved the idea for the film, although none of his policy advisers were involved in its development. Its production was supervised by Rus Walton, publicity director of the Citizens organization and a former executive director of the conservative United Republicans of California. Walton had contacts in the Hollywood film and television industry. All of the clips in the film previously had been shown on television but were now extracted from their original contexts. It included scenes of street rioting and looting, frenzied dancing, and a speeding car—like the one driven by the President—which was intended to link the

Johnson Administration to the theme of creeping national decay. The bare breasts of a girl in a topless bathing suit made national headlines when the film achieved some premature publicity.[81]

The Citizens organization—without clearance from Goldwater's policy group—arranged sponsorship and a national television showing for the film on October 22. Lamb and Smith quote one member of Goldwater's inner circle as observing: "I realize now that we did not know enough about what the Citizens organization was doing. We had confidence in Clif White as a technician; and he was present at the Sunday conferences. We simply assumed that no checkup was needed." Denison Kitchel previewed "Choice," and reacted with fury. But television arrangements were so far advanced that no one but the candidate himself could change the situation, and a showing was arranged. The antennae of the politicians who saw the film at that stage picked up such elements as nudes, pornography, and immorality—all of which can backfire on a candidate. Goldwater faced the crisis courageously. A few days after the showing, he told a reporter in Los Angeles who asked for his reaction to the film: "It is not salacious. It is racist." He said that he had ordered all plans for showing the film canceled, that he repudiated it completely. He granted permission for this observation to be quoted directly.[82]

Apparently, Clifton White and his old associates from the Draft Goldwater Committee had developed their own ideas about how to fight Lyndon Johnson. But the candidate and his advisers vetoed them, finding it less difficult than the technicians to divide the medium from the message.

Theodore White, in fact, points out the difficulties inherent in defining the "ethics" issue from the point of view of political public relations. Doyle Dane Bernbach could, based on Goldwater's public record, expose him in various degrees of extremism. But the problem for their opposite numbers at Interpublic was to attack the President:

> ... how does an advertising firm go about attacking a President? How does one besmirch the majesty and uniform of the office? How, for example, ... do you ask how a Texas Congressman and Senator, never earning more than $22,500 a year, accumulates a fortune of $7 million?[83]

So it would appear that the decision was that instead of attempting to hit the President directly, Goldwater would hammer at such names as Bobby Baker, Billie Sol Estes, and Walter Jenkins. But Baker had not been convicted of anything and it would do a candidate no good to condemn him. The Estes case was much too convoluted, and good for little more than a passing reference. The Jenkins case was a difficult and tragic one, and Goldwater did not relish talking about it. L.B.J. himself had never been on the take—and as for his fortune, this involved the high finance of monopoly broadcasting operations and government licenses. These were matters that could hardly be made clear issues for most voters in campaign oratory and advertising. There was some hope that Goldwater's barbs, even if shallow, might provoke some great intemperate reaction on the part of the President. But Lyndon Johnson, though a sensitive and volatile man, was above all a consummate politician, and too wise politically to engage in any public display of temper and indiscretion.[84]

How, then, to provoke the President? Republican vice presidential candidate William Miller, known as an able partisan debater, was assigned the role of toreador to the Johnson temper. It was hoped that he could excite the President with some sharply barbed abuse and provoke the kind of outburst that would put the Chief Executive on the defensive. Miller did his best, but he played the game by the rules and never got so much as a snort out of either Johnson or Humphrey throughout the campaign. And during his weeks on the road, Miller's skill with the red cape seemed to evaporate. He had provoked no response, had no illusions about the election's outcome, and seemed to have lost his heart for the game.

The Republicans made an illusory and rather questionable public relations pass at the black vote during the Goldwater campaign, when a New Jersey Negro politician, Clay Claiborne, became director of the Minorities Division of the National Committee. Claiborne soon found his division abolished, and he was made special assistant to the director of the campaign organization. A news release on Claiborne's appointment was issued, pointing out that the assignment was a sign of the Goldwater campaign's determination not to abandon any group of voters by default. Claiborne was then assigned to "separate but equal" offices several floors away from the center of the National Committee operation. When he prepared some materials aimed at attracting black votes in the Washington, D.C., area, their distribution was quickly curtailed by a former member of Clifton White's Draft Goldwater Committee staff, "presumably out of fear that Democrats would distribute them among Southern whites. . . ."[85]

The whole façade of interest in the black voter ended sadly when, in the last days of the campaign, it occurred to one Republican tactician that some black votes might be lured away from Johnson in key states by stimulating a phony write-in vote for the Reverend Martin Luther King. The idea seems not to have ever been cleared with Goldwater or Kitchel. Claiborne—reluctantly—issued an order to have handbills printed urging black voters to write in Dr. King. He placed the printing order with a firm in his native state of New Jersey. Democrats there then complained that the handbills violated New Jersey law, in that the organization sponsoring them was not designated on the publications. So Claiborne's career with the Goldwater organization ended with his indictment. He was acquitted when the prosecution failed to establish willful duplicity on his part.[86]

Goldwater's press relations during the campaign showed considerable improvement over those of before and during the convention. The senator now had two new public relations men dealing with the press: Paul Wagner, a professional public relations practitioner, and Victor Gold, a conservative intellectual who had come to the aid of his hero, Barry Goldwater, as he would one day do for another hero, Spiro Agnew. Gold, according to Theodore White, added joy to the campaign trips. He had "joined the campaign to help Goldwater save Western civilization, but discovered the candidate's chief need was some way of getting through to the press." Gold did this in an unconventional manner, which would hardly be found in the textbooks of the public relations profession; he carried reporters' bags, got correspondents to the trains on time, tucked them in and woke them up. His methods worked to the extent that White was able to report that ". . . before they knew it, the correspondents, about 95 percent anti-Goldwater by conviction, had been won to a friendship with the diminutive intellectual which spilled over onto his hero." Although the press buses were often booed by Goldwater supporters, and even stoned on one occasion, a warmth developed aboard as the campaign progressed. Reporters wore a little souvenir Goldwater had had prepared for them, reading "Eastern Liberal Press." And, ". . . at the end, the correspondents permanently assigned to Goldwater were almost protective of him and felt guilty each time they must report those things they could not avoid reporting."[87]

Goldwater's editorial support was another matter. The Republicans can invariably rely upon the endorsement of the bulk of the nation's newspapers and national magazines as a reliable Republican resource (although the value of press endorsements in terms of votes, if any, has never really been established).

But beginning in August, the bastions of the Republican press cut loose from the senator one at a time. Papers that had never before gone Democratic endorsed President Johnson for reelection. The Hearst papers left the Republican fold for the first time since 1932. So did many other major newspapers in cities such as San Francisco, Philadelphia, Denver, and Indianapolis. Some papers were endorsing a Democrat for the first time since their early nineteenth-century beginnings. The *Saturday Evening Post* went Democratic, as did *Life* magazine. As things turned out, the only three major papers in the country that supported Goldwater were the Los Angeles *Times*, the Chicago *Tribune*, and the Cincinnati *Enquirer*. Said Theodore White, "Nothing like this had ever happened before in American political history."[88]

Everyone since 1952 had wound up his campaign with an election eve television show, and Goldwater was no exception. Theodore White characterizes the show as "a dull, contrived family scene." On the last day of the campaign, the senator went to San Francisco, the scene of his triumph at the convention weeks before. There, he proceeded to repeat word for word the same speech with which he had opened his campaign two months earlier in Prescott, Arizona. He admitted to his audience what he was doing:

> ". . . the issues have not changed. I have not changed. The challenge and the choice has not changed."[89]

The Goldwater campaign had ended as it had begun, a campaign run by amateurs. In a sense, many of those who run presidential campaigns are, at best, only apprentices at the job. The professionals—except in a few extraordinary cases—cannot really tell a would-be President what to do. They may advise him on how to do something, but he supposedly tells *them* what it is *he* wants to do. Thus, Barry Goldwater

> . . . was perhaps justified in dismissing Clifton White, who had brought him the nomination, for in White he sensed an appetite and purpose different from his own. But he could not guide by any

sense of his own broader constructive purpose the professionals he later brought in.[90]

Lamb and Smith compare the structure of the Goldwater campaign to the philosophy of a medieval theologian who "orchestrates the theme of the Christian faith to the tune of Greek rationalism." The first principle must be a matter of faith. Once the first principle is accepted, the details seem logical and necessary and the totality convincing. In the Goldwater campaign, belief in the myth of the "hidden conservative vote" was that first article of faith. This basic article, therefore, was not even called into question by the final, grinding, inevitable blow of election night. Goldwater put off his concession statement until enough votes were counted to enable him finally to announce that more than twenty-five million citizens had seen fit to endorse the conservative philosophy.[91]

Unlike the Democratic campaign, the Goldwater organization's commitment to a campaign based on conservative principles—designed to bring a hidden conservative majority running out of the nooks and crannies of America—was remarkably unresponsive to the feedback which forms, by definition, an essential part of the public relations process. The unshakable conviction that conservatism would indeed triumph apparently made no provision for soothing the fear of Goldwater's policies, which had first been raised by his opponents for the nomination and later bolstered by the Democratic campaign.

As the candidate traveled, local party officials asked him to explain again to *their* particular constituency just where he *really* stood on Social Security and nuclear war. The Opinion Research Corporation had revealed that these two issues were of primary concern to the voters. It was obvious that the senator would have to modify his public image on these two issues if he was to make any headway in closing the vast statistical chasm that separated him from the incumbent. Goldwater made a futile effort to remold that image in speeches and statements by "explaining" his "true" position. But his severest critics were a group of his own associates, who were to complain later that if Goldwater just had held rigidly to his basic plan, without modifying his style and position, things would have gone better. Some of Goldwater's close advisers actually devoted a portion of their energies to beating off the efforts of other subordinates to modify the campaign.[92]

Perhaps myths like that of the "hidden conservatives," promoted by these true believers in the Goldwater organization, are understandably tempting for a minority party. Arguments that promise an illusion—of either the right or the left—find willing listeners among underdogs awaiting a Messianic age.

But in this case, the promoters of the illusion were not paid cynics engaged in a professional attempt to dupe the public; they were really true believers and under the same illusion themselves. So much did they believe, that they limited their foci of attention so as to exclude much crucial information. Lamb and Smith's simile is engaging: "As Admiral Yamamoto, speeding toward Midway Island, ignored the possibility that his code had been cracked, Barry Goldwater's policy group ignored or discounted the opinion polls."[93]

The "hidden conservatives," of course, never did emerge. But whence cometh the myth of their existence?

Thomas W. Benham has pointed to the likely frustration of conservatives who were convinced they had found a wide measure of social support and resonance for their views, only to find that "uniquely at election time, and uniquely in vote totals, this vigorous support had a habit of evaporating." The simplest interpretation for the discrepancy between "what one heard" and what went on at the polls is that strong conservatives simply refused to vote in large numbers. As soon as a useful reason was worked out as to why this willful non-voting should occur, a new theory raised its head. It persisted partially because it was a good tactical weapon.

> ... it is not a simple matter of fact vs. fantasy: both worlds are real, and have real effects on the political process. ... if the reality of one of these worlds was manifest on Election Day, 1964, then the reality of the other was equally apparent in the San Francisco Convention.[94]

The "woodwork myth of the hidden conservatives" can, of course, be tested by the techniques of survey research. If one were to prove the hypothesis of conservatives in the woodwork valid, one would have to demonstrate that there were hundreds of thousands of potential Republican voters who had repeatedly sat out elections rather than vote for any of the long string of "moderates" who had appeared on that party's tickets for decades. But as a matter of fact, every reputable examination of the question since at least 1944 has shown that

Republicans vote more frequently than Democrats, and that the turn-out of the most conservative of the Republicans is almost consist-ently high—96 or 98 percent—even when the Republican candidate is a liberal.[95]

And so the Goldwater organization paid the penalty for its own mythology, and its own refusal to heed the evidence that revelation was, indeed, only myth. It resulted in what the liberal Republicans of the Ripon Society have called "one of the most inept and unprofes-sional campaigns in American history," brought about because Gold-water and his advisers, pursuing a "dream of a political world with-out politics,"[96] sought their hidden vote, which was known to be nonexistent not only by journalists and public relations men and pollsters and other observers, but by active, experienced Republicans as well.

But if there are really no conservatives in the woodwork, did Gold-water ever have a chance? Operating under V. O. Key's theory of "acceptable alternatives" cited earlier, a Goldwater victory in the 1964 election would have required a most unlikely combination of Johnson fumbles and Goldwater touchdowns to overcome the basic threat that the Republican candidate seemed to represent to so many Americans. Lyndon Johnson was the President. There was no wide-spread unhappiness with his incumbency. Indeed, the polls showed him mounting the crest of popularity. An active President since the tragedy of the year before, Johnson had established a solid record of accomplishment in a relatively short time. Senator Goldwater, on the other hand, had established another kind of public image, an image he began to build well before he was nominated for the presidency. And it was an image that the American voters were, by a vast major-ity, not willing to associate with the presidency of their country.[97]

## Lyndon Baines Johnson

It is difficult to overemphasize the advantages that accrue to the incumbent who seeks to retain the presidential office. As Theodore White has said, the President wills—and he moves. And as he goes, public attention moves with him. The world's leading journalists fly with him on a moment's notice. They issue advance reports that bring out the crowds to any landing spot the President may choose, banner his comments in the papers, echo his words on the radio, and display him on television. Crowds and public attention are drafted for him. The Signal Corps installs remote communications networks before he even leaves his bedroom in the White House. There is no place too difficult or remote for him to reach, if he only wishes to go. With these kinds of facilities and staff available to him, Lyndon Johnson's formal campaign of 1964 "proceeded almost flawlessly."

> The offensive against Goldwater rolled almost by itself ... the President was free to spread balm and peace around the nation. Never were Republicans denounced as such; the opposition was involved in its own civil war, and the President obeyed Napoleon's maxim: "Never interfere with the enemy when he is in the process of destroying himself.[98]

The Johnson campaign organization was a personal one, and its lines were often confusing. But of one thing there could be no doubt —it was the President's personal campaign, run from the top in a manner unlike any since those of the incumbent FDR. But it was also the most successful presidential campaign in American electoral history. White, from whose description the following p r -related ele ments of the campaign organization are drawn, sketches that organization as structured, like the White House, on a radial mode.[99] The center of the wheel was occupied by those with direct access to the President—Walter Jenkins, Bill Moyers, and Jack Valenti. Jenkins, until his tragic collapse, was "the chief transmission belt" for all presidential directives. Moyers, on the other hand, was "the chief idea channel of the campaign." Valenti was the President's "shadow, companion, counselor and personal attendant." Speech material was all channeled to Moyers. It came in great quantity from all over the government apparatus, going first to Labor Secretary Willard Wirtz, and then to the writers operating under Moyers' direction—such men as Richard Goodwin, Howard Busby, and Douglass Cater. Their finished speeches went through Moyers to the President. This team also controlled the media campaign. Doyle Dane Bernbach (DDB), which worked out of New York, reported to them, and the agency team discussed television strategy with Goodwin and Moyers or the latter's friend and aide at the Democratic National Committee, Lloyd Wright. These three men were generally enthusiastic about what DDB had to suggest.

These younger men in the inner circle were subjected to what

White describes as a kind of "senior review board" of LBJ's oldest cronies: Washington attorneys Clark Clifford, Abe Fortas, and James Rowe. One of them always went over the plans for any major speech or appearance or policy decision, and they were the first to be consulted on any major crisis.

Next in the radial organization was a remnant of John F. Kennedy's "Irish Mafia," Lawrence O'Brien and Kenneth O'Donnell. Any night when both they and the President were in Washington, the three would meet at 6:30 for a campaign review. O'Brien and O'Donnell were the official campaign directors, and all state organizations had instructions to report to them. Mobilizing old Kennedy loyalties, they met with state organizations and directed the President's travel schedule.

White House Special Counsel Myer Feldman had the general function of thinking up ways of embarrassing Barry Goldwater and upsetting Republican campaign offensives. He met each afternoon at his office with a group calling itself the Five O'Clock Club. It consisted of a dozen or so of Washington's bright young Democratic lawyers and junior officials. This group, says White,

> was Johnson's original contribution to Presidential politics. Its franchise was to think about counteroffensive, or what may be called "negative advance." Its purpose was to precede, accompany and follow Barry Goldwater's campaign tour with instant, organized contradiction.[100]

Feldman's group inevitably managed to get a hold of Goldwater's advance schedules, and somehow they had texts of the senator's speeches several hours before the rest of the world. Before Goldwater arrived at the point of delivery, material for the refutation or contradiction was usually in the hands of local Democratic officials. The public relations advantage here was tremendous, in that local news media would carry the Democratic contradiction simultaneously with Goldwater's speech in almost any locality, rather than as a reaction story the following day. There were even instances in which the contradictions of what the senator was going to say made the news before his speech! The Five O'Clock Club was also to be credited with many of the slogans, counter-demonstrations, and hostile placards greeting the senator wherever he went and doing such wonders for his morale.

Finally, as White sketches the organizational plan, there was the

Democratic National Committee, presided over by veteran Connecticut political leader John Bailey. Bailey saw his operation as mainly one of political nitty-gritty. This included the voter registration operation initiated by President Kennedy and carried out by a professional campaign consultant, Matt Reese of West Virginia. Also headquartered at the National Committee was a taping center, designed so as to provide audio material that could be requested by a phone call from any radio station in the country. The committee's research division was directed by another Kennedy man, Fred Dutton, and Louis Martin headed the minorities division.

White makes it clear that President Johnson largely ignored channels in communicating with any of these groups, and that there was much overlap in their work. Occasionally, he would impose an overlay on one or more of the groups, as when he appointed John Hayes, president of the *Post-Newsweek* stations, to serve as final critic on the efforts of the rest of the staff in the area of television and to report his reactions personally to the President.

One additional element in the Democratic campaign structure was, of course, the Hubert Humphrey organization, a personal team with which the vice presidential candidate worked very closely.

The President was looking not only for a high degree of personal control, but for the maximum amount of exhaustive analysis. Both the Oliver Quayle polling organization and Doyle Dane Bernbach helped achieve this latter goal. In the pre-campaign period, DDB formulated a "synoptic plan" for campaign publicity. The agency designed an exhaustive program of research, so as to produce not just an ample plan, but the best that could be turned out. "The President was attracted by this goal, just as he found his professional pollsters providing information that would help him direct a masterful campaign from the White House."[101]

Thus, basic decisions about campaign materials and television advertising were made early and with considerable time and care. Advertising materials were designed even before the convention, complete except for blank lines to be filled with the name of the vice presidential nominee. Careful plans were made to fit even the convention itself into an overall public relations campaign. Considerable energy went into the calculation of convention spending and income as part of the campaign budget, in an effort to make the National Convention "a finely-machined part of [the] campaign."[102]

DDB, for example, produced a design of the convention hall,

which was to lead off the agency's television campaign. The venerable bunting, balloons, and huge heroic portraits that had become an expected cliché at such events were to be replaced by billboards showing various facets of the Great Society. This would allow television cameras to pick up images of the party's social concern and the administration's accomplishments, rather than traditional decorations. The latter, it was thought, would not only be reminiscent of old-style politics, but perhaps emphasize the "wheeler-dealer image" that Johnson and DDB were trying to shake. The agency got the billboards it wanted. But there was some compromise with tradition. Two huge pictures of President Johnson and President Kennedy looked out over the delegates, and when the President was nominated, his supporters were allowed to enjoy a vigorous "spontaneous" demonstration, complete with placards. On top of all this came Johnson's own efforts to insert drama and excitement into the convention with personal appearances at the last minute, his manipulations involving Hubert Humphrey and the vice presidency, a spectacular fireworks-illustrated birthday celebration for himself, and so on. It was obvious that the President was going to be his own press agent, and the decisions that led to his actual projected image went far beyond the careful "logic" of DDB and the other professionals concerned.[103]

Doyle Dane Bernbach, Inc., is a "hot," imaginative, fast-growing New York advertising agency. DDB's accounts have included the Avis Rent-A-Car "Number Two" campaign; the introduction of the Volkswagen to the U.S. market; Levy's Rye, "You don't have to be Jewish" campaign; El Al Airlines, and others. Before 1964 the firm had not been involved in politics. The results of its staff work on the Democratic advertising campaign were a clear indication of the growth of sophistication in the profession—and perhaps of what the American people had come to accept in political advertising and advertising in general. The contrast with the first major broadcast advertising campaign for a President, 1952, was remarkable.

For by now it was apparent that people did not simply *vote* for a presidential candidate. What they really did was *accept* him; in effect, they *bought* him. And once this premise can be acknowledged (if not fully tolerated), it would seem that it was, really, only a matter of time until both politicians and admen did the logical thing and sought one another out.

This is what happened in the case of John F. Kennedy. He had been impressed by DDB's advertising work for commercial products and thought the agency might do well at politics. He asked brother-in-law Stephen Smith, the newly appointed director of the 1964 campaign, to talk with the agency about taking on the Democratic account. According to one reporter, President Kennedy "saw a Volkswagen ad with the headline 'Think Small.' It was the kind of thing that appealed to his sense of humor."[104]

The agency's management was Democratic in its sympathies, and drawn by the new frontier of political advertising. But L.B.J. organized his own campaign, and by February 1964 serious opposition to DDB had developed within the Democratic National Committee. This was particularly true of some of the veteran politicians.[105]

It was not that these Democratic Party leaders did not accept advertising agencies as a political fact of life. Politicians are pragmatists. But their orientation lacked the industrial and commercial basis of the Republicans, many of whom hire and fire p.r. and advertising men and their campaigns as part of their ongoing responsibilities in private life. As we have seen, the fondness of the Republican Party for commercial-style national advertising in presidential campaigns really grew out of a desire to transfer the successful marketing techniques of the business world to politics. But as Lamb and Smith have observed, the Democrats (including such valuable veterans as Chairman John Bailey and Treasurer Richard Maguire) in 1964 were still accustomed to advertising agencies that were unpretentious and inexpensive—two adjectives that do not apply to Doyle Dane Bernbach.

Lloyd Wright began his job as the National Committee's media coordinator in March, just in time to review the advertising agencies being considered for the campaign. He began to advocate retaining DDB. It was Wright's feeling that the quality of their output was superior, that the agency had the respect of the media, that it understood the mysteries of what media deliver which audiences at what times, and that it had the creative ability to develop a variety of campaign materials. The National Committee and other seasoned Democratic leaders could not see paying DDB's high prices—especially in view of the full news coverage automatically commanded by a President in office. Maguire, who controlled the coffers, felt that the election was so secure that there was no point in spending the money. But he did not have Cordiner's unilateral veto power. And Wright disagreed with the Maguire position; he felt DDB's creativity was not only worth the price, but that it was required to increase the size of the President's "mandate" and to raise the educational level of the campaign. Party leaders, skeptical about creativity in political advertising to begin with, were especially dubious about DDB's unconventional plans and saw little need for the additional public support that would have to be purchased at the agency's high fees. They thought in terms of what other aspects of the campaign would have to be cut back in order to pay the Madison Avenue-sized bills. President Johnson, however, apparently impressed with the prospect of more votes, and the correlation of that prospect with the work of Doyle Dane Bernbach, backed Wright.[106]

The decision, in retrospect, was a historical departure for the Democratic Party. As we have seen, the use of the broadcast media and of advertising agencies to manage programming had been an accepted part of Democratic campaigns since that classic contest of 1952. But, as Lamb and Smith emphasize, before 1964 program content for the Democrats had always been within the province of the political leadership. Even the famed "O'Brien Manual" of the 1960 campaign, innovative as it was, stated firmly that although an advertising agency might handle production, only political leaders should determine the content of campaign advertising.

The DDB staff, in April, began to develop campaign themes and story lines, with Wright as its principal point of contact with the party. The agency assigned some forty members of its staff to the Democratic account. Their aim, with which the White House was in agreement, was to "draft a definite plan for the campaign on how to get through to the public." Wright encountered sustained resistance from his colleagues and nominal superiors at the National Committee and eventually bypassed the regular organization to deal directly with Moyers at the White House.[107]

But controversy over the role of DDB raged throughout the campaign. For example, the agency was given early responsibility for designing both print materials and radio and television presentations. In April, DDB began to develop an overall strategy for the campaign, to be implemented consistently through publicity, design, and events. This strategy was developed within the agency after study of public opinion data and briefings from such electoral experts as Richard Scammon and White House researcher Paul Southwick.

DDB decisions were reached in close consultation with Wright and Moyers. Men such as John Hayes, Richard Goodwin, Kenneth O'Donnell, and the Clifford-Fortas-Rowe "appeals board" were involved "to lesser and varying degrees." Nevertheless, experts at the Democratic National Committee felt their advice was going unheard, let alone heeded. Like Wright, DDB eventually established direct linkage with the White House, assuming that the President made the campaign decisions and that his staff had the best access to him.[108]

Experience verified these initial assumptions about access to the President, at least in the early stages of the campaign. For Moyers and Wright had, indeed, prevailed in their efforts to convince the President to choose DDB. At their early meeting wih Johnson, according to one report, agency representatives showed him the first versions of the "nuclear responsibility" films that were to dominate much of his television campaign. According to one report: "He asked a few questions, made the comment, 'You know what you're doing,' and left."[109]

So DDB and its White House liaison took heart from what Moyers and Valenti assured them had been a good meeting with the President and drafted their "definitive plan for the campaign on how to get through to the public." The plan was ready in late July and actually adopted by the White House before the Democratic National Convention met to formally nominate Lyndon Johnson. The plan, according to Lamb and Smith, represented "careful analyses of both political attitude formation and national opinion surveys."[110]

The DDB plan, then, was to come out punching hard at the Republicans. This was to put Goldwater on the defensive as early as possible in the campaign, while at the same time presenting a positive picture of Johnson by simply letting him go on about the business of being President. Only later was the advertising to concentrate on substantive policy issues. It is interesting that this planning was going on while President Johnson was waging a kind of non-campaign—telling the press he was just going to go on being the President and not worry about any formal campaign. It is also interesting to note that this presidential line is exactly what the press reported. There was a remarkable lack of analytical reporting on campaign planning. What was going on behind the scenes in planning the campaign was the *real story* of late summer. *That* was the political process of 1964 in operation, and yet it attracted no media attention at the time.

The planners at the advertising agency wanted television spots to concentrate on Goldwater's weaknesses and emphasize the social virtues of the Great Society program. This approach, and President Johnson's own conduct as a man above politics, were to act to contradict the image of a "wheeler-dealer" which DDB's opinion research said the public attached to the chief executive. Nuclear responsibility and civil rights were to be major campaign issues. But the Republican convention and later polls led Moyers and Wright and the agency people to decide that "civil rights would take care of itself; that the backlash was overrated"; and that Social Security, the TVA, and the fact that so many Republicans opposed Goldwater should be added to the nuclear responsibility issue. But DDB had already produced some civil rights spots, and the party was billed for the unused commercials. This was normal procedure for the agency, but highly irritating to Maguire, and served as confirmation to him and other old-line leaders who had opposed DDB from the start that the firm was an overpriced luxury.[111]

The innovative Democratic television spots were screened and considered for weeks before reaching their fame shortly after the convention. There was a close relationship between the status of the campaign budget and these television decisions. Even when decisions had been made at the White House level, Richard Maguire would delay and threaten to withhold money from projects that he felt were politically unwise. He thought this about a number of the DDB commercials and made strong cases against them before he paid the bills.[112]

Even though the Democrats, like the Republicans, had a recalcitrant hand on the purse strings, there are notable differences between the way in which Maguire and Cordiner operated. In both campaigns, control of the treasury was, as might be expected, of great importance. But Maguire was above all a politician, and when he withheld money it was done as a gesture to emphasize his political judgments. Cordiner, on the other hand, did so simply to run the campaign like a successful business—keeping the campaign budget balanced and finishing in the black.

Eventually, the antagonism of the National Committee toward DDB began to have its effects upon the campaign. There was intense dissatisfaction with the agency's work at National Committee staff meetings, largely because of a feeling that the agency was arrogant —it worked through the White House and considered itself "above" the political professionals. On the other hand, if the National Committee gained White House clearance for one of *its* decisions, the DDB people would still argue the matter with the committee staff.

> Antagonized by being ignored, believing that an agency's function was not to make strategy but to implement it, appalled by the high prices, convinced that some of the "radical" designs were politically harmful, and suspicious of the "hard sell" approach they detected, most of the campaign leaders at the National Committee lobbied against the agency's work.[113]

The committee had some success in cutting down the $9,000,000 DDB package—for example, billboards were eliminated. Miscellaneous materials for the campaign were also able to slip through the definitive DDB plan into other hands, and "a diverse menagerie of pamphlets, brochures, and other materials was ultimately produced, largely in response to the unhappiness of the campaign leaders who needed them."[114]

Theodore White feels that at least three of the DDB television commercials for the Johnson campaign (two of which were quickly aborted) "deserve to go down in history as masterpieces of political television." These were:[115]

1. "Daisy Girl." This sixty-second spot was shown only once, on NBC's "Monday Night at the Movies" on September 7. It began with a close-up of a little girl in a meadow picking petals from a daisy, counting as she went along. A background voice picked up a countdown, and the film faded through the girl's eyes to an atomic testing site, and the entire scene then dissolved into a nuclear mushroom cloud. A voice concluded: "These are the stakes: To make a world in which all of God's children can live or go into the dark. . . ." The film mentioned neither Goldwater nor his party, but the propaganda effect was devastating. As White says, ". . . the shriek of Republican indignation fastened the bomb message on them more tightly than any calculation could have expected."

2. "Ice-Cream Cone." Ten days later, a commercial was televised showing another pretty little girl. This one ate an ice-cream cone while a motherly voice in the background explained that strontium 90 is a fallout product found in milk, and that Senator Goldwater opposed the Nuclear Test Ban Treaty. "This, as cruel a political film as has ever been shown, was also aired but once."

3. "Social Security Card." This showed the fingers of two hands tearing up a Social Security card. It was shown repeatedly throughout the campaign and "probably had greater penetration than any other paid political use of television except for Richard M. Nixon's Checkers broadcast in 1952."

Democratic National Committee leaders tended to be critical of the spots as being too "hard sell." There was one, less overstated, which they liked: "Hot Line." In this one the picture showed a special telephone marked "White House." While the phone rings, a voice says: "This particular phone only rings in a serious crisis. Keep it in the hands of a man who's proven himself responsible. Vote for President Johnson on November 3rd. The stakes are too high for you to stay home."[116]

Even though these films had been previewed by most of the campaign leadership and were applauded when they were shown to Democratic leaders at the National Convention, it was apparent that the Democrats were no more prepared, in public relations terms, for the impact of these commercials than were the Republicans. The Democrats' apparent embarrassment was expressed by Hubert Humphrey, who said on "Meet the Press" that the "Daisy Girl" ad was "unfortunate." An unidentified member of the Moyers-Wright-DDB team, on the other hand, told Lamb and Smith: ". . . When the history of the campaign is written, I think it will be seen as a triumph. Our strategy was to . . . put [Goldwater] on the defense. . . . This worked."[117]

This film was one of fifteen produced for the campaign by Doyle Dane Bernbach as what Lamb and Smith call "a calculated segment of a coherent and sophisticated image strategy worked out by the agency." But it seems incredible, in retrospect, that it had so little to do with the careful, reasoned judgment of the President of the United States. He was using it as a vehicle to help him remain in office on the basis of a "mandate" from the American people. And yet the content of the messages with which he would reach most of those people was left to the technicians to work out.

In this vein, Wright—who, through Moyers, came to represent the President on such matters—was concerned that the campaign advertising be used as an educational medium on the issues. He did tend to agree that the "Daisy Girl" spot "bordered on dirty tactics." Wright actually did veto the "Pregnant Woman" commercial conceived and executed by one of the DDB men. This film showed an expectant mother walking through a park with a little child while a background voice depicted the dangers of fallout to children born and yet-to-be-born, and how the President, unlike Barry Goldwater, supported the Nuclear Test Ban Treaty.[118]

Thus, it would appear that on several significant matters, differences in viewpoints existed not only between the media staff-agency group and the traditional political leaders, but perhaps among the entire group of top White House advisers and staff. The burden of the evidence is that conflicts over basic values and the purposes of the campaign dominated all of the relationships in this crucial area of campaign public relations. And, if the goals of these different kinds of people are analyzed, the development of such serious differences could almost be predicted. As we have pointed out earlier, traditional political leaders are interested in maintaining power and controlling personnel when they are in power. They are also faced with the problems of raising campaign funds and are stuck with the post-campaign debts once the shouting has ended. A fairly small turnout at the polls, if all indications point to a victory for them, is of no great concern. The public relations men and other communications professionals, on the other hand, have no continuity of political ambition. They would like to get the word out as effectively and imaginatively as possible, so that they can take pride in their work and the results they hope it will bring. They are more concerned with control of issues than control of personnel. They would like to get paid, presumably as much as possible, so fund-raising problems are not their cup of tea. And, as a measure of their success, they take pride in evidence that they have begun some soul-searching dialogue on the part of the electorate—and the best confirmation that the dialogue *has* taken place is, from their point of view, a massive turnout on Election Day of people who have come to see things as they do. The campaign, then, becomes for them a sort of massive adult education and marketing operation all rolled up into one.

However, the Doyle Dane Bernbach–Lloyd Wright–Bill Moyers efforts of 1964 were not really adult education; they were based not on substance but on emotion. An important objective was to deliver a personal jolt to Barry Goldwater, and this they apparently did, perhaps even provoking him, in his own defense, to try even harder to defend the positions that were being attacked. And they were, to be sure, somewhat tenuous, and rather scary, positions to begin with.

There was another striking and somewhat precedent-breaking aspect to the DDB commercials: the President, running for reelection, said nothing on any of them. In fact, he was not so much as pictured. There was apparently some criticism of this by certain Democrats, and repeated suggestions were made during the summer for alternative uses of television, most of which were opposed by DDB, Wright, and Moyers. But after the convention and the first bursts of criticism on the "Daisy Girl" and the "Ice-Cream Cone," the White House decided to add two television shows featuring the President himself. Seven films were made, and all were shown toward the end of the campaign. The cost was some $2,000,000—all of it in excess of the allocated television budget. Four of the films were five-minute spots in which Johnson discussed foreign affairs, nuclear responsibility, domestic matters, and economic policy. There were also three half-hour programs in which the President was interviewed by some young people, a ladies' group, and a group of businessmen. As for the DDB commercials, only one ran more than sixty seconds. This was a five-minute "Young Republican" spot in which a Republican voter explained why he would vote for the President and not the senator: "My party made a bad mistake . . . in San Francisco. And I am going to vote against this mistake on November third."[119]

An interesting sidelight on the Democrats' use of television in 1964: the greatest single television drive of the entire campaign was conducted in Texas by the Democratic National Committee to make sure that the Lone Star State stayed with L.B.J. all the way. Of the seventeen states in which the Democrats concentrated the DDB spots, Texas was far in the lead, with 1,345 spots as against 823 spots in California and 410 in New York, each of which is more than half again as large as Texas in population.[120]

The President's mass media campaign was supplemented by a round of personal appearances designed to have maximum political effect. A large staff group hammered out a speaking schedule, but the President's frequent inclination to make last-minute changes in his plans forced many key public relations decisions to be made on a rather uncertain basis—often hastily, in the face of unexpected events. Wilson McCarthy, the chief advance man, attempted to maintain a firm three- or four-day schedule, which he submitted as a daily plan to the White House for President Johnson's approval, for, in the last analysis, it was the President himself who decided where he would go. McCarthy and his thirty-seven-man advance staff had all had experience in 1960 or in earlier campaigns. "They liked to contrast their effectiveness," say Lamb and Smith, "with that of the 167-man Humphrey operation." The advance men and other public relations functionaries apparently did their crowd-drawing work quite well, because the President was most impressed by the size of the crowds at his early appearances. In fact, he responded by expanding his schedule of personal appearances and made a number of unannounced or very hastily arranged stops once he was on the road.[121]

The Johnson campaign was suddenly and unexpectedly faced with a major crisis in political public relations when Walter Jenkins, a leading member of the President's staff and one of his closest confidants, was picked up by the Washington police for alleged homosexual activity in the men's room of a local Y.M.C.A. There was a great deal of anxiety regarding the way in which the Republicans might choose to exploit the incident to their political advantage.

The Democrats first learned of the story on October 14, when an editor at the Washington *Star* called the White House to confirm the rumor of Jenkins' arrest. Jenkins himself took the call. With understandable emotion, he appealed for help to Abe Fortas, who in turn contacted Clark Clifford. Fortas and Clifford moved first to hospitalize Jenkins, who obviously had cracked under the excruciating load of the campaign, as perhaps the hardest-working member of the personal staff of a very demanding President. The two Washington attorneys then spoke personally with Washington editors in an effort to convince them not to publish the story. In some cases, Fortas and Clifford were too late, and in others the editors actually received their first information on the case from the two Johnson cronies. The President and much of his staff were campaigning in New York. Mrs. Johnson, in Washington, made the first public statement in reaction to the case, expressing her sadness and hope for Jenkins' recovery and the well-being of his family. Meanwhile, Fortas, acting on instructions from Johnson, visited Jenkins at the hospital and quickly obtained his resignation from the White House staff.[122]

Also behind the scenes, the Republican National Committee had been tipped off to the circumstances of the arrest before the story came to the attention of the news media. Republican leaders apparently felt that the potential political advantage was too tempting to pass by. Chairman Dean Burch and p.r. director Lou Guylay contacted Midwest newspapers friendly to the Goldwater crusade and told them they planned to hold a news conference regarding a suppressed story. The editors of these papers then put pressure on their news services in Washington to release an accurate version of the incident. Finally, news of the affair moved on the wires, and the Burch news conference proved unnecessary; but the threat of such an event had great effect.[123]

As Theodore White reconstructs the President's reactions to the incident, it appears that one of Johnson's first considerations—after that of national security—was with the public relations implications of the affair. Characteristically, L.B.J. looked to the pollsters for help in deciding how to proceed. Still in New York, where he had spoken at the annual Alfred E. Smith Memorial Dinner, the President had Jack Valenti telephone pollster Oliver Quayle and ask him to appear immediately at the Waldorf. Quayle drove at seventy miles an hour from his Bronxville home and made it to the President's suite in twenty-five minutes. Once there, he was commissioned to do an instant opinion poll designed to determine how many votes could shift to Goldwater as a result of Jenkins' misfortune. Quayle's staff manned the telephones the next morning, as presidential advisers tried to determine whether Johnson should proceed as scheduled with a broadcast on the anniversary of the Nuclear Test Ban Treaty or devote his air time to clarifying the Jenkins matter. By afternoon, the pollsters had enough response for Quayle to reach the presidential party in Brooklyn and report that no significant shift could be detected. The wisest course, he advised, would be to go on campaigning without making the affair appear to be an emergency.[124] The President accepted this advice and conducted himself accordingly.

Although it is difficult to say what considerations other than those of public relations—or even politics—were involved in the President's decision, from a professional public relations point of view the Democratic response to the incident was handled masterfully. As Lamb and Smith point out, "the extensive political experience of both the campaign leaders and staff led them to interpret the event as a bad, but in a sense 'natural' part of politics." Dirty linen turns up in a large percentage of political campaigns. The Eagleton affair is the most recent example. The decision against condemning Jenkins was also a positive one: to treat him with kindness and sympathy, to quickly disassociate him from the presidency, to make no further comments, and to stress once more the central themes of the campaign. The President correctly assumed that citizens were more concerned with his ability to cope with national security than with his association with Jenkins. As one respondent told Lamb and Smith, the President was sympathetic and firm with Jenkins. His response was pragmatic. In effect, he told his associate: "In your position you make me vulnerable; so you have to quit."[125]

Two other comments should be made. One is that, faced with a negative story, a public relations man can always hope that a more monumental news story will break, to shift attention away from his client. He prays for this as one fighting a forest fire prays for rain. The President's luck was with him, and other events began to hit the headlines in a most fortuitous manner. The Premier of the Soviet Union, Nikita S. Khrushchev, was deposed on October 14–15. On October 16 Communist China announced that it had exploded an atomic bomb. And in Great Britain, the Labour Party won the General Election on the 15th for the first time in thirteen years. Meanwhile, the St. Louis Cardinals, defeating the invincible New York Yankees, won the World Series. So almost as quickly as it had come up, the Jenkins crisis passed from the front pages.

Secondly, there is one bit of political shrewdness here not generally discussed in connection with the incident. This is that the political decision-makers really had no way of knowing for sure just how widespread homosexual tendencies, not to mention various other "secret" sexual practices, are among the general population. Aside from practicing homosexuals, many individuals may have had an incident of what our society considers sexual "deviation" somewhere in their lives or harbored longings that went unfulfilled. So a less humane treatment of Jenkins might well have actually antagonized an unpredictably large number of voters.

The incident also clearly reveals how heavily a presidential candidate—and the incumbent Chief Executive of the United States—relied on the outcome of polls (indeed, hasty polls that used relatively small samples) to help him make crucial political decisions.

In fact, at one point during the course of the campaign, President Johnson told a group of correspondents on his airplane that the Democrats had spent half a million dollars on polls. This was a considerable overestimate, but the President was proud to emphasize his reliance on such surveys. He said that President Kennedy had taught him to use polls. They were valuable, he said, only to tell you what the people were thinking about.[126]

The obvious inference is that if you pay for polls to tell you what people are thinking about, you do so because you intend to shape your campaign accordingly. You talk to the voters about what the polls say they have on their minds, and no doubt do your best to tell them what the polls say they want to hear—or at least you avoid telling them what they don't want to hear.

Thus, Lyndon Johnson, very much unlike Barry Goldwater, was expert at structuring his campaign so as to achieve feedback, the two-way communication vital to intelligent, effective public relations. His first concern was with a massive electoral victory, and he wanted to achieve it by exercising personal control over the campaign. To achieve these two goals,

> . . . the President followed the practice of finding the best men for campaign jobs and attaching them as closely as possible to himself. . . . A surprisingly large group of leaders was within the President's immediate purview. He saw them often, even daily, seeking their views and giving them his. Their views and judgments were a rich source of feedback, enabling Johnson to respond quickly and relevantly to a variety of operational problems of the campaign.[127]

So Lyndon Baines Johnson, the thirty-sixth President of the United States, won reelection by a margin of 15,951,083 votes. This was the greatest vote, the greatest margin, and the greatest percentage of the total vote (61 percent) that any President had ever polled.[128]

The Johnson campaign of 1964 had been a somewhat unique form of public relations politics; the public relations practices were an artful combination of the professional and the highly personal. The campaign dealt with issues, but only in such a way as to put the opponent on the defensive, not to bring forward any new ideology. Certainly no programs were introduced that represented anything like a radical departure from what had gone before. With the possible exception of the television spots, which we have reviewed, and the effort to capitalize upon Republican dissent by forming pro-Johnson campaign organizations of Republicans and businessmen, public relations tactics were only refined, not created. Perhaps if the Republican campaign had been more innovative in terms of political public relations, the Democrats would have had to respond in kind. But as things turned out, such was not the case. Furthermore, such creativity as did exist in the Democratic campaign—largely the Doyle Dane Bernbach television spots and publicity material—had been toned down considerably as a result of the active internal dissent of more traditional politicians. And as for speechmaking, Johnson's spontaneous remarks

> . . . served for the most part to translate carefully considered positions into a Johnsonian patois. By this time, Barry Goldwater's analogous statements were cautious and more controlled than Johnson's. But it was too late; Goldwater's efforts to soften his image as an erratic radical made little impression upon the voters.[129]

# Six:
# The 1968 Campaign

It was a year of political chaos. By 1968, the nation, in a sense, had reached the bottom of a decade. Halfway around the world, its young men gave their lives by the thousands to fulfill what the President of the United States insisted was an irrevocable commitment to the uncertain government of a tiny nation on a huge continent where the days of this country's presence were obviously numbered. Simultaneously, the country seemed almost to explode from within. Dissension over an unpopular war combined with the frustration of those who felt that in a society presumably designed to provide the greatest good for the greatest number, too many were simply not doing very well at all.

Suddenly, it seemed as though protest had been heaped upon protest, dissent upon dissent, discontent upon discontent, until, like an abandoned teapot, the country boiled over. To some, the Union itself seemed in greater danger than at any time since the era of the Civil War.

The President of the United States, having lost the "mandate" that had made him the most popularly elected Chief Executive in the history of his country three and a half years before, virtually resigned his office. He would not seek the second term that had seemed not long before to be a foregone conclusion. Lyndon Johnson would not have the nine years in office that he and most of his fellow citizens had for a time assumed would be his destiny. And the nation embarked upon the task of choosing his successor.

# The Pre-Nomination Campaigns

## *The Republicans*

RONALD REAGAN

With the Hollywood star system in operation in American politics, it was perhaps only a matter of time until someone who was an actual, honest-to-goodness, real-life Hollywood star might actually seek to ride that stardom into the White House. In a sense, it seemed perversely logical. All the techniques of the public relations profession and related crafts could be applied to turn a politician into a star, a process not too difficult to accomplish with the right combination of money and talent. So why not start with a star and politicize him to whatever degree might be necessary so as to attract enough box office to put his name in lights on the biggest marquee of them all—1600 Pennsylvania Avenue?

Governor Ronald Reagan of California is such a man. He had been a longtime leader of the Screen Actors Guild and a New Deal liberal of the first order while he was a popular and highly paid film star. But somehow, by the mid-fifties, it seemed that both of these qualities had changed. He had grown a little weak at the box office, he was not in great demand for leading film roles with spectacular salaries, and he had also grown increasingly conservative.

The emergence of this new Right Reagan seemed to have taken place during his work on the General Electric lecture circuit from 1954 to 1962. Reagan was under contract with GE at $125,000 per year (later rising to $150,000) to host the weekly half-hour "General Electric Theatre" on television and to spend twelve weeks annually touring GE's plants. The theory of the corporate public relations and industrial relations men at GE was that the presence of such a Hollywood celebrity, a member of the same big happy family as the night janitor in Schenectady, would enliven workers and management to the benefit of the stockholders. The assumption was that Reagan would reflect upon the Hollywood scene as he lectured, perhaps even sharing a morsel or two of "inside" filmland gossip with his new co-workers. Instead, Reagan chose such topics as "Losing Freedom by

Installments" and "Communist Subversion in Hollywood." Nevertheless, most of Reagan's lectures went over well—or at least until he upset the GE board of directors by using the Tennessee Valley Authority as a classic example of government overinterference in free enterprise. It seemed that TVA was a $50,000,000 client of GE's, and Reagan obligingly dropped the reference when GE chairman Ralph Cordiner said that it "would make my job easier."[1]

Reagan's basic lecture-circuit patois had been stropped to a keen edge by 1964. His ex-boss at GE, Ralph Cordiner, had become the balanced-budget finance chairman of Senator Barry Goldwater's presidential campaign, and that campaign also served to launch Reagan as a political figure. His vehicle was "The Speech," GE Lecture Number One, now redubbed, "A Time for Choosing." It was a sort of latter-day Herbert Hoover single-speech approach to life, combining some free enterprise pyrotechnics with a demolition job on federal expenditures. It made its national television debut on behalf of Goldwater in the closing weeks of the 1964 campaign, and the response was magnificent, even magnanimous. More than half a million dollars in political contributions were attributed to the telecast, and many Republicans "felt that Reagan was wasted as a cheerleader while Goldwater was out there fumbling passes." And, above all, Reagan spoke with great sincerity: "There is no reason to question Reagan's sincerity as a New Dealer, just as there is no reason to doubt his later ardor in the right-wing cause. He is plastic rather than perfidious."[2]

Not long after Reagan's debut as a pitchman in the 1964 campaign, in the days following the inauguration of Goldwater's triumphant opponent, a new California organization called the Friends of Ronald Reagan quietly came into being. Its most vociferous organizer was Henry Salvatori, a developer of oil exploration and drilling equipment and a backer of the Anti-Communist Voters League. Salvatori had both independent wealth and independent ideas about what qualified a man for the presidency. In a rare interview, he outlined those qualifications for Doris Klein of the Associated Press shortly after Reagan's election as governor of California in 1966:

> "People criticize Ronnie for having no political experience, but he has a great image, a way to get through to people. Look at the Goldwater experience. His philosophy was sound, but he didn't articulate it moderately. The Governor has a similar philosophy,

but he can express his thoughts. Look at John F. Kennedy. He didn't have much of a record as a Senator. But he made a great appearance—and had a beautiful wife. So does the Governor. Nancy Reagan doesn't have to take a back seat to anyone. And the Governor has plenty of time between now and the nomination to make a record as an administrator. But I don't believe people in other states really care much about what's happening in California anyway."[3]

Ronald Reagan had been helped in his efforts to become governor of California by our old friends, the Los Angeles firm of Spencer-Roberts & Associates. The professional managers and p.r. men at Spencer-Roberts had set a goal, which they obviously achieved, of making sure that Reagan was accepted by the voters not only as an actor but as a governor. About one million Californians found him more acceptable as a governor than the incumbent, Edmund G. "Pat" Brown. Brown had always been an underdog in the past— especially so four years before when he had rallied to beat former Vice President Richard Nixon and remain in the governor's chair. But this time, Brown came out looking like a bully. He attacked Reagan's right-wing disposition and his obvious absence of political and administrative experience. Spencer-Roberts advised Reagan to ignore Brown's attacks. He did. Brown stepped up his attacks and began to appear increasingly desperate. And by comparison, "Reagan suddenly was, of all things, a statesman."[4]

Spencer-Roberts had been engaged by Reagan in 1965 upon the recommendation of Barry Goldwater, who had been impressed by the job the firm had done against him when working for Nelson Rockefeller in the 1964 California presidential primary. Senator Thomas Kuchel and his staff, along with some other California Republican moderates and liberals, were outraged that Spencer-Roberts would be working for Reagan and would thus be unavailable to them. But Roberts explained the firm's motives: "After all, we have a staff and an overhead here. We need clients."[5]

The firm's efforts were geared to keep Reagan, who showed up first in the polls, in the lead, with no show of anger or temper, and with ample proof that he was a "mainstream Republican." Spencer-Roberts broadened the Goldwaterite group behind the film star to include some of the people who had been associated with Rockefeller in 1964, and threw a few Jews in among the WASPS for good measure.

Reagan committees were created all over the state. Each included at least one Rockefeller and one Kuchel man; if the group was large, a Nixon supporter was added. Thus, the "mainstream" image would emerge by association; Reagan couldn't possibly be a Bircher with such regular guys on his squad. In fact, Spencer-Roberts worked up a seven-hundred-word statement for their client on the subject of the Birch Society. In it, they had him advocate that Birchers should reach a decision concerning "the reckless and imprudent statements of their leader," Robert Welch, although Reagan made no recommendation as to what that decision ought to be. He said he sought no support from the society, did not say that he didn't want it, or that he would reject it if it were volunteered. Whenever Birch-type questions were raised, copies of the statement were on hand.[6]

Spencer-Roberts obviously helped convince a majority of California voters that Ronald Reagan was a responsible man, that he could be trusted as governor, and that he was ideologically acceptable to them. Polls were taken at the outset of the campaign and Reagan's issues and the poll findings were on the same track. He was anti-crime; everyone was. He was for stern measures to put down ghetto violence; so were most people in California—except those who were poor, black, Mexican-American, and/or frustrated, in which case they voted for Pat Brown or stayed home on Election Day.[7]

William E. Roberts, one of the partners in the firm that helped make Ronald Reagan a "statesman," told a Republican National Committee Public Relations Seminar in 1967 how it was done. His statement is worth quoting at some length:

"What were some of [our] public relations problems. . . . we had a candidate who had no experience for public office whatsoever against an opponent who had twenty-three years of public office and eight years as Governor. From the beginning we felt that there was nothing to be gained from . . . trying to become more knowledgeable than he was on a given issue. . . .

"Our answer to that was to be very candid and honest about it and indicate that Governor Reagan was not a professional politician. He was a citizen politician. Therefore, we had an automatic defense. He didn't have to know all the answers. He didn't have to have the experience. A citizen politician's not expected to know all of the answers to all of the issues. . . .

"As a matter of fact, before the end of the campaign, he hit it so well and so hard that Governor Brown was on the defensive for being a professional politician. . . .

"Another problem not quite so serious but still one to be dealt with was the fact that he was an actor. Because he was an actor, it was charged that he was just going through the motions and acting out the part of running for Governor with no sincerity. . . .

"So . . . it was mandatory . . . that a question-and-answer period follow his speech. This strategy immediately told the audience that he did have a grasp of the issues. . . . Not knowing what the questions would be, they were impressed by the fact that he had knowledge on the subject and was able to deliver it to them. . . .

"Nobody who was bloodied and tarred in the '64 race occupied a major front position in the '66 election. Not that they weren't good people. But they weren't involved where the public would see them as far as the frontal operations were concerned.

"We dealt with the issues that we felt the people were interested in. We arrived at that decision via surveys, via the steering committee's own reaction, and, frankly, via the Q-and-A session."[8]

And so on. The point is, Reagan got one million more votes than Brown. And a new Republican star was born. The midwives were Spencer-Roberts & Associates.

It was quite soon after Reagan's election as governor of California that Salvatori and his friends decided to point their new hot property toward the White House. The whole project was circumspect—elaborately so. Chester et al. have said that it required from Reagan himself "considerable talent for what is known in the Presidency-hunting business as 'honest lying.'" The campaign was even to require some undercover work, later described by one of its prime movers as being "like something out of a James Bond movie."[9]

The underground delegate-hunting operation called for the talents of an F. Clifton White, and that is exactly whom Salvatori and the Reagan backers hired for the job. As we have seen, White is not a conventional sort of campaign consultant, if there is such a thing. Political campaigns were not White's full-time job at the time, although he had been lecturing steadily on the subject with his old friend, fellow professional, and political rival Joe Napolitan (who was later to become consultant for Humphrey's presidential campaign, and then to co-found with White a new professional society for campaign consultants). White, after the Goldwater debacle, had gone back to spending a good deal of his time earning fees from corporations as a "public affairs consultant," advising business on government relations. The Reagan campaign, like that of Goldwater, seemed, however, to intrigue him.[10]

But the job was a difficult one, even for a man of White's formidable experience and talent. He needed up-to-date political intelligence and had been away from national politics for three years. The power structure had changed within his own party, and many of those who had been on top back in '64 were now out. Richard Nixon's delegate-hunting system was perhaps one of the most sophisticated ever put together, and White was one bright man fighting a faceless army. He went around the country seeking help from old friends, but there were inevitably those states in which he went to the wrong people. For example, Butch Butler, a Houston oil man who headed Texans for Reagan, appreciated White's help but complained: "It's no good. He's working the wrong side of the street." White's terms of reference were also difficult for him to work with. His plot was the reverse of the Goldwater effect: the senator had seized the convention, but Reagan had to proceed with stealth. He was a non-candidate. So White was cast not in his accustomed role of public proselytizer, but rather had to assume the "objective facade of a taker of soundings."[11]

Meanwhile, in the fall of 1967, Thomas Reed, a millionaire's son who had made a million or two on his own in real estate and oil geology before retiring at age thirty-two to work on Reagan's gubernatorial campaign, left the governor's staff. He announced that he was returning to private life, but, actually, his mission was to start the James Bond phase of the Reagan-for-President operation.[12]

Public relations methods were to be a central phase of the Reed operation. But he was unable to make use of the candidate himself. His solution was to resort instead to films of Reagan. He assembled in November a unit consisting of Greg Snazelle, a San Francisco television commercial producer, and John Mercer, vice president of the San Francisco advertising agency of Meltzer, Aron, and Lemen, Inc. Both men had worked with Reed two years earlier on the gubernatorial campaign. Their function then had been to produce television spots presenting Reagan in a more liberal light in the northern part of the state than he had found necessary or expedient in southern California. But the new project was more ambitious. After all, said Snazelle, "Reagan was the first politician to come along literally tailor-made for the media." But the governor's name was in no way to be associated with the project. The film-makers could shoot the governor in his office and home, but Reed told them that if reporters asked what they were doing they were to say they were "shooting footage for stock." Meanwhile, Reed collected all the existing political film of Reagan he could find. The new film was to be combined with existing footage into a half-hour campaign "biography" of the governor.[13]

The overt side of the campaign was to be initiated by Citizens for Reagan groups around the country. Part of Reed's job was to see to it that such groups would be established firmly by the spring of 1968. They were, however, to have a "self-generated" image, and no one was to know from whence the enterprise emerged. Citizens for Reagan headquarters were ultimately set up in Topeka, Kansas, under a local savings-and-loan executive, Henry Bubb, a veteran of the 1940 Wendell Willkie campaign. All operations were to be centered there. All information about Reagan was to be disseminated from Topeka, C.I.A.-style. So Reed, where secrecy was thought necessary, assumed a new fictional identity, that of a Kansas businessman, John Kurwitz. According to Chester et al., this resulted in such absurdities as Mercer and Snazelle receiving teletype instructions from Kurwitz in Topeka, when they knew Reed was in his California office a few blocks away. They would have to phone Reed, ask for Kurwitz, leave their number with the secretary, and wait five minutes for a call from Reed. There was only minimal contact between the film unit and the governor's staff, although Reagan's press secretary, former Washington newspaperman Lyn Nofziger, would drop by from time to time just to let the operation know it was being supervised.[14]

It was agreed that the Reagan film should emphasize the image of Richard Nixon as a political loser. At the same time, Reagan would be made to come across as a first-rate vote-getter. If such a film were not to boomerang, it needed a good deal of public relations delicacy. For example, it was reluctantly decided not to use any portion of Reed's prize find, a complete videotape of Nixon's unfortunate press conference following his loss of the 1962 California gubernatorial election ("You won't have Dick Nixon to kick around anymore"). That acquisition was, however, to prove useful early in 1968 when some of Nixon's aides thought of entering their man in the California primary against favorite son Reagan and were told by Reagan's staff that some in the governor's camp might feel obliged to rerun the 1962 tape if Nixon came into the race. (The eventual compromise provided that neither Reagan's favorite-son candidacy nor his delegate slate would be challenged in the primary, provided the California delegation reflected all strains of Republican opinion.[15]

The final scenario for the film biography was to show Reagan in all of the roles he had played in the past—orator, union organizer, diligent executive, "slayer of the giant vote-getter Pat Brown"—all the roles except that for which he was best known, that of actor. In a sequence aimed pointedly at President-makers, Brown was shown beating Republican leader William Knowland in 1958, Republican leader Richard Nixon in 1962 (with a shot of the disconsolate Nixon making his concession statement), and finally a triumphantly radiant Reagan toppling Brown. The finished product, entitled "Ronald Reagan: Citizen Governor," was ready in March 1968. It was screened by Nofziger, but not Reagan, on the basis that a sneak preview would cramp his style in disclaiming all interest in such projects on his behalf.[16]

It was decided not to use the film in states holding early primaries. The theory here was that a low vote in those states didn't much matter and could even be advantageous by making later voting results look like a surge for the governor. There were no efforts made in New Hampshire in March, and Reagan got one percent of the vote there. There was some activity on his behalf in Wisconsin, but not much in the way of a public relations program, and there the governor received 11 percent of his party's vote. The film was unveiled in Nebraska, a hawkish, conservative state almost ideal for a Reagan drive. The Californian received 22 percent of the vote when the Republican primary was held there in May.[17]

The big Reagan effort was made in connection with the May 28 Oregon primary. The film unit went to work updating the biography. Reagan's oratorical piece at the end of the film seemed dated in light of the King assassination, the Pueblo capture, and the escalation of law and order rhetoric. The producers suggested that their subject speak out publicly on more newsworthy themes so that they could film that speech as a substitute for some of the old footage. The governor obligingly invited the cameramen to an Oakland fund-raising dinner. It proved a tough assignment. According to one film-unit member, the seventy diners were "smashed out of their minds." Furthermore, Reagan, used to larger, more attentive gatherings, stumbled on his lines. Nevertheless, Snazelle, with a combination of deft editing and canned applause, came up with a version he thought acceptable. Reagan, however, was so concerned about what he was sure had been a clumsy performance that he broke the ground rules, screened the film himself, and give it his final approval. The "honest-lying" stage had reached its apogee.[18]

Reagan's Oregon operation was well financed and included some outstanding local Republican leaders. Operating with an open-ended media budget (Reagan's opponents claim he spent $200,000 in Oregon), the Reagan organization shelled out to televise the "biography" six times—and the ratings and reviews were good. Snazelle and Mercer beefed up the television bombast with a series of sixty-second commercials produced from man-on-the-street interviews (for example, "Nixon's okay, but he's a loser. Now that Reagan . . . !"). Reagan, by the way, never appeared in Oregon. He ended up with 23 percent of the vote, a total that disappointed Reed and the other insiders. The primary operation, now nearing its end, had yielded mediocre results. The strategy, then, moved from public relations at the grass roots to one of building prairie fires among delegates to the Republican convention, southern delegates in particular.[19]

It is interesting to note that the national polls played a negative role in Reagan's drive for the nomination. The strategy was to avoid comparisons with other candidates by keeping him off the polling rosters of Harris, Gallup, et al. Strenuous denials were issued whenever an enterprising reporter sniffed out indications that something might be in the works. Polls, in any case, would have doubtless shown Reagan running behind Nixon and Rockefeller. In fact, one of the latter's secret weapons was a convention-eve poll showing Reagan running almost as badly against Humphrey as Goldwater had done against Johnson in '64. Rockefeller people intended to flood the convention with copies of the poll if the balloting ever polarized into a straight Reagan-Rockefeller battle, which it did not.[20]

Reagan, of course, never made it in 1968, but this is not to say he will not be around for some time. He is a national figure, win or lose. There continue to be powerful interests who are backing him and hiring powerful experts to help him out. Reagan, meanwhile, responds to pressures of the moment and does so with a sense of small-town righteousness.

Chester, Hodgson, and Page sized him up as

> ". . . a public relations man, not a policy-maker. . . . He can sell the policy, but he cannot make it. Playing to the camera, a technique which few politicians or reporters master, is Reagan's forte.

... To ask whether Reagan is good or bad is, in a sense, an irrelevant question. He is a force—whether for good or ill, depending entirely on which direction he is pointed and who is at the controls.[21]

### NELSON ROCKEFELLER

Nelson Rockefeller was at it again in 1968: the graying, dapper, spendthrift pied piper of Republican presidential politics, tripping lightly but steadily toward the White House, scattering in his wake a luxuriant flow of policy pronouncements, position papers, staff analyses, fact-finding trips, speeches, television commercials, pamphlets, campaign biographies, businessmen's committees, and other Rockefeller-type paraphernalia. Rockefeller was not being pretentious. He just operated like a Rockefeller, and more so all the time. The more you want the presidency, the more you spend trying to get it.

All of this had been amply illustrated in Rockefeller's winning gubernatorial campaign of 1966. Bringing him in for a third term and making him the nation's senior governor in years of experience, his 1966 New York campaign was perhaps the most expensive non-presidential campaign in the history of American politics. It was an imaginative effort, utilizing some of the best talent and ideas that the advertising and public relations professions had to offer. It was, as well, a ruthless campaign, sparing not less than an estimated $5,750,000 to steamroller the opponent, New York City Council President Frank O'Connor. Says James Perry:

> Someone else one day will spend as much money and spend it just as well. And, almost certainly, the techniques Rockefeller used in New York will be built into the nation's first new-style Presidential campaign.[23]

The 1966 Rockefeller campaign for reelection as governor of the state of New York is described by Perry in fascinating detail. It was an effort that employed hundreds of people, not only in the campaign, but in a pre-campaign effort to "refurbish the Governor," when the polls showed him slipping. Through one of the Interpublic complex's agencies, Jack Tinker & Partners, television was used in more advanced and technically brilliant ways than had ever been the case in previous political campaigns, whether for the presidency or other offices. The governor appeared in none of his own commercials in '66; they were done by professional actor Ed Binns, the voice of Alka-Seltzer and Gillette, who was also busy recording the Milton Shapp commercials for Joseph Napolitan in the Pennsylvania general election. Eye-catching campaign materials were specially designed for a huge variety of special groups—"It was out of this world," said campaign aide William L. Pfeiffer. "We had something for every group except the Times Square prostitutes."[23]

When it was all over in 1966, Rockefeller had outspent O'Connor about 6 to 1, and beat him 2,690,626 to 2,298,363—figures that seem to imply that Rockefeller could have been beaten had he not had so much money, so much talent on his payroll, so much time to plan. Rockefeller may have been a product in a "battered and dusty package," but he was well marketed. During one October week, seventy-four Rockefeller television spots were run in New York City. They were seen in 91 percent of all the television homes in the city (about 5,600,000 out of 6,000,000 New York City homes had television in 1966) and seen an average of 9.8 times in each home.[24] It was almost surrealistic—"Forget that tired, old Rockefeller," the consumer was being told. "Buy this one instead—bright, new Nelson, more vigorous and able than ever." New Yorkers, of course, bought the new product, and it did perform rather reliably for them, even if some of the wonders promised by the commercials didn't quite materialize and some of the implications about the competition weren't quite accurate. But to sell the delegates to the 1968 Republican National Convention was another matter.

Rockefeller's strategy in seeking his party's presidential nomination in 1968 was to attempt to appeal to the people over the heads of the politicians. But his tactics had to be different from those of Eugene McCarthy, who had chosen the route of the primaries. Rockefeller's decision to enter—or rather, to reenter—the race for the nomination had been made too late to sew up any delegates through the primaries. Nixon had been engaged in a direct and grueling delegate-persuading operation around the country for two years or more. His imminent success was evident. And he had, it should be observed, done the job without much publicity. Rockefeller, on the other hand, had to go to the media. His object was to influence public opinion or, more accurately, to influence the polls. The pollsters talk to Democrats and Independents, as well as Republicans, and the Rockefeller team hoped that the poll results would reflect Rockefeller's rising popularity with voters of all political persuasions as his media exposure escalated. The polls, in turn, could be used as a compelling argument with the delegates. Those polls, therefore, had to show not just that Rockefeller was more popular than Nixon, but that Rockefeller could beat *any* Democrat while Nixon could not.[25]

The primacy of media considerations was evident by the middle of April 1968 when the governor was again seriously considering a bid for the nomination. Midwestern businessman J. Irwin Miller set up a Rockefeller for President Committee, run by Minnesotan Jerry Olsen. For the sake of appearances, then, the committee was given a basically midwestern flavor on the surface. But Rockefeller political adviser George Hinman was again pulling all of the strings from New York behind the scenes. As soon as he thought the governor was in the race, he called Tom Losee, head of the Houston office of McCann-Erickson, the country's second largest group of advertising agencies. Losee had worked in Rockefeller's campaigns in some capacity since 1958. When Losee flew to New York, Hinman told him Rockefeller had not yet made a firm decision, but just might be in the picture. Losee contacted Gene Case, a partner and the top "creative man" at Jack Tinker & Partners of New York, part of the McCann-Erickson/Interpublic Group.[26]

The Tinker agency had been hired by Dr. William Ronan, then dean of the New York University School of Public Administration and Social Services and chief intellectual adviser to the governor, to put together Rockefeller's "exemplary" advertising campaign in connection with his 1966 reelection in New York. Appropriately, the Tinker firm had a record of "restoring" products, Alka-Seltzer and Braniff/International among them.[27]

As we have observed, TV advertising in the 1966 gubernatorial campaign was regarded by professional admen as a model of such efforts. One commercial in particular, in which a largemouth bass was interviewed about water pollution, is regarded as a classic of political advertising. (Other "classic" Tinker projects: the Braniff image pep-up in which the airplanes were painted wild pastels and the stewardesses dressed in exotic garb, and the "breakthrough" Alka-Seltzer commercials showing in quick succession the moving stomachs of many different kinds of people doing many different things, from holding a pneumatic hammer to belly-dancing.)

Losee had worked in the 1966 campaign with Ronan and the Tinker group, and he put together the same team in 1968: Gene Case; Bob Wilvers, the art director; Myron McDonald, the head of the firm and a marketing man specializing in planning; Clifford Botway, and Dr. Herta M. Herzog, a Viennese sociologist. Altogether, about fifty people were made available by the agency to work on the Rockefeller account.[28]

The Tinker group went to work on May 1, and by Memorial Day it was able to present a detailed media plan, budget, and specimen ads at a meeting at the governor's New York City headquarters on West 55th Street. The admen presented a twenty-nine page strategy paper, notable for the way in which these men—competent technicians, even artists, in devising creative ways to sell products—attempted to assess the political situation at that point in time for the governor and would-be President:[29]

> "The American crisis is not the war in Vietnam, nor rioting in the cities, nor inflation, nor deterioration of respect among our friends, nor any specific. It is a failure of leadership. . . . America is, has been and (God Willing) always will be hungry for heroes."

And as for others who would lead, the Tinker people threw in some political character analysis of their own:

> "Eugene McCarthy . . . A Pied Piper who almost bridged the generation gap until the visceral pyrotechnics of Kennedy interrupted the quiet communication. . . . Robert Kennedy . . . A controversial figure. . . . In him, the recollection of a hero who fell in Dallas . . . shorter, more prolific progeny-wise, more enigmatic, less outgoing, but becoming so. . . . Kennedy's problem is to establish himself as a whole hero and not just as a sibling substitute. . . . Richard Nixon . . . It is difficult just now to see him as the leader."

But a client's virtues are without number. Rockefeller, they said, was:

> "The only potential leader . . . the man with the guts to do the right job . . . a man from a famous American family. . . ."

Then this brilliant and original analysis of American political opinion:

> "It is clear today that American society is divided between those who wish slower change and those who wish more rapid change."

The Tinker "strategy paper" went on to cite the preliminary report of Rockefeller house pollster Lloyd Free on public opinion in 1968 as demonstrating that:

> ". . . certain of the Governor's positions coincide with those sought by the majority in many cases. It is also clear that when one cuts through the bafflegab of label rhetoric to real meanings, other of his positions can be seen productive of the actions and consequent results people really want. . . . What is really wanted is better "big government." . . . And in the heart of its Judaeo-Christian economic ethos, the American public really knows it is not going to get something for nothing."

Apparently the Tinker people were trying to tell Rockefeller that the best case he could make for himself, in terms of his image-building activities with the general public, was as a "new leader." As we have seen, he was billed the same way when he was running for re-election in New York in 1966. This seems all the more ironic in view of the fact that Rockefeller had been in the presidential lists at Republican National Conventions since 1960. Nixon had been his rival for the nomination eight years before and would be again this time. But it was a "new" Nixon, so now there would also have to be a "new" Rockefeller. And as he set about making his case, the Tinker strategy was also saying, it would not hurt the governor's ultimate political chances if he would go ahead and tell people that he was a liberal, well, sort of a liberal, anyhow. The governor had been given essentially this same advice by another sage of Madison Avenue (444 Madison Avenue, headquarters of *Newsweek*, for which he did a column), Emmet Hughes. On May 19, Hughes told Rockefeller in a private and profusely underscored memo that he should make clear

> "as *sharply* and *incisively* as possible—*the CHOICE that you are presenting to the Republican Party.*
>
> "This means making clear—without any explicit dealing in personalities as such—that Nelson Rockefeller and Richard Nixon stand for *two profoundly different views.* . . . Nixon does *not* want such a choice defined. His haziness on issues may be natural, but it is not accidental. It is his deliberate *intent* to *blur* issues between you and him. *We must not conspire with him in doing this.* Your *polls—not the presumed preconceptions of delegates.* . . . the decisive favorable influence *on* the delegates *will* be the polls. . . ."[30]

Hughes' language might have been more succinct than that of the Tinker agency—he had been at this sort of thing longer—although whether he expressed himself less pretentiously is debatable. Certainly, he could underscore as well as any adman. It was his *role* to give the governor this sort of advice. As for where he got his information on the certitude of the polls' influence on delegates, that is rather mysterious. But it did serve to determine the strategy of the Rockefeller campaign, a strategy which hardly proved effective. For political commitments are commitments, and a delegate who promises his vote is trading off one of the few political advantages he has, for his own good reasons. So even when the polls did go the governor's way, there seemed to be little excitement about it inside the Rockefeller camp. The in-group there, however, somehow seemed to go on believing, to the last, that if Hughes said delegates were going to be influenced by the polls, then, dammit, they *would* be influenced. Otherwise, something must be wrong with *them* out *there*—boobs from Omaha and whatnot—because the Rockefeller team was too superb and spending too much money to be wrong about the country.

Once the goal of effectively influencing national opinion polls is accepted, then Tinker's media plan   contrasted with its advice on political strategy—was logical. It was designed to focus on:

1. Representative markets of large, movable delegate blocs.

2. Markets representative of population segments which were potentially favorable and could therefore be moved through clear and dramatic statements of the Rockefeller position.

Sixteen big northern states with one-third of the national population and more than one-half of the delegates to the convention were listed as "communication targets." Tinker also suggested a three-pronged attack on public opinion:

1. A campaign of sixty-second evening spot television commercials in thirty major markets, supposedly aimed precisely at voters most likely to react favorably when questioned by poll-takers about Rockefeller.

2. Three minutes a week for seven weeks of national network television advertising. Tinker argued that TV, properly used, "is the most emotionally evocative of all media. Its topicality brings the futility of Vietnam into 50 million homes nightly." They calculated that the three minutes a week of

network time would deliver Rockefeller's story to 90 percent of all American homes.

3. An original newspaper advertising campaign. Said Losee, "People see so much advertising. Fifteen hundred, two thousand messages a day coming in. People think it's bullshit. Political advertising, to get through, has to be simple. It has to be dignified. Not that same old hack political gobbledy-gook." So Tinker recommended a Rockefeller insert in forty papers stating, "in referential, documentary black and white, the Governor's position on the key issues. As contrasted to the general non-positions of Richard Nixon." This done, the ads were bound into a special supplement for the Miami *Herald* and issued at the time of the opening of the convention, thus giving each delegate a bold statement of the Rockefeller positions.[31]

This program, like most of those planned for a Rockefeller, was expensive. The media budget ran some $4,500,000: roughly $2,000,000 for the television spots, $1,000,000 for network television, and $1,500,000 for newspapers. The advertising campaign began in mid-June and was scheduled to peak ten days before the August 5 opening of the convention—on the day when the last Gallup interviews were being taken. Thus, no money would be spent in the days immediately before the Miami Beach gathering, since there would be no point in influencing those already polled.[32]

This, of course, speaks to technique, rather than to what issues all of these messages would deal with. In theory, operating strictly on the basis of public relations politics, polls would identify not only sections of the electorate that could be won, but also the issues that must be stressed to attract those votes winnable. Then a media campaign could be designed to address itself to those issues. But that is not what happened in Rockefeller's campaign. The media campaign was based on polls carried out in February. Lloyd Free, using a national sample of Gallup interviews, asked people to say how worried they were about twenty-one problems or concerns that he had prepared on the basis of earlier polls. Respondents' answers were graded on a four-point scale and used to compose another list of problems worrying the American voters. The resulting list revealed a rather conservative set of priorities. Concerns on the minds of voters, according to the Free surveys, included "law and order," strong military defense, government spending, moral standards, and so on. All of these rated much higher than such characteristically liberal concerns as poverty, racial problems, and the schools, which all came out on the bottom of the list. "Rebuilding our cities," for example, a logical Rockefeller theme, ranked 21 of 21. Based on this list, a public relations adviser or practitioner of the "new politics" would advise a campaign stressing toughness in foreign policy, preparedness in defense, and law and order ahead of social reforms on the domestic scene. Rockefeller's campaign would then have reflected a profile of the voters' state of mind, according to the polls.[33] It might or might not have actually mirrored Rockefeller's own concerns and priorities.

Free attempted to reinforce the twenty-one-item laundry list and its conservative emphasis by pointing out to Rockefeller in a Memorial Day meeting, and at other more private sessions, that it would be worthless for him to go after poor and black votes or even their weight in the opinion polls. Free, a liberal Republican by conviction, apparently made the point as a dispassionate judgment, unrelated to his own conviction or Rockefeller's of what would really be right or wrong except in terms of votes. He pointed out that the black vote represents some 9 percent of the electorate, and that 90 percent of this vote would probably go to the Democrats in November regardless of anything a Republican candidate might say or do. Furthermore, any support that might be won among the blacks or the poor would likely be won at the expense of support from large blocs of white Republicans or Independents. Free's "scientific" judgment was buttressed by that of such politicians as former Republican National Chairman Leonard Hall and New York Lieutenant-Governor Malcolm Wilson, who were in charge of the Rockefeller delegate-wooing operation and viewed any emphasis on liberal issues as counterproductive to what they were attempting to bring off.[34]

Despite advice to the contrary, the Rockefeller ads tended much more to the liberal than the conservative side. For example, Free's polls, as we have seen, had placed "rebuilding our cities" as the last of the concerns of the sampled electorate, but one ad nevertheless showed the candidate talking about urban renewal in Harlem ("We have faith in the heart of Harlem, and we have faith in the people who live there"). He also did a rather "unscientific" one-minute commercial opening with a drum roll and a picture of a dark, wet slum street. Rockefeller himself read the narration:

"Three thousand black men were among those brave Americans who had died so far in Vietnam.

"One hundred thousand black men will come home from Vietnam. What will they make of America, these men who risk their lives for the American Dream, and come home to find the American Slumber? What will they make of the slums where, too often, jobs are as rare as hope?

"This is Nelson Rockefeller, and I say they deserve more than this. I say they deserve an equal chance. They deserve decent housing, decent jobs. And the schooling and training to fill these jobs.

"To those who cry, 'law and order,' I say, 'to keep law and order there must be justice and opportunity!' [As he made this last point, a black man loomed out of the shadows and walked toward one camera.]"[35]

As Chester et al. point out, justice and opportunity were apparently not the first things to occur to some viewers as the strange black man walked quickly out of the dark street. Free called the spot a "flop," and said that "a lot of people, especially women, didn't like it at all. You see, you couldn't really tell who was coming toward you. It was a little alarming for many people." The spot had some quick repercussions, not the least of which was the flood of complaints from professional politicians around the country. Said one Rockefeller staff member:

"Our campaign was pretty schizophrenic. Sometimes our two organizations, the one aimed at the delegates and the other at the polls, were antithetical. If we put out something, say, a full page on the riots, that would appeal to Democrats and liberal Republicans in the northeast, Malcolm Wilson would go out of his mind in the Midwest—and you couldn't blame him."[36]

But the Rockefeller people were apparently undeterred. Said Losee:

"We had our charter, which was to go ahead and influence the polls. The politicians might scream like hell, as they did shout about the riot ad. But that was none of our business."[37]

These statements make some rather interesting points. The first is that in addition to the media campaign, the politics of technique, there was an orthodox campaign, of sorts, under way in an effort to persuade some delegates directly, through personal contact, rather than rely entirely upon the impact of the polls. Secondly, that portion of the campaign devoted to influencing the polls was an interesting switch from previous instances of the influence of public opinion polls on presidential campaigning. Conventionally, the tactics of a public relations-advertising campaign call for *responding* to the polls in such a way as to fall into conformity with the apparent views of the majority of the electorate. In the case of Rockefeller in 1968, however, the approach was not to respond to the polls, but to *influence* public opinion in such a way as to actually *change* the out-come of those polls. Furthermore, the effect of the media campaign upon the delegate-recruiting campaign was of little apparent concern to those in charge.

If a television commercial alienated potential votes for Rockefeller at the convention, it was not the business of the professional communicators who were trying to influence the polls. And yet the purpose of influencing the polls was to sway delegates!

All of this posed a sort of existential dilemma of public relations. In a sense, cold analysis might dictate concentrating media effort on those issues that the public had said were bothering it; therefore, if the people want to hear a conservative approach, that is what the candidate should give them if he wants their votes. But this was countered by an apparently unsentimental, pragmatic argument as well: Hughes and Free felt that the governor could not claim leadership by "out-Nixoning Nixon." He would have to present, to borrow a phrase from Barry Goldwater, "a choice, not an echo." He had to be himself. What was he? Well, Rockefeller was committed by nature to the issues ranking lowest on Free's list of priorities: for example, justice and opportunity for the blacks, rebuilding the cities. Said Free: "Nelson got tangled up in his emotions."[38]

How did all of this come out? First of all, it cost a lot of money. Including the media budget, salaries, transportation, polls, communications, rent, etc., the Rockefeller pre-nomination campaign cost about $7,000,000. As for influence on opinion polls, the results are not too clear. Losee contends the polls *were* influenced, and the Harris data give the claim some support. However, to accept Losee's conclusion, one would have to ignore the possible effects of extrinsic factors and treat Rockefeller-oriented fluctuations in the polls as being in a direct cause-and-effect relationship with the public relations and advertising campaign. Another fallacy is that the possible effects, positive or negative, of the media campaigns of other candidates would have to be ignored. On this basis, Chester et al. point out, the Harris figures show that before the Rockefeller media barrage both the governor and Nixon would have been beaten by Hubert Humphrey. After the public relations onslaught, figures showed Rockefeller leading Humphrey by 6 percent and Nixon trailing the Vice President by 5 percent. However, Gallup polls taken between May 4 and May 8, compared with those taken between June 29 and July 3, do not buttress this point of view. Rockefeller had pinned his hopes on the final Gallup poll to be taken on the eve of the Miami Beach convention, but was bitterly disappointed. The Gallup totals showed Nixon seven points ahead of Humphrey and Rockefeller in a dead heat against the likely Democratic nominee. In an effort to blunt the impact, the Rockefeller forces released the somewhat more favorable (to the governor) results of their own private polls, but without much effect. Two days later, Louis Harris' figures showed Rockefeller leading *all* candidates. The "house polls" were done by Archibald Crossley for Lloyd Free at Rockefeller's expense. They showed Nixon leading the governor nationally by 2 percent, but Rockefeller ahead in seven of the nine key industrial states in which the election would actually be decided. But by this time it was too late to change any minds—all the damage that could have been done by the earlier polls had already taken place.[39]

Chester, Hodgson, and Page feel that the flat contradiction between the Gallup and the Harris polls at such a critical moment in the pre-nomination campaign represented "a landmark in the history of political polls in the United States. It was the first serious blow to their growing credibility since the disaster of 1948 when they predicted that Dewey would beat Truman." Both pollsters, Harris and Gallup, apparently saw this incident as a potential professional crisis and issued a joint statement insisting that both their polls were accurate when the interviewing had been done, concluding from their appraisal of the large industrial states that Governor Rockefeller actually had a better chance of being elected President. But they did not explain their divergence over so short a period. The Gallup data had been gathered between July 20 and 23, and Harris' between July 25 and 29. As Free himself has explained, there are ninety-five chances out of one hundred that any given random sample poll will come within 3 or 4 percent of the true figure. But there are also five chances in one hundred that it will not, so one of the polls might just have been plain wrong. It doesn't really matter, for practical purposes, which one. Rockefeller had staked his efforts on the mystical faith of his advisers that the polls would serve to convince the Republican delegates that the governor could win the election while Nixon could not. The contradiction in the two major polls meant neither of them would convince the delegates of anything—"least of all something they did not want to believe."[40]

So Rockefeller's campaign had failed. But he certainly had tried everything. As Norman Mailer has pointed out in his most colorful fashion:

> [Rockefeller] was like a general who had mounted the most massive offensive of a massive war but had neglected to observe that the enemy was not on his route, and the line of march led into a swamp. Rockefeller took out ads, pushed television, worked with hip musicians and groovy bands (Cannonball Adderly, Lionel Hampton), got out the young at every rally (the adolescents too young to vote), hob-nobbed with governors and senators, made the phone calls, hit the high pressure valve (Bill Miller and Meade Alcorn and Leonard Hall and Thruston Morton called in old debts from old friends), hit the hustings in his plane "Hiya fellow"— did everything but enter the campaign at the right time, fight it out in the primaries, or design his attack for the mollification of Republican fears. He did everything but exercise choice in serving up the best political greens and liver juice for the rehabilitation of Republican pride. In secret he may have detested the Average Republican. . . .[41]

Chester, Hodgson, and Page seem to agree. These astute observers saw the Rockefeller campaign as a rebellion by one segment of the American upper-class establishment against the growing dominance of middle-class Mid-America in the Republican Party. The candidate and his principal backers were scions of the American business and industrial aristocracy. Their principal advisers—Hughes, Free, Hinman, Walter Thayer—had risen to their professional heights as part of that special breed, found mostly in New York, of intellectual servants of large-scale American corporate enterprise and its leading officers. Their proven weapons in the corporate world were public relations, advertising, polls, marketing techniques, computers and planning, and they followed their instinct to duel with the newly dominant national Republican leadership with this particular choice of weapons.[42]

But more conventional political considerations, the real dynamics of the American democratic system, were lost on these men and others like them. They operate in a kind of communications hothouse in New York City, which tends to view most of those west of the Hudson, despite the denials of this sophisticated breed, as boobs or at least as somewhat inferior and as easy prey for their brand of politics and its "scientific" tools. Whether Rockefeller's advisers had to answer for the implied arrogance-ignorance of their approach is really a matter between them and the governor. It is, in a real sense, beyond the ken of the American system to give them any greater punishment than the loss of the prize that they so vigorously sought in their own way.

As Mailer has put it:

> The preliminaries to Miami Beach were simple: Nixon, by dint of an historical vacuum whose presence he was the first to discern, and by the profit of much hard work, early occupied the Republican center—the rest of the history resides in Rockefeller's attempts to clarify his own position to himself. Was he to respond only to a draft of Republicans desperate not to lose to Johnson, then to Kennedy, or was he to enter primaries, and divide the Party? Since he was perfectly capable of winning the election with a divided Republican Party, because his presence as a nominee would divide the Democratic Party even further, the question was academic. But Rockefeller's history cannot be written, for it is to be found in the timing of his advisers and the advice of his intimates, and they are not ready, one would assume, to hang themselves yet.[43]

Two other significant points remain to be made on the subject of Rockefeller's efforts in 1968. One is that the governor's media campaign seemed to rest more upon paid advertising than professional public relations. Put another way, the governor needed to do more than buy time and space. He had to make hard news. As the Kennedys and others had long since discovered, you can't buy time on Walter Cronkite, but a minute on the network news may in other ways cost more than a minute of prime network time bought for cash. It is also more valuable. The governor had to be seen doing vital, exciting things—making speeches, meeting a lot of different kinds of people around the country. He had to react to the statements of others, make his own proposals, put out a stream of releases. Furthermore, the national electorate needed to know more of what the governor was like as a human being. But Rockefeller is an aristocrat, and his press secretary, Leslie Slote, and others, who had the primary responsibility for such matters, are an aristocrat's men. America's aristocrats and their staffs are never anxious to share the customary details of their dinner parties, their wives' wardrobes, or the dreary problems of always opening one house and closing another. So none of them were enthusiastic about sharing little tidbits of personal detail with the public. Rockefeller had been burned before, and besides, he did not think that his personal life was anybody's business. His inclusive definition of privacy, however, lost him the advantage of a good deal of free publicity.

Secondly, and related to this, is the impact of the unsuccessful Rockefeller media campaign upon the future of political public relations and so-called "scientific management" in politics. As Chester et al. have pointed out, a specific lesson of the "schizophrenia" of the Rockefeller media campaign is that the "creative people" involved in such an effort will almost inevitably find it difficult to follow the "grimly logical course" mapped out by polls and computers. It is easier to dramatize highly emotional issues related to social action. People who have the talent "to manipulate the technology of the mass media have ideas of their own." What happened, said one Rockefeller adviser, " . . . was that the executives agreed with the policy indicated by the polls, but then the creative people gathered up the ball and ran with it. What they produced was pretty much what you'd expect from a group of New York intellectuals!"[44]

### GEORGE W. ROMNEY

The brief and early-aborted campaign of Governor George W. Romney of Michigan deserves a degree of scrutiny within the boundaries of this book because it illustrates what amounted to a virtual abdication of the personal judgment of a potential presidential candidate in favor of polls and Ph.D.'s. The Ph.D. came first.

He was Walter D. DeVries, who first became Romney's director of research in 1962. He says he told Romney at the time, "that I would do so only if I had what practically amounted to carte blanche in the use of public opinion polls. And I got it."[45]

In mid-1967, as Romney's bid for the presidential nomination of the Republican Party got under way, DeVries was still ordering and interpreting public opinion polls. In fact, he told James Perry, "We have probably made more use of in-depth polling on issues than any political organization in the country." This, according to Perry, is "no idle boast; it's nothing less than the simple truth. The Romney organization . . . is incontestably the nation's leader in the art of political polling."[46]

DeVries taught political science for five years at Calvin College. Then he went into politics, he told Perry, out of "pure masochism." DeVries sees his profession as a new one, "somewhere between ward heeling and ivory tower." This emerging profession, he feels, improves the quality of political debate and gives the country more adequately equipped political leaders.

> "As a political scientist, I am interested in the development and use of factual information (empirical data, in our jargon). Both political parties need campaigns that are rational in the way they handle the candidate's time, the campaign resources, the issues, and the public-opinion polls. Perhaps the GOP has most often overlooked real public opinion. The opportunity in this Party is magnificent for relating public perceptions to positive policy pro- posals. And let's not forget that the bulk of the American public is not basically liberal; it is moderate-conservative. With imagination and image, the GOP can capture the trust which is necessary to rise to national leadership. It is still satisfying to be part of this."[47]

(Perry is struck with the significance of the fact that all twenty-five Republican governors in office when he wrote *The New Politics* in 1967 employed "professional intellectuals"—"bright, ambitious men like DeVries." The Democrats, he pointed out, have not attracted the same kind of people, but the trend was so "subterranean" as not to have caused much public comment. Democratic intellectuals histori- cally have not worked for governors, but rather on the national level, as speech writers or members of issue-oriented presidential task forces.)[48]

DeVries' polling mania is not satisfied by most public opinion firms, which he contends are basically marketing research organiza- tions. Unlike some of the commercially oriented public relations and advertising men involved in presidential politics, DeVries feels that there *is*, indeed, a difference "between testing style changes on a new Chrysler or preferences for cereal and soap, and doing a thorough in-depth study on people's political attitudes." The problem, he told Perry, is that political polling is often just one small part of a research firm's business. Since it becomes almost an avocation, and is not an ongoing account, there is an understandable tendency to assign the political projects to the less talented members of the firm. For one thing, the firms do not make as much money on political polling as they do on commercial accounts.[49]

DeVries is clear in his belief that a pollster must be viewed as a technician, not as a strategist. He sees public opinion polls as important tools of the democratic process, measuring what the electorate is thinking and wanting, and giving political leaders a sense of direction in providing problem-solving leadership:

> "Polls tell the candidate what are *relevant* issue structures, his standing with the public (the distance to the goal); and polls suggest the campaign pledges and requirements needed to develop candidate image. Polls are at least as relevant as any 'intuitive' assessment of campaign strategy—probably more so than most. And the most effective polls are in-depth image and issue polls taken over a period of time to develop a trend line and to allow campaign strategy shifts as indicated."[50]

Without detailing the events of Romney's campaign, which had little impact upon American presidential politics, it has seemed worthwhile to examine briefly the views of one of his chief advisers —if for no other reason, because of the ethical questions it raises. How much of a trend is there for "scholars" to become involved in political campaigns? Does a scholar cease to be a scholar, a scientist cease to be a scientist, when he becomes so involved, any more than, let us say, an industrial chemist ceases to be a scientist when he works for a profit-making organization rather than a university? Is it a serious mistake to assume that when one hires a Ph.D. he has hired a scholar, a scientist?

Professor Howard White became rather incensed on the subject when former Republican National Chairman Meade Alcorn told a meeting of the American Political Science Association a few years ago that many members had been sent cards listing functions that they might perform in a presidential campaign. One of the principal functions was speech writing. Wrote Professor White:

> Alcorn was very proud of the replies he received. No one on the panel had the effrontery, no one in the audience had the opportunity, to point out to Alcorn that the best campaigns [have been

those] in which the candidates write their own speeches, that no
one ever checked a card affirming his willingness to write speeches
for Abraham Lincoln or Winston Churchill. What kind of neutral-
ity is this, what kind of science, which permits the representative
of a party to affirm, unchallenged, his wish that political scientists
be partisans, and partisans who might help to engineer consent?[51]

However legitimate Professor White's views may be as a defense of
both the tradition of the political virginity of the political scientist
and the tradition of the personal eloquence and thoughtfulness of a
statesman, both traditions seem headed irreversibly, with some notable exceptions, probably more of them in the first category than the
second, toward virtual oblivion. And although institutions of higher
learning may go on protesting that when they produce Ph.D.'s they
are producing research-oriented scholars, there are those—those who
receive the degree and those who hire the recipients—who view it
primarily as a passport to the upper reaches of commercial and political expertise. And although the faculties and admissions offices and
catalogue writers of the graduate schools may have it one way, the
development officers and the independent organizations that bolster
their efforts are fond of quoting statistics on Ph.D.'s "supplied" to
government and industry when soliciting various forms of financial
support. But that is perhaps a topic for another book.

RICHARD NIXON

The story of Richard M. Nixon's campaign for his party's nomination in 1968 is not primarily a story of political public relations. It is
a story of the hard work of rounding up delegates. He had done the
job over most of the past four years, more intensively during the last
one or two preceding the 1968 Republican convention. He moved
slowly and steadily around the country, dutifully making speeches for
the Republican Party, raising funds for his party and for local candidates, meeting lots and lots of the middle-class Republicans in the
small and medium-sized communities of the American heartland—
people and places not really touched by Nelson Rockefeller or
anyone else who might conceivably be nominated by the Republican
Party in 1968.

And during the six months or so before the Miami Beach convention, the presidential primaries gave Nixon one victory after another,

against little or no competition, bringing him toward the nomination on a slow, steady, even keel. As for his relations with the press, which were never very good, he had kept his publicity to a functional minimum in the months leading to the convention. As Norman Mailer has pointed out:

> He had no longer anything much to gain from good interviews, not at least until his nomination was secured; he had everything to lose from a bad interview. A delegate who was slipping could slide further because of an ill-chosen remark.
>
> To the extent that the Press was not Republican, and certainly more than half, privately, were not, he would have few friends and more than a few determined enemies. Even among the Republicans he could expect a better share of the Press to go to Rockefeller. . . . he did not, in comparison with other political candidates, have many reporters who were his personal friends. He was not reputed to smoke or drink so he did not have drinking buddies as Johnson once had, and Goldwater, and Bill Miller, and Humphrey; no brothel legends attached to him, and no outsize admiration to accompany them; no, the Press was a necessary tool to him, a tool he had been obliged to employ for more than twenty years but he could not pretend to be comfortable in his use of the tool, and the tool (since it was composed of men) resented its employment.[52]

If Nixon had been doing some hard, technical work in the pre-nomination days, so had the Republican National Committee. Chairman Ray C. Bliss of Ohio, having expunged all traces of Goldwater influence (despite the senator's "titular" leadership), was "fashioning an effective instrument of persuasion for 1968." As we have indicated, Bliss saw his role as that of a "nuts and bolts" technician and not that of an ideologist. Bliss's commitment to the Republican cause —*any* Republican cause—is one of such intense party loyalty as not to permit any individual discretion whatsoever. He made the committee a technical training institution, and public relations was one of the key areas of training. More than twenty thousand party workers from around the country, under the Bliss leadership, had been brought into seminars on such topics as political public relations, voter registration, research, and women's activities. Speakers at the public relations seminars included representatives of such organizations as Whitaker and Baxter, Campaign Consultants Incorporated,

Spencer-Roberts & Associates, Opinion Research Corporation, Central Surveys, Incorporated, INFOPLAN, Incorporated, and Jack Tinker & Partners.[53]

One of Nixon's pre-nomination moves, through his campaign manager and law partner (and later attorney general) John Mitchell, was to establish an opinion research operation in June 1968 under Professor David R. Derge of the Indiana University department of government. Opinion Research Corporation of Princeton was hired to "undertake perhaps the most elaborate polling operation yet attempted in a Presidential election, at the substantial cost of a quarter of a million dollars." The corporation, like those to which Dr. DeVries referred in the statement quoted above, spends most of its time on market research projects for manufacturing concerns. But it has also had various associations over a period of time with the Republican Party, for which it had done work in 1964 in thirty-eight states.[54]

Opinion Research Corporation took panel polls for Nixon—a derivation of a market research technique in which it specializes. The technique was originally developed by political scientists to study changes in voting intention and the effect of political propaganda. The concept of the panel poll is that rather than interviewing a fresh sample each time, as is done in a conventional poll, the same people are interviewed on successive occasions. As for the validity of the technique, the scholars are not agreed among themselves, but this does not discourage organizations like Opinion Research from using it for profit, nor politicians from paying the bills:

> . . . Certain learned disputes continue in the political science journals over the alleged reinterview effect and the scholarly validity of the concept. In the meantime, panel polling has become an important commercial tool and is used for such things as measuring the effectiveness of one T.V. commercial against another.

As for its ultimate influence on the Nixon campaign:

> It was an enormous amount of information-gathering machinery, but there seems to be some question how much it meant to the people paying for it. "I really doubt," said one of the men involved, "that it led to any serious policy movement in the campaign."[55]

Nixon, in other words, showed early in his pre-nomination drive that he shared the attitude of many old-line politicians toward opinion research "and its attendant subtechnologies—that is, a mixture of fascination and mistrust." Another polling test designed by his research organization was a series of "semantic differential" tests designed to examine the public's perceptions of Nixon and Humphrey. Respondents were asked to review sets of opposing words (e.g., interesting/uninteresting, just/unjust, passive/active) and to place candidates on a scale between each set of opposites, using a seven-point scale to rate first their ideal President, then Humphrey, and then Nixon. Nixon personally requested some additional tests, which provided an interesting indication of what he might have perceived as his own image problems. They included shifty/direct, insincere/sincere, and politician/statesman. Nixon usually came out nearer the statesman end of the scale (7) than the politician end (0), averaging around 3.5. Humphrey, to the Republican candidate's delight, came out with a little under 3, whatever that meant.[56]

Despite Nixon's obvious early anxiety over image, it seemed to stem more from curiosity than a decision to have himself remodeled for the campaign on the basis of the findings. He said at one point: "I'm not going to have any damn image experts coming telling me how to part my hair." And his staff members took pains to explain that polls were confusing as well as occasionally useful, and thus could not become the major factor in decision-making.

> Everybody was anxious to make clear that Nixon would not tailor his politics to fit what the research said people wanted—and, indeed, there is evidence he did not do so. Yet Nixon, like most other politicians, has been content to modify his attitudes according to pressures less scientifically and more intuitively assessed. It is not the idea of finding out what people want and giving it to them which politicians are uneasy about—that, despite pieties to the contrary, has always been the business of politics, and it would be curious if it were otherwise. What does worry them is the idea of doing it precisely and rationally. . . .[57]

The same type of disdain on the part of the candidate for the use of professional techniques has become *pro forma* with regard to television. Presidential candidates have hired professional television advisers ever since Dwight D. Eisenhower took on actor Robert Montgomery to coach him in the 1952 campaign. And yet the candidate, never wanting to appear too slick, avoids admitting to any special knowledge of the medium.

In the words of Joe McGinniss, who was quite close to the Nixon television operation:

> [The candidate] should express distaste for television, suspicion that there is something "phony" about it. This guarantees him a good press, because newspaper reporters, bitter over their loss of prestige to the television men, are certain to stress anti-television remarks. Thus, the sophisticated candidate, while analyzing his own on-the-air technique as carefully as a golf pro studies his swing, will state frequently that there is no place for "public-relations gimmicks" or "those show-business guys" in the campaign. Most of the television men working for him will be unbothered by such remarks. They are willing to accept anonymity, even scorn, as long as the pay is good.[58]

## The Democrats

### EUGENE McCARTHY

Senator McCarthy's early efforts at winning the Democratic nomination were probably characterized most by a lack of organization —and a generalized chaos in whatever organization did exist.

Press relations was one of the early problem areas, and Seymour "Sy" Hersh, a thirty-year-old ex-Associated Press reporter, was an early appointment to McCarthy's national staff. It was hoped that Hersh, who had covered the Pentagon and written a book on chemical and bacteriological warfare, could "make some sense of the Senator's dismal press relations." McCarthy had, according to Chester, Modgson, and Page, themselves journalists, a "cavalier disregard for journalistic obsessions about deadlines. . . . Many reporters approached his campaign with irreverence and were inclined to question whether he was a 'serious' candidate." Hersh was charged with expediting the flow of information, to ensure that the Senator delivered the speeches he said he would so the journalists could get early releases, and, hopefully, to make McCarthy more accessible to the media. Chester et al., in an interesting sidelight, claim that when Hersh was recruited in January 1968 by campaign manager Blair Clark, himself an ex-CBS newsman, Clark told him that, "All we want to do is get Kennedy in."[59]

The bill for McCarthy's television advertising and mailing costs in his successful New Hampshire primary campaign was picked up by one of his major contributors at that stage of the operation, Harold Stein of the Dreyfus Fund. Stein recruited his own advertising man, Julian Koenig of the New York firm of Papert, Koenig, Lois, Inc. He also hired Larry Freundlich of Doubleday, an editor who had worked on Robert Kennedy's book *To Seek a Newer World*. Freundlich soon discovered that McCarthy's own small team of writers was actually underemployed, and that "The Senator had a characteristic almost unique in Presidential politics: an ingrained aversion to prepared texts."[60]

McCarthy was "difficult," from a political public relations man's point of view, in other ways as well. His own staff, more aware of the importance of such considerations, often moved independently. McCarthy would not take political advantage of his Catholicism in New Hampshire, where 65 percent of the ninety thousand registered Democrats are Roman Catholics. The local staff got around this by finding out where the senator was attending mass while in the state, and then tipping off local press photographers. The staff tried other gimmicks as well. Although the senator's personal staff had purposely not packed the candidate's ice skates when he went to New Hampshire, the local campaign staff managed to borrow a pair, and McCarthy spent a very photogenic twenty minutes on a Concord rink playing hockey with a group of semi-pros. Thus, "McCarthy on Ice" broke into the national newsmagazines. A mid-February after-hours party for student volunteers had been declared off-limits to the press by the national staff, but the local staff revoked the order, and "for some of the newsmen present it became a turning point in their perceptions of the campaign."[61]

As for Stein's adman, Julian Koenig, he was

> . . . all for hard-hitting, emotional advertising on the war issue. The subject of burned babies was discussed. The locals persuaded him to cool it. And Koenig did come up with one of the best slogans of the campaign: "New Hampshire can bring America back to its senses," which conveyed the right impression while subtly flattering local pride.[62]

Richard Goodwin, who made his debut as a presidential campaign adviser on John F. Kennedy's staff in 1960, was an unexpected and unrecruited addition to the McCarthy writing staff. He joined it after the 1968 Tet offensive in Vietnam. Reading about the bombings of temples in Hue as he sat in his Boston home, Goodwin made up his mind, threw his typewriter in the back of his car, and drove to the headquarters of the McCarthy wordsmiths, the Wayfarer Hotel in Manchester, New Hampshire. Goodwin, the "first real pro to come on the team," told Hersh, "With these two typewriters, we're going to overthrow the government."[63]

The government remained in power, but the McCarthy triumph in New Hampshire did overthrow some conventional assumptions about Vice President Humphrey being an effortless, automatic shoo-in for 1968's Democratic presidential nomination.

In Oregon, the campaign, especially in its earlier stages, was the responsibility of Howard Morgan, the former state Democratic chairman, and Howard Whipple, a journalist who had sought greener pastures in the real estate business. McCarthy, however, disdained their advice on how to approach Oregon, telling his backers there, "You must accept me for what I am or forget this romance right now." Chester et al. feel the Oregon campaign probably benefited from the absence of McCarthy's national staff, which knew little about the state and was occupied with two disastrous adventures in Nebraska and Indiana during April and May. Morgan and Whipple, who were formally made heads of McCarthy's Oregon campaign, set up fifty headquarters throughout the state and sent out student canvassers to "places which had never seen a political worker." Whipple and Morgan also directed the senator's scheduling, and his radio and television advertising. According to ex-newsman Whipple (now a political public relations man, even if he didn't think of himself as such), the national staff members who did come in wanted to run a five-minute advertisement using quotes from Senators Mark Hatfield and Wayne Morse condemning the war in Vietnam.

> They hadn't realized that this sort of ad would alienate the Democrats who were going to vote against Morse in the Democratic primary and would also give the impression that Hatfield, a Republican, was telling Democrats how to vote. They're very independent voters up here, and they wouldn't have liked that one bit.[64]

If local knowledge was sensibly employed in Oregon, where it helped to produce a well-organized campaign that succeeded in trouncing Senator Robert Kennedy, in California the tables were turned. There, the McCarthy campaign seemed a shambles by comparison. Even the logistics of moving the Minnesotan around, along with his entourage of staff, reporters, cameramen, and so on were never under control. For example, on May 10, McCarthy's plane left Sacramento ten minutes early, leaving behind half a dozen very irate reporters, not to mention four members of the senator's own staff. The candidate next arrived nearly an hour early to speak at Los Angeles' Griffith Park. He finished his speech at 4:20, just the time at which he was supposed to begin, and walked out of the stadium as hundreds of his fans and potential supporters and workers arrived.

> National political reporters, accustomed to associating crispness of travel organization with political viability, were inclined to be contemptuous. Whatever other difficulties might beset the Kennedy campaign, his personal entourage was nearly always on time.[65]

One high-ranking professional in the Democratic Party told the writer that the McCarthy campaign, to a considerable extent, was an exception to the increasing professionalism in the use of commercial public relations, advertising, and related techniques in presidential campaigning. It is also important to remember, however, that a movement of the sort that swept McCarthy to national prominence as a potential President has been a most uncommon phenomenon in recent American political history. This is news in itself. Thus, such a movement would attract a good deal of media attention without trying to do so professionally and without buying vast quantities of time and space for messages controlled by the candidate.[66]

## HUBERT H. HUMPHREY

In May, once Hubert H. Humphrey's intention to seek his party's nomination was evident, one of the first things he did was to retain an advertising agency. At this point in the pre-nomination campaigning, the ad agency scoreboard looked like this:
—Nixon had engaged Fuller & Smith & Ross.
—Rockefeller had retained Jack Tinker & Partners.
—Robert Kennedy had now contracted with Papert, Koenig, and Lois, which had previously worked for McCarthy in New Hampshire.
—McCarthy was now working with the Carl Ally Agency, which before taking on the senator had devoted its talents to Hertz-Rent-a-Car, IBM, and Sleep-Eze, among others.
Humphrey now moved to retain Doyle Dane Bernbach, the agency

that had attracted John F. Kennedy's attention in 1963 with its "Think Small" ads for Volkswagen and had been hired the next year, over the objections of many veteran politicians, to help market Lyndon Johnson. Ironically, one of the principal DDB accounts was Avis Rent-a-Car, the key competitor of Hertz, which retained McCarthy's agency, Carl Ally. Adding further to the irony, DDB, which was now working for the Vice President, had originated for Avis the slogan "We're only Number Two. We have to try harder."[67]

The Vice President's account, at this stage, was entrusted by agency chief William Bernbach to his youngest of many vice presidents, Arie Kopelman, then not yet thirty years old. Kopelman's principal previous responsibilities had been with the Proctor and Gamble Company, handling such products as Joy, Bold, Cinch, Zest, and Mr. Clean. The strength of such products was specialty packaging, which involved "relatively unsubtle, broad-brush creative work, directed by extremely refined statistical analysis, at which Kopelman was universally acknowledged to be brilliant." His major work at DDB was on the H. J. Heinz soup account, and it was evident that Kopelman did not shy away from the idea of packaging presidential candidates like soup and soap. "When I wrote the media plan," he said, "we looked at it as if we were marketing a product for Heinz or Proctor and Gamble." Kopelman and his colleagues were enthusiastic about the Humphrey assignment, and by the time of the Democratic convention in Chicago there were fifty-seven people working on the account and twenty more media specialists standing by to gobble up broadcast time for commercials and documentaries as soon as they got the word. Trial runs were begun with a computer operation, working out "rotation patterns" designed to calculate the value of repeating a given broadcast spot on a particular subject in a certain city $x$ number of days after its original showing. Kopelman went to Chicago for the convention with a group of fifteen copywriters, film directors, and visualizers, and awaited the word to get moving on his production schedule, which called for starting production of Humphrey spots on August 30.[68]

As the Democratic convention got under way, media arrangements for the party were in the hands of Democratic National Committee Public Relations Director Martin Hauan. He had held this post for only a year, but had seventeen years of political public relations experience. Hauan's journalistic career included service as managing editor of a small city daily, owner of a country weekly in Missouri, and news director of radio and television stations in Missouri and Oklahoma. His political career had begun with a stint as press secretary to Governor Johnson Murray of Oklahoma. Toward the end of Murray's term, Hauan launched an agency bearing his own name in Oklahoma City, specializing in political public relations. (It stayed in business when the boss went to work for the Democrats.) He conducted a variety of state and local public relations campaigns and one on the national level: New York Governor Averell Harriman's unsuccessful bid for the Democratic presidential nomination in 1956. His public relations staff at the committee as the convention approached included half a dozen people; about the same number were involved in research. David Banks and Muriel Hart edited the committee's monthly, *The Democrat*; Carl Olexa produced news releases and some radio and television spots for distribution through eight regional substations via telephone call-in arrangements. These people, along with assistants Rosalind Rosenberg and Elaine Tomcheck, went to Chicago with Hauan, where they were supplemented by temporaries and volunteers. The Washington agency of Maurer, Fleisher, Zon & Associates had also done some special production, art, and advertising assignments for the Democrats.[69]

For a professional political public relations man, with considerable journalistic experience in the printed and electronic media, Hauan hardly seemed to be thinking of himself as a champion of communications as the convention approached. *Public Relations News* quoted him on August 26, 1968, as saying of the party's plans: "We are not running a Convention for TV; it's for the delegates and the people."

*P.R. News* also reported that the Democratic public relations planners had sharply reduced the number of floor passes for the press and taken various other measures that antagonized the media, such as moving the customary television and photo island from the middle of the floor to the back of the hall, thus providing more floor space but forcing grumpy photographers and cameramen to rely upon telephoto and zoom lenses.

As a matter of fact, the television networks were generally unhappy with most of the arrangements for the coverage of the Chicago convention. As the date of the event approached, there was a telephone strike in Chicago, and the men who had to install and service the lines into the International Amphitheatre and other locations vital to transmitting television signals were not on the job. The television networks, it is generally agreed, began to apply pressures behind the scenes to move the convention to Miami, where the necessary telephone and television lines were all in. But, as Norman Mailer describes the situation, Chicago Mayor Richard J. Daley

> . . . was not about to let the convention leave his city. Daley promised he would enforce the peace and allow no outrageous demonstrations. Daley hinted that his wrath—if the convention were moved—might burn away whole corners of certain people's support. Since Hubert Humphrey was the one who could most qualify for certain people, he was in no hurry to offend the Mayor. Lyndon Johnson, when beseeched by interested parties to encourage Daley to agree to the move, was rumored to have said, "Miami Beach is not an American city."[70]

It is not difficult to understand the desire of the television people to see the convention moved. Because of the restrictions imposed by the strike, television cameras could be used only in the Amphitheatre and some of the downtown hotels, but not in the streets. There they were restricted to newsfilm cameras, which would mean hours of delay in visual reporting of any action in the streets.

How ambitious the networks—and individual workers, broadcasters, and others—were in looking for opportunities for retribution against Chicago, the mayor, and the Democratic candidate, it is difficult to say with any degree of accuracy. It is safe to say, however, that the strong resentment by the electronic media of the whole affair represented a very serious public relations problem for the Democrats and their nominee. Mailer says it nicely:

> How [the networks] must have focused their pressure on Daley and Johnson. It is to the mayor's curious credit that he was strong enough to withstand them. It should have been proof interior that Daley was no other-directed twentieth-century politician. Any such man would have known the powers of retaliation which resided in the mass media. One did not make an enemy of a television network for nothing; they could repay injury with no more than a Charonic slur in the announcer's voice every time your deadly name was mentioned over the next twelve months, or next twelve years.[71]

So Hubert Humphrey was in the position of beginning his campaign in the face of antagonism by the media—particularly the television networks—for the way they had been treated at the convention, for the stories they had missed, and for the apparent indifference of the Democratic organization to the long-term effect of such action upon its public relationships.

## After the Convention: The Race for the White House

### *Richard M. Nixon*

In the opinion of one professional public relations man, Richard Nixon's image strategists decided at the outset of his 1968 campaign that their man's most severe error in 1960 had been his "failure to realize that politics in America had changed." According to H. Zane Robbins, vice president and general manager of the Chicago firm of Burson-Marsteller Associates, Nixon was presented in 1960 as a "serious, dignified candidate of the Ike and Roosevelt stripe. . . . He got licked by an Irish-Catholic brawler who offered the public a fresh face, bright intellect, great personal charm, and a quick mind." This, according to Robbins, meant to Republican strategists in 1968 that Nixon was an excellent candidate who had been in the past a victim of faulty marketing. This time, "they were determined to present the real Nixon."[72]

If Nixon had been victimized by faulty marketing in 1960, then the electronic precision of his 1968 campaign organization seemed to make up for lost time. Liberal and conservative observers alike came away feeling that the Nixon organization appeared to be a full-fledged example of the politics of manipulation a full four terms ahead of 1984.

For example, Garry Wills, a contributor to the *National Review* and author of *Nixon Agonistes*, described "the minute calibration that marks Nixon, the great calculator." At the other end of the spectrum, *The Progressive* editorialized that Nixon was "the fully automated candidate, programmed to give on each public occasion the performance calculated to win friends and influence people." From a strictly pragmatic point of view, there were also those observers who felt that Nixon's reliance on an assortment of gadgetry contributed to a certain rigidity in his campaign organization which, after all, came close to losing, despite every possible advantage. For,

> Few things in politics are more subtly damaging than a reputation —deserved or not—for chilly efficiency, and so this was deplorable public relations. The Nixon campaign put one in mind of Ettore Bugatti's remark about a particularly elaborate and cumbersome Rolls-Royce of the 20's: the "triumph of workmanship over design."[73]

The Nixon campaign drew heavily on the latest products of the communications and data-processing industries, "and not infrequently a certain institutional enthusiasm about all this hardware slopped right over into self-parody, as when campaign manager John Mitchell declared that it was his job to 'program the candidate'." Nixon's version of "participation politics" was structured around a computer whose memory bank had stored up sixty-seven Nixon positions on public issues. Around the country, visitors to Nixon offices were encouraged to speak into tape recorders and ask brief questions, addressed to the candidate, regarding issues with which they were concerned. Each person who asked the machine a question got a reply: a four-paragraph letter also written by a machine, in this case a computer-directed electric typewriter, and signed by a signature machine. And the replies were not done strictly by rote, for the computer had even been programmed to give a slightly different individualized answer each time. Other candidates, Robert Kennedy, for example, had used personal letter mills before. Nixon, however, had done a more total job of organization than his predecessors. It cost $250,000, more than anyone else had spent before on such an operation. With a touch of unintentional irony, the Nixon organization called the whole thing "participation," which in 1968 was also the rallying cry for insurgent candidates, for whom it had an entirely different meaning.[74]

On the hard-core advertising side, the Fuller & Smith & Ross agency was hired to promote Nixon. The firm was told not to bother with any material aimed at securing the nomination, but to look straight toward the campaign itself in drawing up its plans. John S. Poister, a vice president of the firm, ran the operation and was under a mandate to work out a plan for reaching every voter in the United States who owned a television or radio set. The cost—which eventually ran to more than $11,000,000—turned out not to be a problem. In fact, the contrast between the Democratic and Republican ability to handle the costs of their media campaigns has seldom been stronger than in 1968. As the Republicans considered their ambitious plan, the Democrats puzzled over their party's inability to find more than $2,000,000.[75]

When it came to television, something we might call the pseudo-video-event had become a dominant feature of Nixon's campaign schedule. Since television is the way you get to the most voters, the reasoning went, public events are not held for reasons of content or validity, but mainly to provide television with something to report. Nixon's ideal day always contained such an event. It usually came early, allowing ample time for TV film processing and editing before the six o'clock news. The events themselves and the audiences that turned out for them might be largely irrelevant at times. The candidate might, for example, spend an afternoon at a rally of students all under voting age. This schoolchildren device is often effective, in that the pupils, having been given time off from classes to attend, are usually quite high-spirited and enthusiastic. Furthermore, it gives the candidate an association with young people while permitting him to sidestep a confrontation with truly militant college youth. The cameras constantly demanded new and original forms of sustenance. But, according to Chester, Hodgson, and Page, "this was not always easily managed with Nixon, on whom, to his credit, hokum sits ill."[76]

Having said this, the three authors go on to cite an instance of obvious hokum, and one with which Nixon apparently got a bit carried away. In Seattle, on October 25, the candidate, on a visit to the harbor, climbed into the prow of a hydrofoil, and the boat proceeded to rush around the harbor, spurting jets of water. Then, according to Chester et al., Nixon

> . . . assumed a curious attitude apparently modeled upon that of stout Cortes . . . Nixon apparently got carried away; three-quarters of an hour later, a glance down any of the numerous vistas of the Seattle dockside was apt to reveal in the middle distance the hydrofoil buzzing past, with the tiny figure of the Presidential candidate gesticulating in the bow. The effect, in the end, of the numerous passings and repassings was oddly like some slapstick movie of the twenties, and parties of people in boats were in danger of falling overboard in sheer hilarity.[77]

In retrospect, it seems clear that the influence of television in the Nixon campaign of 1968 was all-pervasive. Not only was it an important factor in campaigning for the candidate, and an important tool in covering the campaign for the media, it had also by now become the silent midwife of a continuous chain of pseudo-events unrelated to the presidency or to one's qualification for that office. Television was no longer even just a medium for reaching the electorate. Now a presidential candidate was performing for the medium. McLuhanism had blossomed much more effusively in this presidential campaign than in any of its previous quadrennial flowerings.

The Nixon organization, in addition to regularly producing such telegenic events for local and national news programs, gave a great deal of time to special appearances on local and regional television, through a combination of news interviews and paid commercial spots. However, two television features that had been common to most previous campaigns were missing this time: the customary "background" interviews with the national press and the periodic confrontations with national television cameras, in one way or another. The Nixon organization did, however, produce its own programs, and the candidate's evenings were periodically given over to private videotaping sessions. So pervasive had the medium now become that several days during the campaign were used for virtually nothing but private television broadcasts and taping sessions. For example, Chester et al. cite Nixon's schedule for September 20:[78]

> "9:15—Baggage should be at 450 Park Avenue for transporting to airport.
> 10:55—Depart New York City en route Philadelphia, Pa., flying time 35 minutes. HOTEL HEADQUARTERS: Marriott Motor Hotel, City Line and Monument Aves.
> 11:30 a.m.—Arrive Philadelphia International Airport.
> 11:50—Depart airport en route downtown Philadelphia.
> 12:10—Motorcade in downtown Philadelphia.
> 12:50—Arrive Marriott Motor Hotel.
> 7:00 p.m.—Depart hotel en route WCAU-TV (Across the street from hotel).
> 7:05—Arrive WCAU-TV studio, City Line and Monument. Viewing room will be provided for the press.
> 7:30—Mr. Nixon will appear on live Pennsylvania television.
> 8:30—Conclusion of television program.
> 8:40—Return to Marriott Motor Hotel for overnight."

The one area in which Nixon seemed most generous with his time was in the granting of interviews to local television stations. His accessibility this time out contrasted markedly with what had been the case in the 1960 campaign. The questions asked on these stations around the country, however, were usually less than frightening. And if they were occasionally more penetrating, Nixon (who by now had much experience in such matters) was usually much more expert in handling the queries than many local newsmen seemed to be in pursuing their subject.

On September 26, for example, in Louisville, Kentucky, the candidate was asked:

> "Mr. Nixon, at this point in the campaign, what do you find as the greatest concerns of the people? . . .
>
> "Have you encountered any surprises at all? I suppose not? . . .
>
> "The polls that we have seen show you ahead nationally. Is there any hazard at all to being a leader?"[79]

Even these examples, however, appear as the Everest of free intellectual exchange when contrasted with the new "Nixon Format" used for television on a number of occasions throughout the campaign. These were periods of purchased, slickly produced television time on which Nixon appeared with a pre-selected panel and his own "house moderator," former University of Oklahoma football coach Bud Wilkinson. The programs were produced for regional audiences. The program cited in the above schedule, for example, reached Pennsylvania, Delaware, and New Jersey. The panelists, selected for appearance and safety's sake, were not known for stirring up controversy.[80]

The Nixon organization included a number of men with their own brand of enthusiasm about the political uses of television. They and their operation are described with shattering detail by reporter Joe McGinniss in his book *The Selling of the President 1968*. One of the men so involved was Harry Treleaven, who was hired by Leonard Garment, Nixon's law partner, in the fall of 1967 as creative director of advertising, after eighteen years with the J. Walter Thompson advertising agency. Initially, he was to consider Nixon's "personality problems." Of the candidate's alleged lack of warmth, Treleaven said:

> "He can be helped greatly in this respect by how he is handled. . . .
> Give him words to say that will show his *emotional* involvement in

the issues. . . . He should be presented in some kind of 'situation' rather than cold in a studio. The 'situation' should look unstaged even if it's not."[81]

To Treleaven, logic and rationality seemed to play very little part in convincing a voter to choose his man. When, in 1952, Rosser Reeves mounted the classic spot advertising campaign for General Eisenhower, there was a stir about merchandising a presidential candidate like a tube of toothpaste. But by 1968 there was no question to men like Treleaven that this is exactly what you have to do: appeal not to logic, but to illogic; not to rationality, but to emotion. As he has written:

"There'll be few opportunities for logical persuasion, which is all right—because probably more people vote for irrational, emotional reasons than professional politicians suspect. . . .

"Political candidates are celebrities, and today with television taking them into everybody's home right along with Johnny Carson and Batman, they're more of a public attraction than ever."[82]

William Gavin, a staff man with a very different sort of background, apparently seemed attractive to Nixon because he shared some of these same ideas. Gavin, a young English teacher from Abington, Pennsylvania, was hired, so the story goes, after he wrote Nixon a letter in 1967 urging him to run and base his campaign on television. A conservative Irish Catholic, Gavin had published some essays in the *National Review*. He wrote his fan letter to Nixon on letterhead borrowed from the University of Pennsylvania, on the theory that the candidate would pay more attention to the communication if it seemed to be coming from a professor. During the course of the 1968 campaign, Gavin wrote think pieces on image, and the means through which Nixon might improve his through television. His approach was amazingly close to Treleaven's:

"Voters are basically lazy, basically uninterested in making an effort to understand what we're talking about. . . . Reason requires a high degree of discipline, of concentration; impression is easier. . . . It's the aura that surrounds the charismatic figure more than it is the figure itself that draws the followers. Our task is to build that aura. . . ."

Gavin, by the way, went to work in the White House as a presidential speech writer in January 1969.[83]

Raymond K. Price, Jr., was known as the most accomplished writer in the Nixon campaign. A former editorial-page editor of the New York *Herald Tribune*, he had been working on a novel on February 22, 1967, when Nixon invited him for lunch and offered him a job, which he accepted after a week's thought. Price, who also went to work in the White House after the election, seemed to be on precisely the same wicket as his newfound colleagues. He suggested that the campaign attack "personal factors" rather than "historical factors," which formed the basis of the low esteem in which many people apparently held Nixon: Wrote Price:

> "These tend to be more a gut reaction, unarticulated, nonanalytical, a product of the particular chemistry between the voter and the *image* of the candidate. *We have to be very clear on this point: that the response is to the image, not to the man. . . .*"

Thus, concludes McGinniss,

> there would not have to be a "new Nixon." Simply a new approach to television. . . . It was as if they were building not a President but an Astrodome, where the wind would never blow, the temperature never rise or fall, and the ball never bounce erratically on the artificial grass.[84]

Frank Shakespeare, along with Treleaven and Garment, made up what was to be called the campaign's "media and advertising group." Shakespeare, who was in his forties, had spent eighteen years as an executive at the Columbia Broadcasting System, where he had worked closely with the CBS Television Network president, James Aubrey, who had since been discharged, while Shakespeare stayed on.[85]

For Shakespeare, according to McGinniss, television was the totality of the Nixon campaign. Little else mattered. He had nothing but disdain for other techniques, even public relations insofar as it applied to cultivating the print media, toward which he was hostile.

> " 'Without television,' Shakespeare said during the course of the campaign, 'Richard Nixon would not have a chance.' Nixon, he continued, ' . . . would not have a prayer of being elected because the press would not let him get through to the people. But because he is so good on television he will get through despite the press. The press doesn't matter anymore.
>
> "We're going to carry New York State despite the *Times* and the *Post*. The age of the columnist is over. Television reaches so many

more people. You can see it in our attitude toward print advertising. It's used only as a supplement. TV is carrying our campaign.
And Nixon loves it. He's overjoyed that he no longer has to
depend upon the press. . . . He has a great hostility toward the
press and as President he should be shielded.' "[86]

After Nixon's election, Shakespeare was made director of the
United States Information Agency. Shortly thereafter, it was
announced that some reorganization would be undertaken at USIA
to place greater stress on the use of television, as opposed to the print
media.

Nixon's one-hour television programs were produced during the
course of the campaign by Roger Ailes, the twenty-eight-year-old
executive producer of the Mike Douglas Show, which was syndicated
out of Philadelphia by the Westinghouse Broadcasting Company.
Ailes had started as a prop boy on the Douglas show in 1965, and
three years later he was the boss. According to McGinniss, who
worked with him closely during the campaign, Ailes

> . . . was good. When he left, Douglas' rating declined. But not
> everyone he passed on his way up remained his friend. Not even
> Douglas. Richard Nixon had been a guest on the show in the fall
> of 1967. While waiting to go on, he fell into conversation with
> Roger Ailes.
> "It's a shame a man has to use gimmicks like this to get
> elected," Nixon said.
> "Television is not a gimmick," Ailes said.
> Richard Nixon liked that kind of thinking. He told Len Gar-
> ment to hire the man.[87]

At a press conference several days after his nomination, Richard
Nixon told reporters, "I am not going to barricade myself into a television studio and make this an antiseptic campaign." Then he flew to
Chicago and opened his campaign with one of those full days—built
around a television program. He had indeed barricaded himself, and
he stayed behind the barricade even when ten thousand people con-
gregated in front of his hotel and screamed for a glimpse, a greeting.
And Chicago was only the first of ten places from which Ailes-pro-
duced "Nixon Format" shows were to emanate.[88]

Each one-hour show was broadcast live, in front of a carefully
selected studio audience, which, as McGinniss describes the scene,
would provide wild enthusiasm on cue from Ailes' assistant, hope-

fully infecting the home audience as well. The press was barred from rehearsals, able to see only the same sterilized version of the programs that were made available to the general public. In fact, at Shakespeare's insistence, no press representatives were ever allowed in the studio with the audience while the show was on the air. Thus, no one would be in a position to say what went on before air time, or just what it was like during the whole process of confronting the American people with the man who wished to be their President, and was, indeed, to have his wish fulfilled.

Press secretary Herbert Klein, to his credit, argued with Shakespeare's anti-press decree. If this was how it was going to start, McGinniss quotes him as saying before the first show in Chicago, it was going to be like 1960 all over again. Treleaven and Ailes sipped coffee (presumably in McGinniss company) in the automated third-floor snack shop at the WBBM (CBS) studios in the old Chicago Arena building, and Ailes figured it this way:

> "Goddam it . . . the problem is that this is an electronic election. The first there's ever been. TV has the power now. Some of the guys get arrogant and rub the reporters' faces in it and then the reporters get pissed and go out of their way to rap anything they consider staged for TV. And you know damn well that's what they'd do if they saw this from the studio. You let them in with the regular audience and they see the warm-up. They see Jack Rourke (Ailes' assistant) out there telling the audience to applaud and to mob Nixon at the end, and that's all they'd write about. You know damn well it is."[89]

Nixon's prose on these programs was pretty much as bland as one would expect in such a setting. Actually, things were well designed so as to obviate the necessity for the candidate's appearance to be anything but antiseptic. Nixon could even muse, lose himself in "amusing" digressions. For example, in one program, which was beamed to Texas, Arkansas, New Mexico, and Oklahoma from KLRD-TV in Dallas on October 11, Nixon got involved in a lengthy discussion of football with Bud Wilkinson. After a long dissertation, which covered the University of Oklahoma football team, the Dallas Cowboys, and the Super Bowl, Nixon made his political point by saying:

> "I'm digressing on football again, but that's my favorite subject. But to go on with the other question. What I'm going to say is this. We are going to have an offense and a defense. We are going to

sock it to them on the offense and defend on the defense. How's that?"

Panelist Field Scovell, a businessman, responded with aplomb: "I think you've got a pretty good hand in Bud, and I think old Bud's got a pretty good hand in you."[90]

Helping to render the television programs, and thereby the campaign, even more sterile was the fact that each show would be seen only by the people who lived in the particular state or region to which each program was beamed. This meant, as McGinniss points out, that the candidate could repeat the same statement, phrase for phrase, and even gesture for gesture, in response to a variety of questions, everywhere he was on the air. Those in the press entourage might be bored, but as we have seen, they were not expected to be great friends of Nixon, who could thus "get through the campaign with a dozen or so carefully worded responses that would cover all the problems of America in 1968."

The final Nixon telethon on the last night of the campaign was, however, a coast-to-coast production, emanating from NBC's Television City in Burbank, California. Poor Roger Ailes had sprained his ankle, having decided to try skydiving for the first time on the day before the telethon, so McGinniss describes him as running the show with his foot in a bucket of ice. As final preparations were under way for the grand finale, Ailes made his contribution to American political thought:

> "This is the beginning of a whole new concept. This is it. This is the way they'll be elected forevermore. The next guys up will have to be performers. The interesting question is, how sincere is a TV set? If you take a cold guy and stage him warm, can you get away with it? I don't know. But I felt a lot better about jumping out of that plane yesterday than I do about this thing tonight."

And as Nixon concluded his telethon later that evening, he told the audience: "I'm not a showman. I'm not a television personality."[91]

From the standpoint of the whole body of political thought available to man, this kind of campaign lends itself to a rather thorough indictment on a long list of counts. It represented an abdication of responsibility. One might say it represented an abdication of judgment on the part of the candidate. In another sense, however, Nixon wanted to get elected, and it was his judgment, based on the advice of those whom he had hired to advise him, that this was the way to do it

—and it all worked. It was the ultimate pragmatism. From the point of view of public relations—notwithstanding the fact that the Public Relations Society of America Code of Ethics forbids members to "corrupt the channels of communication"—it was technically quite well done.

The vice president of one large public relations agency, for example, has said that Nixon's 1968 campaign was a reflection of a conscious effort to present himself in informal television situations. It worked well, according to this professional. No longer did the public see that somber, heavily shadowed face peering into the camera. Now Nixon was standing, moving easily around, answering unrehearsed (if predictably safe) questions from an uninhibited (if well-directed, well-chosen and predictably enthusiastic) audience. All of this

> . . . successfully dispelled in the minds of most voters the idea that Nixon is a stiff, humorless automaton. It convinced most viewers —whether or not they supported Nixon—that the candidate was well versed on domestic and world affairs and well equipped for the Presidency.[92]

Although newsmen could not get into the television studios, Nixon's overall press relations in 1968 were characterized, in marked contrast to 1960, by considerable attention to the physical comforts of news media representatives. Although the press this time around suffered no discomfort, which they might be prone to take out on Nixon, they nevertheless found themselves pretty well cut off from the candidate. Once Herbert Klein went around telling newsmen at the luxurious Key Biscayne Hotel that they should all relax happily and forget about competition since no one was going to get anything out of the candidate during his stay on the key. Meanwhile, devoted Nixon supporters put Lincolns, Cadillacs, and Imperials at the disposal of the press. There were also free yacht trips, water skiing facilities, and entertainment with lots of free food and drink at night. One of the more exciting news developments was the awarding of the name "Snakehips" to Congressman Melvin Laird of Wisconsin—later to become Secretary of Defense—because of the "elegant, olde-world manner of his rotations on the dance floor with Nixon's private secretary, Rose Mary Woods." The Florida stay wound up with a lavish party on October 14, more lavish, according to Chester, than anything the Kennedys had ever put on earlier in the decade.[93]

The problem in public relations terms with this sort of procedure is that reporters, who enjoy fun and games as much as, if not more than, the next man, don't really enjoy themselves all that much when the games are work-related and the ration of food and drink far outweighs that of information. And even if the correspondents can do with a bit of loafing and luxury, the editors back home, who don't smell the salt air and the bubbly champagne and have to do with a noticeable lack of meaningful stories on a presidential candidate, are not likely to be overjoyed by the campaign party's generosity to working newsmen.

Chester et al. came away feeling that the reporters really didn't get on much better with Nixon than they had in 1960:

> The relationship between Nixon and the reporters who were supposed to be conveying the propositions to the electorate was of such frigidity as to make any act of communication difficult. After a few weeks of campaigning, the newsmen scarcely bothered to maintain even the mask of professional camaraderie which is usually the last barrier between their feelings and their subject.[94]

Once again, the press coverage of the presidential campaign in 1968 illustrated that it is virtually impossible for a candidate to say anything at all to any kind of group in any location without bringing on widespread national publicity. This fact of political life apparently bothered Nixon, as it had in 1960, and as it had irritated Senator Goldwater even more in 1964, and as it had plagued even General Eisenhower, not only during campaigns but throughout the presidency, and as it would upset George McGovern in 1972.

Nixon, for example, was talking to a relatively small group, about two hundred persons in the obscure town of Hampton, New Hampshire, when he said that he had "a plan to end the war"; but he was not about to reveal his "plan" unless and until he became President. Said one Democratic staff member:

> This could have slipped by without notice with that kind of audience in so remote a city if the media hadn't been right there—but the media are always with the candidate these days, and the candidate who forgets it is making a serious public relations mistake. As it was, Nixon's statement got a national audience, and the Democrats jumped on it. The Republicans realized it was unfortunate, and also understood that the Democrats would take political advantage.[95]

Republican public relations machinery, however, jumped into action in the case of some widely quoted and less-than-fortunate statements by vice presidential candidate Spiro Agnew. Unfortunately for the Republicans, the damage had already been done, and the work was focused mainly on the prevention of future *faux pas* by the candidate, who was taking a rather unusual approach to making Spiro Agnew "a household word."

Soon after Agnew called Vice President Hubert Humphrey "squishy-soft on Communism," Stephen Hess, an experienced Republican intellectual, was dispatched to join the Agnew staff. Columnists Evans and Novak correctly observed that Hess was being sent to look after Agnew. Hess found that the candidate and most of his staff, to Hess's amazement, were delighted with the effect of the "squishy-soft" address. Said Chester et al.:

> Apparently, they were infected by the Billy Rose approach to publicity: don't read it, measure it. Hess arrived just in time to stall more diatribes on the same subject. Such crowd-pleasing gambits as "Communists in our midst" and "lists of names" were under consideration. At this point, it emerged that Agnew genuinely did not know that these phrases were the slogans of McCarthyism. Indeed, he may not have known what McCarthyism was. He was vaguely aware that Joe McCarthy had been a bad guy of some kind, but he had no idea why. In 1953, Agnew had been an apolitical manager of a supermarket, and in the years since he hadn't bothered to find out about McCarthy.[96]

Nixon generally seemed less concerned with his visibility than he had been in 1960, when he had insisted on fulfilling his convention promise to take his campaign to all fifty states. As we have seen, there were periods such as those at Key Biscayne, when he spent most of his time vanishing from public view. Nixon took a two-day vacation at the end of September, and his three-day break in mid-October came when there were only three weeks left to the campaign. The effect on the press corps was something other than copacetic. The scheduling appeared to be, at least in part, a reaction to the overenthusiastic effort to visit each state in 1960, which had contributed then to the candidate's general state of physical exhaustion and to the tired appearance that was thought to have contributed to his less than vigorous appearance on television next to the robust John F. Kennedy.[97]

There is also some evidence that in 1968 Nixon and campaign manager Mitchell had in mind more than a simple urge to protect the candidate from the usual barbarities of the campaign. They had apparently decided that a good deal of what goes into the conventional presidential campaign is wasted effort. For example, they had decided that the customary big nighttime rallies, while they might occasionally prove useful, should not again become the object of the detailed energies they had received in 1960, because of the simple fact that such meetings were usually held too late in the day to get on the television news programs.[98]

Nixon's public meetings during the campaign, from a newsman's point of view, tended to distill into three general categories:[99]

1. The airport stops outside small cities. The nominee usually appeared on a flatbed truck with local Republican office seekers before audiences of 300 to 400 people. Such meetings were usually held in solid Republican areas, where Nixon was almost certain to win. The real aim was to aid the local candidates. These meetings usually ran about half an hour. Balloons and high-school bands were standard features. Nixon would offer a brief version of his standard speech, often just a collection of proven applause lines: "a small but serviceable bouquet of axioms and witticisms, selected apparently for the fact that they remained comprehensible almost irrespective of the order in which they were put together. . . . These well-tried lines became so familiar that the waiting reporters tended to mouth them in a chorus, finishing slightly ahead of the candidate."

2. The major daytime rallies, usually scheduled for states where Nixon needed to consolidate his support. These were occasions for the full version of the standard campaign speech, after a warming-up by Peanuts Hucko's jazz band or its equivalent and the girlish cheers of the Nixonaires (who were off-duty airline hostesses) and the Nixonettes (who were mostly daughters of local Republican vestrymen).

3. The huge indoor rallies, before large audiences. Admission was restricted so as to give the Nixon people control of the audience, which was composed so as to conform with their concept of good public relations. Aside from a suitable sprinkling of students, tickets were given only to citizens felt to be solid and reliable. In St. Louis, a city which is 45 percent black, the crowd of three thousand apparently contained six black people. At Madison Square Garden on November 1, New York state Republican committeeman Fred Carlin

said, "Anyone who doesn't look right is pulled from the line." Those who flunked the "eye test" included Negroes in African garb, some people with beards, some people without ties, and three Hasidic Jews. These "standards" were a remarkable implementation of Nixon's September 19 radio address, in which he said, "The lamps of enlightenment are lit by the spark of controversy; their flame can be snuffed out by the blanket of consensus."

These big rallies usually opened with a big brass band and perhaps a thousand-voice choir, which would sing the "Battle Hymn of the Republic," climaxing with a big balloon shower. The carefully selected audiences appeared to bolster the candidate's self-assurance, as he told his listeners that *they* were the *real* Americans. The speeches were not usually focused on very specific issues, with the exception of the "Crusade Against Crime." However, in specific areas where the matter of federal largess was important to the voters, Nixon advocated such programs as apparently in no way inimicable to the American virtues of self-reliance which he proclaimed in the abstract. In the important swing state of Texas, for example, the candidate supported continuation of oil-depletion allowances at current levels. In Austin, he supported the space program as "a national imperative." In East Tennessee, he praised the TVA and the Oak Ridge National Laboratory. In North Carolina, he was in favor of protecting the U.S. textile industry. In Johnstown, Pennsylvania, he promised vigorous action to deal with rising foreign steel imports. The Nixon organization was considerably less specific in its promises to minority groups. A candidate can probably be forgiven for focusing on regional interests as he travels a country as vast as the United States. But some statements were made, such as those about bringing private enterprise more closely into the problems of domestic poverty, which can hardly be said to have been explicitly detailed.[100]

An example of a Nixonesque attempt at minority group appeal in his campaign took place in Texas. This state seemed particularly bothersome to the Republicans, especially after the leaders of the traditionally feuding liberal and conservative factions of the Texas Democratic Party gathered under one roof at the Houston Astrodome to see Hubert Humphrey receive the laying on of hands from Lyndon Johnson. The Republicans felt the Mexican-American (Chicano) vote, some six hundred thousand strong in Texas (about half of it located in and around San Antonio), was likely to be crucial. But

Nixon, in trying to cut down the proportion of the expected Chicano vote of four hundred thousand which would go to Humphrey, could point to no record of achievement on behalf of Mexican-Americans. In fact, one of his campaign problems had been his inability to attract any kind of non-white support. But Nixon did his best when, before sixty-five hundred people in San Antonio, he introduced the Cuban couple who had been his and his wife's personal servants for several years. He told the audience that both his daughters had studied Spanish, and that he and Pat had gone to New Mexico for their honeymoon. The pitch fitted in with Nixon's appeal to the white middle class. "They have not been rioting," he said of the Chicanos. "They have not been breaking the law." It also appeared that none of them attended the San Antonio meeting.[101]

Again, the appeal of the man who sought to be President of *all* the people betrayed a lack of understanding of the problems of a significant minority group. Nixon could appeal to such groups only in such a way as not to antagonize the reasonably prosperous, white, middle-class, suburban-type voters who really needed no conversion, who were Nixon's for the asking, because they felt that finally one of *them* could be *their* President. But for public relations purposes, for the sake of appearances, it made good sense to at least go on record on behalf of the oppressed and dispossessed. No commitments were made. Those who were already committed to the Nixon cause would understand; they too might believe that private enterprise and "black capitalism" could solve the poverty problem; they too believe that even if people like black Americans and Mexican-Americans, in general, are not to be trusted; after all, *their* servants are certainly *different,* not bums like "the rest of *them."* Of course, there would be Mexican-Americans and black Americans and others on whom all this would have a negative effect. But such people probably wouldn't be Nixon voters to begin with, and in the meantime the candidate has made some p.r. capital out of the whole thing.

Speech writers have a good deal to do with the way these and other issues are articulated. Speech-writing—consistently good speech-writing—is an uncommon talent, even among the finest p.r. men, who, with their corporate heads, are frequently in search of the best practitioners. Nixon's dependence on such men is typical of heads of state, actual and aspiring, around the world. Although some may be sufficiently gifted to write well, none really have the time in which to do so. Abraham Lincoln, of course, wrote his own materials, but he was unique, and the presidency one hundred years ago was a considerably different institution. Some modern Presidents, as well as potential Presidents, men like Franklin Delano Roosevelt and Adlai Stevenson, have employed writers, and then frequently outshone them in preparing their own material and certainly in creating phrases. But these men, too, were exceptional.

Nixon's staff included not only a stable of writers but a managing editor to coordinate them. James Keogh, a former executive editor of *Time* magazine, was to play this same editorial role on the White House staff—scheduling, supervising, editing. During the campaign, Nixon would have conferences with his writers, outlining some of his speech ideas, suggesting some sources of information, perhaps citing one or two earlier statements in the same vein. The assigned writer would then follow up his leads, try a draft, discuss it with Keogh and maybe another writer, and then submit the material to Nixon. The candidate might then discuss the matter further with the writer then or make notes in the margin. Not that there was always time to do this in the campaign. Once, for example, Nixon picked up a speech written by a writer he hardly knew—someone who was not a regular member of his staff—and recited it on the air word for word. This was probably a rather serious public relations error in that the text turned out to be the much-attacked radio address on law and order. It had been prepared by Jeffrey Hart, a young Dartmouth English professor and former associate editor of the *National Review*, who had been a speech writer for Ronald Reagan until after the Republican convention.[102]

In addition to men like Keogh, Price, and Gavin, the Nixon speech-writing staff included, and still includes, an interesting assortment of individuals. Perhaps the most seasoned public relations man among them is William Safire, the proprietor of his own thriving p.r. agency until after the election and the author of three books, including *The Relations Explosion* and *The New Language of Politics*. Safire was rather unique among his colleagues in being Jewish, a native New Yorker, and a liberal Republican. He met Richard Nixon in Moscow in 1959, where Safire had stage-managed—without Nixon's knowledge of his role—the famous Nixon-Khrushchev "kitchen debate." At the time of that confrontation, Safire was working for New York publicist Tex McCrary, handling the account of the construction company which had built the "typical model house" on display at the U.S. exhibition in Moscow. As Nixon and the Soviet Premier strolled through the entrance to the model home, Safire opened an exit door, sending a crowd he had previously assembled into the model, trapping Nixon and Khrushchev near the kitchen. Nixon, seeing the good crowd, was tempted to seize the moment to rebut Khrushchev with some views about the American Way. An Associated Press photographer, unable to get close enough to shoot a picture, tossed Safire his camera over the heads of the Russian guards, and Safire took the only news photo of the event, the famous AP "kitchen debate" picture. Of course, public relations men with an eye for keeping as many clients as possible simultaneously content might have noticed that the picture also included the model home, another client's washing machine, boxes of Dash and SOS on top of the washer, and, importantly, the wife of Safire's boss, Jinx Falkenberg. The following year, back in New York, Safire joined the Nixon-Lodge volunteers and worked intermittently for Nixon, Rockefeller, and Senator Jacob Javits.[103] In early 1973 he announced his departure from the White House staff to become a columnist for *The New York Times.*

Another of the professional communicators on Nixon's staff, and also the youngest, is Patrick J. Buchanan, former editorial writer for the conservative St. Louis *Globe-Democrat*, a job he landed at twenty-three. Buchanan is an Irish Catholic and, like Gavin, a strong Buckley-type conservative. He had first run into Richard Nixon at a Belleville, Illinois, cocktail party in 1965 and told him that if he was going to run for President, he, twenty-six-year-old Mr. Buchanan, wanted to "get aboard early." Nixon hedged at the time, but Buchanan angled an interview in New York, where he convinced Nixon, in a three-hour conversation, to put him on the payroll. His specialty in the campaign was the daily changeable-with-the-news opening for the basic stump speech. Buchanan was also ghost-writer for Nixon's syndicated column, "The Loyal Opposition." Nixon, who used Buchanan for advice as well as for writing and continues to do so, once called the young man "one of the most brilliant political analysts in the nation today."[104]

The place of these and other public relations men and professional communicators in the campaign was especially evident when Nixon retired for his three-day campaign pause in Key Biscayne during mid-October. There had been a decision to launch a new series of major speeches during the last phase of the Nixon campaign ("It was as near as he got to a concession that the campaign had not been sufficiently active"). Those who met during the pause included Bryce Harlow (who had written the "security gap" speech, borrowing from Kennedy's "missile gap" speech of August 1958), Richard Allen (who did the "research gap" speech and after the election became assistant to National Security adviser Henry Kissinger), Alan Greenspan (the head of a successful economic consulting firm who describes himself as "a nineteenth-century liberal" and headed economic research for the campaign), Garment, Price, and Keogh. The enterprise was called "Operation Extra Effort," and Garment was authorized to purchase ten additional radio network slots to give vent to its products.[105]

The retention of so many of these people on the White House staff in similar capacities following Mr. Nixon's inauguration seems quite significant. It indicates that once a candidate credits public relations practitioners and their skills and the various subtechnologies which they employ with helping to put him in the White House, it is unlikely that he will in any way curtail the use of those individuals, those skills, those subtechnologies once he becomes Chief Executive.

Public relations professional H. Zane Robbins, for example, felt that the Nixon team was evidently so convinced of the value of the various polling and research devices used during the campaign that their continuing employment after Nixon became President was being very seriously considered. Such research, said Robbins, would probably involve in-depth taped interviews on major issues. These would have the effect of both gathering data and flattering the interviewee with an opportunity for a "curbside chat with the President." This, said Robbins, would be "not only informative but a masterful p.r. stroke as well."[106]

Thus, perhaps the ultimate in self-fulfillment for political public relations technology: the technique serves not only as a tool of measurement but as a public relations device in and of itself.

## Hubert H. Humphrey

When the Democratic National Convention ended in Chicago, Hubert Humphrey and his associates had nothing like the well-planned, gimmick-laden campaign that the Nixon organization had begun laying out long before the Republicans made their official choice. Rather, the Humphrey campaign had to fight for its life from the first moments of birth.

One of Humphrey's managers described it this way:

> "We had no money. We had no organization. We were 15 points behind in the polls. We did have a media plan, but we didn't have the money to go with it. And we were going to have to change our ad agency anyway. The worst thing was that we didn't have enough time. The candidate approved the campaign plan in Chicago on August 30. That was the Friday before Labor Day, which is the day the campaign begins, traditionally. Instead of having three or four weeks to mount a campaign, we had three days. And so the candidate went on the road, and he was a disaster."[107]

Lawrence O'Brien, who had come along with Humphrey to run the pre-convention campaign, now wanted to retire from politics to his pick of several high-paying jobs. Humphrey had planned to hand the management of his campaign over to Kenneth O'Donnell, another member of the old Kennedy "Irish Mafia." Finally, however, the Vice President succeeded in convincing O'Brien, who had perhaps by now become the consummate professional Democrat, to stay on. But before he had done so, a power vacuum had developed, with half a dozen other staff members vying for authority. O'Brien went to work with his two associates, Joseph Napolitan and Ira Kappenstein, to draft the campaign's media plan. There was simply no one else to do the job. At this late point in the campaign, all this team had to go on was a brief that had been prepared by another aspiring campaign manager, Secretary of Agriculture Orville Freeman, Humphrey's fellow Minnesotan. Freeman's original concept, however, now seemed overly elaborate in view of the financial straits in which the Humphrey campaign found itself. So O'Brien cut it back and got the candidate's approval of the rough draft on August 29, as the Vice President was waiting to deliver his acceptance speech.[108]

Both Kappenstein and Napolitan were getting their first exposure to the public relations of a presidential campaign. Kappenstein had been a bright young reporter for the Milwaukee *Journal* when a fellow Wisconsinite, John Gronouski, was appointed Postmaster-General and asked Kappenstein to join him in Washington. Kappenstein accepted. Later when Gronouski was made ambassador to

Poland, and Lyndon Johnson appointed O'Brien Postmaster-General, Kappenstein stayed on as O'Brien's assistant, which he remained, despite his boss's varying capacities, until his untimely death. Napolitan, it will be recalled, was the pro who had astounded the Democratic regulars in Pennsylvania two years before with his management of the Milton Shapp campaign. Now he was working for Humphrey. Napolitan had some strong views of his own, and he was in a position to implement them during the Humphrey campaign. It might be well to consider the views of this professional's professional on some of the basic public relations devices which we have been discussing as common threads running through most recent presidential campaigns.

"Effective use of television," says Napolitan, "is the key" to a successful campaign. He contends that even though everyone now makes use of television as a campaign device, some candidates still have not realized that they can *lose* votes on television. Buying television time does not automatically put you ahead with the voters:

> "You lose them when you put your guy in front of a camera, the kind, you know, where he starts out, 'Good evening ladies and gentlemen, my name is Joe Blow and I want to talk to you tonight about taxes.' When you do that you can hear the click of sets being switched or turned off all over the state. That sort of program is just radio with a light to read by."

Napolitan, furthermore, believes in allotting a "substantial part" of the campaign budget to the production costs of television programs and spots.

> "When some candidates have, say, $100,000 for TV, they put maybe $5,000 into production so they can spend more on [TV] time. I'd rather spend $30,000 on production and only $70,000 on time. The truth is that you just can't made good, cheap films."[109]

As might be expected, in listing campaign advertising priorities, Napolitan puts television first, dividing his second choice about evenly between direct mail and radio. Radio has the advantages of simplicity of production and economy of cost, by comparison with its sister medium. Sometimes, in fact, the audio from a telecast can be used on radio with only minor changes. This is done, for example, with programs such as "Meet the Press" and "Face the Nation." Direct mail is another matter; to many people, political "junk mail" gets the same cursory treatment as more commercial solicitations. As James Perry points out, however, Napolitan is in the company of most of the contemporary professional campaign consultants and managers in the belief that *good* direct mail can achieve notable results in a political campaign. One argument made in favor of this device is the increasing mobility of the population, the fall-off in person-to-person contact on political matters, and the fact that whole blocks or groups of blocks in many areas of the country now lack the kind of recognized group leadership that they have traditionally had. Direct mail coming into a new housing subdivision in this kind of situation, for example, might help fill a communications gap.[110] In 1972 direct mail was perhaps the most effectively used public relations tool in the McGovern campaign. Used to solicit funds more than votes, it brought results from "little people" which underwrote a substantial portion of McGovern's campaign costs.

Napolitan is unenthusiastic about the results of newspaper advertising in political campaigns. It also bothers him that the same newspapers that preach in their news and editorial columns about the tragedy of the rising costs of political campaigns often raise their rates for political ads far above what they charge their other customers. At times, "the political rate is double the regular advertising rate, with no discounts allowed, and cash on the barrelhead. . . ."[111]

As for polls, says Joe Napolitan, they "never won an election. But you can win an election with what you do with your polls." The first poll of the campaign, the basic poll, is the most important one to Napolitan, because it determines the messages to be carried to the voters in campaign literature, TV and radio spots, billboards, and so on. Such basic polls are increasingly expensive. They cover a lot of ground, sometimes requiring forty-five minutes or more to complete an interview. The cost, therefore, runs between $6 and $10 per person interviewed.[112]

It is worth underlining once again the assumption implicit in Napolitan's comments about polls—an assumption which we suspect is so banal to the campaign consultant fraternity as to have already passed beyond the pale of serious discussion. This is the automatic procedure whereby a candidate determines the issues which he will discuss and the positions he will take on the basis of what the polls indicate the voters want to hear.

A further assumption is that a candidate is courting disaster should he decide to fly in the face of such data and set his campaign priorities on what he believes to be important.

Napolitan's ideas about television and advertising were to come into direct conflict with those of young Arie Kopelman of Doyle Dane Bernbach, who now reenters the scene. Kopelman felt that by September 5 he had the go-ahead he needed on the Humphrey advertising. The creative people at DDB went to work on three commercials, preparing storyboards (captioned drawings of proposed television films, mounted in sequence on boards) to be shown to Napolitan. On September 13 William Bernbach, who was then in Mexico, received a cable reporting that the Humphrey account was being taken away and given to Campaign Planning Associates, an outfit being jerrybuilt for the purpose by Napolitan in cooperation with another New York advertising agency, Lennen & Newell. As Chester et al. (to whom we are indebted for much of the account which follows) point out, all of the exact reasons for this action were not entirely clear.[113]

One reason was apparently financial. The DDB proposal called for a campaign costing $6,000,000 to $7,000,000. This might have been more than reasonable in 1968 by Republican standards, but was out of the question for the Democrats, who did not know whether or when they would be able to buy any half-hours on network television. They did almost no advertising until late September. Humphrey had no full-length programs, very few television spots, and no radio or newspaper ads at a time when Nixon was burning up the airwaves. Furthermore, DDB, as is customary in the advertising business, and as had been the case in 1964, expected to get a regular percentage of the advertising billings as a commission, while Lennen & Newell were prepared to work on a flat fee basis. Nevertheless, when Lennen & Newell did come into the picture, its representative, Allan Gardner, was aghast at the seriousness of Humphrey's cash position. He talked with the campaign treasurer, Robert Short, and mapped out ideas for a "very conservative" campaign, to cost $6,500,000—about the same amount as the Doyle Dane Bernbach campaign had called for. Short told Gardner he might be able to give the agency $2,500,000, but he was not entirely sure of that; he had to get on the telephone that week to raise enough money to meet the payroll.

But a more basic professional conflict between Napolitan and DDB is perhaps more significant for our purposes. This is the essen-

tial difference between two concepts of professionalism in the conduct of a presidential campaign. Men like those at Doyle Dane Bernbach make their livings as expert communicators. They bring
together a variety of creative skills ordinarily used for commercial
products and put them to work in marketing a candidate for the presidency. Napolitan, as we have seen, is another kind of new professional. This new breed of campaign consultants are necessarily p.r.
men in the first instance, as were Whitaker and Baxter, for example,
but see themselves as having much broader expertise in the deploy-
ment of a variety of public relations, organizational, and political
techniques. They use p.r. people, ad agencies, film-makers, pollsters, and so on. Napolitan had done his precedent-shattering job
for Milton Shapp largely through polls and a television documentary
produced by free-lancer Shelby Storck (who later made "The Mind
Changer," the highly personal half-hour film of Hubert Humphrey
shown on election eve). Napolitan had made his name and his career
in Pennsylvania. By 1972-1973, he was involved in the New York City
mayoral contest, and in campaigns in Venezuela. Chester et al. refer
to him as a "gruff, abrupt fellow with no patience for what he considers irrelevant." He was supposed to have horrified the Doyle Dane
Bernbach men when, after watching one of their presentations, he
barked, "That's not an effective use of television, and I think it's terri-
ble." Said one of the agency men: "You just don't talk to Mr. *Bernbach* that way!"

There is also some evidence of an ideological split between Napolitan and the DDB people (if one interprets "ideology" rather
broadly). The admen felt they were on the side of principle. Napolitan felt that he was on the side of the party that was paying the bills.
Some of the DDB staff had been involved personally as volunteers for
McCarthy earlier in the year, and this was enough to cause some suspicion in the Democratic National Committee, which, despite the
success of DDB's campaign for Johnson in 1964, were still not convinced of the value of a "high class" advertising agency. Some of the
party regulars may have also still smarted from some of the organizational difficulties that had taken place vis-à-vis DDB in 1964. Furthermore, the party had been split wide open by the Chicago convention and the events that surrounded it, and many conflicts, which
might ordinarily have been suppressed, were now out in the open. A
regular party man—the Vice President of the United States—had

been nominated, and the dissenters no longer had a place in his campaign.

Thus, the fears of Napolitan and the Democratic regulars were hardly allayed when several of the ad agency men began grilling the Humphrey people with questions on the order of "Why didn't Humphrey come out against Daley?" Some Democrats began to suspect "incipient sabotage" at DDB. For example, the agency produced a mock-up of a "law-and-order" commercial for the Democrats. One DDB staff member said: "We had some rather liberal ideas, stressing the dimension of social justice. Well, Joe Napolitan actually said, 'I don't want to see any black faces in this stuff. I don't want to argue about it. No black faces!' "[114]

The incident is also of interest because it sheds some light on a more subtle but very salient point. the advertising agency appears to have been given a good deal of latitude in making an initial determination of the approach that the Vice President might take to a whole set of issues during the course of his campaign. Even if others closer to the candidate had veto and editorial power, the agency was still operating under a mandate that was considerably more than technical in nature. DDB was apparently in a position to recommend what the candidate's position might be, for purposes of his television spots, rather than simply ascertaining first-hand the Vice President's views and using communications skills to present them as they were. Once again, the difference between selling and marketing was at work. But it was not just a case of telling the people what they "wanted" to hear; it also was telling them what the advertising men wanted them to hear.

Furthermore, Napolitan, who exercised veto power on behalf of the candidate and felt that he was in a position to issue directives about such matters as the color of people appearing in commercials, was not the candidate. He was not running for President. He is, in fact, a mercenary. There is nothing pejorative implied in our use of that term. Traditional politicians also had to make a living. So do professionals who work for a variety of worthwhile causes. Our point is that Napolitan, and growing numbers of his colleagues, are just that: paid professionals. Napolitan, given his growing stature in his profession, may be able to pick his clients, but he is at the service of the preachers of a variety of political gospels, so long as they are Democrats. But just where the man who wanted to be President figured in this is unclear. Although some of the gimmickry of the Nixon campaign may have been absent in the Humphrey effort (for one thing, the Democrats couldn't afford it), available evidence would seem to indicate that the Vice President had been afflicted with the same variety of abdication of judgment in favor of the professionals that seems to be increasingly endemic in political campaigns.

In any case, during the initial weeks after Chicago, Napolitan also had some more positive assignments. He had to produce and stockpile the ammunition for the counterattack. Shelby Storck was brought in on faith to make his documentary—no one really knew where the money to show it would be coming from. (And the potential financial sacrifice should be noted.) Napolitan also commissioned some private polls designed to show Humphrey with a somewhat less negative image than the national polls seemed to indicate he had.[115]

By the time the campaign reached midpoint, the Democrats found themselves with an unexpected natural public relations asset: the obvious contrast between the two vice presidential candidates, Governor Spiro Agnew and Senator Edmund Muskie. For a vice presidential candidate to provide such a boon as Muskie did for the Democrats is a rare occurrence; in 1968 this may have been even more remarkable than usual because of the general feeling that both presidential candidates were simply not very popular. Thus the media, looking for exciting copy, began to contrast Muskie and Agnew, with the senator before long emerging as the obvious journalistic front-runner.

Muskie had never roused man to great heights of intellectual revelation with impassioned or thoughtful or original or even moderately stimulating political oratory. One highly placed Johnson Administration official told the writer that the only time he could recall Muskie really getting excited about an issue was when it might have had some effect on potato growers in Maine. Muskie had sided, for a time, with the hawk majority in his party and was a cautious and competent politician with a reasonably good presence.

But the contrast with the then politically untalented Agnew was almost immediately evident. Muskie only had to be mannerly while Agnew was off and running with gaffes like "Polack" and "Fat Jap." The Humphrey advertising and public relations people, by the end of the campaign, played the Agnew image to the hilt. One of the most telling of the commercials—used on both television and radio —said simply: "Spiro Agnew for Vice President" and was followed by a long burst of near hysterical laughter and the words "This would be serious if it wasn't so funny."[116]

One official of the Democratic organization told the writer that there was some concern among the campaign leadership that Humphrey's "depth of feeling about things was not being communicated to the voters." According to this respondent:

> Humphrey *is* a man who has deep, emotional reactions to important issues. One of the most effective bits in the campaign was that television documentary showing the human side of Humphrey's life. You saw him in Waverly, how he was when he relaxed at home. One of the most touching pieces of film was the scene with his retarded grandchild.[117]

McGinniss had some reservations about the taste of this half-hour film ("The Mind Changer"), although he reluctantly agrees that it succeeded in its goal of further humanizing the Vice President:

> It was awful in many ways. It showed Hubert Humphrey and Edmund Muskie crawling down a bowling alley in their shirt sleeves. It showed Humphrey wearing a stupid fisherman's hat and getting his lines snarled on a lake near his home and it took shameless advantage of the fact he has a mentally retarded granddaughter. It was contrived and tasteless. But it was the most effective single piece of advertising of the campaign.
>
> . . . It began with the assumption that of course he had faults as a politician and of course he had made a lot of mistakes, but it said again and again that Hubert Humphrey, at least, is a person. Here he is sweating, laughing, crying out in the open air. . . . Nixon . . . depended on a studio the way a polio victim relied on an iron lung.
>
> That one Humphrey film made a mockery of Richard Nixon's year-long quest for warmth. You can't create humanity, it said. You either have it or you don't. Hubert Humphrey has it. Guess who does not.[118]

Financial problems continued to plague the Humphrey campaign almost down to the wire. During the last ten days or so, the polls showed a considerable surge in the Democrats' strength. Some of the Democratic National Committee officials relate this upswing to the question of finances. It is, they say, a cause-and-effect relationship. The polls began to show Humphrey coming up as more money had become available for television time. As the polls improved, more money came in. This enabled the organization to purchase still more television time, and the polls continued to improve. The availability of additional cash also helped the Democrats make a more exciting production of their final election eve telethon, which the Republicans acknowledged grudgingly was well done and probably quite effective.[119]

This chain of events brings to mind the events that followed Harry S Truman's upset victory in 1948. Suddenly, the day after the election results were known, a great many checks with dates a few weeks old began to arrive at party headquarters from loyal Democrats who had somehow forgotten to put them into the mail before Election Day.

Humphrey's rise in the polls was indeed a dramatic one. The public relations aspects of the campaign were geared, after a certain point, precisely to affect the polls and produce a bandwagon effect, and the efforts apparently met with considerable success.

A Gallup poll on September 22 had shown the Vice President fifteen points behind Nixon. The Humphrey operation then began to prepare for the Harris poll of October 7 in a "classic illustration of the way polls, press, and politicians interact in a Presidential campaign." The danger, from the point of view of Humphrey's advisers, was that the Gallup results would influence the media to write off the Vice President (as they largely did with McGovern in 1972), and their coverage and editorial comments would then be reflected both in more low poll figures and dwindling financial contributions. This, as we have indicated, would mean less advertising and media exposure, thus producing a more rapid downward spiral. William Connell, Humphrey's executive assistant, prepared a memo proposing that the campaign attempt not only to counteract Gallup, but to discredit him altogether. Connell argued impressively that the polls Napolitan had commissioned for Humphrey at the time of the first blow from Gallup showed that he had a "fighting chance" to go over the top in the electoral college. Connell stressed that if the October 7 Harris poll showed improvement, Humphrey could point not only to that improvement but also to a *remarkable* change from the Gallup results. On October 22 Connell wrote a memo headed "Gallup's Credibility Gap." His idea was that

> "the polls should not be meekly awaited as Acts of God. We should prepare a full-swing orchestration on the theme: 'The swing is on to Humphrey.' We should hit key columnists, writers,

and financial people with the news that we were already in the ball game at the time the bad Gallup poll was taken, and with this new national upsurge, we have strengthened ourselves . . . in enough states to win the election in the Electoral College."[120]

The effect of the Humphrey organization's line on the polls, and its implications for the public relations program of an "underdog" candidate for the presidency, was well illustrated by the interesting difference between two stores in *The New York Times*. On October 6 the *Times* carried a story by Warren Weaver, Jr., who said he based his statements on "interviews with several hundred political leaders." The story held that in Electoral College votes Humphrey was running not second but third, well behind George Wallace and Richard Nixon. Weaver gave Humphrey 28 electoral votes, to 66 for Wallace and 380 for Nixon. (The final totals were: Nixon, 301; Humphrey, 191; Wallace, 46.) The headline on Weaver's story read: "Humphrey leading in 4 [States] as He Drops Further Behind." Three days later, the *Times* ran a story by White House correspondent Max Frankel under an eight-column headline, "Democratic Leaders, Calling Polls Misleading, Say Humphrey Can Win." It made no reference to the glum predictions that had been carried in the same paper three days before. The Frankel story said that "After an extensive state-by-state survey, including many polls that cost $250,000," the Humphrey people had become convinced that their candidate "retains a fair chance to win the Presidency."[121]

Just what had taken place during the intervening three days? The *Times* and other papers had been given the results of polls commissioned by Joseph Napolitan, with the concurrence of O'Brien, at the time of the Gallup poll shock waves. On October 9, the same day the *Times* published them, Connell put the figures into a memo to be shown to selected reporters for the less favored newspapers. The memo was headed, "Humphrey on the Upswing, Gallup or Not!" Chester et al. say that the memorandum "was by no means composed in a spirit of disinterested scientific research. . . . It was a selling document." The memo used two categories of evidence:

1. Results of telephone polls conducted for the Democratic National Committee by Sindlinger and Company. Connell drew attention to a "sharp rise in the undecided vote following the Democratic Convention, and the gradual swing back to Humphrey of that undecided vote since mid-September."

2. Other evidence from still more private polls commissioned by the Democrats. Connell didn't mention that the five polls cited in the memo had been carried out by Joe Napolitan himself or that additional polls by Oliver Quayle and others had not been released. Said Connell:

> "The central point is this. . . . Somebody is wrong—either Gallup is wrong or *all* of the five state polls [Napolitan's] are radically wrong and Sindlinger is wrong as well."

A note from Connell to O'Brien the next day, enclosing more of the same, said:

> "Larry, the attached memorandum prepared by our polling people should be used with selected columnists, etc. I think it is highly significant and persuasive."[122]

Not all media representatives reacted the same way to the Humphrey polls. Columnists Rowland Evans and Robert Novak condemned what they called "dubious" surveys, "not taken seriously by the polling fraternity or the Democratic National Committee's own research division," and "releasing questionable data to bolster nagging morale." Although the Humphrey people denied such charges, Chester and his fellow British reporters call the Napolitan-Connell effort a "trick"—"a desperate attempt to bolster morale." And morale *was* low. In any case, the operation was highly successful— "most newspapers swallowed it hook, line and sinker." The operation was not aimed solely at the press, but at potential financial contributors as well. Wires went off to state Democratic chairmen and Citizens for Humphrey coordinators saying that the public polls showing Humphrey trailing Nixon might be wrong. The private polls, said the telegrams, tell a different story, and since we need money for TV commercials, go tell the good news about "our" polls to potential donors. And sure enough, the financial appeals began to have effect.[123]

Thus, it appears that the Humphrey campaign had degenerated a good deal beyond those campaigns that choose issues and positions based on poll results, as most now do. It had gone further down the road than a campaign in which a candidate selects personal mannerisms and dress and speech patterns according to poll results, as John F. Kennedy seems to have done in 1960. It went even further than a campaign designed solely to influence the polls and thereby change men's minds with several percentage points, as Rockefeller had attempted to do in his 1968 campaign for the Republican nomination. The Humphrey campaign, not content with what the major national polls said about the Democratic candidate's chances, ran its own polls, of a limited and questionable nature. It did so not in order to provide the campaign organization with information, but rather to build an arsenal of dubious data with which to mislead the mass media, and through them potential Humphrey voters and contributors. And to a considerable extent, the media bought what the Humphrey professionals were peddling.

## Some 1968 Miscellany

The presidential campaigns of 1968 in some ways presented a kind of phantasmagoria of American politics. The year was not without its share of bizarre elements. Although we shall not attempt to account for these phenomena here, or to trace their development, it might be interesting to look at one or two of the proceedings taking place on the fringe of the two-party action.

One such activity was the campaign of George Wallace, former governor of Alabama, and in 1968 the candidate of his own creation, the American Independent Party. One of the ways in which the Wallace campaign was distinctive is that it operated without the benefit of any professional public relations assistance. This probably helps account for the fact that Wallace's campaign bumbled along during the first half of 1968 without being taken seriously either by press or politicians; and that when it really began to attract massive attention, the Wallace organization was not able to cope with its newfound popularity, let alone channel this public attention to ultimate political advantage.

The press began to overcompensate for its lack of interest in Wallace by July, when "television crews began to burrow through the crowds at Wallace rallies looking for trouble." Reporters started to turn out in force for the Wallace meetings, and columnists and commentators puzzled over his proposals (frequently missing the real point) and pontificated about his significance. So without any organized public relations campaign, in the sense in which we have been discussing such efforts, by the time of the major party conventions,

Wallace had established himself as a national candidate. It was evident that he would have some serious support in the North. Furthermore, Wllace had probably had some influence in the supplanting of Vietnam as the number one campaign issue by the more dubious theme of "law 'n' order." The major candidates, in any case, could no longer ignore him, his statements, and his professed presidential ambitions.[124]

However, the Wallace organization's disregard of the rudiments of professional public relations (probably more out of naïveté than disdain) was so basic as to turn the working conditions for the press assigned to cover his campaign into complete chaos. Press arrangements usually were simply nonexistent. At one point things had grown so bad that a delegation from the press corps approached Wallace and said that if he would appoint a press liaison man, the reporters would get together and pay his salary. Although meant as a joke, the serious intent of the gesture was evident. Eventually, and incredibly, press problems for the candidate became the domain of the senior Secret Service man on the detail assigned to travel with Wallace, David Frarex. ". . . He was not only a kind of press liaison man; he seemed just about to run the campaign."[125]

The brief, localized, and inconsequential campaign of Roger D. Branigan, governor of Indiana and favorite son candidate for the Democratic presidential nomination, demonstrated that the political advantages of divorcing content from style were not entirely a creation of Madison Avenue. Branigan's empty campaign also illustrated that the fine old American tradition of political hokum gets along fine at times with more sophisticated mass-media techniques. Branigan was advised by Robert Montgomery, an Indianapolis adman and a veteran of the 1960 Kennedy campaign. Montgomery, who had also done some of the media work in Branigan's successful gubernatorial campaign, admired the Hoosier politician's content-void techniques. Said Montgomery: 'Running for governor, he didn't make a political speech. And so far as I know, he hasn't made a political speech this time. But, I'm happy to say, no one has noticed the omission."[126]

The Youth International Party (Yippies) convened in Chicago's Lincoln Park during the Democratic National Convention, where it nominated (before the tear gas cannisters began to fly) a pig as its candidate. Abbie Hoffman, head of the party, demonstrated an interesting degree of sophistication about the uses of the mass media and the possibilities for manipulation in a presidential campaign. The

Walker Report, *Rights in Conflict,* quotes Hoffman on the creation of his party as follows:

> "... And so, YIPPIE was born, the Youth International Party. What about if we create a myth, program it into the media, you know ... when that myth goes in, it's always connected to Chicago August 25 ... come and do our thing, excitement, bullshit, everything, anything ... commitment, engagement, Democrats, pigs, the whole thing. All you do is change the H in Hippie to a Y for Yippie, and you got it ... you can study the media and you say, well, the H is switching, now they're talking about Yippies. New phenomena, a new thing on the American scene. ... Why? That's our question. Our slogan is 'Why?' You know as long as we can make up a story about it that's exciting, full of shit, mystical, magical, you have to accuse us of going to Chicago to perform magic."[127]

As Chester et al. point out, Hoffman's basic revolutionary text seems to come quite a bit closer to Marshall McLuhan than Karl Marx.

> ... and with the creation of YIPPIE, they developed a new revolutionary premise for the electronic era: when the might of a society cannot be challenged, strike at its myths. Power in this situation does not proceed out of the barrel of a gun, but, in Hoffman's words, out of "charisma, myth and put-on—the triple-barreled YIP shotgun."

Hoffman and the Yippies and others in their coalition at Chicago had become acutely aware of the kind of phenomena that Daniel Boorstin wrote of in *The Image*—that is, the gap between the way in which most American people perceive their society and its underlying realities. It was psychological warfare of the kind that Hoffman and his group were well-equipped to wage.

> They were in themselves mockeries of traditional American conceptions of clean-cut young manhood, yet their very bizarreness made them news. They lived with an awareness usually vouchsafed to politicians after years of bitter experience and sometimes never: the absolute noncorrelation between news value and moral values.[128]

And that, some cynics might say, is just what political public relations is all about.

# Seven:

# The Meaning of Political Public Relations to the Process of Choosing a President

Hail to B.B.D. & O.
It told the nation how to go!
It managed by advertisement
To sell us a new President . . .
Philip Morris, Lucky Strike,
Alka-Seltzer, I like Ike.

This bit of doggerel was written by Marya Mannes in 1952 about the packaging of Dwight D. Eisenhower for the American public. And when Miss Mannes wrote it, the idea of selling a potential President with the same professional skills—indeed, by the same professionals —used to sell deodorants, cigarettes, and headache remedies was per- haps vaguely amusing to some, vaguely scandalous to others. Televi- sion was still something of a novelty, more a family plaything than its principal medium of communication. But by 1968 Chester, Hodgson, and Page were able to say that "people had become used to the idea";[1] and S. I. Hayakawa that "In the age of television, image becomes more important than substance."[2]

Our attempt in this book has not been to prove that presidential politics and public relations are now one and the same. We would still hold with Stanley Kelley's hypothesis of 1956 that skill is only one element of politics, and public relations skills are only a part of the total range of those skills needed in campaigning. As he has pointed out, the public relations man is essentially a specialist in communication.[3]

But to the degree that presidential campaigning is now essentially a process of communication to broad publics, the public relations man and other related professionals hold sway. His profession has become increasingly "scientific," and, as we have seen, he now routinely makes broad use of a whole range of devices and skills, including research, advertising, public opinion polling, data processing, and so on. From the concept of a need to consult with the public relations man in his special areas of expertise has evolved a broader and yet more special profession of campaign consulting and campaign management. Thus, some of the broader skills called for in the waging of a political campaign—organization, negotiation, the syntheses of substantive programs out of the supposed needs and articulated demands of conflicting publics—have now become the dominion of the professional's study and advice, rather than simply the candidate's judgment.

So even if the political expertise of the public relations man and others in related professions remains just one part of the total required, the evidence is that it is an increasingly dominant part. Even when the professional himself is not involved in central decision-making, considerations that have their origin in public relations techniques still play a major part in the decisions and actions of the candidates and their closest advisers, even when those advisers are thought to be primarily political in nature. The implications of all this for the American political system are serious and pervasive. For this reason, we have attempted, extracting from the limited literature on the subject, to give a clear picture of a certain kind of political animal, to demonstrate the character of his thinking, to portray the essence of his skills, to illustrate the techniques that he uses, to discuss the conditions under which he works, and to trace the nature of his relationships to other political figures and organizations—and the considerations on the part of those individuals and groups that guide them in their use of public relations techniques and practitioners.

As for the technical need of professional communications advice in the conduct of a presidential campaign—and most other political campaigns, for that matter—there can be little doubt. We have seen that the means for disseminating the news of a political campaign have become increasingly complex. There is no reason to assume that a statement by a presidential candidate, or even of an incumbent President, will automatically warrant a couple of columns on the front page or a couple of minutes in the opening segment of a network newscast. As the pressures of competition for such space and time become increasingly intense, the public relations consultant becomes more of a right arm to the political candidate, as he has to so many businessmen. Some editorial decisions by the media are no more predictable than world events. But to the extent that there are methods for deriving the greatest possible impact from a particular story, the public relations professional makes his business out of knowing them. And, along with the advertising man, this expertise is not limited to major daily newspapers and radio and television, but extends to specialized publications, foreign language and ethnic newspapers, labor periodicals, pamphlets, brochures, posters, billboards, newsletters—maybe even skywriting and signs towed by blimps—and all manner of special events. Further, as a broad-gauged individual, his expertise now extends well beyond the media into broad areas which might be termed "creative programming."

So, what Kelley observed in 1956 is more true than ever today: we are not dealing with a phenomenon that will go away, any more than the media will go away or become less complex. It is not just that the professional sells his services; they are loudly demanded by the politicians. The question of a commitment to the use of mass media is no longer discussed in planning a presidential campaign, it is assumed. But the mechanisms are costly, and sometimes their technical requirements appear esoteric to the uninitiated. They are, as Kelley has said, manned by personnel

> linked in an intricate network to each other and to the outside world. . . . Each message that is sent through the communication system must compete successfully with thousands of others, if it is to reach the consumer at all. The audience's receptivity to different kinds of appeals may, and does, undergo constant change.[4]

Nevertheless, Kelley contends, there is still some "magic" involved in this demand for public relations services. Public relations men themselves, and their clients, political and otherwise, frequently find themselves in difficulty when it comes time to assess the general effectiveness of public relations techniques in the achievement of a desired objective. Similarly, any evaluation of a particular public relations technique as opposed to another in terms of cost effectiveness is difficult to achieve with any substantial degree of scientific accuracy. Such questions are the subject of considerable ongoing discussion among p.r. professionals.

The politician, however, is by definition a compulsive. He *must* win. So he is in the position of having to look favorably upon almost anyone who seems to have at his disposal some skills or information that might be used to help him win. Even the most confident of campaigners may "run scared" at times (for example, Lyndon Johnson at the time of the Jenkins incident in 1964). The need for crisis management, born of competitive politics, is wind in the sails of the effective public relations man, just as it would be in similar situations in the business world.

Of course, this is not quite the way things were supposed to work out, according to classical democratic theory. John Stuart Mill, for example, did not envision the use of professional public relations men, but rather a free press when he wrote that ". . . without publicity . . . how could [the public] either check or encourage what they were not permitted to see?" This "intelligence service," this objective enlightenment, was to be provided for the people by the press. Jefferson, too, saw it as a great device for public education. But now the control of the press and other informational media has become increasingly centralized. It has been physically and financially impossible for most media to staff up in such a way as to keep pace in quantity and substance with the increasing complexity of the world around them. At the same time, the public relations profession has grown. And although many of those who run the media wish it could be otherwise, they also know, even if only the most forthright will publicly admit to it, that they are dependent upon public relations men for a major share of their news, derisive remarks at press club symposia notwithstanding. So the classical view of the role of the press simply is no longer adequate. Furthermore, the economic and other problems that have helped bring the media to increasing dependence upon the public relations profession show signs of intensifying rather than abating and, as this happens, the value of the practitioner to the presidential candidate can only increase.[5]

Since public relations men are not about to get out of presidential politics, it becomes pertinent to consider their long-range impact on the American political system. Some public relations men have themselves been thinking along these lines. In some cases, they have reached rather disgraceful conclusions, as witness this conclusion by H. Zane Robbins of Burson-Marsteller Associates:

> "When you stop to think about it, the art of politics is really a lot simpler than it seems. Despite the seeming complexity, all it

requires for success is the application of common sense in defining the problem, followed by hard, grubby work to solve it. In this, *political persuasion is no different from any other public relations project.*"[6]

In point of fact, it *is* as different as it can be. The danger to the American democratic system lies not so much in the use of political public relations as it does in the persistence of this kind of commercial thinking in political situations. It has caused justifiable outrage among thoughtful scholars and other political observers, to wit, Professor Howard White:

> What Rosser Reeves is reported to have said in 1952, that he looked upon the voter in a booth as he did upon a man who was trying to choose between two brands of toothpaste, has been transformed into the assumption not so much that the voter chooses between commodities but that he himself is a commodity, to be packaged and processed and stored away until inventories are counted on Election Day. Commodities, of course, do not choose; they are chosen. And while the press is not really blunt and clear about what is new in present-day campaigns, it seems that it is the processed voter, the voter who does not choose but is chosen.[7]

What Dr. White has in mind is the maneuvering, the manipulating of public opinion, called by Edward Bernays and others "the engineering of consent." In a sense, many small "d" democrats would share with public relations men a general approval of at least one phenomenon that has been associated with their ascent—that is, the rising power of public opinion. After all, as Kelley has pointed out, population growth, universal suffrage, increasing educational levels, all have meant more democracy and less aristocracy in America, in that it is increasingly difficult to resolve political matters through agreements among members of a limited ruling group that derives its prestige not only from who is "in," but from the power it has to keep others "out." Mass media, too, are inherently democratic insofar as they make it possible to engage in instantaneous and simultaneous communication with people who are all over the place not only geographically, but in socioeconomic terms.

If all of this is a boon to democracy, then the problem for democracy is that the system of mass communications in the United States makes it possible, as we have tried to illustrate in preceding chapters, to focus national attention on personalities and events in a manner that becomes increasingly effective as the infusion of capital and technical skills becomes more massive.

Perry, for example, illustrates this point with Nelson Rockefeller's victory over Frank O'Connor in the 1966 New York gubernatorial election. In this contest, it will be recalled, Rockefeller's massive organization outspent O'Connor's more conventional campaign group by about 6 to 1, and in the end beat the City Council president by a fairly small margin, 2,690,626 to 2,298,363, with the Liberal and the Conservative party candidates each getting more than 500,000 votes. These figures, says Perry, "show that Rockefeller could have been beaten; he *should* have been beaten; he won only because he had so much money, so much talent working for him. . . ." This, to Perry, suggests some patterns for the future:[8]

    1. The need for money—to be spent wisely, "even ruthlessly." You must have it early, and spend it often.

    2. Television. "The premier instrument for political campaigning. It penetrates into almost every home; it sways and angers and even converts."

    3. Experts. "No one wins any more with amateurs."

    4. Time. It takes time to put together a "new-style" campaign.

There is also, of course, the question of the candidate himself. Perry, despite his studies of the technology of the "new politics," refuses to believe that *anyone* can be elected, given money, lots of television exposure, expert help, and time to deploy them. Even though Rockefeller had all of this in spades in 1966, says Perry, "There was, in all the confusion and bitterness, a genuine product to be marketed, albeit in a battered and dusty package."

In a report on the first conference to be sponsored by the American Association of Political Consultants, *Newsweek* magazine indicated that some participants did admit that there are just some candidates who cannot be helped by packaging techniques. The reasons, as one might guess, do not necessarily have anything to do with political competence. It is just that a candidate who has a "hot" or "hard" television image no longer has a chance in a major election. George Romney is a case in point. "You just couldn't change George Romney by TV advertising," according to Frederic Papert of Papert,

Koenig, Lois. "Romney was the instance where we applied every technique and none of them worked," an unnamed consultant was quoted as saying.[9]

So we are again back to marketing and packaging. One is almost forced to conclude that public opinion, to the degree that it has become a more powerful factor in the choosing of Presidents, is only powerful in the sense that it can now be manipulated in support of a given objective, at least for the short term, with the proper inputs of money and technique. Thus, public opinion is not really a weapon that the people can confidently hold in reserve as part of their revolutionary arsenal. Instead, it has become a factor subject to professional management. Supporters of public opinion polls might hold that the opposite is the case. It is their contention that the polls work to the greater glory of the democratic process; they highlight the issues, state them in simple terms, cover the electorate continuously, and thus help to approach the concept of the people consulting together in the choice of a leader. They hold that polls uncover the major concerns of the electorate and determine the will of the majority. Thus, according to this point of view, the polls give people a chance to address themselves to matters troubling the electorate, so that a kind of dialogue actually does take place.

The effect of such polls on the election of the President and on other of our democratic processes is really a more significant question than the perpetually discussed matter of the scientific accuracy of the surveys. For not every thoughtful citizen would agree that checking and rechecking and publishing and broadcasting the results of small samples of the shifting preferences of the public during the heat of a presidential campaign is necessarily a wise procedure. For there seems to be serious evidence that the results of such polls have done little to raise the level of political campaigning. On the contrary, they have destroyed the political courage and leadership and potential eloquence of more than one presidential campaign. It may even be said that the polls are no help to political progress. For, as Ogden and Peterson have pointed out, they tend to give voice to a public tendency toward complacency and conservatism. The polls, in their abbreviated and simplistic approach to the issues of the day, serve to mask the complexities of our decision-making processes and are to a very great extent based on a serious misconception of American democracy.[10]

The illustrations that we have drawn from various presidential campaigns would tend to bear out this hypothesis. Barry Goldwater —despite what one might feel about his positions on crucial issues, and regardless of whether one could conscientiously vote for him or not—is notable as the noble exception to the tendency toward the sterilization of presidential campaigns, which has been making steady progress since 1952. His disregard for the polls in shaping his positions may have been based in part upon an erroneous assumption about a "hidden" conservative majority. But Goldwater nevertheless determined at the outset to articulate his conservative philosophy during the course of the campaign, and that he did—to his own political detriment. With that single exception, and with some exceptions in the case of Adlai Stevenson, the general tendency is for presidential candidates to be quite willing to modify their own judgments (if indeed, they still have any) to fit what the polls indicate they "should" say and do in order to get elected.

Thus, public relations politics can generally be associated with moderate, middle-of-the-road, fence-sitting politics. With the refreshing exception of the YIPPIE campaign of 1968, which was a kind of burlesque of the whole process, the new political technology and the professional exploitation of the mass media in presidential campaigning can be said to have nothing to do with radicalism and substantial political innovation. For one thing, radicals do not tend to be wealthy, and the wealthy do not tend to finance political innovators. And this technology and these professional services—involving data processing, public opinion polls, film, videotape, television and radio time, advertising agencies, and the services of bright, highly trained and experienced people—are not cheap. As Perry has said, "The professional managers are mercenaries. They are willing to go almost anywhere for a buck."[11]

Not many of those bucks are to be earned working for the poor, the young, the black, or any of those generally thought to be in the forefront of social and political change. Indeed, to the extent that history has borne out V. O. Key's contention that, temporally, Democrats can generally be shown to have been responsible for more change when in office than Republicans, this whole matter of public relations and technological politics may prove to be basically detrimental to the two-party system. For as we have seen, Joseph Napolitan is one of the few of those professional campaign consultants and managers who makes a living working for Democrats. These men must get paid. And, as Chester et al. have pointed out:

> In general, it is naïve to suppose that techniques which can be used only by those with access to enormous financial resources will often be available for any really damaging assault on the *status quo.* . . . There is only one circumstance in which the poor, the black, and indeed the young are going to find computers, polls, and scientific campaign management used on their behalf: that is when a wealthy candidate appoints himself as their champion. The user of technology should not be confused with his clients. It is one thing to say that Robert Kennedy, who could and did afford to use the full range of modern techniques for mass communication, felt a genuine concern for the disinherited. It is quite another to say that, because of this, the blacks of Watts or Bedford-Stuyvesant or the Mexican migrant workers acquired control of computers and pollsters and advertising agencies. And in politics, it is control that counts.[12]

There has, as our accounts of several presidential campaigns have implicitly demonstrated, been something of an imbalance between the Democrats and the Republicans in using the full measure of the new techniques and the new professionals. Perry goes so far as to contend that the Republicans have preempted the new technology, and that the upsurge in Republican strength since 1964 is attributable at least in part to that party's readiness and greater financial ability to employ public relations, advertising, and other techniques in their campaigns. Ironically, it amounts to a use of innovative techniques to mount campaigns desiged to promote the status quo. Although he is sure that the Democrats will ultimately catch on and thus restore the balance, Perry also predicts that "Meanwhile . . . the Republicans will continue to win elections they should, by all rights, be losing."[13]

This very area of whether one "should not" or "does not deserve to" win elections (when victory is assumed to be a result of the manipulation of the voters through the devices which we have been discussing) is a difficult area, and one that gets right down to the heart of democratic theory. What is "fair" and "right" and "ethical" in this field? We are dealing with a gray area of American politics, the only resolution of which to many calls for a kind of censorship of campaign techniques, which in its own way would raise a number of new questions about the American democratic system. Can we impose a kind of "arms control" in political campaigning? If public opinion, as eventually expressed in the vote itself, is the "ultimate weapon" of the electorate, to what extent can techniques for manipulating and defusing that ultimate weapon be controlled? And who can really represent the people in negotiating any form of "political arms control"? It is probably safe to assume that the American democratic system in general, and the system of electing a President in particular, are strong enough to survive the onslaught, and to survive without much basic change in form. It is not the form but the substance that is in the greatest danger. We face a loss of vitality in the political dialogue, a vitality that is invaluable, irreplaceable, and immeasurable.

One indication of this anti-party, anti-deliberative tendency of public relations politics is the overwhelming evidence that the United States has entered an era of personalized politics. As Perry points out, few of the men who have made full use of communications techniques are the traditional old-party loyalists. Eisenhower does not fit into this traditional mold, nor do the Rockefellers, Romney, Reagan, John F. Kennedy, Goldwater, or McGovern. Richard Nixon, who may have been in that category the first time around, changed his approach considerably between 1960 and 1968, as we have seen. Each of these candidates has created his own campaign organization, in most cases, as an actual substitute for the official party mechanism.

The professional political consulting or campaign management firm also serves as a kind of surrogate for the old-line party organization. Spencer-Roberts might be hired by a Nelson Rockefeller for a California primary campaign because of the temporary nature of the operation and the need for intensive first-rate local expertise. Other candidates might use such a firm because of limitations of time or money, which prohibit the building of an equivalent personal organization. Perry has, in fact, ventured a prediction that the day is coming when consulting and management firms will work for candidates of either party, just as poll-taking firms do now. There is no reason to believe that this will not happen. In the commercial world, a public relations firm presumably will not take on a client in whom a principal of the firm simply does not believe, nor one whose interests directly conflict with those of a current paying client. But with those possible exceptions, it can be said that one can generally find a "reputable," technically competent public relations firm to help preach virtually any gospel for the proper fee.

None of this means the downfall of the *form* of the two-party system. Candidates for the presidency build their personal organizations and hire their consultants, but those organizations are always pitted against one another within the structure of the existing political party system. This is generally true even when the candidate does not feel the strongest of loyalties to his party of record and its prevailing ideology. Recent primary campaigns of individuals like Nelson Rockefeller, Eugene McCarthy, and Robert Kennedy all fit into this category. They appear to further illustrate that the really significant fragmentation of the party system by personal organizations at election time takes place at the level of the presidential primary. But, as Perry points out, much of this sort of speculation

> . . . rests solidly upon a presumption—that the regular party organizations will be unwilling or unable to seize upon these new techniques themselves. It is not, I admit, an entirely comfortable presumption . . . [However,] regular party organizations frequently stand aside during a contested primary and only go to work thereafter. Then, of course, it's often too late to develop a winning campaign.[14]

So the advantages enumerated earlier—money, talent, time—clearly lie with a Rockefeller or a Kennedy, who can build an expert personal organization over a period of months or years, along with the proper public relations and advertising buildup, market research, and so on—and simply pay the bills. The man with the greatest advantage, then, becomes the one who has the resources to muster the new techniques of politics, the most sophisticated advice of the public relations profession, the most advantageous approach to the media—and the loyalties of other powerful, wealthy men who will seek one another out. Perry feels that together, in the right hands, these assets become a "juggernaut." To the extent that the tradition of American democracy favors equality of opportunity, even where a chance at the presidency is concerned, the odds should be a bit more even. With this in mind, Perry and others have proposed a number of reforms: matching grants in the primaries; tax deductibility of moderate-sized political contributions to encourage more giving from "little" people; a more stringent regulation of spending and reporting; a requirement for more free time to be supplied by radio and television stations; subsidies to such stations and others supplying campaign services; free mailing privileges for candidates; even government subsidies of advertising agencies. But in the last analysis, power and money will always have a good deal to do with one another, and it is unlikely that any program of reforms will be instituted that will eliminate the wealthy candidate's advantages.[15]

After all, creating a political star through a systematic buildup requires money and professional skill, just as the creation of a Hollywood star has traditionally called for the same requirements. Even between-film and between-campaign publicity is expensive. It is no new story that the advantages in such a system go the wealthy man or, certainly, to those who can, like Richard Nixon, depend on the reliable support of well-to-do supporters. This was, at least in part, the significance of the controversy over Nixon's "fund" in the 1952 campaign. Essentially, the Nixon fund was put together to provide seed money for a continuing buildup of the young senator. As Kelley has pointed out, the name of Murray Chotiner, Nixon's number one (if not sole) public relations consultant at the time, figured prominently in the reported expenditures of the controversial funds.[16]

So the candidate must have the means to communicate his point of view widely and strongly. It is not difficult to speak, but the problem in the age of mass communications is one of being heard. A candidate's attempt to be listened to when he is selling must also be conceived in economic terms; that is, the goal is to reach the most people for the smallest relative expenditure. Thus, the techniques of market research used in commercial advertising become relevant in yet another way to presidential campaigning. Which television stations located in major markets, for example, offer the best bargain in cost per thousand viewers reached?

The traditional conception of the place of discussion in a democracy, as we have pointed out, implies more or less equal opportunity for participation in the dialogue. But we must hold with Stanley Kelley that under modern conditions, this is no longer a practical goal. Perhaps the best that we might be able to hope for is some form of distribution of the limited opportunities for participation according to some principle of equity.[17]

But any system is likely to run counter to the goals of the public relations practitioner. Walter Lippmann once pointed out that behind the constitutionally guaranteed right of free speech there stands a view that debate "is a procedure for attaining moral and political truth."[18] Such a debate, obviously, implies the presentation of various sides of a question alternately to the same audience and under precisely equitable, dispassionately monitored conditions. With this, the political public relations man disagrees. From his point of view, it is good strategy for one side or the other to avoid this aspect of debate. After all, he is hired not only to try to sell a particular candidate, but to attempt to gain some differential advantage in that candidate's exposure. Thus, if he succeeds in gaining greater exclusivity of access to a particular audience, he is in a position to "give them his particular picture of reality, free of the natural check of competing facts and interpretations."[19]

Gaining such a differential advantage has a good deal to do with the candidate's personality. Clinton Rossiter, in his classic work *The American Presidency*, posited a whole set of "availability criteria" for potential Presidents, rule-of-thumb generalizations regarding the factors that operate to make some men candidates more readily than others.[20] The public relations man, on the other hand, tends to gauge availability by other means—for example, measures of the currency of a candidate's name with the public, the success with which he has projected his public personality, the way he performs on television, the attitudes excited by that personality; in other words, his image, actual and potential, and the public's reaction to it. The nomination of a man such as General Eisenhower seems to have grown largely out of such considerations. His supporters argued that his personal popularity was so immense as to be an advantage that the party would be politically unwise to reject. Such arguments were heeded, apparently, in determining his selection in 1952 over Taft, a man who would sit much better with more delegates in terms of his party regularity.

One could, however, make a case for the fact that one's personal popularity has to be immense indeed before it will succeed in giving one preference over a more regular party man. In 1968, for example, delegates did not choose to heed Nelson Rockefeller's argument that even if Nixon was most popular with party regulars, he, Rockefeller, deserved the nomination because only he could win the presidency for the Republicans.

Television presence also is an increasingly important "availability factor." Edmund Muskie's success with the tube in 1968 loomed large in his political future. His tearful outburst in front of newsfilm cameras during the 1972 New Hampshire primary had much to do with altering the course of that future. Similarly, participants in a September 1969 political consultants conference attributed Hubert Humphrey's loss in 1968 to his shortcomings as a television personality. They sized him up as a "hot" pitchman, tending to overplay on the "cool" video medium. "The biggest mistake of his campaign may have been that he never learned to use television right," according to one of his own television advisers. On the other hand, Richard Nixon was seen as a man whose video aplomb soared between 1960 and 1968. Not that Nixon was personally enthusiastic about his extensive use of the medium. Said Joe McGinniss: "The hardest job on the past campaign was not selling Nixon to the U.S., but selling Nixon on TV."[22]

So the general currency of one's name; the general outlines of his positive image; his skill at utilizing the mass media; the power that he possesses to buy or otherwise bring under his control the skill required for his pre-convention buildup, all become significant "availability criteria" in the political parlance of the public relations man. Furthermore, the public relations man and various other consultants —advertising executives, copywriters, film producers, television directors, time buyers, advance men, pollsters, data procesing experts, and, yes, political scientists—*themselves* become increasingly important political actors, and their crafts an increasingly important part of the political process. This is particularly true of the presidency, where personal organizations centered around the candidate appear to be decreasing the importance of political "regularity" in the traditional sense.

Indeed, Theodore White contends that the higher the office, the more important is the candidate and the less important the organization. He points out that at the ward level in some major cities, virtually anyone can still be carried to victory by sheer muscle. Campaigns for the governor's mansion, he argues, tend to be more issue-oriented than those for the White House; gubernatorial candidates, White feels, must project their proposals, not just themselves. At the presidential level, however, the candidate and his actions outweigh all other elements of a campaign. The candidate's words, travels, behavior, all aspects of his conduct, are watched intensely. His top team of advisers is, of necessity, a highly personal team.

> The national press corps follows *him* from dawn to dusk; the television networks invest the greatest part of the news resources and

energies in trailing *him.* One unguarded remark of a candidate, or one felicitous thrust, will reach more people than any accumulation of position papers, or pamphlets. For it is not what gets written down in platforms or pamphlets that counts; it is what gets into people's heads to move their emotions.[23]

This is no new story. Before television, even before the pioneering Charles Michelson became the director of publicity for the Democratic National Committee, he perceived that the system itself tends to make imaginary characters out of presidential candidates:

> "The American people will elect as President of the United States in November a nonexistent person—and defeat likewise a mythical identity.
> "They will vote for and against a picture that has been painted for them by protagonists and antagonists in a myriad of publications, a picture that must be either a caricature or an idealization."[24]

The electorate really does not know a candidate—particularly a Presidential candidate—except through his projected image. Most candidates thus tend to become mythical characters in almost the same sense as many Hollywood stars. The analogy may be too severe, although perhaps not. It might be possible for Hollywood to make a trollop into a love goddess, or even "the girl next door," while we like to think that a presidential candidate has *something* on the ball not created for the occasion of his campaign. We may be dealing with managed mythology in both cases, but a presidential candidate, unlike many performers, is likely to be placed in *some* situations where he must rely upon his own character and intellect and resourcefulness in order to acquit himself decently.

Even so, as Kelley has correctly pointed out, the public relations man (and his technically oriented colleagues) can go to work on a candidate in order to nurture and modify those characteristics of the candidate most likely to draw a positive reaction from the audience. His smile can be coached. His grooming and dress can be changed. He can be kept in front of microphone and cameras for hours, just like an actor, in order to produce a result that satisfies the producer and the director. Scores of photographs can be taken in order to get the properly salable product for the billboards.[25]

Interestingly, it seems possible to package, test-market, re-package, and re-market the same man several times over. And when the job is finished, the voters will apparently buy a variety of images, even if self-contradictory. Thus, aristocrats like Franklin Delano Roosevelt and John F. Kennedy became "men of the people"; Dwight Eisenhower became a simple, homespun, down-to-earth fellow who simultaneously was a national hero who had the wisdom to "go to Korea" and single-handedly figure out how to resolve a highly complex matter of foreign affairs; Ronald Reagan would make a good governor precisely because he had no relevant experience; Lyndon Johnson was an old-fashioned liberal with an old-fashioned conservative record, and so on.

Sometimes, of course, the candidate himself can cause a hitch in the building of his own image. In that way, if no other, he is different from a tube of toothpaste. The famous Clem Whitaker once lamented this fact:

> ". . . an automobile is an inanimate object; it can't object to sales talk—and if you step on the starter, it usually runs. *A candidate on the other hand can and does talk back—and can sometimes TALK YOU OUT OF AN ELECTION, DESPITE THE BEST YOU CAN DO IN CAMPAIGN HEADQUARTERS.*"[26]

With all of this emphasis on personality and image, one is tempted, of course, to ask what role *issues* play in a presidential campaign. Is it true of the process of choosing a President in American democracy that, as Pericles told the people of Athens, "We do not look upon discussion as a stumbling block in the way of political action, but as an indispensable preliminary to any wise action at all"?

When Stanley Kelley published his outstanding work in the field of political public relations in 1956, he was of the opinion that the entry of the professional public relations man into the political arena bode well for the serious discussion of issues in the course of election campaigns. It was an improvement, at least, from the era of bossism. For under that traditional system, the boss's appeal to the voter seldom was based upon issues, especially not national issues. It is difficult, Kelley correctly pointed out, to justify such a system on the basis of the democratic theory of government. For the heart and soul of democracy rest upon the ability of men to understand issues of policy, to discuss, and to govern themselves. The public relations man, on the other hand, is not so chary about injecting issues into campaigns, because this is one of the principal means by which he strives to organize opinion and action. After all, the public relations man is a communicator, and one belief he sincerely holds is that words and images can influence the minds and action of men. Says Kelley:

> Often the critiques of the public relations man's activities have a highly moralistic tone. There are no myths to justify his role as a policy-maker in political life. There is no authority to sanctify it. There is only the bare fact of his skill in using words and making himself heard. . . . There is truth in such criticisms, but what one is criticizing cannot be contrasted with a past age in American politics when public issues were sincerely presented and soundly argued. To the contrary, it is the politics of the public relations man, and not traditional practical politics, which posits discussion as real—real in the sense that it can decide a course of events. The public, as well as the propagandist, must accept responsibility for the level and value of that discussion. To criticize political public relations, to explore the problems it presents, is to examine the problems that result from the closer approach of democracy to its own ideal.[27]

To the extent that this conclusion was valid in 1956, the passing of years, the developments of the media, and the refinements—if that is the word—of five more presidential election campaigns have opened it to serious question. True, the traditional practice of public relations began as a kind of intentionally nonobjective journalism. There was no denying that the point of view was, almost by definition, highly subjective. But the approach was journalistic—the conveying of information, the encouragement of discussion, the utilization of facts as the basis for argument.

But, as we have seen, the use of the term *public relations* in the conventional sense no longer adequately covers the kinds of techniques used to promote presidential candidates. When Daniel Boorstin wrote his well-known book *The Image* in 1961, he discussed what he called pseudo-events and pseudo-candidates and suggested that show business had taken over American politics. According to this theory, political public relations, indeed, political campaigning as a whole, is primarily an exercise in press-agentry.[28] There are, of course, political campaigns in which this has been true. Ronald Reagan's efforts may be a case in point, and perhaps those of other show biz people-turned-politicians, such as George Murphy and Shirley Temple Black.

But by 1968 James Perry's observations had led him to the conclusion that it is not really show biz or press-agentry or public relations, in the traditional sense, that is taking over in politics, but, rather, the technology of business and industry:

> This new technology, which is changing the way all of us live, is finally being applied to the most disorganized and unsystematic endeavor in American life—politics. Things will never be the same again. The new technology is already at work in politics, though most people, politicians among them, have chosen to overlook it.[29]

Such technology has, of course, nothing whatsoever to do with political issues. Raising such issues too vigorously may even "cross-pressure" the electorate; in other words, a candidate who tries to make his case through issues, according to the technologists, can so disturb and confuse the voters as to cause them to react against the candidate who has caused them all this unsettling bewilderment.

For market-oriented technologists—such men as Harry Treleaven, one of Richard Nixon's key media advisers—genuine issues are of virtually no significance in a presidential campaign. The question is only one of who does the sharpest job of packaging and marketing the product. As McGinniss has pointed out, there is for men of such background only one's own product, that of the competition, and advertising. Most national issues today, Treleaven has written, ". . . are so complicated, so difficult to understand and have opinions on, that they either intimidate, or more often, bore the average voter. . . . Few politicians recognize this fact."[30]

A somewhat more traditional political official, from his vantage point at the Democratic National Committee, is essentially in agreement:

> Campaigns are concentrating more strongly on personalities than issues. Issues are complex, and it is hard to do more than just highlight them, and perhaps develop the *major* issues. . . . Poll-taking has had a tremendous effect in determining the issues. . . . We are also evolving new techniques to deal with complex issues—after all, you can't hide them . . . they're there. But television is so important, and television will always be tied more to *events* than

issues. Therefore a campaign should focus on those issues which
are most newsworthy. . . . Vietnam, for example, is a highly complex newsworthy issue. During the '68 campaign [a Democratic
National Committee staff member] suggested the production of a
television documentary explaining *all* of the U.S. programs in Vietnam—and just why the United States is involved there—tracing the
whole history from the early part of this century. Humphrey would
have been the narrator. But the idea was never accepted.[31]

Short of moralizing, at least one significant conclusion to be drawn
is that if campaigns really do not deal with the issues, then the election itself really resolves no important question. The fact that more
people buy your soap or vote for your candidate than that of the
competitor does not really mean that you have settled anything more
than the matter of whose marketing and packaging and advertising
techniques brought superior results.

This lack of resolution of basic issues is, then, the product—or
nonproduct—of the sterilization of political campaigning. Which
candidate *really* said anything at all in the 1968 presidential campaign, for example, which would have convinced a rational voter that
he had a clear-cut choice between candidates representing distin-
guishably different approaches on any major question? One wag said
that choosing between Humphrey and Nixon that year was like choosing between Sodom and Gomorrah. And in 1964 was a vote for Lyndon
Johnson supposed to be a vote for or against more fighting in Vietnam? And in 1960 just which policies of Richard Nixon did the
electorate reject when it chose John F. Kennedy?

To the three British observers, Chester, Hodgson, and Page, this
very area—which they call "the gap between rhetoric and reality"—
is "the most disturbing problem in American politics":

> The President is an elected politician. . . . Like any other politician
> in a democracy, he is supported by people who think he will
> uphold their interests. . . . But the President is not only an elected
> politician. He is also magic. He is the monarch, emblem, and pro-
> tector of national unity, defender of the American faith. And so the
> gap opens again between the rhetoric and reality. It is not enough
> that he should be a decent, honorable, sensible man who has suc-
> ceeded, as Disraeli said when he became Prime Minister "in climb-
> ing to the top of the greasy pole." He must be the divinely
> ordained leader.[32]

But the reality is closer to a confidence game than it is to divine ordination. Candidates hire people to work on their behalf not so much to convince citizens that a vote for candidate A is a more rational act than a vote for candidate B, but rather that candidate A is a more appealing purchase. Television, and the techniques surrounding it, have made the selection of a presidential candidate as much a centralized process as the purchase of consumer goods. Just as the once-eloquent salesmanship of the corner grocer has given way to the sales messages that television beams into the living room, so the eloquence of a potential President has been supplanted by precisely the same techniques.

The spot commercial is one of the most notable of these techniques. Ten to sixty seconds is enough time in which to say hardly anything at all, and to force whatever is said to be grossly oversimplified and inevitably distorted.

When Nelson Rockefeller mounted his reelection campaign for governor of New York in 1966, for example, he began with a series of sixty-second spots. They were not inherently unethical, provided one was not upset by the fact that the candidate himself never appeared on the screen. But as the campaign moved into its final phases, the commercials became ten- and twenty-second unsubstantiated attacks on Frank O'Connor (attacks that O'Connor simply lacked the funds to rebut even if the time were available). One commercial went like this: "Frank O'Connor, the man who led the fight against the New York State Thruway [as a state senator], is running for governor. Get in your car. Drive down to the polls, and vote." Actually, what O'Connor and his fellow Democrats had opposed was the idea of a toll road. They had wanted a free highway. Another twenty-second commercial, aired only in upstate New York, implied that O'Connor advocated free subways in New York City, the expense to be born by all state taxpayers. Actually, O'Connor never made any specific proposal to eliminate New York subway fares; he had only reflected at one point about long-term prospects for subway lines in *all* cities.[33]

As we have seen, the massive use of television spots in political campaigns can be traced to the formula originally worked out by Rosser Reeves of Ted Bates & Co., Inc., for the 1952 Eisenhower campaign. Within the advertising field, Bates had been known as "the spot agency." Reeves originated the famous Anacin commercial that featured hammers and lightning pounding away inside of an exposed cranium; the Rolaids commercial showing stomach acid burning a hole in a tablecloth, and the Colgate Dental Cream (with Gardol) commercial that hurled baseballs at the viewer nightly. He fought the Hot Cigarette Habit with Kool, made Viceroy the Thinking Man's Cigarette, and then turned his attention to the presidency. A former colleague sized up Reeves' effort:

> . . . a great howl went up in the liberal press about merchandising the Presidency like toothpaste. The fact is that Rosser started something that every Presidential candidate since has used, and the organization of spot-TV campaigns aimed at specific audiences in critical areas has become a permanent part of American national politics.[34]

Spot commercials for presidential candidates, because they are not necessarily vicious or obviously dishonest, may not always seem a positively objectionable campaign device. "Yet, in their distortion, they are . . . contributors to lowering the level of communication."[35]

One form of such distortion, which can only detract from the quality of the political dialogue, is the pattern of commercials without candidates. Such campaigns, which began on a large scale with the Democrats' "Ice-Cream Cone," "Social Security Card," and "Daisy Girl" spots of 1964, seemed well established by 1968. These commercials are yet another step in the march toward political sterilization. There is really no way of tracing such a spot to the judgment and viewpoint of the candidate, who has had little or nothing to do with producing the commercial, and may not even be mentioned until the closing line, if at all.

Ted van Dyk, former public relations adviser to Hubert Humphrey, told the writer that there is growing apprehension about the use of such commercials among a number of those actively involved in political campaigns. Apparently, some of the "new professionals" have come to feel that legislation, or at least an agreement of some sort, is necessary to assure that candidates for high office put in an appearance on their own commercials, so that viewers could get at least a somewhat clearer indication of the man and his relationship to the issues.[36] On the other hand, it seems unrealistic to expect this to really happen. Commercials without candidates have proven successful, and potential candidates don't like to foreclose any options.

Furthermore, requiring a man to appear on his own spots smacks more of the "old politics" than the "new politics." In any event, the Rosser Reeves effort of 1952 demonstrated that it is possible to put a candidate in all of his spots and still not have him say anything.

Another Democratic professional with experience in presidential campaigns points out that the advertising and public relations men often have to do a lot of convincing to make a candidate believe that he should *not* appear in all of his commercials.[37] Candidates who wouldn't be running if they disdained the limelight tend to feel they should appear on everything. It is usually the professional who makes the determination that such appearances would be of no help to the candidate and convinces him to let the image-makers use the television time in their own way. Candidates, reluctantly or not, have apparently allowed themselves to be convinced—some of them in a big way. In 1966, for example, Nelson Rockefeller spent more on television commercials on which he did not appear than his opponent, Frank O'Connor, spent on his entire campaign to become governor of New York.

Howard White has suggested that political science professors and other groups might recommend legislation setting forth a minimal length for political broadcasts and telecasts.[38] Even if such demands were made, the passage of such legislation also seems a remote possibility. First of all, Professor White feels that such legislation should be based on the ground that an appeal to reason in less than fifteen minutes is likely to be spurious. But advertising is seldom, if ever, designed to appeal to *reason*. Secondly, controlling the length of a commercial does nothing about its content, and there is no reason to believe content is likely to be any better in fifteen minutes than in one —it might be fifteen times as bad. Thirdly, such a measure would force candidates to pay a great deal more for television time than they might wish or be able to do; and that money would all be spent in reaching one audience for fifteen minutes, not fifteen audiences for one minute.

It is possible, however, to make certain other predictions about the use of television in presidential campaigns. The increased use of regional television is an evident trend. A candidate can get the greatest mileage out of area-oriented issues by appearing on regional television hookups in various places around the country. Such appearances are financial compromises, in that they cost somewhat more than a strictly local show, but not anywhere near as much as a network program. The cost-per-thousand-viewers reached, all important in the advertising business, is usually relatively low. Furthermore, these telecasts save the candidate and his party a good deal of barnstorming to small and medium-sized communities once they have arrived in a given area of the country. The use of regional television also allows a candidate to repeat himself a good deal on certain matters as he moves around the country, each time attracting new viewing audiences and receiving coverage from the local press just as though he were saying something fresh and original. All of this helps satisfy the public relations objectives of a campaign, without imposing any additional intellectual burden upon the candidate and his writers. Only the television advisers and technicians have their workload increased. It should be pointed out that the increased role of regional television has the advantage of removing the concentration of the means of production in New York, where costs are high and logistical problems abound. There is some question, however, as to whether it accomplishes, voluntarily, what Theodore White said after 1964 might have to be done by law: to disperse production "by law, into the less competent, less artistic hands of regional talents, hoping that dispersion will give diversity and that diversity will be more valuable than artistry."[39] The great burden of the evidence is that although local facilities are used, all of the production skills, short of routine technical jobs, are supplied by the candidate's central television staffs, drawn largely from New York.

The enormous cost of television time is a serious problem for almost all political candidates. For example, one might spent $100,-000 on a Senatorial campaign in one state, while the same campaign conducted in another, more populous state would cost $2,000,000. There is a good deal of interest in this problem on the part of political leaders. Discussions about potential federal legislation have been under way at various levels for some time. The three major national television networks have made a number of attempts to allay the possibility of such legislation. As of this writing, they have announced discounts of about 25 percent on commercial time to be granted to bona fide political candidates.[40] Such measures seem long overdue. The demands of the networks and local stations for cash on the line in advance of political broadcasts have caused some disgraceful incidents, some of which we have recited. How is one to even guess at the serious ways in which such demands can affect the whole political process?

For instance, a Democratic National Committee representative told the writer that at one point in 1956 Adlai Stevenson needed some $80,000 for a particularly crucial television program and waited in the studio, uncertain of his own plans, because the money did not come in until thirty minutes before air time. "Some phone calls had to be made. For a while, it looked as though he might not go on. And he was running for President of the United States."[41]

Such fund-raising problems, along with the general difficulty of the escalating costs of network time, also seem to point in the direction of increased use of regional television, and relatively low-cost national and regional radio, as the wave of the future, particularly during the earlier stages of presidential campaigns. Such limited media use gives a candidate and the professionals who work for him more of a chance to try out new images, audition new techniques, and assess the results without "blowing" a network television time period and the money and effort that it requires.

Even if one does resort to the odious comparison of marketing toothpaste with marketing presidential candidates, it becomes evident that the toothpaste can at least be test-marketed before an attempt is made at a national campaign. To the extent that it is not possible for a presidential candidate to proceed this way, the country is penalized by making it nearly impossible for men who may have the most solid credentials but the shakiest financial resources and public relations to run for office.

Indeed, as has been pointed out earlier, increasing campaign costs have been a major factor in convincing candidates at all levels of the need for public relations counsel. It becomes a practical matter of obtaining the greatest effectiveness from a limited budget. Those who give the money, as well as those who spend it, are interested in seeing the funds used to produce the best results.

There is, of course, always the possibility that at some point in the future, some candidate will simply break the mold. In fact, it seems fairly safe to venture a prediction that the "slick approach" to the American public is likely, in and of itself, to become a campaign issue. A courageous candidate, or one with a clever staff, will at some point probably attempt to reveal the public relations and advertising and merchandising techniques for what they really are. A candidate might use an ad within an ad, go behind the scenes and analyze a commercial or technique used by his opponent. The people might be shown by one candidate exactly what goes into producing a political spot, starting from the early development of an idea. The point of such a campaign, if handled well, might help attract the loyalties of the young and alienated. The point of the exercise presumably would be that candidates are dealing with an electorate faced with the matter of choosing a Chief Executive of the United States of America and not a market of potential soap-buyers. The irony is that the media themselves would have to be used extensively to put across such an anti-media campaign. It would require the same resources, human, financial, and communications, as the campaign whose techniques it is criticizing and the agreement of the media managers to sell time and space for the purpose.

The press itself has not done a very thorough job of probing into the vitals of presidential campaigning and letting the voters know just what is going on behind the scenes. Perry has pointed out that most political reporters

> ... still tend to dog the candidate's footsteps, reporting almost stenographically what he says in his public appearances. But that is just a segment of the total campaign, and probably not even the most important segment. It is a mass-media campaign ... the battle is waged in the voters' homes. The voter reacts to what he sees on television and to the campaign material he receives in the mail.[42]

Thus, few voters see candidates in the flesh, and not all that many are likely to consume the written details of what each candidate has to say as those speeches are reported in news dispatches. The press, it would seem, has been noticeably lax in turning up stories of the inner workings of presidential campaigns. Indeed, manipulation might not be nearly so prevalent a technique if investigative and interpretative reporting on the part of the professional journalists assigned to the campaigns, and their editors, played a greater part in the overall pattern of news coverage emerging from campaigns and elections.

Were the press to truly play the independent role that it says that it does, it might not be nearly so easy for the new political professionals to play the electorate like some kind of musical instrument, pressing keys and valves and pedals and striking exactly the chord they wish.

For if there is blame to be assessed for much of what we have been discussing, all of it cannot fall upon the professionals. Always those who allow something to be done to them must share the blame with those involved in the actual *doing*. The public, however, does not have the stimulus and ammunition required for such a reaction because the media, with rare exceptions, simply go along with the wishes of the professionals and report only on that portion of a campaign that is visible above the surface. And even at that, they have not done a complete job. It would seem reasonable, for example, to expect political reporters to report on and analyze new radio and television spots as they are introduced, along with reactions from the opposing candidate.

We have seen how it is possible to do rather well politically by using "superior" professional techniques. From the point of view of the public relations men, the advertising men, the market researchers, the packagers, the consultants, and the managers, all of these techniques are rational. It is quite rational to make liberals conservatives, conservatives moderates, moderates indefinable—if that is what gets more votes. It is "rational" for Spencer-Roberts to pass off Ronald Reagan's political ignorance at the time of his debut as a candidate by calling him a "citizen politician." It is "rational" for Nelson Rockefeller and his "team" to destroy Frank O'Connor with $6,000,000 spent on attacking him for positions he had never taken. For brother Winthrop, it was rational for tens of thousands of voters to be impressed by finding a Rockefeller name signed by a computer to computer-printed "personal letters." As Perry points out, this is the creed of the technologists; they sincerely believe that what they are doing is making politics a rational exercise.[43]

The public relations pioneers—Whitaker and Baxter and others like them—based their decisions not upon technically gathered and processed empirical data. They relied more heavily upon their intuition, intellectual assets, and "seat-of-the-pants" judgment, which remain the chief tools of the most successful public relations men.

Now that so much of the field has gone so thoroughly technical, now that the technique is so widespread as to change the basic nature of political campaigning, it is clear that some very basic ethical questions must be raised. One would expect that these developments would be reported more closely, and that the consequent public reaction would serve as a modifying force. But there has been little or no reaction at all. The research difficulties to which we referred early in this book are symptomatic of the dearth of literature on the subject. Books by Perry (probably the first political reporter to describe in depth the basic changes in political campaigning) and McGinniss dealing with some aspects of this problem are the first to appear since Stanley Kelley's pathfinding work in 1956. Other material has been culled from comprehensive accounts of campaigns, published long after the winners had taken office. But even this literature, interesting as it is, falls far short of the kind of hard-hitting, day-to-day reporting that is necessary to make the voting public aware of the fact that each time they vote for a President, they are being more thoroughly bamboozled than the time before.

We have now reached the point where voters are hardly voting for a real man any more; the image built during the campaign grows farther and farther away from the real human being who is running for office. And when the man is elected, the country, those who voted for him and those who did not, can no longer be reasonably sure of what to expect from the man once he is sitting in the White House.

McGinniss, who worked with Richard Nixon's television team in 1968, was able to say almost a year after the campaign that at least "Humphrey, for all his faults, was on TV an extension of his real self." But, he says, "The TV spots on Nixon were dishonest—they tried to create something that wasn't there." Another Republican media consultant saw it differently when he said at a professional conference: "The qualities that make a good President may make a bad TV performer. So, is it not the height of morality to create an image to put the good man across?"[44]

It is perhaps hard to believe that anyone really thinks that way; it is especially painful when one considers that he is talking about electing someone to the presidency of the United States, with all that it implies.

But who attempted before Election Day in 1968 to analyze for the American people the nature of Richard Nixon's television campaign, and what it said and did not say about the kind of President he would make? There was really no such analysis available to the conscientious voter. By the same token, as Perry points out with justifiable indignation, no newspaper in New York State challenged Governor Rockefeller for the basic unfairness, if not downright dishonesty, of the last stages of his 1966 gubernatorial campaign. Nor was that an issue two years later when he made bid number three for the presidency. Nor did any of the television stations with whom his organization was dealing refuse to accept the highly questionable last-minute material which it was peddling. Nor did any paper in Arkansas challenge brother Winthrop for his computer-printed letters or even note that this sort of campaign was going on. Perry puts it this way:

> Each of these new-style campaigns is a little like a magician's act. What you see is the candidate out there on the stump, delivering speeches and making statements. It is almost exclusively this high-level campaign that the reporters and commentators observe. But what the reporters and commentators don't see—what they don't report or assess—is that hand under the table, selling the voters through the mass media in their homes. . . . This second campaign is just as important as the first. Probably more important, for the dirt is usually found under the table . . . and, the dirt these days is usually part of this second, and largely unobserved, campaign, while in days gone by it was all part of one campaign. To this extent, the new techniques are responsible for a new and subtle kind of political dirt.[45]

Such statements are disturbing enough in and of themselves. It is even more disturbing to realize that we are faced with an excruciating paradox. On the one hand, the media techniques of the professionals are so sophisticated as to open up an entirely new and quite involved series of ethical problems in political campaigning. Those involved in these very media, however—the reporters and editors who follow the campaigns for the public—are generally not seeing in macrocosm what has happened to their own field. Thus, they go on reporting the more conventional and traditional aspects of political campaigning. This is really the part of the campaign that is staged precisely for the newsmen to see and report, and they fall right into the trap like a duck for a bobbing decoy and a rubberized whistle.

Reporters and editors go on judging the quality of campaign coverage by such conventional journalistic criteria as accessibility of the candidate, "scoops" and exclusive quotations, an occasional "zinger" of a line in a routine day of speech-making, an advance peek at a "major" policy address, and so on. Theodore White and other reporters write at length about the difficulty of reporting on a campaign when candidates retreat for strategy meetings, resist press conferences, reject private interviews.

But the reporters are themselves resisting the real story:

1. First, that the nature of campaigning has changed and that what they are waiting around for the candidate to say is probably one of the least important aspects of the campaign.

2. Secondly, that the role which the media play in a campaign has also changed drastically and that they, the press, may be the last to realize that the candidate may not really need them in the same sense as his predecessors once did. In a sense, they are being had. For the candidate and his advisers know that if they buy television time and completely stage a broadcast so as to make the aspirant look as good as possible, not only will the people watch it, but the press will show up and report the questions and answers, and more people will read about it the next morning. And if an occasional James Reston or Max Lerner should write two or three hundred words of dissent—well, a bad column may have been a stab in the heart in the old days, but now it's more like a mosquito bite.

As all of this takes place, the public relations man and the new professional managers inevitably become actors of more central importance on the political stage. Kelley has pointed out:

> As those who aim at control of government come to regard mass persuasion as their central problem, then the specialist in mass persuasion will rise correspondingly in influence. When the businessman and the politician turn for help to the mass media technician, it means they are seeking to exploit the power potentialities of the mass media to the fullest possible extent. . . . The public relations man is both a beneficiary of this change and a kind of signal that it is taking place.[46]

There is no question that public relations men and their colleagues have moved into positions of great influence and have been delegated the power to make important decisions, which enable them to leave a firm imprint on the American political process. They have, as Kelley accurately predicted, affected some of the basic relationships between the public and its government.

This ascendancy of the public relations man to a policy role was predictable because, as we pointed out early in this book, political public relations men have generally followed, with some lag, their colleagues and counterparts in the business world. In business, the policy-making role is an aspiration that public relations men now attain with increasing frequency. It is one of the dogmas of the profession that public relations is a management function and that management must always be convinced and reminded of the fact. "Better public relations for public relations" has, in a few years, attained the status of a professional cliché. In practice, it means that those who begin as technicians often end up as vice presidents or trusted outside counsel reporting directly to the chief executive. There is even a professional award given annually to p.r. men who "make it" to positions of overall management responsibility. Thus, the same trends that brought the public relations man into politics in the first place have acted to help him rise in the hierarchy of decision-makers. "His services are valuable because effective use of the mass media is one of the roads to power in contemporary society, and it is difficult clearly to separate strategic and tactical considerations in that use."[47]

The general problem of political apathy also has made a substantial contribution to the rise of the public relations man, for "he talks to people the majority of whom he believes to be radically uninterested in the problems of government." Kelley underlines the fact that the professional communicator knows as well as any social scientist that rational discussion is necessarily discursive. He knows that this means analyzing all of the elements of complex problems and presenting them in a logical sequence of reasoning. "But he also believes that if one is to 'hit' the mass-media consumer with maximum economy, arguments must be capsulized and sloganized."[48] Thus, the public relations man tends to set up a campaign for a citizen assumed in advance to be apathetic and irregular in his devotion to political discussion of any sort.

This same apathy has perhaps been one reason for a noticeable lack of any outcry on the part of the American voters. A public used to being conned into a new car every two or three years, the raising and lowering of hemlines and necklines, the natural relationship between a variety of chemical and cosmetic preparations and the quality and quantity of love, may simply see nothing outrageous about being sold a President in the same fashion—and, indeed, making its "purchase" with about the same depth of consideration. After all, things have always worked out.

So the new techniques are directed to this kind of voter. Who pays for the techniques that reach him, how much is paid for them, and why are things done this way—these are not questions to which he gives much thought. After all, if Proctor and Gamble spends huge amounts selling him soap and toothpaste, what is so strange about Nelson Rockefeller spending some vast part of his considerably more vast fortune, or a lot of rich people giving money to President Nixon, to help get them elected?

The result is a citizenry which, in some respects, has the potential of behaving more like a herd than an electorate; not necessarily because people are stupid; it's just that they have their own priorities. Says Perry:

> A pessimist would suggest that it is simply too much. Most voters aren't all that interested in their political system. They're struggling to make a living, to raise their children, to pay *their* bills. So they will be polled and simulated and prodded and pushed.[49]

In fairness, it must be pointed out that there are, within the public relations profession, large numbers of people who would not consider certain aspects of what we have been discussing here as a responsible use of public relations expertise. They are serious about ethics, and if a client will not take their advice and live right, they will not take his money and try to convince anyone that he is doing so. They will, in short, present their clients, political and otherwise, only in terms of what they actually are. True, they will attempt to present that client or candidate in the most favorable light possible, but only by way of communicating that which is true but perhaps not widely known. They believe that a sow's ear is a sow's ear, they do not see the Emperor's clothes when he is naked, and they do not see themselves as makers of kings, wizards, or soothsayers. By and large, public relations professionals are intellectually agile, creative human beings and are no more greedy or venal than anyone else.

Public relations consultant Roy Fenton has told fellow professionals that it is precisely because of the political public relations man's somewhat "shadowy" role that his responsibility must extend beyond that of the normal client relationship to include the best interests of the electorate. The stakes are too high for the professional to plead immunity, or for the customer to always be right. The professional must, in fact, appreciate and understand that

> unless the ability of men to understand and discuss issues of government and to govern for themselves is fully utilized, we must

admit that the focal points of democratic thought—and of the hopes and dreams of all levels of society—are a sham and a cruel pretense. . . . failure to establish a rather rigid code of ethics in political public relations does a disservice not only to the profession but also to the nation.[50]

It might also be pointed out, to the credit of the competent public relations professional, that he is well aware of the general apathy of the electorate and in his own way he fights against it. Insofar as increasing political participation is a valid goal for American democracy, the public relations man does make his own contribution. He tries to reach large masses of people with his messages. True, he is often seeking to control attitudes, but he wants also to arouse the normally apathetic voter. He knows that if he is the one to succeed in reaching normally nonparticipating voters, it is likely that they will go his way. Often, he guides himself by the advice of Aristotle's *Rhetoric* (which, like everyone else, he may or may not have read) and attempts to arouse those strong emotions, fear, indignation, anger, contempt, that have the power to overcome apathy and indifference.

Such strategy might find itself implemented by tactics ranging from ordinary oratory to esoteric electronics. This strategy was the object, in fact, of Winthrop Rockefeller's extensive keypunching operation in connection with his 1966 election as governor of Arkansas. The computer's first job was to isolate those people who displayed some interest in the candidate but did not register to vote. The computers sent two letters to such persons, one with the magic Rockefeller signature. After volunteers followed up by telephone with a personal appeal to the unregistered voters, Arkansas registration jumped by 60,000. As Perry points out, this is a significant development in a southern state where many thousands of literate citizens have never bothered to vote because there has been one-party rule, and the policy of that one party is to keep the vote down.[51] So whatever one's reaction might be to Winthrop Rockefeller's computer-based campaign, it did help contribute to an opening of the political process in Arkansas, and the involvement of thousands who might otherwise never have gone to the polls.

Such recent cases seem to bear witness to a hypothesis we share with Stanley Kelley, that the tendency of public relations politics runs counter to that of local bossism. In fact, the "new politics" of public relations and technology runs counter to political decentralization in general. As we have illustrated, it is only a national party or other large and well-financed group gathered around a particular candidate that can really afford the best in communications talent and reap the economics of large-scale production. Thus, the balance of political power, which once resided at the local level, tends to concentrate at higher levels in the party hierarchy. Leaders at the national level, once dependent on local organizations as their basic point of contact with the electorate, now go directly to the voter through the mass media. National committees and candidate-centered organizations, once concerned chiefly with mediating among the coalitions of local groups which traditionally have formed American political parties, are now more concerned with policy: which advertising agency shall we retain, how do we pay them, and when can we have a look at those films?

V. O. Key's perceptive and prophetic observation back in 1947 was that:

> Political power has been based on a stable network of the party machine, around each member of which was clustered a little group loyal through thick and thin. For this there seems to be in the process of substitution a power structure broadly based on mass consent and support. . . . And in the midst of these changes in opinion manipulation the old-time politician is at sea and men are bewildered and a little afraid.[52]

The question today is whether the American system, which has shown over nearly 200 years and forty-seven presidential elections the ability to survive and prosper and rise above its problems and shortcomings, will be basically altered by the vast, revolutionary changes we have been discussing. It is safe to predict that the system will survive. It will continue to change, as it has already, in substance, but very little in form. Whether it will be more or less rational than in the past is debatable.

Plato could speak of rational criteria for choosing rulers, especially if philosophers were to be kings. Here in the United States of America, rational choice has never been a particularly noteworthy aspect of national elections. We cannot look back upon a day in which candidates were indeed chosen on a rational basis and then conclude that mass media, public relations, and the "new politics" of technology and professional management have changed all of that. Ballot boxes no longer float down the Hudson River, as they did the day after Abraham Lincoln's election; nominations do not emerge from smoke-filled rooms, and local potentates no longer rise to power through their ability to "deliver" huge blocks of votes. Whether things are "better" or "worse" is more a matter for individual taste than scientific determination.

The change in substance with which we are faced is one that removes the electorate one step further from the Chief of State, makes the whole system that much more remote and inaccessible, and runs the risk of increased alienation, apathy, and indifference. The gap between political rhetoric and reality is widening. And more and more citizens perceive that a man and a man's "image" are not at all the same thing; and the images, it seems, have a tendency to blur. Nothing memorable is said in a presidential campaign any more because the effort is to avoid saying anything memorable. Presidential candidates have become political eunuchs. Paradoxically, in an age where the means for transmitting political excellence and eloquence to every citizen of the republic are readily at our disposal, it is the whimper of mediocrity that is being heard in the land.

# An Afterword:
# The 1972 Campaign

These words, first intended as a public relations man's instant analysis of the 1972 presidential campaign, have made the author wonder whether any analysis can go far enough. I think not. Not yet. For it is now well into 1973, and several drafts and many thoughts have been discarded as at once profoundly superficial and inordinately depressing.

This book began as an attempt to assess the impact of a body of professional thoughts, techniques, and practitioners on the process of choosing a President. It was pervaded by and concluded with a hypothesis that this pivot-point in American democracy had been sadly, perhaps irreversibly eroded.

Now even that seems too mild. For now we have seen the bottom of the barrel. There is talk of impeachment in the land. The office of the presidency has been badly shaken; the process of filling it has become a cause not only for concern, but for widespread cynicism.

Even at the beginning, before the worms crawled out of the barrel, there were indications that public disdain of the whole candidate-selling process had reached new depths.

*Newsweek*, attributing the apparent growth in doubt and indifference to McGinniss' popular "exposure" of the Nixon media campaign of 1968, contended that this fact was itself dominating the thinking of those who were planning public relations strategy for President Nixon and Senator McGovern in the summer of 1972. Both groups expressed "abhorrence for antiseptic presentations," and their hopes to sell their candidates "in a low-key manner that maintains their credibility." But all disclaimers to the contrary, there was little to indicate that the job would be done any less commercially, less professionally, less slickly.[1]

Most changes in public relations approaches, initially, seemed superficial at best. One such procedural change was that both the

Republicans and Democrats chose to ignore existing commercial advertising agencies, and instead assembled their own large professional groups as "in-house agencies." Mr. Nixon's, in an early display of confidence in self-evident goals, was called the "November Group"; Senator McGovern's, simply "Charles E. Guggenheim Productions."

The creative director of the November group was William Taylor, otherwise of Ogilvie & Mather. He headed a staff for which ideological uniformity was a major qualification. "If you hand-pick people who are *for* the President, . . . you have a single-mindedness and can work better," he explained.[2]

And so, background investigations were done on every potential employee. The sanitation process was thorough. The Republicans did not want "another Joe McGinniss in their midst." The man who made sure was James McCord, now in a federal prison for his role as a leader of the Watergate burglary and bugging brigade.[3]

Los Angeles adman Peter M. Dailey, who headed the November Group, also decided to "innovate" in the use of documentary film as a communications technique. He hired a fellow Californian, preeminent documentary-maker David Wolper, to put together films on "the Nixon Years." His task was to show the President not as candidate, but as statesman.

Another new development in 1972 was the rediscovery of radio. Both parties battled to see which could get the upper hand in the form of tape recordings distributed to the nation's 11,400 radio stations for use on local broadcasts. The Democrats allotted a larger budget to the cause, but the Committee for the Re-Election of the President used every major figure in the government, including some who were supposedly nonpartisan, such as Federal Reserve Board Chairman Arthur Burns. Joseph White, McGovern's broadcast news coordinator, developed the capacity to feed an average of one thirty-second news tape a day to every station in the country. McGovern's voice was used almost exclusively. The goal was the equivalent of $12 million in free air time during the seventy-day campaign. White's budget of some $100,000 was about $25,000 higher than that of the Republicans, who taped six to ten officials a day. Since broadcasters, for understandable reasons, are reluctant to admit to regular use of such tapes, the total amount of free air time made available during the campaign is a matter of some dispute.[4]

What were the issues in 1972?

When the Democrats nominated McGovern, he said that the central issue of the campaign was Richard Nixon. When the Republican Party nominated Richard Nixon five weeks later, he said that the central issue was George McGovern.

## The McGovern Campaign

What the 1972 campaign comes down to, said McGovern's p.r. man Ted van Dyk (who in the previous campaign had lent his skills to Hubert Humphrey), is: "Would a voter rather buy a used car from Richard Nixon or George McGovern?"[5]

The image, in other words, was to be one of righteousness, sincerity, honesty, goodness, arrayed against the forces of evil.

But McGovern was not to be an aloof "good guy." A further public relations objective was to portray him as "a man of the people"—in warm, personal terms, making honest points to "plain folks." He was not at ease in front of the camera, and Charles Guggenheim's objective was to bring him across as attractive and sincere. "For McGovern," he said, "television is really not an audience of 1,000, but 1,000 audiences of one." "Straight and square" was the way one adman described both candidates' public relations campaigns.[6]

McGovern opened his national television campaign on September 10 with a commercial he had used since the New Hampshire primary. Even though the new television material for the general campaign was not yet ready, the Democrats were anxious to get on the air. It was another three weeks before the first of the Committee for the Re-Election of the President commercials were to be telecast.

McGovern's initial television spot was five minutes long—a film shot in a Wisconsin veterans' hospital the previous January, in which embittered disabled veterans discussed their problems with the senator.

"I love the United States," he told the vets as the film closed. "But I love it enough so that I want to see some changes made. The American people want to believe in their government, they want to believe in their country, and I'd like to be one of those that provides the kind of leadership that would restore that kind of faith." The spot concluded with the slogan: "McGovern . . . for the people."

By the time of the election, the McGovern organization had produced some forty commercials in five-minute, one-minute, and thirty-second lengths, filling almost all of the $3.5 million worth of prime time the networks made available to the candidates. McGovern's television campaign moved in other directions as well: telethons, a filmed biography, a major speech on Vietnam, a panel discussion, and, finally, last-minute spots attacking the President.[7]

For the latter, McGovern came up with a new television producer in the closing days of his campaign. Encouraged by Democratic advisers who felt that the Guggenheim commercials were too low-key, the senator engaged Tony Schwartz, a New York consultant who had worked for Senator Edmund Muskie in the primaries, to take a more aggressive approach. Schwartz was the maker of some of the famous spots employed by Lyndon Johnson in 1964—such as the "Daisy Girl" and the "Social Security Card."[8]

Guggenheim, by this time, had turned out some two dozen spots depicting McGovern in "spontaneous" conversations with voters. The most prominent of the Schwartz spots, by contrast, showed one man inside a voting booth, having a crisis of decision and breathing heavily as he says:

> Well, either way it won't be a disaster. What am I looking for? I mean, so I'll vote for Nixon. Why rock the boat? I'm not crazy about him, though. I gotta make up my mind. I don't have that much time. I can't keep people waiting. The fellas are for Nixon, they expect me to vote for him, too. Me vote for Nixon! My father'd roll over in his grave. The fellas say they are. Maybe they're not. Crime? I don't feel safer. Prices up. Gotta feeling: Don't vote for Nixon. I'm confused. Who am I measuring McGovern against? My gut feeling, my gut feeling: McGovern. This hand [as he raises it] voted for Kennedy. I mean, it's just possible McGovern's straight. Maybe he can . . . [He pulls the Democratic lever, sighing] That's the way.

There was no issue, no indication of the McGovern position, no real indication of the Nixon position, no real "pitch," let alone a contribution to the dialogue of democracy.

But another Schwartz spot was more to the point. It led off with a series of headlines about what the administration was then referring to as "the so-called Watergate caper," and then a voice, over the background of a teletype machine, said: "This is about bugging, this is about spying, this is about thieving, this is about lying, this is about payoffs . . ." The voice concluded: "This is how you stop it—with your vote." The spot ended with the single word "McGovern."

Schwartz had all of ten days in which to produce his new material, and much of what he developed simply could not get duplicated, distributed, and on the air in time for the election. One such spot showed George Washington's face on a dollar bill changing to Nixon's as the economy worsened. Another focused on vivid descriptions of destruction and death in Vietnam. Still another introduced a note of whimsy as it depicted a butcher slicing big chunks from a small sausage to depict how taxes and high prices cut back income: "Now look at what the big baloneys pay in income tax," the announcer's voice said as the butcher substituted a fat sausage and delicately sliced paper-thin wafers off one end, "a fraction of the fair share they should be paying."

This spot was part of McGovern's effort to associate his candidacy with the interests of the consumer and the "little guy," and to place the administration definitely on the other side of the fence. As he told the Western States Water and Power Consumer Conference on September 25: "You would have to go back at least as far as the administration of Warren G. Harding to find an administration so beholden to the special interests and big business. . . ."[9]

The McGovern organization seemed proud of its television campaign . . . so much so that on the Sunday before the election, the campaign committee took the unusual step of buying newspaper ads lauding another aspect of its own television programs, McGovern's "fireside chats." The ad, headlined "How George McGovern Won the Election," stated:

> As late as early October, millions of Americans knew George McGovern only from 30-second appearances on television. Then, beginning October 10, McGovern started making a series of 30-minute fireside chats to the American people. He talked quietly about Vietnam, inflation and the economy, morality in government. Suddenly people began finding out and talking about the fact that McGovern was far more sensible, strong, decent and steady than they had realized.[10]

It was a dangerous ad, because it also implied that had it not been for his "chats," McGovern would have come across as obtuse, weak, indecent, and shaky.

McGovern's concentration on television grew progressively heavier as the campaign entered its final phase. He cut back on live appearances in an attempt to reach millions of viewers electronically and turn the tide. On October 22 he appeared on ABC's "Issues and Answers"; on the twenty-third he did an hour-long telethon tied to a network of stations in New York State, Connecticut, and New Jersey; on October 24 he appeared on a similar program in Milwaukee; on October 25, on a nationwide paid-political broadcast on ABC, and so on. In one of these appearances McGovern suggested a new format, complaining about the President's refusal to debate him on television: "Maybe we could run some of Mr. Nixon's old films and I could at least answer him that way. In fact, we're thinking about doing that. We'd try to take fair statements of his positions, and then I would answer them."[11]

The "debate issue" hardly seemed the most likely matter about which the American public was going to become exercised in October 1972. After all, there had been no presidential "debates" in twelve years. And it seemed unlikely that any sitting President, least of all one who had good personal reason for abhorring the whole format, would open himself to another such experience. McGovern issued his first challenge in early August, and it was obvious that the President had decided long before that he was not about to lend that publicity vehicle to anyone who was after his job.

Nevertheless, on October 18, McGovern offered to pay for national television time for a series of pre-election encounters. Presidential Press Secretary Ronald L. Ziegler announced the President's refusal: "Our position is unchanged."

Actually, the most *recent* Nixon position on debates had not changed; but *that* position *did* represent a change from his earlier point of view. As President, Mr. Nixon had said, he had changed his view about debates. He now felt strongly that the Chief Executive should not participate. His contention was that the President makes national policy whenever he speaks, and that debates were a bad place to make policy.

McGovern campaign chief Lawrence O'Brien, alert to the switch, called a news conference to describe the Democratic challenge. For the occasion he had readied newsfilm clips of the President's previous statements on debates, including a Nixon response to a question on the subject in Anaheim, California, on September 16, 1968, in which he said: "I believe that nationally televised debates between the two major candidates . . . would serve the public interest. I seem to be always anxious to debate. I'll be glad to take on anybody."[12]

But now it was McGovern who needed the exposure. One device which the McGovern p.r. people introduced in 1972 to increase it was instant videotaped campaign news. It was first used in the California primary, when the media staff, displeased with the low returns they were getting from their television spots, used a videotape recorder to follow the candidate on his personal appearance tours, rushing tapes of his comments to local stations for possible inclusion in their news programs.

But the general campaign is a national campaign, and a day in Los Angeles in October illustrated how it was possible for McGovern to have considerable impact on local media, but much less elsewhere in the country. On the twenty-seventh he had a full schedule of six events, designed to corner the attention of all seven television channels in that media-conscious city. But despite his success locally, voters around the country saw little of the candidate. One network ignored him, and the other two noted his Los Angeles blitz only briefly.[13]

As we have observed earlier, and as Warren Weaver, Jr., pointed out in *The New York Times* of October 29, "In presidential campaigning today, success in attracting media coverage is the single most important goal of any candidate's schedule." The impact of that crucial point is total: In other words, a presidential campaign *is* a public relations campaign. One can posit that it is also many other things, but public relations is the existential reality . . . media is what running for President is all about. To the extent that this hypothesis is correct, American democracy is in a state of crisis.

Nevertheless, as Weaver pointed out, both Nixon and McGovern continued to take the "traditional public stance that they are seeking in their travels to take their message directly to the voters. . . . In fact, the indirect message is vastly more important." The gap between rhetoric and reality was as wide as ever.

After all, McGovern, on October 27, was seen in the flesh by some 7,500 people in Los Angeles. But in California alone, his potential audience of television viewers, radio listeners, and newspaper readers was in the millions—and much higher in the rest of the country. In local television shows monitored by *The New York Times* over a twelve-hour period that day, McGovern's activities received more than twenty minutes of free time.[14]

On a national basis, the President's strategy of bidding for media attention by staying put in Washington was working. The three network thirty-minute evening news shows on that same day devoted 14½ minutes to Vietnam peace initiatives, 3½ to the President's vetoes of the day, and 3 to McGovern's campaign activities. This, in spite of a well-programmed McGovern effort to make all of the hard news early in the day in order to allow enough time for reporters to make their late-afternoon deadlines back East.[15]

Television was not McGovern's only media problem. Democratic candidates are, of course, used to having newspaper publishers aligned against them. But for some forty years they have usually been able to count on having the "working press" in their corner. But somehow, 1972 was different.

McGovern not only had the owners against him. Many of the writers—especially the "pundits"—seemed less than enthusiastic about his candidacy. Clayton Fritchey, a pro-McGovern pundit, theorized that this was a new tendency to which Democratic political p.r. men had better be alert. The working press, he contended—especially well-paid political reporters and columnists—were upwardly mobile, and had now moved from the working class to the "Establishment" themselves. Thus, they had developed vested interests in their contacts with the Establishment—contacts which were of little help in anticipating or understanding the "McGovern phenomenon, which developed and flourished outside the old-time political Establishment." Thus, they tended to brush off the McGovern candidacy for some time, and were less than happy to be proven wrong before their readers and employers upon his nomination.[16]

And if the press had some problems with the McGovern image, the candidate seemed, by early October, to be having some trouble with it himself. He felt that one of his reasons for showing so poorly against the President in the polls was ". . . a failure by me to communicate my real character and veracity to the voters." Another problem, James Reston pointed out, was a "masterful political selling job by Mr. Nixon." And there was, thirdly, "a possible inability by some of the press to bring the same critical examination to the two candidates."[17]

Whether the press was rougher on McGovern than the President was problematical. As Reston put it, ". . . you couldn't get many votes for that proposition around the White House, where the old Nixon aides will never forgive the reporters for telling the truth about Mr. Nixon's record of political dirty tricks."[18]

The application of public relations techniques to fund raising on a mass scale was a notable innovation of the McGovern campaign. The techniques of direct mail were the key to the unprecedented effort to finance a presidential campaign with a lot of little contributions from a lot of little people . . . what many political and other professional fund raisers tend to scoff at as "low-end giving." Political public relations men, accustomed to using direct mail techniques for persuasion, now used them to finance the campaign—and their own media efforts.

The technique had worked well in funding McGovern's early anti-Vietnam and primary campaigns, and now it was being used in an effort to elect a President . . . and it worked again. Now, with the flight of many large contributors from the Democratic Party by early August, it was crucial to the success of the expensive media program already in the works.

"Direct mail has made my candidate possible," one McGovern leader said. "Without direct mail, we would not have been able to afford paid television. Without television, we would have had no hope of reaching the American voters." The results astonished even the McGovern optimists, as the direct mail campaign brought in as much as $850,000 in a single mid-October day.[19]

McGovern also broke political fund-raising precedent after Labor Day, when it was obvious that funds were sorely needed. He made direct, emotional appeals for cash to almost every audience addressed. The tradition in presidential politics is for the candidate to attend private fund-raising events and "prime" large givers, while his staff and other well-heeled supporters do the actual fund raising.

And, although both the public relations people and the fund raisers on the McGovern staff denied that this was a purpose of his appeals, the public fund raising was an inspired p.r. ploy. For it contrasted his campaign in the public mind with the well-financed efforts to re-elect the President. Indeed, McGovern himself drew that contrast in each of his appeals. It is interesting that he drew it on the basis of his public relations budget, because he was short of the cash sorely needed to commit printing costs and radio and television advertising. As he told a Seattle audience on September 4: "They've filled the White House, not with servants of the people of this country, but with clever public relations experts whose function is to manipulate the people of America." Therefore, he said, he needed the help of his listeners in raising funds to counter the millions being spent on the Republican public relations campaign.[20]

By late September, the McGovern organization also had produced four new television spots aimed specifically at fund raising. They featured actor Paul Newman and three contributors—two workers and an elderly woman.

There seems little question that the pivotal factor in McGovern's public relations problems in 1972 was the case of Senator Thomas Eagleton. It was, of course, an unanticipated story, upsetting, once again—like the Jenkins case in 1964—the best planning of journalists and p.r. men.

The case was forced into the open by a team of newsmen from the Knight newspaper chain—a piece of investigative reporting which was to win them a Pulitzer Prize in May 1973. The irony for these reporters, Bob Boyd and Clark Hoyt, was that they and their papers lost their scoop when they decided to give McGovern and his staff an opportunity to think over the evidence which they had accumulated.

Their thanks from the McGovern high command was a delay until such time as the leaders could make a public pronouncement. Their hopes for a news beat went on the rocks when Eagleton arrived in South Dakota to confer with the man at the top of the ticket, and McGovern aide Frank Mankiewicz told the reporters that Eagleton was about to have a news conference. As a consolation prize, Boyd and Hoyt were granted an exclusive interview with Eagleton afterward. He told them then that the timing of his announcement was, "frankly because of you guys."[21]

The damage of the Eagleton revelations to the McGovern presidential image was incalculable. Furthermore, there is evidence to indicate that McGovern's decision to withdraw from his "one thousand percent support" of his hand-picked vice presidential nominee and ask him to resign from the ticket may have tarnished that image still further.

Louis Harris found that the most significant fact in the Eagleton affair was that in dropping him McGovern took a course which most pleased people over fifty, and which was in sharp disagreement with what had been assumed to be his strongest constituency—voters under age thirty. While people over fifty indicated by 58 to 29 percent in a Harris poll that "any man with a background of mental disorders should disqualify himself from running for President or Vice President," young people disagreed with that proposition by 60 to 30 percent.[22]

Harris' findings indicate the public did not panic at the news of Eagleton's psychiatric history. Thus, there appears to have been a failure of an important aspect of public relations thinking in the way in which the whole matter was handled by the McGovern organization. For public relations is a *two*-way process. And it is perhaps a viable hypothesis that McGovern and his staff, in calling for Eagleton's head, gave the American public much less credit for resiliency than that public was willing to give the senator from Missouri.

Harris' findings, indeed, indicated that in dropping Eagleton, McGovern lost the gains he had scored for being candid about his colleague's difficulties, at the same time showing loyalty to an associate in trouble. "As it is," Harris said at the time, "Senator McGovern not only has lost the momentum in these early stages of the campaign, but has created some problems with his one best hope for ultimately achieving victory—the new voters under thirty years of age."[23]

When McGovern tried to gain face by making a full explanation on nationwide television on August 1 of his reasons for asking for Eagleton's resignation, he was rebuffed by the television networks. In their judgment, his statement would not be "newsworthy" until and unless he was prepared to announce his new choice for the vice presidential slot. But there was yet to follow a week of humiliation and rejection by at least six potential vice presidents before McGovern would be prepared to go on the air and announce that his candidate would be R. Sargent Shriver, an attractive and articulate man who had never run for office, and whose primary virtue at the time seemed to be his willingness to accept the nomination.

Another important aspect of the democratic process had been eroded. And it is possible to lay much of the blame for that erosion at the door of overzealous public relations thinking which had resulted in a serious confusion of priorities. For, as James Reston put it, the

time before the Democratic convention, which might have been used
to make a careful study of potential vice presidential candidates,

> was devoted to polling in order to see which candidate had the
> right "image" to add votes to the ticket, and very little to the ques-
> tion of finding the man whose character and record would, in an
> emergency, enable him to unify and govern the country. . . .
>
> The Democrats have powerful issues and new political forces on
> their side, but they are now so preoccupied . . . that they have little
> time or energy to think about the fundamental problems of the
> Republic. . . .
>
> The Republicans are playing it all very quiet and cool, and
> allowing the reporters of the press, radio, and TV, whom they
> have vilified for four years as partisans of the opposition Demo-
> crats, to report Mr. McGovern's troubles, and dramatize the re-
> election of Mr. Nixon and Mr. Agnew.
>
> It is all very normal, sad and ironic, but there are still great
> issues to be discussed, and a campaign for the American Presi-
> dency to be waged.[24]

The McGovern image was badly damaged. There was no doubt
about it. He had brought off a *tour de force*, winning his party's nomination in the face of odds which appeared overwhelming. He had
thrown away the book on how to succeed in the presidential sweep-
stakes. And now . . . with the agonizing decision on Eagleton and the
week of grasping for a replacement . . . now he was open to accusations of ineptitude, of indecisiveness, of the inability—as one
observer put it—to organize a phone booth, let alone the United
States.

The electorate was cheated. The American democratic process had
been robbed. For McGovern had taken the stance of a neo-Populist
in the primaries. His leftish image was in clear contrast to the middle-of-the-road stance of adversaries like Muskie and Humphrey.
And if McGovern strove for a more moderate image during and
immediately after the convention, at least the lines had been drawn
for a "far more valid referendum on national directions than presidential elections usually offer. Voters were to have an opportunity to
choose between obviously divergent paths on such crucial issues as
defense spending, welfare policy, and tax reform."[25]

Furthermore, the impact of the Eagleton affair did not die easily.
Even McGovern's p.r. people admitted it—and publicly. On October

6 his press secretary, Richard A. Dougherty, said he thought there were still 10 or 12 million people angry with McGovern because of the incident. "What I don't know," he said, "is if, when they go into that voting booth, they're still going to be mad enough to vote for Richard Nixon."[26]

Russell Baker found amusing this clamor that the Eagleton crisis be quickly gotten out of the way so that the campaign could proceed to deal with the "real issues." There was more reality than humor in his observation that the way in which McGovern handled that crisis might actually be a better opportunity than any other in which the public could perceive the Democratic candidate as he might actually behave in the White House.

In 1956, he observed, when Adlai Stevenson spoke for a nuclear test ban and an end to the draft, President Eisenhower mused, "Sometimes you sure get tired of all this clackety-clack," as he took his ovations and cocked his ear to shouts of "I like Ike." In 1960 the "Great Debates" focused on Quemoy and Matsu . . . and who was better, Nixon or J.F.K., to get Castro out of Cuba. In 1964 the issues were clear. If you wanted peace in Vientam, you voted for Lyndon Johnson. And in 1968, of course, Mr. Nixon had a secret plan to end the war. A. J. Liebling, said Baker, told the "quintessential issue story" in his book *The Earl of Louisiana.* Earl Long had run successfully for governor on his pledge for a tax cut. His first request to the legislature was for a tax increase. An adviser told the governor he couldn't do that, because he had promised in his campaign to cut taxes if elected. Replied Long, "I lied."[27]

The Eagleton crisis was not so great, either, as to put a stop to campaign hoopla. It was press agentry at its best on July 28 while, as he wrestled with his conscience, Senator McGovern donned a Stetson and fringed suede jacket to join the annual Gold Discovery Day Parade in Custer, South Dakota.

With Mrs. McGovern, the senator mounted a maroon and white Continental to join in the spectacle celebrating the Custer gold strike of ninety-eight years before. A press corps of fifty, complete with television crews, crowded into the town of two thousand, fascinated not only with McGovern and thoughts of a possible dark horse replacement for Eagleton, but with horses of a different color—dyed blue and gold and red, mingling with the Lions and 4-H Club floats.

And as Senator and Mrs. McGovern dismounted in front of the

Gold Pan and Wagon Wheel saloons to shake hands for the cameras, a campaign worker suggested hopefully to reporters, "An overwhelming reception? An underwhelming reception?" Earlier, he had been heard to remark that the Custer crowds were "as much as one deep in some places."[28]

And by August 9 it was clear that there were benefits from the Eagleton affair to at least two important groups which undoubtedly crossed party lines—collectors and makers of campaign buttons. McGovern-Eagleton buttons, free in unlimited quantities only days before, were being advertised at $1.00 each ... "Losing Combination Becomes Winning Combination for Collectors!"


## The Nixon Campaign


If it was more clear than ever in 1972 that for the vast majority of the American people, the media *were* the campaign, it was equally evident that the President of the United States understood this well.

For, in the words of Herbert Teison, "In a post-graduate course of eight years, Richard Nixon and his team learned that it is not what the candidate is, but what he can be made to appear that will pay off at the polls."[29]

And so, while McGovern spent his time and energy and campaign funds attempting to generate media attention through his appearances around the country, the President's p.r. strategy consisted basically of sitting in the White House. Thus, he would reach as many or more voters through media coverage not of a scrappy Republican office-seeker, but of a cool and powerful Chief Executive.

The decision to seek maximum exposure as the man running the country and minimal attention as a man running for office was an ingenious one, for it led to a dual focus in the media. Since Mr. Nixon was not being covered as a *candidate*, but rather as *President*, the media had no campaign style to criticize, or campaign blunders in which to catch him.

McGovern, on the other hand, was closely scrutinized—his organization, his methods, his program, his promises ... all were fair game. And the view from the hustings is considerably different than the perspective from the White House press room.

Senator McGovern was an aspirant. President Nixon was a sacerdotal figure. An aspirant's ability to run the country is a perpetual question mark. The President chose not to raise any questions about his organizational or decision-making skills. He just went on being President.

But as we have seen, clever public relations does not very often mean good democratic dialogue. And 1972 added more evidence in support of this hypothesis, for issues were again of minimal importance in the public mind. As R. W. Apple, Jr., pointed out in *The New York Times*: "What does it matter if a voter questions Mr. Nixon's commitment to economic betterment for blue-collar workers if the same voter is unable to picture Mr. McGovern in the White House?"

One McGovern adviser put it this way: "Most voters never even get to the question of issues until they have decided, in some mysterious way, that both candidates are basically qualified to handle the Presidency."[30]

None of this is meant to imply any lack of public relations machinery or activity in the Nixon campaign. The mechanism was there, it was well oiled, and it was hard at work on the American voter.

The entire governmental public relations network is virtually at the President's disposal. Mr. Nixon had tightened that control by appointing Herbert Klein as Director of Communications for the Executive Branch. He worked across the street from the White House itself, concentrating on Cabinet-level departments, with a staff of twelve.

In the White House, Ronald Ziegler, the presidential press secretary, who had handled the Disneyland and 7-Up accounts for White House Chief of Staff Harry Robbins Haldeman when the latter managed the Los Angeles office of the J. Walter Thompson advertising agency, had fourteen people of his own. And, since 1968, the White House speech-writing team had grown to sixteen. Then there were media monitors, television advisers, photographers. One writer estimated conservatively that, all categories included, the permanent Nixon public relations staff in the White House numbered some sixty people.[31]

The President, of course, is in a position to manipulate television, the most important public relations tool of the campaign, more dramatically than anyone else in the country. For he is the only person in the country who can command virtually automatic and unlimited access. And Mr. Nixon was no slouch. He knew, for example, that 9:00 P.M. on Mondays is one of the primest slices of prime time, and chose that hour and day for many of his major appearances. There was simply no way McGovern or, before his nomination, other potential Democratic challengers could even hope to compete with the free opportunities for television exposure available to the incumbent. It is a political fact of life which has profound implications for American democracy, increasing the advantage of the incumbent incalculably.

But the Republican campaign organization also told its story on paid broadcast time:

> 1. The Committee for the Re-Election of the President produced a series of five-minute commercials, stressing the President's positive achievements, showing Mr. Nixon at work, and never mentioning either the Republican Party or its adversaries.
>
> 2. Sixty-second spots under the imprimatur of "Democrats for Nixon" attacked McGovern head-on for his proposed welfare program (one version of it, at any rate), his advocacy of cutbacks in defense spending, and his supposed difficulties in reaching decisions.
>
> 3. In a series of radio speeches, the candidate himself appeared, dealing with several substantive issues.

Meanwhile, the Committee conducted "one of the most ambitious efforts in political history to woo voters by personally addressed mail appeals, running to 10 or 15 million," that went to all Republicans and selected Democrats and independents in several key states.[32]

The rediscovery of radio was an interesting phenomenon. Warren Weaver, Jr. (whose excellent coverage of the media campaigns of both candidates for *The New York Times* in 1972 was an innovative and significant contribution to political journalism) contended that there was no pretense of any substantial numbers of real listeners. Rather, he pointed out, the radio text served to underline the presidential message and promoted it from the status of a press release to a media event.[33]

Raymond K. Price did make a pretense of a national audience in his introduction to a volume of the President's radio talks, which was published by the Committee for the Re-Election of the President, and widely distributed by direct mail with a covering letter, on White House stationery, signed by Herbert G. Klein, dated February 7, 1973.

"The audience of a nationwide radio speech is smaller than for a nationwide television speech," said Price, in masterful understatement, "but still very substantial: estimates of the 'live' audience for each of the 1972 radio speeches ran from two to six million . . ."[34]

Price called the President's extensive use of radio an "innovation" which helped him to present "his views on the often complex issues facing the American people. . . . For years," Price continued,

> the conventional wisdom had been that with the advent of television, radio was dead as a medium for political speeches. [Nixon] thought otherwise. In many respects, radio is better than television for the delivery of a thoughtful speech—the attention of the audience is entirely on the content, not on such irrelevancies as staging. Also, radio is a less intrusive medium than television. It does not require pre-emption of the viewers' favorite programs . . . it is a great deal less expensive. . . .[35]

Still, it seemed odd for one of the most innovative users of the mass media in the history of the American presidency to put his public relations eggs in such an old and tattered basket. But he apparently felt comfortable with it, and once he was back in office, the White House indicated his intentions to make it an integral part of his communications program—for example, in a series of addresses which replaced the traditional State of the Union message in early 1973.

Jules Witcover pointed out that Mr. Nixon apparently prefers radio to television because it requires less preparation on his part, less time, less electronic equipment, and no makeup. Radio does not make him perspire, to the best of our knowledge, nor would it reveal the famous heavy Nixon beard. The President could usually get by with one advance read-through of his copy, and had no need to be concerned with his gestures. Furthermore, radio allowed him to wear his reading glasses, the existence of which was a secret to his television audiences. Mr. Nixon's staff, Witcover indicated, had not forgotten surveys taken after the "Great Debates" of 1960, indicating that those who heard them on radio but had not seen them on television thought J.F.K had lost.[36]

The President's television campaign had actually begun with the Republican convention in August, where his nomination was a foregone conclusion, and planners faced the problem of holding audience interest in what had evolved from an integral part of the democratic process to a long television show.

Republican National Committee Chairman Robert Dole called it "a prime-time Convention." So instead of traditional speeches, viewers were treated to a film festival. The opening night included a film on the President's achievements, another paying tribute to Dwight D. Eisenhower, and a two-minute special on *Mrs.* Nixon, narrated by James Stewart. On the night of Mr. Nixon's nomination, viewers were shown another film, "Nixon the Man," narrated by John Wayne. All four films had been produced by David Wolper under his contract with the November Group.

The Committee for the Re-Election of the President opened its official television campaign on September 25, with a low-key five-minute documentary on the President's visit to the Soviet Union—an edited version of the longer film shown at the convention. The sole political assertion was the closing tag, "This is why we need President Nixon more than ever."

The film followed the first of the McGovern commercials by two weeks. In the same week the film on the Russian trip and another five-minute documentary on senior citizens were shown twice each for a total investment of some $60,000. The Republicans were taking only partial advantage of the carefully balanced time schedule of slots which each party could buy at reduced rates, as laid out by the networks in the summer of 1971. They did not exercise their rights to buy the first two weeks' worth of time, and bought only part of the available package in the second week.[37]

Peter Dailey, the head of the November Group, called the first two films "reasonably typical" of the television material to appear during the rest of the campaign. They were positive in their approach, he said.

> You're dealing with a sitting President here, recording the achievements of his Administration over the past three years and his plans for the next four. In 1968 you had two candidates, and the political burden of proof was on both of them. *But in 1972 we have one candidate* and the burden of proof is on George McGovern to prove his executive ability and to prove that his policies are

meaningful enough to be more effective than those of the President.[38]

The edited film on the Soviet trip, which made its debut following the NBC Monday night movie, was narrated by Richard Basehart, and referred to the President's journey to Russia as "an historic first step." The week's other five-minute commercial, on senior citizens, stressed the fact that there had been a 51 percent rise in Social Security benefits since Mr. Nixon had taken office. But, as Weaver pointed out, it neglected to mention the not inconsiderable role of the Democratic-controlled Congress in the new Social Security legislation.[39]

While the Committee's official television spots stressed only the positive virtues of the man whose re-election they advocated, and McGovern's spots used unrehearsed voter questions, with little criticism of the opposition, another Republican television operation was on the attack. The "Democrats for Nixon," spearheaded by former Treasury Secretary John Connally (who would become a Republican in May 1973, when the Watergate scandal seemed to be peaking), launched a head-on offensive against George McGovern.

Connally, the star of the opening shot by the Democrats for Nixon, in a five-minute statement that debuted September 19 on ABC, accused McGovern of refusing to support the "basic principle of foreign policy—that the United States should not become a second-rate power." The Texan said that he found this "frightening and dangerous":

> Five American Presidents, Roosevelt, Truman, Eisenhower, Kennedy and Johnson, believed our country must have a strong defense if we were to have any hope of an enduring peace. President Nixon has kept us on this wise course. George McGovern has demonstrated that he will not. Five American Presidents gave people the world over the only beacon of hope for freedom and safety in the atomic age. President Nixon has kept that commitment. George McGovern has demonstrated that he will not.[40]

Interestingly, plans for the Democrats for Nixon spots were discussed with reporters by Kenneth Clawson, Herbert Klein's Deputy Director of Communications for the Executive Branch. Although he said the group would run its own independent operation, he seemed thoroughly conversant with its plans. He agreed that the commercials were aimed squarely at McGovern, attempting to build an image of the Democratic contender as a man who had taken contradictory and —in Connally's terms—"dangerous" positions on key issues. Said Clawson, "McGovern is the star of the show."[41]

The Democrats for Nixon, whose spots Dailey called "more comparative" than those of the President's re-election committee, became even more heavily partisan by early October. On October 3 the organization aired a commercial symbolizing McGovern's proposed defense-spending cuts with a hand sweeping away miniature soldiers and ships. The toys fell away as a drum rolled and an unidentified voice announced: "The McGovern defense plan: He would cut the Marines by one-third. He would cut Air Force personnel by one-fourth, the Navy fleet by one-half, and carriers from sixteen to six." The announcer recalled Hubert Humphrey's statement about McGovern's proposed defense economies during the Democratic primary battles: "It isn't just cutting into the fat, it's cutting into the very security of the country." The spot then shifted to a scene of the President aboard a Navy ship, and visiting troops in Vietnam, with "Hail to the Chief" playing in the background, as the announcer concluded: "President Nixon doesn't believe we should play games with our national security. He believes in a strong America to negotiate for peace from strength. That's why we need him now more than ever."[42]

McGovern's public relations people were quick to counter the new spot by pointing out that their man's defense plan did not call for a 33-1/3 percent reduction in the Marine Corps, but 29 percent; that he advocated a 21 percent cut in Navy personnel, not 25 percent; that his projections for reducing the interceptor squadrons of the Air Force were only slightly different than the President's own timetable, and that the attack on the matter of aircraft carriers was misleading because only five of sixteen existing carriers were being maintained on active duty, and McGovern advocated a force of six, with three on active duty.[43]

The Democrats for Nixon spots broke with public relations precedent in the 1972 campaign not only because they were the first which attacked the opposition head-on, rather than stressing the virtues and ideas of the candidates, but also because they were the first produced so as to make use of symbols rather than the candidates themselves. Guggenheim, on the Democratic side, had vowed to stay away from such an approach to television, and had by this time made twenty-four spots based on McGovern's conversations with voters. The dissatisfaction of many in the Democratic camp with spots which did not capitalize on the alleged distrust and/or dislike of Mr. Nixon on the part of large segments of the American public apparently led to the decision a short time later to retain Tony Schwartz to produce the commercials discussed earlier.

Just what *is* most effective in a television spot designed to move voters? There have been few attempts to find out. In fact, the public relations profession generally suffers from a lack of sound evaluative mechanisms. This lacuna in the field causes many public relations people vast difficulties in convincing the hard-nosed pragmatists within their own organizations of the impact of what they are about. Although attempts may be made to relate an upward trend in sales figures to a masterful new public relations compaign, in the last analysis the p.r. practitioner must rely on the judgment of those he serves to appreciate his efforts in "setting climate" through effective communication. He looks to advise his management on the public relations implications of their activities and decisions, to appeal to their taste to appreciate his more creative and imaginative efforts, and, occasionally, to pander to their egos as they see the name of their company, their product, their program, or—best of all—their very own selves in lights.

Whenever an employer or a client tells a p.r. person, "Of course, I'm not interested in any personal publicity," the p.r. man starts to worry. He knows he's going to have to hustle, because what is meant is almost inevitably precisely the opposite of what is being said.

Following the 1972 campaign, in a rare attempt to gauge the actual impact of television spots on the final election returns, two Syracuse University political scientists revealed some conclusions based on the responses of some 175 of 625 voters interviewed three times during the course of the campaign.

Robert D. McClure and Thomas E. Patterson released evidence which indicated that Democratic voters who had made a decision to vote for Mr. Nixon in 1972 were confirmed in that new allegiance by the Republican television commercials. As might be expected, they remembered more about those spots than other groups of voters, and responded more favorably to them than other groups. Of the Democrats favoring the President, 73 percent were able to recall the

Republican commercials. The same spots were remembered by 67 percent of other Democrats, 63 percent of independents, and 58 percent of the Republicans interviewed. It also came as no surprise that the McClure and Patterson study showed McGovern voters to be more antagonistic toward the Nixon commercials attacking their candidate than Nixon voters were to the more low-key McGovern spots. The scholars concluded:

> Defecting Democrats found reinforcement for their voting decisions in the Nixon commercials. . . . Most of those voters were voting against George McGovern as much as for Richard Nixon and the direct attack on George McGovern of many "Democrats for Nixon" commercials provided reasons for their decisions—and the comfort of knowing there were many other Democrats like them.[11]

The Republican p.r. strategy would appear to have been notably effective. Although evidence is scanty, the campaign was apparently sufficiently partisan to reinforce defecting Democrats in their decision, and not so highly partisan as to discourage those defections in the first place. The campaign, as the President had reportedly told Republican leaders in early August, was directed not against Democrats, but against "McGovernites." This meant stressing the record heavily, avoiding squabbles, and laying off the press. "We may not like the way the press handles the campaign," Mr. Nixon reportedly said, "but we want no quarrels with the press."[45]

It was obvious that the word was out. White House aide Patrick Buchanan said, " . . . there is little disposition around here to make an issue of the media in the campaign." And, as early as July 22, Vice President Spiro Agnew, the administration's foremost media critic, urged an audience in Portland, Oregon, to "forego harangue and cliché in favor of discussion based on reason," and suggested that "bygone conflicts between state and press be put aside."[46]

The idea for the truce with the press is credited to two former newsmen in the administration—Clawson, who had been a reporter for the Washington *Post*, and John Scali, a former ABC newsman who was about to become Ambassador to the United Nations. The press peace policy was endorsed by Klein and Ziegler, who, with other observers, had been perceiving a change in the tone of McGovern's press coverage since Hubert Humphrey had begun asking rapier-like questions about the South Dakotan's policies in such areas as income distribution and defense. Newsmen found increasing accessibility to the Klein-Clawson communications complex, and when Clark McGregor succeeded the later-to-be-indicted former Attorney General John Mitchell as campaign manager, he began meeting often with reporters, in sharp constrast to his predecessor.[47]

The development was an interesting one. For nearly four years, with Mr. Agnew as its principal spokesman, the administration had been trying to convince the American people of the alleged liberal bias of the nation's press. In point of fact, the newspapers of the United States are overwhelmingly Republican and Conservative. Earlier in the Nixon Administration, the Vice President had demanded that " a broader spectrum of national opinion should be represented in the press." It appeared that in 1972, however, if a broader spectrum was needed, it was needed in precisely the opposite direction of that which the administration had in mind.

On October 6 *Editor and Publisher* magazine reported that 726 daily newspapers had responded to its survey of 1,764 papers, inquiring as to which presidential candidate the paper was endorsing. Mr. Nixon was endorsed by 688 of the newspapers responding, with a combined circulation of 17.5 million copies. Those backing McGovern—38 to be exact—had a circulation total of 1.4 million.

It was not an unusual development. Of those daily papers which endorsed a presidential candidate in 1960, 84 percent backed Richard Nixon. In 1968, 80 percent of the papers endorsed him. The pro-Nixon papers in 1960 represented 83 percent of all daily circulation; in 1968, 78 percent. And in some of the major cities—Detroit, Cleveland, Philadelphia, Los Angeles, Chicago—*all* major papers endorsed Mr. Nixon.[48]

Yet, *First Monday,* the Republican Party's house organ, feigned pleasant surprise at the press's entirely predictable repeat performance in 1972. Reporting in November that 80 percent of the nation's dailies had once again endorsed the President, it said:

> One of the most remarkable developments . . . has been the deep and amazing support of the President and his programs by the Nation's press—*amazing,* because the American free press is generally tough on Presidents no matter who occupies the hot seat in the Oval Office; *more* amazing because Richard Nixon and the

editorial community have had more than their share of Mexican stand-offs through the years.⁴⁹

What is it in the media which the administration found so objectionable? The newspapers were overwhelmingly in its support, and off the editorial pages more often than not accepted the administration's version of events as spelled out in public relations handouts. As for television . . . well, Ben Bagdikian calls it "the President's medium." What the Republicans could not or did not buy in the way of television time, the President could co-opt for the asking, with more certainty than any other man in the country that he would get it. And he could be assured of direct and instantaneous impact, unmarred by the interpretation of reporters or editors.

What the Nixon Administration objected to was really the same thing that bothered Lyndon B. Johnson, John F. Kennedy, Eisenhower, Truman, and probably all of their predecessors—the occasional effort of competent journalists to do their job . . . to cut through the public relations cosmetics while those in power and their p.r. staffs tried to present their best profile to the voters.

And that function of a free press in a free society operated in 1972 under the shadow of repeated administration efforts at intimidation and manipulation. The FBI had investigated reporters. Daniel Ellsberg and Anthony Russo went on trial for releasing to the press materials which, as testimony at their abortive trial later indicated, had long since been in the hands of the Russian Embassy. There were efforts to subpoena Earl Caldwell of *The New York Times*, and the government of the United States, for the first time in history, was requesting and obtaining injunctions against newspapers. And then—although, for reasons which might be fascinating to investigate, it was not widely reported and analyzed—there was the spectacle of the Chief Justice of the United States greeting two Washington *Post* reporters at the door to his home late one night with a shotgun in his hand.⁵⁰

For voters around the country, the missing element in the Republican presidential campaign was its star. Not only did the President's decision to leave the campaign to a laundry list of surrogates communicate that he was preoccupied with the business of running the country. It also communicated the President's desire to demean his opponent. In his few low-key radio speeches, severely limited public appearances, and single campaign address on television, Mr. Nixon was able to make his way through the campaign without even mentioning George McGovern's name. By the same token, he left the Democratic candidate on the battlefield to joust not with the man he was challenging for the White House, but with that man's second string.

The ranks of this group of stand-ins grew to scores as they spread out across the country "to celebrate and defend the presidency of Richard M. Nixon." They ranged in geography and ideology and personality from Governor Rockefeller to Governor Reagan; from familiar faces like Herb Klein to new ones like the newly appointed Acting Director of the FBI (a nonpartisan position), L. Patrick Gray; from expected political figures like Republican Chairman Robert Dole to novel ones like the President's daughter, Mrs. Edward Cox. All played a key role in the Republican campaign strategy . . . a plan "more elaborate and richly funded than traditional efforts by incumbent Presidents to use the leading lights in their party and Administrations to campaign for them."[51]

The surrogates made news wherever they went. They cheered the administration at local civic clubs and on local interview shows, their schedules coordinated by computer to see to it that the right people got to the right places at the right time.

The technique also gave the Republicans the opportunity to present spokesmen with specialized expertise in areas where their specialties were political issues. Thus, Secretary of Health, Education, and Welfare Elliot Richardson could deal with bussing, Interior Secretary Rogers C. B. Morton with ecology, and Vice President Agnew with just about anything.

With the surrogates all over the map, and the President yet to emerge from the White House, McGovern countered mainly with himself, scheduling his campaign to provide a maximum of variety in geography and in subject matter. In one September week, Monday found him in West Virginia calling for an end to strip-mining; Tuesday he was in Chicago, promoting a tax-credit system and federal aid to parochial schools in that heavily Catholic city; Wednesday he went east to New Jersey, advocating billions in new aid to the aged; by Friday he was back in the Midwest, accusing the President, in Detroit, of demagogy and cynicism in exploiting the bussing issue . . . and then, into seclusion to work on his "fireside chats" for television.

The campaign featured not only surrogate people, but surrogate phraseology. Not only was there an absence of debate on the issues, but, as Max Frankel lucidly observed, the candidates and their writers relied persistently on symbolic code words as a substitute for a genuine exhange of views. To wit:

> —Mr. Nixon pledged to save the country from those who would stain its "honor"; Senator McGovern blasted those who would slay its "soul."
>
> —Senator McGovern spoke about placing national economic policy in the hands of the "special, grasping, greedy interests" who would only make the rich richer; the President condemned "those who call for a confiscation of wealth."
>
> —On the defense issue, where opposing budgets might have provided the underpinning for a genuine discussion of what level of military strength the country actually required, the Republicans spoke only of "weakness," the Democrats of "waste."
>
> —McGovern attacked the President for "hiding" from the people, and not campaigning in their midst; Mr. Nixon said he was doing an important job—that he was busy being President, and countered McGovern's statements with demonstrations of "statecraft."[52]

Not only was the democratic process stultified by such non-debate, it was dulled. It was difficult for large numbers of voters to get very excited about the campaign, and difficult for the public relations operatives on either side to stimulate them.

But there were occasional flashes of novelty in the Agnew camp. The man chiefly responsible for them was one of the more interesting faces on the political public relations scene, Victor Gold, press secretary to the Vice President. A colorful component of the campaign, he amused reporters with his frequent and vociferous public insults of bus drivers, pilots, cameramen, Secret Service agents, local police, potential voters, and the newsmen themselves. He was even known to pretend to be a reporter in order to end a news conference with the traditional benediction, "Thank you, Mr. Vice President," when he considered the line of questioning inappropriate. "But," said *The New York Times'* James Wooten, "he has nevertheless gone about the care and feeding of the press with a zeal and an expertise that have won him endorsements from some journalists as the best in the business. A native of Birmingham, Alabama, who had come to Washington for a public relations job, and served as a deputy press secretary for the Goldwater campaign in 1964, Gold was described by one reporter as "Spiro Agnew's Spiro Agnew."[53]

If there were new faces in the campaign, there were also some old ones, some of which seemed to be lurking in the shadows. As we have seen earlier, Mr. Nixon entered public life with political adviser and lawyer Murray Chotiner prominently in the wings. In 1956, while Mr. Nixon was serving as Vice President, a Senate investigation showed that Chotiner had been involved in influence peddling, and he faded farther into the background. Two years later, the then Vice President told Stewart Alsop, "It was a tragedy that [Chotiner] had to get involved in the kind of law business that does not mix with politics." But when Mr. Nixon took over the White House in 1969, Chotiner was back with him again. He left his official position before the 1972 campaign, and, according to columnist William V. Shannon, was once again practicing "the kind of law business he always had," handling "secret political tasks" for the President. It was depressing. And with him in "the Nixon entourage," wrote Shannon, "are a number of other political fixers, wiretapping hatchetmen and propaganda peddlers, as seedy a crowd as ever surrounded any Chief Executive."[54]

By the spring of 1973 it was clear that Shannon had been more of a prophet than many supporters of either candidate might have liked to believe during the campaign. The revelations of just how "seedy" some of the crowd was; the fixing and the spying and the wiretapping and the lying; the resignations and dismissals and defections from the inner core of trusted advisers with whom the President had surrounded himself placed the prestige of the presidency in jeopardy, and forced one to reflect upon the various Nixons, new and old, from "Tricky Dick" to Mr. President, with whom the people of the United States had been confronted for more than two decades, and what had happened to that people and that country during those twenty years and more.

To most of us Americans, it must seem as though Richard Nixon has always been with us. We have grown up with him. We can remember vividly the "Checkers" speech of 1952, stimulated by revelations of a "secret fund" of $18,000. Now we were confronted by another alleged "secret fund" of $10 million, supplied by wealthy donors whose names the President would not release.

We can remember Richard Nixon denouncing Harry Truman and his administration for not "standing up" to Communist China, and describing Adlai Stevenson as "Adlai the Appeaser . . . who got a Ph.D. from Dean Acheson's College of Cowardly Communist Containment." And now we were confronted by films of Mr. Nixon's journeys to Peking and Moscow.

We can remember electing Richard Nixon on a "pledge" to end the war in Vietnam, and his references to his "secret plan" to do just that. And we can remember Mr. Nixon, in 1954, urging that the United States intervene to save the French in Vietnam . . . Vietnam, which, as late as 1967, he called "the cork in the bottle of Chinese expansion."

In 1972 the War was still on, and Mr. Nixon's Democratic critics were lamenting the fact that 20,000 more Americans had lost their lives in Vietnam under the Republican Administration. So H. R. Haldeman, the White House Chief of Staff, went on a television interview show and described Edmund Muskie and other of the President's opponents in terms much like the Constitutional definition of treason: "consciously aiding and abetting the enemy." Herb Klein characterized Muskie, at the time considered by the Republicans the man who would be most difficult to beat in 1972, as "bolting beyond the bounds of criticism and dissent." And then, the new Nixon, his colleagues having said their piece, said, "I do not question the patriotism or the sincerity of those who disagree with my policies to bring peace."[55]

Against the background of 1952, the *déjà vu* aspects of H. R. Haldeman and the "secret fund" issue in 1972 were almost too much for the mind to bear. It is worth reviewing how the issue was handled in the context of a potential public relations crisis during the course of the campaign.

It was late in the campaign before the White House began to show signs of restiveness over the whole "corruption" issue, and what the administration chose to call "the so-called Watergate Caper." On October 25 Ronald Ziegler heatedly denied a Washington *Post* story linking Haldeman to a "secret fund" allegedly used to underwrite a large-scale effort at political espionage. He called the *Post* story "shabby journalism" and "a blatant effort at character assassination."

It seemed that bets were now off in terms of the earlier White House directives that the administration would remain at peace with the Fourth Estate, at least until the President had been safely assured of four more years in Washington.

For simultaneously, over at the Committee to Re-elect the President, campaign manager Clark McGregor joined Ziegler in attributing political motives to the *Post*'s coverage of the espionage episode —coverage which would win a Pulitzer Prize the following May 7.

McGregor accused the paper of "operating in close philosophical and strategic cooperation" with the McGovern organization—a statement presumably part of the large group of pronouncements which Ziegler rendered categorically "inoperative" in April 1973. Ziegler's earlier tactic had been to denounce both the charges and the *Post* without denying the accusations. For example, he did not deny allegations which linked the Watergate affair with Dwight Chapin, a White House aide with close ties to the President and Haldeman. However, on October 25, Ziegler said that the counsel to the President, John W. Dean III, "informed me that there was no special fund."[56]

Although it was not clear at the time just how much criminality was involved in the whole episode, and how deeply it had permeated the campaign, the lid was coming off, and the can of worms was not pretty. In October the Fair Campaign Practices Committee disclosed that more complaints of unethical political practices had been lodged in 1972 than "at any time in recent history."

Political public relations is a game played by clever men for high stakes, and like most such games, it lends itself to dirty tricks. And the lines between clever maneuvers, dirty tricks, and outright criminality had become blurred.

For example, when James W. McCord, presently serving his term in a national institution of another sort, was arrested inside the headquarters of the Democratic National Committee, he was carrying a sheaf of applications for college press passes, a memo on housing and accreditation of college press representatives, and a staff memorandum on arrangements for other youth groups. A source close to the investigation told *Newsweek*: "It was a complete package, enough material to forge college press credentials." A harmless trick? Well, a former CIA agent explained it this way: "The psy-war opportunities were endless. You pass off bogus tickets to a bunch of young people; you've got a mini-riot when they try to get in—and with media coverage, you've supported a thesis of party disarray."[57]

There was more. In October McGovern's political director, Frank Mankiewicz, released a list of ten specific acts of alleged sabotage. Among them was a telephone call from someone claiming to be campaign executive Gary Hart to AFL-CIO President George Meany, imperiously ordering him to appear in New York for a meeting with McGovern—a call Hart says he never made. Another call went to Walter Cronkite of CBS, from someone identifying himself as Mankiewicz, thanking Cronkite for loading the network's newscasts in McGovern's favor—apparently hoping Cronkite would admit to intentional and elaborate bias. Instead, Cronkite, a good reporter, called Mankiewicz and confirmed that the call was a hoax. Still another call went to CBS from someone claiming to be McGovern's media buyer, asking for cancellation of the time buy for the Democratic candidate's major Vietnam address.[58]

Now some of the earlier incidents, going back to the primaries, began to fall into place. One of the most elaborate took place at a Muskie fund-raising affair at the Washington Hilton in April. There, according to Muskie finance chairman James Goodbody, $300 worth of liquor, a $50 floral arrangement, cakes from—of all places— the Watergate pastry shop, and 200 steaming and delectable pizza pies all arrived C.O.D. African diplomats were invited to the event by people claiming to be members of the Maine senator's staff, and limousines and drivers were ordered to pick them up. Two magicians, one of them who had flown in for the occasion from the Virgin Islands, arrived with orders to "entertain the children," none of whom were there.[59]

And in the spring of 1973, more revelations were scraped from the bottom of the p.r. barrel in the wake of the Watergate affair.

By late April, it had come to light that:

1. As the public awaited reaction to the President's decision to mine Haiphong Harbor in May 1972, the Committee to Re-elect the President had laid out $4,400 in $100 bills for an intentionally amateurish-appearing ad in *The New York Times* stating that

"the people" supported the President. The first of ten names on the list of obscure signatories was one Patricia O'Leary, secretary to the Nixon campaign's advertising agency.

2. Also in May 1972, Nixon campaign workers deluged station WTTG-TV in Washington with as many as 4,000 extra responses to a survey of public support for the mining decision. One campaign worker told the *Times* that "work ground to a halt in the press room while everyone filled out 10 postcards." This was vigorously denied by De Van Shumway, public relations man for the campaign committee, who asserted that "only 2,000" postcards were mailed from headquarters.

3. Another senior campaign aide managed to recall that he had organized a flow of congratulatory wires to the President from veterans' groups, thinking it strange anyone should take exception to the procedure. "Except for this insane environment we're in now because of Watergate, those are the sort of tricks you'd tell Teddy White about after the election," he said. (Meanwhile, Watergate developments had forced White to postpone his deadline for publication of *The Making of the President 1972.*)

4. At least one Washington, D.C., student was discovered to have been receiving $150 a week to disrupt and spy on antiwar picketers in front of the White House. In April 1973 the student's boss, who had headed up Nixon's campus campaign, lost his job in the Department of the Interior.[60]

And so, Richard Nixon had been re-elected. More *déjà vu.* He scored his victory on exactly the tenth anniversary of his "good-bye to public life" address, delivered the morning following his loss of the California gubernatorial election to Edmund "Pat" Brown. And with him that day in his Beverly Hills hotel as he bade the press farewell forever, reminding newsmen that they would not "have Nixon to kick around anymore," were his trusted aides, Herbert Klein, Ronald Ziegler, John Ehrlichman, and H. R. Haldeman.

Any analysis of the public relations aspects of the Nixon campaign must inevitably conclude that it was masterfully handled, and it is difficult to see why anyone associated with it might have felt the need to help assure the President his re-election by dealing under the table. He just didn't need that kind of help.

The advantages of the incumbent have been spelled out at length

elsewhere in this book. And there is no question about the fact that
Mr. Nixon out-orchestrated the old master, L.B.J., and any other President in modern history in coolly pacing the policies of his administration to the tempo of his re-election campaign. One new development
after another went off like loud reports in a series of well-timed fire-
works, with the flame rushing lustily along the powder-laden fuse
from one skyrocket to another. Finally, John Ehrlichman modestly
admitted, "A lot of things are coming together at a point. And it is a
point, frankly, which we selected as a target time as a matter of
enlightened self-interest."[61]

The President substituted management for charisma ... and
McGovern seemed to be displaying neither. Mr. Nixon had conducted an impersonal campaign. He was a kind of closet candidate
who successfully replaced his body with events. His occasional flashes
of flesh-and-blood were almost ritualistic, from his renomination at
Miami Beach to his vastly restricted outdoor campaigning, motorcad-
ing through the friendly byways of Atlanta or New York's affluent
Westchester County. His very few addresses were given before
filtered and purified audiences of GOP enthusiasts, his television
approach limited to film clips of himself doing his job, and his
nationwide campaign speeches delivered on radio, "as if to remove
the visual reminders of the pre-Presidential Nixon."[62]

And George McGovern, for all the evangelical appeal he and his
campaign carried to the true believers, seemed somehow almost life-
less. One sympathizer said, "I can't help it, for the life of me, but he
comes off like Liberace." A reporter observed, "His voice struggles
for passion and sounds like grace at a Rotary luncheon." He was a
schoolmaster, a minister, convinced of the rightness of his lessons and
his sermons. As the campaign came down to the wire, and the poll
curves were as flat as the candidate's eyes on TV, his teaching had
given way to preaching, and his campaign became a struggle between
good and evil. The platform seemed to evaporate as the issues coa-
lesced into what he called "a coalition of conscience and decency"
against an old guard willing to nominate almost *any*one else. And so,

The Democratic Convention had begun it all in a crusade-like
atmosphere—McGovernites willing to nominate no one else, arrayed
against an old guard willing to nominate almost *any*one else. And so,
McGovern made Nixon the prime issue, and in so doing became an
issue himself. On other issues, his approach emerged first as radical,

then as muddled. The handling of the Eagleton issue was clumsy, compounding the clumsiness with which the Missouri senator apparently had been tapped for the ticket in the first place. The search for a successor was a humiliating one, and the staff struggles along the way a kind of unprecedented issue of organizational skills, bringing McGovern's competence and finally his credibility into question.

When McGovern talked of "restoring the Presidency to a position of moral leadership worthy of a great people with great ideals," people scoffed. But somehow, by the spring of 1973, with a scandal a day coming out of the campaign garbage can and impeachment a favorite topic of coffee-break conversation, it began to make more sense. Perhaps McGovern was telling the American public more than it wanted to hear. For to level charges of racism and genocide and injustice is to charge the American *people*, not just their Chief Executive. Perhaps, just perhaps, the problem was not that the preacher was too preachy, but that his congregation was too full of sinners.

All in all, it was a campaign which seemed dull, without a life of its own, and certainly without even the humor which is often a saving grace in American presidential politics.

One *New York Times* correspondent, when asked by his editor for a sampling of Nixon campaign humor, responded: "Your request for a memo on Nixon's humor is possibly the most humorous aspect of the whole situation." Spiro Agnew, despite his reputation as something of a humorist, got in little more than an occasional obligatory one-liner, with Sargent Shriver a favorite target for barbs such as "He knew the burdens of a childhood in which there were eight mouths to feed in his family: himself, his parents, and five polo ponies." Shriver himself always traveled with Bob Hagen, his one-liner man, who came up with such thigh-slappers as "President Nixon is courting the Catholic vote so hard I wouldn't be at all surprised to hear that he's begun playing bingo in the White House every Thursday night." As for McGovern himself . . . well, McGovern had a mission, and missions don't lend themselves to comic relief . . . although when he announced the support of some black political leaders, he got in some inadvertent guffaws when he made light of some criticisms with the revelation that "When I was twelve years old, I stole a watermelon."[64]

In the words of Art Buchwald: "This was the most exciting of all Presidential elections. . . . Nothing could compare with it except the recent fight for the presidency of the Prudential Life Insurance Company."

# Notes

NOTES TO INTRODUCTION

1. Scott M. Cutlip and Allen H. Center, *Effective Public Relations*, 2nd ed. (Englewood Cliffs, N.J.: Prentice-Hall, Inc., 1958), pp. 54–55.

2. *Ibid.*, p. 4.

3. *Ibid.*

4. Robert L. Heilbroner, "Public Relations—The Invisible Sell," *Harper's*, Vol. 214 (June 1957).

5. Cutlip and Center, *op. cit.*, pp. 4–5. Italics those of the authors.

6. Stanley Kelley, Jr., *Professional Public Relations and Political Power* (Baltimore: The Johns Hopkins Press, 1956).

7. *Ibid.*, pp. 7–8.

8. Ray W. Fenton, "The Candidate, Campaign and Ballot Box," *Public Relations Journal* (March 1966), p. 25. Mr. Fenton is director of Public Relations Associates, Great Falls, Montana.

9. Kelley, *op. cit.*, p. 3.

10. Harold D. Lasswell and Abraham Kaplan, *Power and Society* (New Haven: Yale University Press, 1950), p. 158.

11. June 25, 1969.

12. Howard B. White, "The Processed Voter and the New Political Science," *Social Research*, Vol. 28, No. 2 (Summer 1961), p. 128.

13. Theodore H. White, *The Making of the President 1964* (New York: Signet Books, The New American Library, 1965), p. 383.

14. Theodore H. White, *The Making of the President 1960* (New York: Signet Books, The New American Library, 1961), p. vii.


NOTES TO CHAPTER I

1. See Arthur and Lila Weinberg, *The Muckrakers* (New York: Simon and Schuster, 1961).

2. *Ibid.*, p. 300.

3. Ivy L. Lee, *Publicity* (New York: Industries, 1925), pp. 7–8. Quoted in Stanley Kelley, *Professional Public Relations and Political Power* (Baltimore: The Johns Hopkins Press, 1956), pp. 17–18.

4. Philip Davidson, *Propaganda and the American Revolution, 1763–1783* (Chapel Hill, N.C.: University of North Carolina Press, 1941), p. 3.

5. Alfred McClung Lee, *The Daily Newspaper in America* (New York: Macmillan, 1937), p. 40.

6. Scott M.Cutlip and Allen H. Center, *Effective Public Relations*, 2nd ed. (Englewood Cliffs, N.J.: Prentice-Hall, Inc., 1958), p. 20.

7. See *Autobiography of Amos Kendall* (Micro-Offset Books, 1949, reprinted); Arthur M. Schlesinger, Jr., *The Age of Jackson*, and Cutlip and Center, *op. cit.*, pp. 20–22, for details of Kendall's methods and the extent of his influence.

8. Luther B. Little, "The Printing Press in Politics," *Munsey's Magazine*, Vol. 23 (September 1900), pp. 740–744. Quoted in Cutlip and Center, *op. cit.*, p. 25.

9. Cutlip and Center, *op. cit.*, p. 25.

10. Pendleton Dudley, "Current Beginnings of PR," *Public Relations Journal* (April 1952), pp. 9–10.

11. Cutlip and Center, *op. cit.*, p. 36.

12. Frank Parker Stockbridge, "How Woodrow Wilson Won His Nomination," *Current History* (July 1924), p. 561. Quoted in Kelley, *op. cit.*, pp. 29–30. See Arthur S. Link, *Wilson: The Road to the White House* (Princeton: Princeton University Press, 1947).

13. George Creel, *Rebel at Large* (New York: Putnam, 1947), pp. 157–58. Italics Creel's.

14. Charles Michelson, *The Ghost Talks* (New York: Putnam, 1944), p. 22. See also Kelley, *op. cit.*, p. 31.

15. Kelley, *op. cit.*, pp.31–32.

16. *Ibid.* See also Ralph D. Casey, "Republican Propaganda in the 1936 Campaign," *Public Opinion Quarterly*, Vol. I, No. 2 (April 1937), pp. 27–45.

17. Elisha Hanson, "Official Propaganda and the New Deal," *The Annals of the American Academy of Political and Social Science*, 179 (May 1935), p. 178. Quoted in Kelley, *op. cit.*, pp. 14–15.

18. Pendleton Herring, *The Politics of Democracy* (New York: Norton, 1940), p. 259.

19. Curtis D. Macdougall, *Understanding Public Opinion* (New York: The Macmillan Company, 1952), pp. 554–557. We are indebted to Dr. Macdougall for most of this account of the Willkie campaign, pp. 554–557, 575. See also Kelley, *op. cit.*, pp. 34–35.

20. *Ibid.*, p. 555.

21. *Ibid.*, p. 557.

22. Harwood L. Childs, *An Introduction to Public Opinion* (New York: John Wiley, 1940), p. 10.

NOTES TO CHAPTER II

1. Stanley Kelley, Jr., *Professional Public Relations and Political Power* (Baltimore: The Johns Hopkins Press, 1956), p. 3.

2. Robert C. Brooks, *Political Parties and Electoral Problems* (New York: Harper, 1922), p. 327, quoted in Kelley, *op. cit.*, p. 27.

3. Edward L. Bernays, *Crystallizing Public Opinion* (New York: Boni and Liveright, 1923), pp. 52–53.

4. "Madison Avenue's Hand in Politics," *Business Week* (June 30, 1956), p. 93.

5. *Ibid.*

6. Kelley, *op. cit.*, p. 35.

7. *Business Week, op. cit.*

8. Morton B. Lawrence, "Public Relations—A Major Force in Political Campaigns," *Public Relations Quarterly* (April 1959), p. 31.

9. Paul A. Theis, "Publicity and Politics," *Public Relations Journal* (September 1968), p. 8.

10. Ray W. Fenton, "Candidate, Campaign and Ballot Box," *Public Relations Journal* (March 1966), p. 26.

11. "Preparing Employees for Their Citizenship Role," *Public Relations News* (July 13, 1964), p. 3. Also see Committee for Economic Development, *Financing a Better Electoral System* (New York: CED, 1968).

12. Hearings before Special Committee to Investigate Campaign Expenditures, House of Representatives, 82nd Congress, Second Session, p. 12. The actual final figure was about $140,000,000. See CED, *op. cit.*, p. 15.

13. *Ibid.*, p. 76.

14. CED, *op. cit.*, pp. 16–17, 67–68.

15. Lawrence, *op. cit.*, p. 30.

16. Samuel J. Archibald, "Public Relations, Politics and Government," *Public Relations Journal* (June 1967), p. 38. Also see H. Zane Robbins, "Public Relations and Politics" (Chicago: Durson-Marsteller Associates, 1968), mimeographed, p. 2.

17. Letter from Paul Cain, The Cain Organization, Dallas, Texas, to Shirley D. Smith, Executive Director, Public Relations Society of America, Inc., New York (November 11, 1957), pp. 1–2.

18. Theis, *op. cit.*, p. 8.

19. James M. Perry, *The New Politics: The Expanding Technology of Political Manipulation* (New York: Clarkson N. Potter, Inc., 1968), p. 8.

20. *Ibid.*, pp. 8–10. See also Kelley, *op. cit.*, *passim.*

21. Perry, *op. cit.*, p. 11.

22. *Ibid.*

23. *Ibid.*

24. *Ibid.*, p. 13.

25. Interview with Nick Kostopulos, Special Assistant to the Chairman, Democratic National Committee, June 25, 1969.

26. Perry, *op. cit.*, p. 42.

27. *Ibid.*, p. 48.

28. *Ibid.*, pp. 33–40.

29. *Ibid.*, p. 33.

30. Quoted in *ibid.*, pp. 32-33.

31. Clem Whitaker, address before the Los Angeles Area Chapter of the Public Relations Society of America, July 13, 1948, quoted in Kelley, *op. cit.*, p. 46. Italics and capitalization Whitaker's.

32. Lawrence, *op. cit.*, p. 31.

33. Theis, *op. cit.*, pp. 8–9.

34. Lawrence, *op. cit.*, p. 32.

35. *Public Relations News*, Vol. 24, No. 35 (August 26, 1968), p. 2. Hauan also predicted at the time that the biggest public relations problem to be faced by the Democratic National Convention in Chicago would be the expected demonstrations. "All we can do is trust in the Lord—and Mayor Daley."

36. Howard B. White, "The Processed Voter and the New Political Science," *Social Research*, Vol. 28, No. 2 (Summer 1961), pp. 129–130.

37. Lawrence, *op. cit.*, p. 30.

38. Kelley, *op. cit.*, pp. 47–48.

39. Theis, *op. cit.*, p. 10.

40. Lawrence, *op. cit.*, p. 31.

41. *Business Week*, *op. cit.*

42. Robbins, *op. cit.*, p. 10.

43. Theis, *op cit.*, p. 8.

44. Theodore H. White, *The Making of the President 1960* (New York: Signet Books, The New American Library, 1961), p. 46. Capitalization White's.

45. Lewis Chester, Godfrey Hodgson, and Bruce Page, *An American Melodrama: The Presidential Campaign of 1968* (New York: The Viking Press, 1969), p. 47.

46. Robbins, *op. cit.*, p. 14.

47. *Ibid.*, pp. 16–17.

48. Howard White, *op. cit.*, p. 135.

49. Theodore H. White, *The Making of the President 1964* (New York: Signet Books, The New American Library, 1965), p. 392.

50. Theodore H. White, *The Making of the President 1960, op. cit.*, pp. 290–291.

51. *Ibid.*, p. 291.

52. *Ibid.*, p. 283.

53. Theis, *op. cit.*, p. 9.

54. Perry, *op. cit.*, pp. 102–103.

55. *Ibid.*, p. 139.

56. *Ibid.*, p. 140.

57. *Ibid.*, p. 159.

58. *Ibid.*

59. *Ibid.*, pp. 161–164.

60. *Ibid.*, p. 165.

61. *Ibid.*, p. 6.

NOTES TO CHAPTER III

1. Press release, Republican National Committee, January 17, 1953. Quoted in Stanley Kelley, Jr., *Professional Public Relations and Political Power* (Baltimore: The Johns Hopkins Press, 1956), p. 1.

2. Kelley, *op. cit.*, p. 1.

3. Quoted in *ibid.*, p. 151. Italics in plan.

4. *The New York Times* (September 13, 1952).

5. *Ibid.*

6. Quoted in Kelley, *op. cit.*, pp. 154–155.

7. Kelley, *op. cit.*, p. 155.

8. Quoted in *ibid.*, p. 156.

9. Angus Campbell, Gerald Gurin, and Warren E. Miller, *The Voter Decides* (Evanston, Ill., and White Plains, N.Y.: Row, Peterson, and Company, 1954), p. 16.

10. Kelley, *op. cit.*, p. 199.

11. Quoted in *ibid.*, pp. 145–146. Brochure's italics.

12. *The New York Times* (July 12, 1952).

13. Louis Harris, *Is There a Republican Majority?* (New York: Harper, 1954), p. 25.

14. Kelley, *op. cit.*, pp. 200–201.

15. Harris, *op. cit.*, p. 32.

16. *Ibid.*, p. 33.

17. *The New York Times* (October 29, 1952).

18. Kelley, *op. cit.*, p. 192.

19. Adlai E. Stevenson, *Major Campaign Speeches, 1952* (New York: Random House, 1953), p. 302.

20. Kelley, *op. cit.*, pp. 148–149.

21. *Ibid.*

22. *Ibid.*, pp. 149–150.

23. *Ibid.*, pp. 149–151.

24. *Ibid.*, p. 151.

25. *Ibid.*, p. 172–173.

26. *The New York Times* (August 21, 1952).

27. Harris, *op. cit.*, p. 49.

28. "Admen Analyze the Campaign Strategy," *Tide* (November 7, 1952), p. 15.

29. Kelley, *op. cit.*, p. 174.

30. *Ibid.*, p. 175.

31. Quoted in *ibid.*, p. 161.

32. *Ibid.*, pp. 161–162.

33. Herbert R. Craig, "Distinctive Features of Radio-TV in the 1952 Presidential Campaign," unpublished M.A. thesis, University of Iowa, 1954, p. 104, quoted in *ibid.*, p. 162.

34. *Ibid.*, pp. 163–164.

35. Jock Elliott, Address to the BBD&O Annual Meeting, February 27, 1953, quoted in *ibid.*, p. 197.

36. *Ibid.*, pp. 187–188.

37. Gordon Cotter, "That Plague of Spots from Madison Avenue," *The Reporter* (November 25, 1952), pp. 7–8.

38. Kelley, *op. cit.*, p. 189.

39. *Ibid.*, p. 193.

40. *Ibid.*, pp. 194–196.

41. *Ibid.*, p. 197.

42. *Ibid.*, p. 164.

43. *Ibid.*, p. 165.

44. *Ibid.*, p. 166.

45. *Ibid.*, p. 167.

46. "Madison Avenue's Hand in Politics," *Business Week* (June 30, 1956), p. 95.

47. Kelley, *op. cit.*, pp. 168-169.

48. *Ibid.*, p. 179; *The New York Times* (September 15, 1955).

49. Kelley, *op. cit.*, pp. 179–180; *The New York Times* (September 22 and 23, 1952).

50. Kelley, *op. cit.*, p. 180.

51. Quotes from the speech here and in the following paragraphs excerpted from text which appeared in *U.S. News & World Report* (October 3, 1952), pp. 66–70.

52. *Ibid.*, p. 74. See also Kelley, *op. cit.*, pp. 183–184.

53. Kelley, *op. cit.*, pp. 224–225 (note); p. 227.

54. *Ibid.*, p. 193.

55. *The World Almanac and Book of Facts*, 1970 ed. (New York: Newspaper Enterprise Association, 1969), p. 366.

56. See such post-election accounts as Walter Johnson, *How We Drafted Adlai Stevenson* (New York: Knopf, 1955); Jacob M. Arvey and John Madigan, "The Reluctant Candidate—An Inside Story," *The Reporter* (November 24, 1953), pp. 19–26; and Kelley, *op. cit.*, pp. 156ff.

57. Kelley, *op. cit.*, pp. 159.

58. *Ibid.*, p. 157.

59. *Ibid.*, pp. 158–159.

60. *Tide, op. cit.*

61. Kelley, *op. cit.*, p. 190 (note).

62. *Tide, op. cit.*

63. *The New York Times* (October 19, 1952); Kelley, *op. cit.*, p. 186.

64. Adlai Stevenson, *Major Campaign Speeches, 1952* (New York: Random House, 1953), p. 272.

65. *Ibid.*, p. 269.

66. *Ibid.*, pp. 314–316.

67. Kelley, *op. cit.*, p. 172.

68. Kelley, *op. cit.*, p. 167.

69. Manly Mumford, "The 'Blunt Truth' Technique," *Public Relations Journal* (March 1953), pp. 8–10.

70. Kelley, *op. cit.*, pp. 185–186.

71. See V. O. Key, Jr., *The Responsible Electorate* (Cambridge: Harvard University Press, 1966), pp. 67–79.

72. *Ibid.*, pp. 78–79.

73. See Kelley, *op. cit.*, pp. 197–198.

74. *Ibid.*, pp. 195–196.

75. Ray W. Fenton, "Candidate, Campaign and Ballot Box," *Public Relations Journal* (March 1966), p. 27.

76. *Business Week, op. cit.*, pp. 93, 95 96.

77. Scott M. Cutlip and Allen H. Center, *Effective Public Relations*, 2nd ed. (Englewood Cliffs, N.J.: Prentice-Hall, Inc., 1958), p. 25.

78. *Business Week, op. cit.*, p. 96. Italics Norman's.

79. *Public Relations News*, Case Study No. 581, 1956.

80. *Ibid.*

81. *Ibid.*

82. *Ibid.*

83. Democratic National Committee, *A Campaign Guide to Political Publicity*, p. 5.

84. *Public Relations News, op. cit.*

85. *Ibid.*

## NOTES TO CHAPTER IV

1. Theodore H. White, *The Making of the President 1960* (New York: Signet Books, The New American Library, 1961), p. 51.

2. *Ibid.*, p. 144.

3. *Ibid.*, pp. 144–145.

4. *Ibid.*, pp. 44–45. Italics mine.

5. See *ibid.*, p. 283, and Daniel M. Ogden, Jr., and Arthur L. Peterson, *Electing the President: 1964* (San Francisco: Chandler, 1964), p. 76.

6. *Ibid.*, p. 122.

7. *Ibid.*

8. *Ibid.*, p. 66.

9. Quoted in H. Zane Robbins, "Public Relations and Politics" (Chicago: Burson-Marsteller Associates, 1968), mimeographed, p. 16.

10. Ogden and Peterson, *op. cit.*, p. 149.

11. White, *op. cit.*, pp. 111–112.

12. *Ibid.*

13. *Ibid.*, p. 112.

14. *Ibid.*, p. 124.

15. *Ibid.*, pp. 128–129.

16. *Ibid.*, p. 127.

17. *Ibid.*, pp. 130–131.

18. *Ibid.*, p. 131.

19. *Ibid.*, pp. 132–133.

20. *Ibid.*, p. 205.

21. *Ibid.*, p. 85.

22. *Ibid.*

23. *Ibid.*, p. 91.

24. *Ibid.*, p. 211.

25. *Ibid.*, p. 213.
26. *Ibid.*, p. 214–216.
27. Ogden and Peterson, *op. cit.*, p. 150.
28. White, *op. cit.*, p. 79.
29. Ogden and Peterson, *op. cit.*, pp. 150–151.
30. White, *op. cit.*, pp. 226–227.
31. Karl A. Lamb and Paul A. Smith, *Campaign Decision-Making: The Presidential Election of 1964* (Belmont, Calif.: Wadsworth, 1968), p. 52.
32. White, *op. cit.*, p. 366.
33. Ogden and Peterson, *op. cit.*, p. 156.
34. *Ibid.*, pp. 156–157.
35. *Ibid.*, p. 158.
36. White, *op. cit.*, p. 322 (note 2).
37. Herbert E. Alexander, *Financing the 1960 Election* (Princeton, N.J.: Citizens' Research Foundation, 1962), p. 31.
38. Ogden and Peterson, *op. cit.*, p. 155.
39. White, *op. cit.*, pp. 292, 294–295.
40. *Ibid.*, p. 292.
41. Ogden and Peterson, *op. cit.*, p. 146.
42. White, *op. cit.*, pp. 378–380.
43. *Ibid.*, p. 364. See also note 2.
44. *Ibid.*, p. 294 (note 4).
45. This and other information in the following paragraphs concerning the use of simulation is from James M. Perry, *The New Politics: The Expanding Technology of Political Manipulation* (New York: Clarkson N. Potter, Inc., 1968), pp. 165–170.
46. Theodore C. Sorensen, *Kennedy* (New York: Harper & Row, 1965), p. 184.
47. White, *op. cit.*, p. 396.
48. *Ibid.*, pp. 359–360.
49. *Ibid.*, pp. 295–296, 298.
50. *Ibid.*, pp. 362–364.
51. *Ibid.*, p. 13.
52. Ogden and Peterson, *op. cit.*, p. 151.
53. White, *op. cit.*, pp. 303–304.
54. *Ibid.*, pp. 335–336.
55. Ogden and Peterson, *op. cit.*, p. 151.
56. *Ibid.*, pp. 152–153.
57. White, *op. cit.*, p. 300.
58. *Ibid.*
59. *Ibid.*, pp. 334–335.
60. *Ibid.*, pp. 301–302. White characterizes Newton as "one of the most fertile and imaginative minds in the use of modern TV," and Rogers as "one of the most skilled and experienced practitioners of political TV."
61. *Ibid.*, pp. 339–340.
62. *Ibid.*, pp. 341–342.
63. *Ibid.*, pp. 302–303, p. 303 (note 1).

64. *Ibid.*, pp. 311–312.
65. *Ibid.*, p. 339 (note).
66. *Ibid.*, pp. 377–378.
67. *Ibid.*
68. Ogden and Peterson, *op. cit.*, pp. 152–153 (note).
69. Alexander, *op. cit.*, p. 31.
70. Ogden and Peterson, *op. cit.*, pp. 153–154.
71. White, *op. cit.*, pp. 336–338, 343–344.
72. *Ibid.*, pp. 347–348.
73. *Ibid.*, pp. 349–350.
74. *Ibid.*, pp. 351–352.
75. *Ibid.*, p. 352.
76. *Ibid.*, pp. 352–353.
77. *Ibid.*, pp. 354–355.
78. *Ibid.*, pp. 316–317.
79. Ogden and Peterson, *op. cit.*, pp. 160–162.
80. White, *op. cit.*, pp. 320–321.
81. *Ibid.*, p. 321.
82. *Ibid.*, pp. 322–324.
83. *Ibid.*, pp. 329–332.
84. *Ibid.*, pp. 332–333.
85. Ogden and Peterson, *op. cit.*, p. 165.
86. Committee for Economic Development, *Financing a Better Election System* (New York: CED, 1968), p. 70.


NOTES TO CHAPTER V

1. Quoted in Daniel M. Ogden, Jr., and Arthur L. Peterson, *Electing the President: 1964* (San Francisco: Chandler, 1964), p. 169.
2. *Ibid.*, pp. 169–170.
3. Theodore H. White, *The Making of the President 1964* (New York: Signet Books, The New American Library, 1965), p. 123.
4. *Ibid*, p. 135.
5. *Ibid.*, pp. 135–136.
6. *Ibid.*, p. 136.
7. *Ibid.*, pp. 136–137.
8. *Ibid.*, p. 137.
9. *Ibid.*, pp. 137–138.
10. *Ibid.*, pp. 138–139.
11. *Ibid.*, p. 135.
12. *Ibid.*, p. 93.
13. *Ibid.*, pp. 93–94.
14. *Ibid.*, pp. 141–143.
15. James M. Perry, *The New Politics: The Expanding Technology of Political Manipulation* (New York: Clarkson N. Potter, Inc., 1968), pp. 15–17. See also White, *op. cit.*, p. 150.

16. *Ibid.*, p. 17.
17. *Ibid.*, p. 18.
18. *Ibid.*, pp. 31–32.
19. *Ibid.*, pp. 19–20.
20. *Ibid.*, pp. 20–22. See also White, *op. cit.*, p. 150.
21. White, *op. cit.*, pp. 150–152.
22. *Ibid.*, pp. 152–153; see also Perry, *op. cit.*, pp. 22–23.
23. White, *op. cit.*, p. 153.
24. Perry, *op. cit.*, p. 19 (note).
25. *Ibid.*, pp. 22–23.
26. *Ibid.*, p. 24.
27. White, *op. cit.*, pp. 160–162.
28. *Ibid.*, pp. 114–115.
29. *Ibid.*, pp. 115–116.
30. *Ibid.*, pp. 116–117.
31. *Ibid.*, p. 117.
32. *Ibid.*, pp. 117–118.
33. *Ibid.*, pp. 118–119.
34. *Ibid.*, pp. 121–122.
35. *Ibid.*, p. 129.
36. *Ibid.*, pp. 130–131.
37. Karl A. Lamb and Paul A. Smith, *Campaign Decision-Making: The Presidential Election of 1964* (Belmont, Calif.: Wadsworth, 1968), pp. 69–70.
38. Quoted in White, *op. cit.*, pp. 133–134.
39. *Ibid.*, pp. 146–147.
40. *Ibid.*, pp. 154–156.
41. *Ibid.*, p. 133.
42. *Ibid.*, pp. 61, 72.
43. *Ibid.*, pp. 72–73.
44. *Ibid.*, p. 63.
45. *Ibid.*, pp. 73, 296.
46. *Ibid.*, pp. 301–302.
47. *Ibid.*, pp. 305, 309.
48. Lamb and Smith, *op. cit.*, p. 165.
49. White, *op. cit.*, pp. 306–307.
50. *Ibid.*, pp. 308–309.
51. *Ibid.*, pp. 307–308.
52. *Ibid.*, pp. 338–340.
53. *Ibid.*, pp. 340ff.
54. *Ibid.*, p. 337.
55. Lamb and Smith, *op. cit.*, pp. 78–80.
56. White, *op. cit.*, pp. 242–243.
57. Lamb and Smith, *op. cit.*, p. 79; Clifton White, *Suite 3505* (New Rochelle, N.Y.: Arlington House, 1967), p. 398.
58. Theodore H. White, *op. cit.*, p. 191.
59. Philip E. Converse, Aage R. Clausen, and Warren E. Miller, "Electoral

Myth and Reality: The 1964 Election," *American Political Science Review*, Vol. 59 (June 1965), p. 325.

60. Raymond Moley, *The Republican Opportunity in 1964* (New York: Duell, 1964), p. 89.
61. Lamb and Smith, *op. cit.*, p. 93.
62. *Ibid.*, p. 94.
63. *Ibid.*, p. 93.
64. *Ibid.*, pp. 123–124; Theodore H. White, *op. cit.*, p. 379.
65. Theodore H. White, *op. cit.*, p. 375.
66. Theodore H. White, *op. cit.*, p. 377–379; Lamb and Smith, *op. cit.*, p. 89.
67. Lamb and Smith, *op. cit.*, p. 71.
68. Theodore H. White, *op. cit.*, pp. 248.
69. *Ibid.*, p. 383.
70. Lamb and Smith, *op. cit.*, pp. 93–94.
71. Theodore H. White, *op. cit.*, p. 393.
72. *Ibid.*, pp. 380–381.
73. *Ibid.*, p. 398.
74. *Ibid.*, p. 387.
75. *Ibid.*, pp. 388–390.
76. *Ibid.*, p. 393.
77. Lamb and Smith, *op. cit.*, pp. 90–92.
78. Theodore H. White, *op. cit.*, pp. 391–392.
79. *Ibid.*, p. 392 (and note).
80. Lamb and Smith, *op. cit.*, p. 130; Theodore H. White, *op. cit.*, p. 395 (note 9).
81. Lamb and Smith, *op. cit.*, p. 130.
82. *Ibid.*, pp. 131–132.
83. Theodore H. White, *op. cit.*, p. 396.
84. *Ibid.*
85. Lamb and Smith, *op. cit.*, p. 101.
86. *Ibid.*, p. 101.
87. Theodore H. White, *op. cit.*, p. 385 (note 3).
88. *Ibid.*, pp. 397–398.
89. *Ibid.*, p. 405.
90. *Ibid.*, p. 410.
91. Lamb and Smith, *op. cit.*, p. 135.
92. *Ibid.*, p. 219. (The same point is emphasized by Stephen Shadegg in *What Happened to Goldwater?* (New York: Holt, 1965), pp. 221–241. Shadegg contends that the presumed attraction of a campaign speech which the then film star Ronald Reagan made for Goldwater was that it made Reagan sound like "the old Goldwater" (p. 253).
93. Lamb and Smith, *op. cit.*, p. 133.
94. Thomas W. Benham, "Polling for a Presidential Candidate: Some Observations on the 1964 Campaign," *Public Opinion Quarterly*, Vol. 29 (Summer 1965), pp. 195–196.

95. Converse *et al.*, *op. cit.*, p. 323. See also Lamb and Smith, *op. cit.*, p. 54. For an example of the "woodwork theory" see H. Zane Robbins, "Public Relations and Politics," mimeographed (Chicago: Burson-Marsteller Associates, 1968), p. 20.

96. The Ripon Society, *From Disaster to Distinction: A Republican Rebirth* (New York: Pocket Books, 1966), pp. 18–22.

97. Lamb and Smith, *op. cit.*, p. 6.

98. Theodore H. White, *op. cit.*, pp. 421–423.

99. *Ibid.*, pp. 414–417.

100. *Ibid.,* pp. 415–416.

101. Lamb and Smith, *op. cit.*, p. 176.

102. *Ibid.*, pp. 186–188.

103. *Ibid.*, pp. 197–198.

104. Peter Hamill, "When the Client Is a Candidate," *New York Times Magazine* (Octover 25, 1964), p. 31.

105. Lamb and Smith, *op. cit.*, p. 159.

106. *Ibid.*, p. 160.

107. *Ibid.*, pp. 160–161.

108. *Ibid.*, pp. 194–195.

109. Shirley V. Robson, "Advertising and Politics: A Case Study of the Relationship between Doyle Dane Bernbach, Inc., and the Democratic National Committee during the 1964 Presidential Campaign" (M.A. thesis, The American University, Washington, D.C., April 1, 1966), p. 61: quoted in Lamb and Smith, *op. cit.*, p. 195.

110. Lamb and Smith, *op. cit.*, p. 195.

111. Robson, *op. cit.*, pp. 27–28; 32; quoted in *ibid.*, p. 197.

112. Lamb and Smith, *op. cit.*, p. 198.

113. *Ibid.*, pp. 195–196.

114. *Ibid.*, p. 196.

115. Theodore H. White, *op. cit.*, p. 384.

116. Lamb and Smith, *op. cit.*, p. 198 (footnote).

117. *Ibid.*, p. 199.

118. *Ibid.*, pp. 199–200.

119. *Ibid.,* p. 200 (and footnote).

120. Theodore H. White, *op. cit.*, p. 402 (footnote 11).

121. Lamb and Smith, *op. cit.*, pp. 201–202 (and footnote).

122. *Ibid.*, pp. 203–204.

123. *Ibid.*, p. 107.

124. Theodore H. White, *op. cit.*, p. 439.

125. Lamb and Smith, *op. cit.*, p. 204.

126. Theodore H. White, *op. cit.*, p. 446.

127. Lamb and Smith, *op. cit.*, pp. 205–206.

128. *Politics in America 1945–1966,* 2nd ed. (Washington, D.C.: Congressional Quarterly Service, 1967), p. 59.

129. Lamb and Smith, *op. cit.*, p. 207. See also Benham, *op. cit.*, pp. 191ff.

NOTES TO CHAPTER VI

1. Lewis Chester, Godfrey Hodgson, and Bruce Page. *An American Melodrama: The Presidential Campaign of 1968* (New York: The Viking Press, 1969), p. 193.
2. *Ibid.*, pp. 193–194.
3. Quoted in *ibid.*, p. 194.
4. James M. Perry, *The New Politics: The Expanding Technology of Political Manipulation* (New York: Clarkson N. Potter, Inc., 1968), p. 25.
5. *Ibid.*, p. 26.
6. *Ibid.*, pp. 27–28.
7. *Ibid.*, pp. 28–29.
8. *The Art of Winning Elections* (Washington, D.C.: The Republican National Committee, 1968), pp. 89–90.
9. Chester *et al., op. cit.*, p. 197.
10. *Ibid.*, p. 201.
11. *Ibid.*
12. *Ibid.*, p. 203.
13. *Ibid.*, pp. 204–205.
14. *Ibid.*, p. 205.
15. *Ibid.*, pp. 205–206.
16. *Ibid.*, p. 206.
17. *Ibid.*, pp. 206–207.
18. *Ibid.*, p. 207.
19. *Ibid.*, pp. 207–208.
20. *Ibid.*, p. 198.
21. *Ibid.*, pp. 196–198.
22. Perry, *op. cit.*, p. 107–108.
23. *Ibid.*, pp. 107–137.
24. *Ibid.*, pp. 136–137.
25. Chester *et al., op. cit.*, pp. 381–382.
26. *Ibid.*, pp. 381; 383.
27. Perry, *op. cit.*, pp. 112–113.
28. Chester *et al., op. cit.*, p. 383.
29. All quoted in *ibid.*, pp. 383–385.
30. Quoted in *ibid.*, pp. 385–386. Italics Hughes'.
31. *Ibid.*, pp. 386–387.
32. *Ibid.*, p. 387.
33. *Ibid.*, pp. 387–388.
34. *Ibid.*, pp. 388–389.
35. Quoted in *ibid.*, p. 389.
36. *Ibid.*, pp. 389–390.
37. Quoted in *ibid.*, p. 390.
38. *Ibid.*, p. 390.
39. All poll data from tables in *ibid.*, pp. 391–392.
40. *Ibid.*, p. 393.

41. Norman Mailer, *Miami and the Siege of Chicago* (New York: Signet Books, The New American Library, 1968), p. 37.

42. Chester *et al., op. cit.,* p. 393.

43. Mailer, *op. cit.,* p. 102.

44. Chester *et al., op. cit.,* pp. 390–391.

45. Perry, *op. cit.,* p. 71.

46. *Ibid.*

47. *Ibid.,* pp. 72–73.

48. *Ibid.,* p. 73 (and note).

49. *Ibid.,* pp. 77–78.

50. *Ibid.,* pp. 78–79.

51. Howard B. White, "The Processed Voter and the New Political Science," *Social Research,* Vol. 28, No. 2 (Summer 1961), p. 132.

52. Mailer, *op. cit.,* p. 43.

53. See *The Art of Winning Elections, op. cit., passim; 1968 Spring Catalogue of Republican Campaign Materials* (Washington, D.C.: Republican National Committee, 1968), p. 59; and Chester, *et al., op. cit.,* p. 186.

54. Chester *et al., op. cit.,* pp. 617–618.

55. *Ibid.,* p. 618.

56. *Ibid.,* p. 619. For a sample of the semantic differential test, see Perry, *op. cit.,* p. 84.

57. *Ibid.,* pp. 619–620.

58. Joe McGinniss, *The Selling of the President 1968* (New York: Trident Press, a division of Simon & Schuster, Inc., 1969), p. 31.

59. Chester, *et al., op. cit.,* p. 90.

60. *Ibid.,* p. 91.

61. *Ibid.,* p. 92.

62. *Ibid.*

63. *Ibid.,* p. 93.

64. *Ibid.,* p. 299.

65. *Ibid.,* pp. 328–329.

66. Interview with Nick Kostopulos, Special Assistant to the Chairman, Democratic National Committee, June 25, 1969.

67. Chester *et al., op. cit.,* p. 637.

68. *Ibid.,* p. 638.

69. *Public Relations News,* Vol. XXIV, No. 35 (August 26, 1968). p. 1.

70. Mailer, *op. cit.,* p. 103.

71. *Ibid.,* p. 104.

72. H. Zane Robbins, "Public Relations and Politics" (Chicago; Burson-Marsteller Associates, 1968), mimeographed, p. 11.

73. Chester *et al., op. cit.,* p. 614.

74. *Ibid.,* p. 613.

75. *Ibid.,* p. 617.

76. *Ibid.,* pp. 676–677.

77. *Ibid.,* p. 677.

78. *Ibid.,* pp. 677–678.

79. *Ibid.*, p. 687.

80. For details on these productions, see McGinniss, *op. cit.* A former columnist with the Philadelphia *Inquirer*, McGinniss worked with the advertising staff of the Nixon campaign.

81. *Ibid.*, p. 37.

82. Harry Treleaven, "Upset: The Story of a Modern Political Campaign," quoted in *Ibid.*, p. 45.

83. *Ibid.* See also William H. Honan, "The Men Behind Nixon's Speeches," *New York Times Magazine* (January 19, 1969), p. 63.

84. *Ibid.*, pp. 46–47. Italics Price's. See also Honan, *op. cit.*, pp. 20–21.

85. *Ibid.*, p. 48.

86. Quoted in *Ibid.*, p. 58.

87. *Ibid.*, p. 63.

88. *Ibid.*

89. *Ibid.*, p. 66.

90. Chester *et al.*, *op. cit.*, pp. 688–689.

91. McGinniss, *op. cit.*, p. 155.

92. Robbins, *op. cit.*, p. 12.

93. Chester *et al.*, *op. cit.*, pp. 678–679.

94. *Ibid.*, pp. 673–674.

95. Kostopulos interview, *op. cit.*

96. Chester *et al.*, *op. cit.*, pp. 628–629.

97. *Ibid.*, p. 676.

98. *Ibid.*

99. *Ibid.*, pp. 679–684.

100. *Ibid.*, pp. 684–687.

101. *Ibid.*, pp. 750–751.

102. Honan, *op. cit.*, pp. 63, 65.

103. *Ibid.*, p. 63.

104. *Ibid.*, pp. 21; 63.

105. Chester *et al.*, *op. cit.*, p. 721; see also Honan, *op. cit.*, p. 63.

106. Robbins, *op. cit.*, p. 17.

107. Chester *et al.*, *op. cit.*, p. 632.

108. *Ibid.*, pp. 638–639.

109. Perry, *op. cit.*, p. 54.

110. *Ibid.*, pp. 58–59.

111. *Ibid.*, p. 58 (note).

112. *Ibid.*, p. 52.

113. Chester *et al.*, *op. cit.*, pp. 639–640.

114. *Ibid.*, p. 640.

115. *Ibid.*

116. *Ibid.*, pp. 717–719.

117. Kostopulos interview, *op. cit.*

118. McGinniss, *op. cit.*, p. 137.

119. Kostopulos interview, *op. cit.*

120. Chester *et al.*, *op. cit.*, pp. 711–712. Connell's italics.

121. *Ibid.*, pp. 712–713. See also *The New York Times* (October 6 and. October 9, 1968).

122. *Ibid.*, p. 713.

123. *Ibid.*, pp. 713–714.

124. *Ibid.*, pp. 293–294.

125. *Ibid.*, p. 701.

126. *Ibid.*, p. 170.

127. Quoted in *ibid.*, p. 514.

128. *Ibid.*, p. 515.

NOTES TO CHAPTER VII

1. Lewis Chester, Godfrey Hodgson, and Bruce Page, *An American Melodrama: The Presidential Campaign of 1968* (New York: Viking Press, 1969), p. 637.

2. *Time* (July 18, 1969), p. 53.

3. Stanley Kelley, Jr., *Public Relations and Political Power* (Baltimore: The Johns Hopkins Press, 1956), pp. 4–5.

4. *Ibid.*, pp. 202–203.

5. *Ibid.*, pp. 204–205.

6. H. Zane Robbins, "Public Relations and Politics" (Chicago: Burson-Marsteller Associates, 1968), mimeographed, p. 18. Italics mine.

7. Howard B. White, "The Processed Voter and the New Political Science," *Social Research*, Vol. 28, No. 2 (Summer 1961), p. 127.

8. James M. Perry, *The New Politics: The Expanding Technology of Political Manipulation* (New York: Clarkson N. Potter, Inc., 1968), pp. 136–137.

9. "How to Get that Good 'Media Image,' " *Newsweek* (September 29, 1969), p. 35.

10. Daniel M. Ogden, Jr., and Arthur L. Peterson, *Electing the President: 1964* (San Francisco: Chandler, 1964), p. 171.

11. Perry, *op. cit.*, p. 217.

12. Chester *et al.*, *op. cit.*, pp. 378–379.

13. Perry, *op. cit.*, pp. 215–216.

14. *Ibid.*, p. 219.

15. *Ibid.*, pp. 219–221. Cf. Committee for Economic Development, *Financing a Better Election System* (New York: CED, 1968), *passim.*

16. Kelley, *op. cit.*, p. 224.

17. *Ibid.*, p. 229.

18. Walter Lippmann, *Essays in the Public Philosophy* (Boston and Toronto: Little, Brown, 1955), p. 127.

19. Kelley, *op. cit.*, p. 230.

20. Clinton Rossiter, *The American Presidency*, rev. ed. (New York: Harcourt, Brace & World, 1960), pp. 200–204.

21. Kelley, *op. cit.*, p. 219.

22. *Newsweek, op. cit.*, p. 35.

23. Theodore H. White, *The Making of the President 1964* (New York: Signet Books, The New American Library, 1965), p. 380.

24. Quoted in V. O. Key, Jr., *Politics, Parties, and Pressure Groups*, 5th ed. (New York: Thomas Y. Crowell, 1964), p. 470.

25. Kelley, *op. cit.*, pp. 221–222.

26. Clem Whitaker, address before the Los Angeles Chapter of the Public Relations Society of America, July 13, 1948. Quoted in *ibid.*, p. 222. Italics Whitaker's.

27. Kelley, *op. cit.*, pp. 217–219.

28. Daniel J. Boorstin, *The Image: A Guide to Pseudo-Events in America* (New York and Evanston: Harper Colophon Books, 1961).

29. Perry, *op. cit.*, p. 4.

30. Quoted in Joe McGinniss, *The Selling of the President 1968* (New York: Trident Press, a division of Simon & Schuster, Inc., 1969), p. 44.

31. Interview with Nick Kostopulos, Special Assistant to the Chairman, Democratic National Committee, June 25, 1969.

32. Chester *et al., op. cit.*, p. 608.

33. Perry, *op. cit.*, pp. 129–130.

34. Thomas Whiteside, "Annals of Television—The Man from Iron City." *New Yorker* (September 27, 1969), pp. 47–48; 86.

35. Howard B. White, *op. cit.*, p. 146.

36. Interview with Ted van Dyk, former staff member, Vice President Hubert H. Humphrey, June 13, 1969.

37. Kostopulos interview, *op. cit.*

38. Howard B. White, *op. cit.*, pp. 146–147.

39. Theodore H. White, *op. cit.*, 1964, p. 478.

40. *The New York Times*, October 3, 1969.

41. Kostopulos interview, *op. cit.*

42. Perry, *op. cit.*, pp. 55–56.

43. *Ibid.*, pp. 212–213.

44. *Newsweek, op. cit.*, p. 35.

45. Perry, *op. cit.*, pp. 214–215.

46. Kelley, *op. cit.*, p. 210.

47. *Ibid.*, pp. 212–213.

48. *Ibid.*, pp. 231–232.

49. Perry, *op. cit.*, pp. 221–222.

50. Roy W. Fenton, "The Candidate, Campaign and Ballot Box," *Public Relations Journal* (March 1966), p. 28.

51. Perry, *op. cit.*, pp. 144–145.

52. V. O. Key, Jr., *Politics, Parties, and Pressure Groups* (New York: Thomas Y. Crowell, 1942), pp. 570–571.


NOTES TO AFTERWORD

1. "Selling the President '72," *Newsweek*, July 31, 1972, p. 55B.

2. *Ibid.*

3. *Ibid.*

4. Eileen Shanahan, "Two Rival Campaigns Vie for Free Radio Time," *The New York Times*, August 8, 1972, p. 18.

5. Harriet Van Horne, "Making Them Honest," *The New York Post*, August 4, 1972, p. 34.

6. *Newsweek, op. cit.*

7. Warren Weaver, Jr., "How to Tune in the Voters," *The New York Times*, News of the Week in Review, October 22, 1972, p. 3.

8. Warren Weaver, Jr., "New McGovern TV Ads Sharpen Attack on Nixon," *The New York Times*, November 11, 1972, p. 49. Commercial scripts quoted below from same source.

9. James M. Naugton, "McGovern Calls Nixon Ally of Business," *The New York Times*, September 26, 1972, pp. 1, 36.

10. *The New York Times*, November 5, 1972, p. 5.

11. "McGovern Ties Nixon to War Hawks," *The New York Times*, October 25, 1972, p. 32.

12. Bill Kovach, "McGovern Would Pay for Debates; Offer Rejected," *The New York Times*, October 19, 1972, p. 52.

13. Warren Weaver, Jr., "McGovern Ahead in Coast Media," *The New York Times*, October 29, 1972, p. 46.

14. *Ibid.*

15. *Ibid.*

16. Clayton Fritchey, "McGovern and the Working Press," *The New York Post*, August 12, 1972, p. 25.

17. James Reston, "McGovern's Self-Analysis," *The New York Times*, October 4, 1972, p. 47.

18. *Ibid.*

19. Warren Weaver, Jr., "How to Tune in the Voters," *op. cit.*

20. Douglas E. Kneeland, "McGovern Adopts Fund-Raising Role," *The New York Times*, September 7, 1972, p. 38.

21. "The Best and the Worst," *Newsweek*, August 7, 1972, p. 58.

22. Louis Harris, Harris Survey; "The Young Oppose Eagleton Move," *The Standard-Star* (New Rochelle, N.Y.), August 14, 1972, p. 6.

23. *Ibid.*

24. James Reston, "McGovern's Misjudgments," *The New York Times*, July 28, 1973, p. 31.

25. Jack Germond, "The Real Victims of Eagleton," *The Standard-Star*, July 29, 1972, p. 4.

26. James M. Naughton, "The Eagleton Impact," *The New York Times*, October 7, 1972, p. 18.

27. Russell Baker, "Gee, Maw, Not Those Old Classes Again!", *The New York Times*, August 10, 1972, p. 35.

28. Douglas E. Kneeland, "Western Parade Saves McGovern," *The New York Times,* July 29, 1972, p. 10.

29. Herbert Teison, "Campaign Politics," *The Saturday Review*, October 18, 1969, p. 39.

30. R. W. Apple, Jr., "The Nixon Strategy," *The New York Times*, September 30, 1972, p. 16.

31. David Wise, "Are You Worried About Your Image, Mr. President?", *Esquire,* May 1973, p. 190.

32. Warren Weaver, Jr., "How to Tune in the Voters," *op. cit.*

33. *Ibid.*

34. Raymond K. Price, Introduction to *The Clearest Choice* (Washington: Committee to Re-Elect the President, 1972).

35. *Ibid.*

36. Jules Witcover, "Nixon Discovers a New Gadget Called Radio," *The New York Post*, February 15, 1973, p. 11.

37. Warren Weaver, Jr., "Nixon's TV Drive Opens with Film on Soviet Trips," *The New York Times,* September 26, 1972, p. 36.

38. *Ibid.* Italics mine.

39. *Ibid.*

40. Warren Weaver, Jr., "GOP Begins a Drive on TV to Counter Democrats," *The New York Times,* September 22, 1972, p. 30.

41. *Ibid,* p. 30.

42. Warren Weaver, Jr., "GOP Switches TV Campaign to Attack on McGovern," *The New York Times*, October 4, 1972, p. 32.

43. *Ibid.*

44. Warren Weaver, Jr., "Nixon Gain Found from his TV Ads," *The New York Times*, November 26, 1972, p. 39

45. Jack Anderson, "Nixon Plans a Lofty Campaign," *The Standard-Star,* August 17, 1972, p. 8.

46. Robert B. Semple, Jr., "Nixon Orders Cease-Fire in Conflict with the Press," *The New York Times,* August 10, 1972, p. 24.

47. *Ibid.*

48. Ben H. Bagdikian, *The Effete Conspiracy and Other Crimes by the Press* (New York: Harper & Row, 1972), pp. 145–146.

49. "The President and the Press," *First Monday,* November 6, 1972, p. 10.

50. Theodore J. Jacobs, review of *The Effete Conspiracy and Other Crimes by the Press, The New York Times* Review of Books, July 30, 1972, p. 17.

51. James L. Wooten, "President's Surrogates to Step Up Campaign Tempo," *The New York Times,* September 6, 1972, p. 32.

52. Max Frankel, "Nixon, McGovern, and a Campaign of Symbolic Code Words," *The New York Times,* September 29, 1972, p. 30.

53. James T. Wooten, "Agnew's Press Secretary a Touchy Zealot," *The New York Times*, November 3, 1972, p. 21.

54. William V. Shannon, "The One and Only Nixon," *The New York Times*, September 22, 1972, p. 43.

55. *Ibid.*

56. Robert B. Semple, Jr., "Ziegler Denies an Article Linking Haldeman to Fund, *The New York Times*, October 26, 1972, p. 32.

57. "Watergate: Very Offensive Security," *Newsweek,* October 23, 1972, pp. 35–36.

58. *Ibid.*

59. *Ibid.*

60. Christopher Lydon, "Big Money, Dirty Tricks," *The New York Times*, News of the Week in Review, April 29, 1973, p. 1.

61. Richard Boeth and Henry Hubbard, "Nixon: The Remaking of the President," *Newsweek,* November 6, 1972, pp. 44–45.

62. *Ibid.*

63. Peter Goldman and Richard Stout, "McGovern's Politics of Righteousness," *Newsweek,* November 6, 1973, pp. 43–44.

64. "You're Supposed to Laugh," *The New York Times*, News of the Week in Review, October 22, 1972, p. 2.

# Bibliography

"Admen Analyze the Campaign Strategy." *Tide* (November 7, 1952).

Archibald, Samuel J., "Public Relations, Politics and Government." *Public Relations Journal* (June 1967).

Arvey, Jacob M., and Madigan, John, "The Reluctant Candidate—An Inside Story." *The Reporter* (November 24, 1953).

Benham, Thomas W., "Polling for a Presidential Candidate: Some Observations on the 1964 Campaign." *Public Opinion Quarterly*, Vol. 29 (Summer 1965).

Bernays, Edward L., *Crystallizing Public Opinion*. New York: Boni and Liveright, 1923.

————, *Propaganda*. New York: Horace Liveright, 1928.

Boorstin, Daniel J., *The Image: A Guide to Pseudo-Events in America*. New York and Evanston: Harper Colophon Books, 1961.

Brooks, Robert C., *Political Parties and Electoral Problems*. New York: Harper, 1922.

Burdick, Eugene, and Brodbeck, A. J., *American Voting Behavior*. Glencoe, Ill.: The Free Press, 1959.

Campbell, Angus, Gurin, Gerald, and Miller, Warren E., *The Voter Decides*. Evanston, Ill., and White Plains, N.Y.: Row, Peterson & Co., 1954.

Casey, Ralph D., "Republican Propaganda in the 1936 Campaign." *Public Opinion Quarterly*, Vol. 1, No. 2 (April 1937).

Chester, Lewis, Hodgson, Godfrey, and Page, Bruce, *An American Melodrama: The Presidential Campaign of 1968*. New York: The Viking Press, 1969.

Childs, Harwood L., *An Introduction to Public Opinion*. New York: John Wiley, 1940.

Committee for Economic Development, *Financing A Better Election System*. New York: CED, 1968.

Converse, Philip E., Clausen, Aage R., and Miller, Warren E., "Electoral Myth and Reality: The 1964 Election." *American Political Science Review*, Vol. 59 (June 1965).

Cotter, Gordon, "That Plague of Spots from Madison Avenue." *The Reporter* (November 25, 1952).

Creel, George, *Rebel at Large*. New York: Putnam, 1947.

Cutlip, Scott M., and Center, Allen H., *Effective Public Relations*, 2nd Ed. Englewood Cliffs, N.J.: Prentice-Hall, 1958.

Davenport, Marcia, *Too Strong for Fantasy*. New York: Charles Scribner's Sons, 1967.

Davidson, Philip, *Propaganda and the American Revolution 1763–1783*. Chapel Hill, N.C.: University of North Carolina Press, 1941.

*The Democrat* (June 2, 1952). Washington, D.C.: Democratic National Committee.

de Sola Pool, Ithiel; Abelson, Robert; and Popkin, Samuel, *Candidates, Issues, and Strategies*. Boston: MIT Press, 1965.

Draft Questionnaire on Political Public Relations Services. Public Relations Society of America (November 26, 1957).

Dudley, Pendleton, "Current Beginnings of Public Relations." *Public Relations Journal* (April 1952).

"Election Year Oratory: The Case for the Qualitative Argument." *Burson-Marsteller Report*, No. 10 (April 1969). Burson-Marsteller Public Relations, New York.

Fenton, Ray W., "Candidate, Campaign and Ballot Box." *Public Relations Journal* (March 1966).

Hamill, Peter, "When the Client Is a Candidate." *New York Times Magazine* (October 25, 1964).

Harris, Louis, *Is There a Republican Majority?* New York: Harper, 1954.

Heilbroner, Robert L., "Public Relations—The Invisible Sell." *Harper's*, Vol. 214 (June 1957).

Herring, Pendleton, *The Politics of Democracy*. New York: Norton, 1940.

Hillman, William, *Mr. President*. New York: Farrar, Straus & Cudahy, 1952.

Honan, William H., "The Men Behind Nixon's Speeches." *New York Times Magazine* (January 19, 1969).

"How to Get that Good 'Media Image,' " *Newsweek* (September 29, 1969).

Johnson, Walter, *How We Drafted Adlai Stevenson*. New York: Knopf, 1955.

Jonas, Frank H., "The Art of Political Dynamiting." *Western Political Quarterly*, Vol. 10 (June 1957).

Kelley, Stanley, Jr., *Professional Public Relations and Political Power*. Baltimore: The Johns Hopkins Press, 1956.

Kendall, Amos, *Autobiography*. Micro-Offset Books, 1949, reprinted.

Key, V. O., Jr., *Politics, Parties, and Pressure Groups*, 5th ed. New York: Thomas Y. Crowell, 1964.

———, with the assistance of Milton C. Cummings, Jr., *The Responsible Electorate*. New York: Vintage Books, 1968.

Lamb, Karl A., and Smith, Paul A., *Campaign Decision-Making: The Presidential Election of 1964*. Belmont, Calif.: Wadsworth, 1968.

Lasswell, Harold D., and Kaplan, Abraham, *Power and Security*. New Haven: Yale University Press, 1950.

Lawrence, Morton B., "Public Relations—A Major Force in Political Campaigns." *Public Relations Quarterly* (April 1959).

Lee, Alfred McClung, *The Daily Newspaper in America.* New York: Macmillan, 1937.

Link, Arthur S., *Wilson: The Road to the White House.* Princeton: Princeton University Press, 1947.

Lippmann, Walter, *Essays in the Public Philosophy.* Boston and Toronto: Little, Brown, 1955.

Little, Luther B., "The Printing Press in Politics." *Munsey's Magazine,* Vol. 23 (September 1900).

Macdougall, Curtis D., *Understanding Public Opinion.* New York: Macmillan, 1952.

McGinniss, Joe, "Packaging the President: The New Political Values." *New York* (September 8, 1969).

———, *The Selling of the President 1968.* New York: Trident Press, a division of Simon & Schuster, Inc., 1969.

"Madison Avenue's Hand in Politics." *Business Week* (June 30, 1956)

Mailer, Norman, *Miami and the Siege of Chicago.* New York: Signet Books, The New American Library, 1968.

Michelson, Charles, *The Ghost Talks.* New York: Putnam, 1944.

Miller, William Lee, "Can Government be Merchandised?" *The Reporter* (October 27, 1953).

Moley, Raymond, *The Republican Opportunity in 1964.* New York: Duell, 1964.

Mumford, Manly, "The 'Blunt Truth' Technique." *Public Relations Journal* (March 1953).

Ogden, Daniel M., Jr., and Peterson, Arthur L., *Electing the President: 1964.* San Francisco: Chandler, 1964.

Perry, James M., *The New Politics: The Expanding Technology of Political Manipulation.* New York: Clarkson N. Potter, Inc., 1968.

Pitchell, Robert J., "The Influence of Professional Campaign Management Firms in Partisan Elections in California." *Western Political Quarterly* (June 1958).

*Politics in America 1945–1966,* 2nd ed. Washington, D.C.: Congressional Quarterly Service, 1967.

"P.R. Advisers to Taft." *Public Relations Journal* (June 1952).

"Preparing Employees for Their Citizenship Role." *Public Relations News,* (July 13, 1964).

*Public Relations News* (1956), Case Study Number 581.

*Public Relations News* (August 26, 1968), V. XXIV, n. 35.

Republican National Committee, *From the Firing Line: The Art of Winning Elections.* Washington, D.C., 1968.

———, *1968 Spring Catalogue of Republican Campaign Materials.* Washington, D.C., 1968.

Riezler, Kurt, "Political Decisions in Modern Society." *Ethics,* Vol. 64 (January 1954), Number 2, Part II.

The Ripon Society, *From Disaster to Distinction: A Republican Rebirth.* New York: Pocket Books, 1966.

Robbins, H. Zane, "Public Relations and Politics." Chicago: Burson-Marsteller Associates, 1968. Mimeographed.

Robson, Shirley V., "Advertising and Politics: A Case Study of the Relationship Between Doyle Dane Bernbach, Inc., and the Democratic National Committee During the 1964 Presidential Campaign." M.A. thesis, The American University, Washington, D.C. April 1, 1966.

Rossiter, Clinton, *The American Presidency.* New York: Harcourt, Brace & World, 1960.

Schlesinger, Arthur M., Jr., *The Age of Jackson.* Boston and Toronto: Little, Brown, 1945.

"Secret Fund Bared," *New York Post* (September 18, 1952).

Shadegg, Stephen C., *How to Win an Election.* New York: Taplinger, 1964.

————, *What Happened to Goldwater?* New York: Holt, 1965.

Stevenson, Adlai E., *Major Campaign Speeches, 1952.* New York: Random House, 1953.

Theis, Paul A., "Publicity and Politics." *Public Relations Journal* (September 1968).

Thomson, Charles A. H., *Television and Presidential Politics: The Experience in 1952 and Problems Ahead.* Washington, D.C.: The Brookings Institution, 1956.

White, Clifton, *Suite 3505.* New Rochelle, N.Y.: Arlington House, 1967.

White, Howard B., "The Processed Voter and the New Political Science." *Social Research,* Vol. 28, No. 2 (Summer 1961).

White, Theodore H., *The Making of the President 1960.* New York: Atheneum Publishers, 1961; New American Library (Signet Books) reprint, 1967.

————, *The Making of the President 1964.* New York: Atheneum Publishers, 1965; Signet reprint, 1965.

"The White House: Authentic Voice." *Time* (January 27, 1958).

Whiteside, Thomas, "Annals of Television—The Man from Iron City." *New Yorker* (September 27, 1969).

Williams, Richard L., "The Advance Men." *Life* (October 6, 1952).

# Index

Grateful acknowledgment is made to the following for permission to reprint excerpts from published material:

*Business Week*: "Madison Avenue's Hand in Politics," June 30, 1956 (copyright © 1956 by McGraw-Hill, Inc.).

Chandler Publishing Co.: *Electing the President: 1964* by Daniel M. Ogden, Jr., and Arthur L. Peterson (copyright © 1964 by Chandler Publishing Co.).

New American Library, New York, N.Y.: *Miami and the Siege of Chicago* by Norman Mailer (copyright © 1968 by Norman Mailer).

*The New York Times*: "The Men Behind Nixon's Speeches" by William H. Honan, Magazine of January 19, 1969 (copyright © 1969 by The New York Times Co.).

Clarkson N. Potter, Inc.: *The New Politics* by James M. Perry (copyright © 1968 by James M. Perry).

Prentice-Hall, Inc.: *Effective Public Relations*, 2nd ed., by Scott M. Cutlip and Allen H. Center (copyright © 1958 by Prentice-Hall, Inc., Englewood Cliffs, N.J.).

*Public Relations Journal*: "Public Relations, Politics, and Government" by Samuel J. Archibald, June 1967 (copyright © 1967 by Public Relations Journal); *Public Relations Journal* and Ray W. Fenton: "The Candidate, Campaign and Ballot Box" by Ray W. Fenton, March 1966 (copyright © 1966 by Public Relations Journal); *Public Relations Journal* and Paul A. Theis: "Publicity and Politics" by Paul A. Theis, September 1968 (copyright © 1968 by Public Relations Journal).

*Public Relations News*: Case Study No. 581 (1956); "Preparing Employees for Their Citizenship Role" (July 13, 1964); and issue of August 26, 1968, p. 2 (copyright © 1956, 1964, 1968, respectively, by Public Relations News, 127 E. 80th St., New York, N.Y. 10021).

*Public Relations Quarterly*: "Public Relations — A Major Force in Political Campaigns" by Morton B. Lawrence, April 1959 (copyright © 1959 by Public Relations Quarterly, 305 E. 45th St., New York, N.Y. 10017).

Trident Press, division of Simon & Schuster, Inc.: *The Selling of the President 1968* by Joe McGinniss (copyright © 1969 by JoeMac, Inc.).

The Viking Press, Inc.: *An American Melodrama:The Presidential Campaign of 1968* by Lewis Chester, Godfrey Hodgson, and Bruce Page (copyright © 1969 by Times Newspapers, Inc.).

Wadsworth Publishing Co., Inc.: *Campaign Decision Making: The Presidential Election of 1964* by Karl A. Lamb and Paul A. Smith (copyright © 1968 by Wadsworth Publishing Co., Inc., Belmont, Calif.).

Theodore H. White and Atheneum Publishers: *The Making of the President 1960* by Theodore H. White (copyright © 1961 by Atheneum House, Inc.); *The Making of the President 1964* by Theodore H. White (copyright © 1965 by Theodore H. White).